83-2338

83-2338

LC2142   Patchen, Martin
.P37   Black-white contact in
         schools.

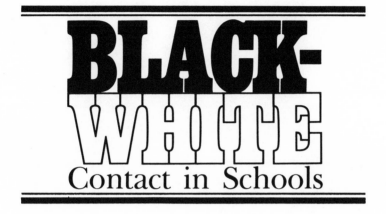

BLACK-WHITE

Contact in Schools

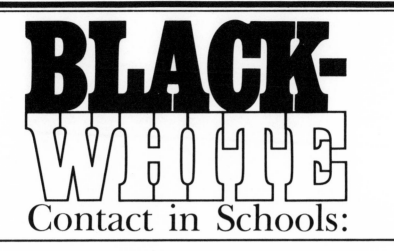

Contact in Schools:

Its Social
and Academic
Effects

by Martin Patchen

Purdue University Press
West Lafayette, Indiana

Library of Congress Card Catalog Number 80–83511
International Standard Book Numbers
  clothbound edition 0–911198–61–X
  paperbound edition 0–911198–64–4
Printed in the United States of America

To the memory of my father,
William Patchen

Contents

PREFACE   ix

ACKNOWLEDGMENTS   xi

BACKGROUND AND SETTING

1. The Study in Context   3
2. The Schools Studied and Study Methods   16

SOCIAL RELATIONS BETWEEN THE RACES

3. Interracial Attitudes   37
4. Interracial Behavior   56

DETERMINANTS OF SOCIAL RELATIONS

5. Students' Early Experiences   83
6. Student Characteristics   115
7. Opportunity for Interracial Contact   138
8. School Situation   164
9. What Counts Most for Each Social Outcome?   208

INTERRACIAL CONTACT AND ACADEMIC OUTCOMES

10. Race and Academic Performance   235
11. Contact and Academic Outcomes: Black Students   257
12. Contact and Academic Outcomes: White Students   295

OVERVIEW

13. Summary and Policy Implications   329

APPENDICES   353

NOTES   363

REFERENCES   377

SUBJECT INDEX   385

Preface

This book reports the results of an extensive study of race relations in the public high schools of Indianapolis, Indiana, which was conducted at the beginning of the 1970s. Although the study covered a variety of types of schools and types of students, the question of its generalizability quickly arises. How relevant are the findings to race relations in schools in other localities and at a later time?

Certainly, I would not expect the descriptive picture of interracial attitudes and behavior which is presented to reflect exactly the situation in other schools at other times (or even of the Indianapolis schools at the present time). For example, the frequency of interracial friendships and of fighting between the races will differ among schools in different cities, just as they did among the schools we studied.

However, both recent research and accounts in the media indicate that the basic kinds of problems which occur in racially mixed schools are, throughout the country today, similar to what they were in the schools which we studied in 1970–72. For example, black students typically continue to be disturbed by lack of acceptance by white schoolmates, by what they perceive as discrimination by administrators and teachers, and by underrepresentation of their race in prestigeful school positions, such as cheerleaders and class officers. White students typically continue to complain of physical attacks by some blacks and of what they see as disruptive behavior by blacks in the schools. In most schools, the average achievement test score of black students continues to be far below that of whites. Thus, while the exact proportions of students who behave in a certain way (such as getting into interracial fights) or who score below average on achievement tests will vary somewhat by time and location, the basic context and issues of race relations in the schools have remained very much the same. Both the schools and society as a whole still confront the problems of how we can maximize the positive social and academic effects of interracial contact and minimize any negative effects.

My basic aim is *not* to describe race relations in particular schools at a particular time. It is, rather, to contribute to the development of general principles which will permit us to understand the social and academic effects of interracial contact. Therefore, while I describe and try to explain race relations among students in a specific set of schools, my main interest throughout is in general concepts and principles. Generalizations which are made are intended to apply to a broad spectrum of school situations, and probably to intergroup relations in other settings as well. Of course, the extent to which these generalizations are valid must be tested by further systematic research and by further experience in other schools.

We were very fortunate to be able to obtain very extensive information in the schools we studied. So far as I know, it is the most comprehensive set of data about race relations in a school system which ever has been gathered. This body of data provides the opportunity to learn much more about interracial contact in schools than has been known previously. I hope that I have made good use of the materials at hand.

The book is intended to be of interest both to social scientists and to practitioners in education and government. Though some policy recommendations are made in the final chapter, the book does not provide practitioners with detailed procedures for making interracial contact yield the best social and academic results. However, by giving the reader a better understanding of the general factors which affect social and academic outcomes in racially mixed schools, it may help him or her to devise specific solutions which fit particular situations.

The book is a lengthy one, with many tables and figures. For some readers, all of the detail will be of interest, at least in some chapters. Other readers, who want to get the main findings and conclusions quickly, may want to look first at the summary of each chapter and/or the final summary chapter.

Acknowledgments

The study reported in this book was a team effort. James D. Davidson, a colleague at Purdue, and I initiated the basic ideas for the study. We were joined shortly by Gerhard Hofmann and William R. Brown, then graduate students at Purdue. The four of us collaborated in further planning, construction of questionnaires, field work, and processing of the data. We also have collaborated, in groups of three or four, on a number of professional papers which have reported limited portions of the study results.

Because the others have become involved in other activities, and because of practical difficulties in further collaboration, it has fallen on me to conduct additional analyses of the data and to prepare the present volume, which presents a comprehensive view of the study findings. However, this volume would never have been possible without the contribution of the other three men to the total project.

The fact that we were able to obtain data of unusual scope and completeness is due in no small measure to the full cooperation and backing which was given to us by Stanley C. Campbell, who was superintendent of the Indianapolis public schools when the study started. We are grateful also for their cooperation to Karl R. Kalp, who succeeded Dr. Campbell as superintendent; to other members of the central school administration; to the principals and assistant principals at each of the high schools; and to the teachers and students who contributed their time and good will to the study.

The study was financed originally by a grant from the U.S. Office of Education (project 561). An additional grant from the National Science Foundation (GS33357) enabled us to continue analyses of the data. We are grateful for both grants.

The support of many people and units at Purdue also has been invaluable. The Institute for Social Research of the Department of Sociology and Anthropology, under three directors (Harvey Marshall, Kay

Johnsen, and Robert Eichhorn), has been generous in providing help in preparing computer programs and typing assistance. While the computer assistants and typists who have helped over the years are by now too numerous to list, I am grateful to each of them for their assistance. Purdue University also has played an important role by providing access to the university computers to perform important analyses after money from grants had run out.

The manuscript has been read and critiqued by William R. Brown, Gerhard Hofmann, and David Armor. I am grateful to them for their helpful comments. The responsibility for the manuscript is, of course, my own.

Background
and Setting

1 | *The Study in Context*

The question of racial desegregation is a central one for our society. While efforts to end the separation of blacks and whites (as well as other groups) are being made in many areas—including housing and jobs—the public school has been a focal point of such efforts.

Two basic rationales have been offered for the effort to bring black and white children together in schools. One rationale centers on the social benefits which are expected to follow from greater contact between the races. Black children and white children—it is hoped—will get to know one another better, will learn to get along with each other, and will change the negative attitudes which they may have acquired from prejudiced families and communities.

Discussing the importance of school desegregation, the U.S. Commission on Civil Rights has said: "We must now look to our children to develop a sense of respect and appreciation for individual worth, regardless of race or ethnic origin, which we, their parents, somehow have been unable to develop. . . . If the schools are to be a positive influence in shaping the nation's future, they must first meet their fundamental obligation to bring our children together" (U.C.C.R., 1973, p. 12).

A second basic rationale for promoting greater contact between black students and white students concerns the academic achievement of black students. Research has shown consistently that average scores of blacks on standardized achievement tests are considerably below those of whites. It has been argued that racial integration in the schools is an important—perhaps crucial—tool for improving the academic achievement of blacks.

For example, Bouma and Hoffman explained the importance of desegregated schools in the following words: "The fundamental function of the American school has been to transmit to the young the values and competencies needed to function significantly in the culture. There is a

3

growing concern that this function is not being adequately performed in respect to that negro percentage in the inner city. The pattern of segregated education increasingly characteristic of large northern cities is one of the major roadblocks to the effective operation of the socialization process" (Bouma and Hoffman, 1968, p. 11).

In a more recent report, the U.S. Commission on Civil Rights stated flatly: "Desegregation is the means through which children of all races are provided equal educational opportunity" (U.C.C.R., 1976, p. 12).

Although arguments for the social and academic benefits of interracial contact may be plausible, the results of relevant research have been mixed. With regard to the social effects of interracial contact, primary attention has been devoted to attitude change. In some instances, the racial attitudes of white students, or of black students, or of both, have changed in a positive direction following interracial contact in school. However, in other cases, no attitude change, or even negative attitude change, has been reported for students of one or both races.

After a review of studies concerning school desegregation and racial cleavage, Carithers concluded: "Some studies have found heightened tolerance; some heightened resistance; some no change. There seems to be, however, a general agreement that racial contact *per se* will not bring about increased tolerance or acceptance" (Carithers, 1970, p. 41).

Similarly, after a careful review of research, St. John concluded: "This review of research on racial attitudes and behavior in schools indicates that desegregation sometimes reduces prejudice and promotes interracial friendship and sometimes promotes, instead, stereotyping and interracial cleavage and conflict" (St. John, 1975, p. 85).

With respect to the academic achievement of blacks, research results again are mixed. Some studies have indicated greater gains in achievement for blacks attending racially mixed classes than for those attending segregated classes (e.g., Rock et al., 1968; Zdep and Joyce, 1967; Morrison and Stivers, 1971). On the basis of such results, some writers (O'Reilly, 1970; Pettigrew et al., 1973) have concluded that the academic achievement of black children is generally higher in desegregated classes—at least under favorable conditions.

However, other studies show no positive benefits, mixed outcomes, or even negative academic effects of interracial mixing on black students' achievement (e.g., White Plains, 1967; Mahan, 1968; Carrigan, 1969). Such results have led some social scientists (e.g., Armor, 1972b) to conclude that induced school integration (especially by busing) does not have benefits that justify its use.

In a careful review of research in this area, St. John (1975, Chapter 2) focused on the best-designed studies—those using longitudinal or quasi-experimental designs. After reviewing fourteen longitudinal studies in three Southern and five Northern states, including the large-scale Riverside study, she concluded that "neither the Riverside evidence nor that of any of the other longitudinal studies provides strong support for the hypothesis that desegregated schooling benefits minority group children." In addition, she writes, thirty-six quasi-experimental studies "suggest that the achievement of black children is rarely harmed thereby, but they provide no strong or clear evidence that such desegregation boosts their achievement. A countdown by grade level and achievement tests, rather than by cities, reveals that a report of no difference is more common than a report of significant gains. Even studies over several years are as often negative as positive in their findings. And where gains are established, we are left to wonder whether the effective agent was the quality of desegregated schools, the selection of the busing program by children of mobility-oriented families, or contact with middle-class or white schoolmates" (St. John, 1975, p. 31).

The evidence seems clear, then, that the hoped-for benefits of interracial contact in the schools will not occur automatically, nor even commonly perhaps. What is needed is an understanding of the circumstances under which positive social and academic outcomes will occur and those under which no effects or negative effects will occur.

A number of scholars who have reviewed school desegregation studies have recognized this need. Thus, Carithers has suggested that more attention should be given to the conditions under which desegregation occurs, writing: "What are the group processes and inter-group relationships under different conditions of desegregation? What happens to whom under what conditions? In short, we need to look in a more differentiated way at the individuals embedded within a school community, responding to each other and to the school environment" (Carithers, 1970, p. 42).

In the same vein, St. John has said: "The pressing need now is to discover the school conditions under which the benefits of mixed schooling are maximized and its hardships minimized" (St. John, 1975, p. 122).

What does existing theory and research have to tell us on this subject? In trying to answer this question, we will consider first the social effects, and then the academic effects, of interracial contact in the schools. In each case, we will review briefly the theoretical ideas which have been proposed and the research which has been done. (More extensive reviews of previous work on specific topics are found in later chapters.) We also will indicate the intended contributions of this study.

The Social Effects of Interracial Contact

The effects of intergroup contact have been discussed from the perspective of a variety of theories (Feagin, 1978). However, the most influential set of ideas on this topic are those which have come to be called "contact theory."

Contact Theory. An early statement concerning the conditions of "successful" contact was made by Gordon Allport in his classic book *The Nature of Prejudice.* He said: "Prejudice (unless deeply rooted in the character structure of the individual) may be reduced by equal-status contact between majority and minority groups in the pursuit of common goals.

The effect is greatly enhanced if this contact is sanctioned by institutional supports (i.e., by law, custom, or local atmosphere), and if it is of the sort that leads to the perception of common interests and common humanity between members of the two groups" (Allport, 1958, p. 267).

Note that Allport's statement points to two conditions—equal status and common goals—as crucial. A third condition—institutional support for positive relations—is said to be helpful. The conditions that would lead to "the perception of common interests and common humanity" are not specified by Allport.

Other writers also have discussed the conditions which may affect the social outcomes of intergroup contact (Pettigrew, 1969b; Cook, 1970). The three basic aspects of the contact situation highlighted by Allport—equal status, common goals, and social support—have almost always been accepted, although Amir (1976) and Riordan (1975) recently have questioned whether research evidence really supports the importance of equal status. In addition to these three aspects of the situation, other writers have pointed to additional aspects of the contact situation as important. Probably the most systematic discussion of this topic is presented by Stuart Cook (1970). In addition to the variables mentioned by Allport, Cook lists as potentially important the following aspects of the contact situation:

1. The numerical proportions of the two groups
2. The degree to which minority group members have attributes which correspond to the negative stereotypes of the majority
3. The possession of valued traits by members of each group
4. Similarity in beliefs between members of the two groups
5. The acquaintance potential of the situation
6. Physical proximity.

Although the ideas of contact theory—especially those originally proposed by Allport—have been widely discussed, there has been little effort to test these ideas systematically.

Reviewing research on school desegregation, Schofield comments:

> Although contact theory is routinely invoked in reports on desegregation research, it has, in actuality, had a remarkably small impact on the design and reporting of that research. For example, contact theory appears to have had extremely little impact on the kind of information given in published reports about the effects of desegregation. Researchers often tip their hats to contact theory in the introductory passages of a research report and then fail entirely to give information on topics which the theory suggests should be vital to predicting the likely outcomes of the interracial experience. [Schofield, 1978, p. 335]

Some of the research on racial desegregation in the schools has provided information which is relevant to particular ideas of "contact theory." This includes data concerning the effects on students' racial attitudes of (1) the racial attitudes of important others—teachers, parents, and peers; (2) participation by those of different races in cooperative activities; and (3) the numerical proportions of the majority and minority groups. (Results on these topics, along with other research results, are reviewed in later chapters.) However, the effects of particular aspects of the contact situation have usually been considered in isolation from the effects of other aspects of the situation.

Schofield comments:

> First, much remains to be done in working out conceptually the way in which the rather general concepts employed by contact theory apply to and operate in the school situation. Second, more work and study is needed on the effects of contact theory variables taken one at a time . . . studies such as those reviewed earlier (Cook, 1970; Lachet, 1972; Schofield and Sager, 1977) suggest that when all or most of the conditions specified by contact theory are met, attitude or behavioral change tends to occur. However, as Cook (1970) and Weissback (1976) have pointed out, this sort of work does not allow one to determine which of the variables specified by contact theory, or which combinations of these variables, are instrumental in bringing about the changes that do occur. [Schofield, 1978, p. 351]

Just as we know little about the combined effects of different aspects of the contact situation, we also know little about the combined effects of the contact situation and characteristics of the students. A number of writers have pointed out that personal and background characteristics of those who come into contact may affect the social outcomes of such contact (Cook, 1970; Amir, 1976). Research on interracial contact in schools has considered the relation of interracial attitudes to such personal traits as sex, initial attitude toward the other group, social class, academic ability and achievement. (See Chapters 5 and 6 for a brief review of this literature.) However, there has been little effort to investigate the ways in which the effects of various student characteristics may combine with aspects of the contact situation.

These limitations of existing research are not unique to studies done in schools. In his general review of studies of intergroup contact, Amir states: "There are two major difficulties in trying to analyze the studies conducted on ethnic contact and to arrive at some generalizations. First, the variables involved in many studies are not or cannot be specified. Sometimes it is clear that a number of variables are included, but they cannot be differentiated from each other. Another difficulty stems from the type of research conducted in this area. As most of the studies are field investigations, analyses of interactions between variables are almost non-existent" (Amir, 1976, p. 8).

Intended Contributions. In the present study, we have tried to overcome some of these limitations of previous research. One of our major purposes is to understand better the ways in which variables which have been discussed under the rubric of "contact theory" (as well as other variables) affect the social relations between black students and white students.

We will examine the separate and independent effect of each of many aspects of:

1. *The opportunity for interracial contact.* (Class racial composition, contact with teachers of another race, etc.)
2. *The school situation.* (Racial attitudes of peers and teachers; similarity of students to their other-race schoolmates; participation in activities involving common goals, etc.)
3. *Students' backgrounds.* (Social class; family racial attitudes, interracial contact in grade school, etc.)
4. *Students' personal characteristics.* (Sex; general aggressiveness, educational aspirations, etc.).

This broad coverage of situational and student characteristics permits us to provide information relevant to all aspects of the contact situation discussed by Allport and by Cook (though we will not always use their terminology). Also, we will consider the effects of some additional factors (e.g., relative power of the two groups, favoritism by authorities) which have been mentioned by other workers as important or which our preliminary acquaintance with biracial high schools suggested might be relevant.

In addition to considering the impact of each separate factor on students' interracial attitudes and behaviors, we will examine the impact of various *combinations* of factors. This will be done both within each of the sets of variables indicated above (e.g., combinations of several aspects of the school situation) and across these sets (e.g., combinations of situational variations and variations in students' backgrounds).

Another way in which the present study is intended to advance work on the social effects of interracial contact in schools is by its focus on interracial behavior, in addition to interracial attitudes. Previous research on the social effects of interracial contact in schools has focused almost exclusively on students' racial attitudes.

St. John's (1975) review lists nineteen studies which purportedly deal with the relationship between desegregated schools and intergroup behavior. But, as Schofield (1978) points out, "only one of these studies involved actual observation of intergroup behavior in a desegregated school. The large majority use variants on traditional sociometric techniques (Moreno, 1934) which involve asking people to report whom they would choose to interact with in various situations, rather than observation of actual choice behavior." While sociometric choices may indicate positive feelings, there is little evidence that such choices have a strong association with actual friendly interactions.

In addition to limitations in measuring friendly interaction, there has been an almost total absence of evidence about negative interracial behavior. Schofield has pointed out the absence of such information, saying "the clear effect of ethical and practical constraints against openly investigating really negative intergroup relations can be seen in an examination of the sociometric measures used to explore intergroup relations in desegregated schools. Although there are notable exceptions (Shaw, 1973), recent studies using sociometric peer nomination techniques almost invariably ask children to name those they want to interact with most but avoid asking for the names of those with whom they are least likely to want to interact" (Schofield, 1978, p. 346). We might add that evidence about negative behavior (as opposed to negative sociometric responses) has been almost nonexistent.

A few studies have obtained information by actually observing the behavior of students in interracial settings—e.g., by observing who sits with whom in the school cafeteria. This type of information, while useful, has been limited essentially to the interaction which takes place in publicly visible places. Information about the nature of the interracial interactions which occur in a wide range of other situations, including those outside the school, are not easily obtained by such methods.[1]

The present study goes beyond most previous work in presenting data about a variety of both positive and negative interactions between black and white students. These include data on reported avoidance, friendly contacts, friendship relations and unfriendly contacts (see Chapter 4). These data permit us not only to provide a broad descriptive picture of the interactions which occur between the races but, more important, to compare the factors which affect positive behaviors, negative behaviors, attitudes, and attitude change. As we shall see, the determinants of interracial attitudes and interracial behavior are not always the same. Nor are the factors which affect one type of interracial behavior necessarily the same as those which affect another type of behavior. Thus, it is hoped that this investigation will provide a broader understanding of the determinants of race relations in schools than is possible when only limited aspects of such relations are studied.

In all, we will present an extensive set of results concerning the social outcomes of interracial contact. We will not attempt to integrate these findings with other work to develop a comprehensive or formal theory of race relations. Such an effort would go far beyond the scope of an already extensive project. However, we will draw from the results many generalizations about conditions that promote or impede good race relations. Such empirically-based generalizations, it is hoped, may help to provide the base on which further theoretical work can build.

Effects of Interracial Contact on Academic Performance

The second major topic of our study is the relation between interracial contact and students' academic performance.

In the middle 1960s, the national Equal Educational Opportunity Survey (EEOS) suggested that attendance at majority-white schools might raise the academic achievement of black students (Coleman et al., 1966). As we indicated above, the research done since then has shown only small and inconsistent effects of racial composition on students' achievements.[2] However, a number of writers have argued that it is not mere physical mixing of the races, but the circumstances under which interracial contact takes place, that may be crucial.

Social Acceptance. One major idea running through a number of discussions on this topic is that contact with the white majority will raise the achievement of blacks (and other nonwhite minorities) only when the minority is socially accepted (Katz, 1968; Gerard et al., 1975; Spady, 1976; Cohen et al., 1972; Lewis and St. John, 1974). When minority students have good social relations with the majority whites, it is argued, they will be more likely to accept the majority as a reference group. This may involve accepting the presumably more pro-academic norms of the majority; and/or learning effective school behavior from majority role models; and/or accepting whites as a group against which to compare their achievement. Social acceptance also has been seen as reducing "social threat" and anxiety, which may interfere with students' intellectual functioning.

Evidence concerning the actual effect of social relationships between the races on student achievement is limited. Analysis of the EEOS ("Coleman") data showed that black students' achievement was higher in desegregated schools where teachers reported no racial tension, and that verbal achievement was higher among black students who had a close white friend (U.S. Commission on Civil Rights, 1967). However, evidence from several other studies does not, on the whole, support the expectation that a combination of being in a primarily white setting and having friendly relations with the whites will *raise* achievement (Lewis, 1971; Narot, 1973; Gerard et al., 1975). In general, blacks' achievement in these circumstances was about what it was in majority-black settings. There does, however, appear to be a *decrease* in the achievement of minority students when they are placed in majority-white settings in which the white majority rejects them socially. The evidence from previous studies concerning white students is too sparse to draw any general conclusions about how their social relations with blacks, in settings with different racial compositions, may affect their achievement.

Academic Values of White Peers. As we have noted, the expectation that black achievement will be raised in majority-white settings is based, in part, on the assumption that black students will be influenced in such settings by whites who place a high value on academic success and demonstrate such values with a high level of academic effort (e.g., Katz, 1968; Spady, 1976). Thus, positive effects should not occur if the white majority does *not* value academic success highly. However, there has been, to our knowledge, no evidence bearing directly on this issue.

Relative Ability of White Peers. The initial academic ability of a black student, relative to the ability of his white peers, should affect his ability to compete with these schoolmates and thus his expectancy of being able to do well at his studies (O'Connor et al., 1966; Katz, 1968; St. John, 1975). The minority student who has developed his academic skills relatively well may feel challenged and stimulated to greater effort by being placed in a primarily white class, where the level of performance usually is above that of the primarily minority class. On the other hand, the minority students whose basic academic skills are low may see little hope of competing successfully in the majority-white class and, therefore, may stop trying.

Again, the available evidence is limited. Several studies reviewed by St. John (1975, pp. 111–117) found inconsistent results concerning the effects of desegregation on black students with different initial ability levels. In another study of particular interest, Gerard et al. (1975) first categorized minority (black and Mexican-American) children into those above and those below the median in pre-desegregation verbal achievement. Their assumption was "that a child above the median would be more likely to perceive himself as having a higher probability of academic success than would a child below the median." The Gerard group found that the achievement of low-ability minority students did not change following desegregation. However, contrary to their expectation of an achievement gain among the high-ability minority students, the achievement of this group actually declined. This drop in achievement was greatest among those who were not accepted by the "Anglos," but even high-ability minority students who were socially accepted did not improve in achievement. Thus, research to date provides little support for the expectation that high-ability black students will benefit most from attending majority-white classes.

Social Class of Students. Discussion of the impact of school peers on students' performance, both in racially integrated and other settings, often has focused on the social class of the students involved. It has been suggested by some that black students will benefit from attending school with white peers who are of higher socioeconomic status, because middle-class whites are most likely to manifest the academically oriented values and behaviors which lower SES black students may then adopt (e.g., Pettigrew, 1969a; St. John, 1975; Spady, 1976). However, some writers have pointed out that contact with peers of higher status may have two separate and conflicting effects on lower-status students. On the one hand, there may be the positive normative and/or role-model effect just described. On the other hand, contact with peers who are generally higher in academic ability may lower the academic self-image of the student and his expectancy of being able to compete successfully with his peers, and therefore lower his motivation. These normative and comparative effects may tend to cancel each other out (Bain and Anderson, 1975; Nelson, 1972; St. John, 1975).

There is only limited evidence about whether the effect of interracial contact on the performance of black students varies with the SES of white peers or with their own SES. Analysis of the EEOS ("Coleman") data by McPartland and York (1967) indicated that the benefit to blacks of being in majority-white classrooms was greater when the SES of the whites was high. Their analysis indicated too that black students with better-educated parents benefited more academically from contact with whites than did lower-SES blacks. In another relevant study, Lewis and St. John (1974) stratified majority-white sixth grade classes by socioeconomic status. They found that friendship with whites was associated with higher black achievement in middle-class schools, but not in working-class schools (though only among black girls). Their assumption was that middle-class whites and white girls were high in academic orientation. However, as noted above, there has been little or no direct evidence concerning how the academic values and behavior of students of each race affect the achievement of classmates of the other race.

Teacher Behavior. Student achievement in racially integrated settings may depend also on the attitudes and behaviors of school staff, especially teachers. Just as a student's peers may influence his academic values, his academic skills (through modeling), his expectancy of academic success, and his level of anxiety in the school situation, teachers also can influence these outcomes. A study by the System Development Corporation of a national program to racially integrate schools found that reading achievement gains were lower in schools where teachers gave minority students a disproportionate amount of negative feedback. Gains in achievement were associated with a greater use of "cultural enrichment" activities—i.e., those concerned with minority themes and materials (Coulson, 1977). Additional, though tentative, evidence of teachers' influence on minority achievement in integrated settings comes from the NORC study of the federal Emergency School Assistance Program (ESAP), which was intended to facilitate racial integration (NORC, 1973). Black male students scored higher on achievement tests in high schools receiving ESAP funds than did those in non-ESAP high schools (though there was no gain for elementary school students or for high school females in ESAP schools). The researchers present evidence which suggests that the programs to improve race relations in ESAP schools resulted in black students perceiving teachers as more pro-integration, which was associated with greater liking for school among blacks, which, in turn, was associated with higher black achievement. However, another study of school desegregation by the Education Testing Service did not find student achievement scores associated with teacher racial attitudes or teacher support for integration (Forehand et al., 1976). While it seems plausible that teacher behavior may affect outcomes in racially integrated settings, there seems little theoretical reason to expect that supportive teacher behavior will have better effects in mostly white than in mostly minority classes. Nor is there much, if any, evidence on this point.

Limitations of Previous Research. Our brief review of previous work indicates that the effect of interracial contact on student achievement has been thought to depend especially on (1) the social acceptance of minority students by the white majority, (2) characteristics of the white students, and (3) characteristics of the minority students.

There are several limitations of the previous body of work. First, there is only limited evidence concerning the relationship of achievement to these aspects of interracial contact with peers. The evidence concerning how the characteristics of students involved in interracial contact affect the results of the contact is especially sparse. Although a basic assumption of much research is that minority students will acquire the academic values and habits of the majority whites, almost no direct evidence concerning these traits of majority students has been available. Similarly, evidence concerning the values, academic behavior, and abilities of minority students has been rare or entirely absent.

A second limitation of previous work is the paucity of evidence concerning the *combined effects* of relevant student body variables. For example, we know little about whether high-quality minority students will do better academically in majority-white classes when the whites also are relatively high in academic ability (compared to other whites) or when the whites are closer to the average black in academic ability. To take another example, we don't know whether black students who are friends with academically oriented white schoolmates will benefit equally when the whites are the majority group numerically and when the whites are a numerical minority.

Third, work to date has, understandably, focused on the achievement of minority students. But it is important also to know more about the impact of interracial contact on white achievement. While the available evidence has indicated no detrimental effect on whites in most cases, several studies have indicated that white achievement drops in majority-black settings (St. John and Lewis, 1971; Wrightstone et al., 1966). If this result does occur, is it likely to occur only under certain circumstances—e.g., when whites in majority-black settings are socially close to blacks who have low academic motivation?

Intended Contributions. In this study, we hope to contribute to greater understanding of such issues. In particular, we will present evidence concerning the relation of achievement to the racial composition of students' classes, to the social relations of students with schoolmates of the other race, and to the characteristics (e.g., values, school behavior, social class, and ability) of students of each race. We also will consider the ways in which these possible determinants of achievement may combine in their effects.

In addition, we will explore the extent to which the effects of interracial contact differ for boys as compared to girls;[3] for those in different curriculum programs (e.g., college preparatory versus other programs); and for students who perceive varying degrees of discrimination and supportiveness by teachers. Evidence of how class racial composition is related to academic performance under these varying coniditons has been extremely limited.

We will not attempt to provide a comprehensive explanation of students' academic performance. Such an overall explanation would require, in addition to considering interracial contact, full attention to a wide range of other factors—e.g., home background, curriculum content, teacher methods—which may affect academic outcomes. We will consider a variety of such factors, but our interest in them will center primarily on how they may condition the effects of interracial contact. The effects of additional factors will be considered also to provide a comparison in judging the academic effects of interracial contact. But our focus will be on the latter throughout.

Our study has some important advantages for the study of the relationship between interracial contact and academic performance. First, whereas the information of many studies concerning the amount, the nature, and the conditions of interracial contact has been limited, we have considerable data on these matters (e.g., class racial composition, interracial friendship, the values and abilities of students of each race). Secondly, as Lewis and St. John have pointed out (1974, p. 89), it is desirable to have alternative measures of academic performance. Our measures include not only grades and standardized achievement scores, but also a measure of students' effort. Motivation and effort have received attention in theoretical discussions (e.g., Katz, 1968) and are probably affected more readily by the student's experiences in school than is his achievement level. Yet most studies of interracial contact and achievement have not had effort measures available.

Third, we have other available data which can be used as controls on the interracial contact–performance relation. As St. John (1975) has emphasized, one of the key deficiencies of many studies in this area is that it is not clear whether students in classes of certain racial compositions tended to be of higher ability *prior to* their interracial contacts. While most of our data are not longitudinal, we have available data on students' abilities prior to high school, as well as on other student characteristics (e.g., social class), which can be held constant when studying the relationship between interracial contact and academic performance.

We also have data on large samples of both black students and white students. This permits us to study the contact–performance relation among those of both races, rather than—as has often been the case—only for the minority students.

Summary

Available evidence indicates that interracial contact in schools does not have consistent positive effects on students' racial attitudes and behavior or on the academic performance of minority students. It is important, therefore, to try to discover the conditions under which racially mixed schooling has the most positive social and academic effects.

The work which has come to be called "contact theory" has specified a number of aspects of the contact situation, and of those persons who come into contact, which may affect the social outcomes of intergroup contact. However, research in the schools and elsewhere has not provided us with sufficient evidence about the independent effects of these supposed determinants nor about their effects in combination.

This study attempts to advance our understanding of the effects on students' interracial attitudes and behavior of various aspects of the contact situation (e.g., racial proportions, similarity of status, racial attitudes of others) and of various characteristics of the students coming into contact (e.g., prior interracial experiences, social class). In addition, this study investigates the *combined* effects of various aspects of the school situation and of students' characteristics.

The second major focus of our study is on the relationship between interracial contact and the academic performance of students. Previous research results generally have shown only small and inconsistent associations between school (or classroom) racial composition and student achievement. However, it has been argued by others that interracial mixing will have a beneficial impact on minority students' performance only under certain circumstances. The literature on this subject suggests the hypotheses that the effects of interracial mixing on minority student performance will depend on (1) the friendliness of the interracial contact; (2) the characteristics of the majority group (e.g., their social class background, academic values, and ability level); and (3) the characteristics of the minority students (e.g., social class, initial ability, sex). Previous evidence concerning the extent to which the relation between interracial mixing and student performance varies with such factors—and especially with various combinations of such factors—has been sparse. This book presents evidence which is intended to throw some additional light on these issues.

In the next chapter, we describe the background and general nature of the study from which our data come.

2 | *The Schools Studied and Study Methods*

The Context

As the decade of the 1970s began, the matter of racial integration was at the top of the agenda of the Indianapolis Public Schools, as it was in many school systems around the country. In part, this was the result of pressures both outside of, and within, the community. The city recently had been sued by the U.S. Justice Department on charges of maintaining racially segregated schools. A trial on these charges was pending before a federal judge. For several years, a citizens' group called Non-Partisans for Better Schools had been campaigning for an end to alleged racial discrimination in the schools. Its chairman had stated: "We believe a first-rate school system is a racially integrated system" (*Indianapolis Star,* May 10, 1970). There also had been pressure from within the school board to speed racial integration.

Faced with these pressures, and with much pro-integration sentiment within its own ranks, the school administration moved to promote greater racial integration. Various plans to promote racial integration were developed by school planners during the 1970–71 school year. These proposals were debated by the school board and within the community. In May 1971, the school board rejected plans to integrate city elementary schools but approved a plan to provide integrated experiences for students in eleven inner-city elementary schools. The board also approved implementation in the fall of plans to integrate the freshman class of a previously all-black high school (Carver).[1] Changes in the system of pupil assignments to a second high school (Jefferson) also were planned for the fall to greatly increase the proportion of black freshmen at that school. During this period, efforts also were being made to increase the number of blacks in supervisory positions within the school system and plans for greater racial balance in assignment of teachers were beginning to be formulated.

In addition to concern about increasing racial integration, the school administration also was concerned about problems of human relations, including race relations, in the schools. These problems were found especially in the high schools. There were a number of assaults, robberies, and other law violations which were serious enough to result in the police being called. Two items taken from newspaper stories illustrate: "Six pupils were arrested and another was beaten at three high schools yesterday, police said" (*Star*, October 25, 1970); "Police will patrol [Harrison] High School in heavier force today following a melee yesterday in which twenty-three youths were arrested. . . . Some pupils were being told to pay money if they wanted to pass safely between buildings on the campus" (*Star*, November 20, 1970).

In some cases, fights and other frictions within the high schools did not involve interracial hositility, but in some cases they did. An example in which such interracial friction was involved is contained in this newspaper item: "Police yesterday arrested 13 youths and broke up a fight near the east entrance of [Jefferson] High School. . . . The school principal said he learned from a teacher that the 9 a.m. fight resulted from a remark by a Negro youth to a white girl in art class Friday. The teacher told [the principal] that the girl reported the incident to her boyfriend who recruited other youths so he could get even" (*Star*, September 23, 1971). At another high school, the *Star* later reported, "Between 200 and 300 [Hillcrest] High School pupils walked out of class yesterday in what they said was an attempt to get school officials to do something to increase pupil safety at school and extra-curricular events. The pupils said the walkout was triggered by racial incidents at the Northside School, culminating last Friday night following the [Hillcrest–Adams] football game at [Hillcrest] when a white pupil allegedly was beaten by Negro youths" (*Star*, September 25, 1971).

School administrators took a number of actions to try to reduce frictions, including interracial frictions, within the schools. A series of workshops on human relations was initiated for school staff members. Keynoting one program, the school superintendent said "human relations problems are most urgent in the area of race relations, for there is a serious undercurrent of racial strain in our general population" (*Star*, September 4, 1970). At each school (at both elementary and high school levels) a staff human relations committee was formed. Not relying completely on promotion of good will, the administration also increased the number of security guards in the high schools.

It was in this milieu—a time of movement toward increased racial integration but also concern with interracial frictions already occurring in the schools—that we approached the Indianapolis Public School administration with a proposal to study interracial contact in the high schools. The school superintendent promised to make available to us information available at central school offices and asked all of the eleven high school principals to grant us entrée to, and assistance in, each school. With the cooperation of the school system thus assured, we then obtained a grant for the study from the U.S. Office of Education and made plans to begin the study in the fall of 1970.

Description of High Schools

Aside from the willingness of school officials to cooperate fully (a vital asset) and the relative closeness of these schools to Purdue, the Indianapolis high schools offered important other advantages for the study of interracial contact. A wide range of racial compositions, types of academic programs, social class compositions, and other variations among and within twelve high school sites ensured that we could study interracial contact under a variety of different conditions. Also, the presence of one all-black school and one amost-all-white school meant that we could contrast some outcomes in monoracial settings with those in biracial situations.

The total population of the Indianapolis metropolitan area in 1970 was just under 800,000. Eighty-three percent were white and 17% were black. However, the Indianapolis Public School system covered only the central portion of the city (Center Township), which had a population of slightly under 275,000. Of this number, 61% were white and 39% were black.[2]

There were eleven high schools in the Indianapolis Public School system. One of these schools—Carver High School—was divided into two geographically separate locations, one for freshmen, the other for upperclassmen. Because these two Carver sites differed drastically in racial composition and in other ways, we will treat them (for our purposes) as separate schools, making a total of twelve school sites.

Racial Composition and Transportation. During the 1970–71 school year, schools varied widely in racial composition, from 1.1% nonwhite at Pershing to 99.8% nonwhite at Carver (see Table 2.1). (Because the number of nonwhites who were not black was insignificant, the percentage of nonwhites given is essentially the same as the percentage of blacks.) Eight of the twelve school sites had white majorities of varying sizes. Two school sites (Harrison and Lakeview) had a small black majority, while one racially mixed school (Highland) had a student body which was over 70% black.

As the black population of the inner city had risen, the proportion of black students in most of the high schools also had risen over the previous five years, from 1965 to 1970 (see Table 2.1). These increases were largest at Emerson and at Hillcrest. At both of these schools, located in middle-class areas at the fringes of the central city, the size of the black student minority had gone from almost zero six years earlier to a large and growing proportion (one-quarter and one-third respectively) by 1970. These changes were due to efforts by school authorities to desegregate the high schools. They involved substantial redistricting and the busing of large proportions of the black students at these schools (see Table 2.2). The effort to desegregate the high schools had resulted also in substantial changes in the freshman class at Jefferson. Ninety-nine percent of the student body at Jefferson had been white prior to 1970. In the fall of 1970, 22% of the freshman class was black. A majority of the blacks at

Table 2.1. Racial Composition of High Schools in Study (Sept. 1970)[1]

School	Total Enrollment	Percent Nonwhite	Change in Nonwhite Percentage 1965–70	Change in Nonwhite Percentage 1969–70
Pershing	2,550	1.1	0	0
Jefferson	1,865	8.7*	+8	+8
Eastern	2,705	13.6	+13	+4
Southwest	2,452	13.9	+6	+1
Emerson	2,676	26.6	+26	+7
Hillcrest	1,965	35.5	+34	+10
Roosevelt	2,033	36.9	+17	+3
John Price	1,533	36.9	+16	+8
Harrison	4,952	53.0	+20	+1
Lakeview	306	53.3	†	†
Highland	1,709	71.2	+6	+4
Carver	1,383	99.8	‡	‡

1. Data from records of Indianapolis Public Schools.

* At Jefferson, 22% of freshmen were nonwhite, but only 1% of other classes were nonwhite.
† New school site.
‡ Change less than .5%.

Jefferson were brought by school buses, but most seemed reluctant to go there. Only 17% of the blacks at Jefferson said that they had preferred to enter that school (see Table 2.2).

Fairly large increases in the proportions of blacks also had occurred at Harrison, Roosevelt, John Price, and Eastern in the years since 1965. However, the increases in black enrollment in these schools occurred through changes in neighborhood composition and/or changes in "feeder" grade schools, rather than through a large school-busing program. Moreover, three of these schools (Harrison, Roosevelt, and John Price) already had a sizable proportion of blacks as far back as 1965.

The greatest change initiated in the fall of 1970 was the desegregation of Carver, which traditionally had been the black high school of the city. To try to make the transition easier, a new school campus (Lakeview) was set up for a freshman class which was planned to be about evenly balanced between whites and blacks. White students who would otherwise have gone to other schools were assigned to this new campus of the previously all-black school over the vociferous protests of many of their parents. About one-third of the whites, as well as a majority of the blacks, attending this new school site had to be bused by the schools (see Table 2.2). Lakeview was the school which was least preferred by white students, only 5% of whom said they had wanted to go there; in addition, it was one of the least preferred schools among blacks. The reluctance of whites to attend Lakeview, a school with a slight black majority, was in marked con-

Table 2.2. Method and Time for Transportation to School and Student Preference for Present School, by School and Race[1]

	Percent Traveling More than 15 Min.		Percent Riding School Bus		Percent Who Preferred Present High School	
	Blacks	Whites	Blacks	Whites	Blacks	Whites
Pershing	55	17	6	4	38	87
Jefferson	84	20	54	6	17	76
Eastern	79	13	10	4	43	80
Southwest	58	19	17	2	35	84
Emerson	48	19	51	11	38	80
Hillcrest	64	15	37	3	50	64
Roosevelt	52	22	17	4	46	76
John Price	64	45	5	1	44	54
Harrison	78	38	8	1	74	73
Lakeview	37	64	61	33	20	5
Highland	38	29	7	1	75	83
Carver	51	—	2	—	82	—

1. Data based on responses of students in our sample. See Appendix A for numbers (*N*s) of samples.

trast to the feelings of white students who attended Harrison and Highland, both of which also had black majorities. The contrast between Lakeview and Highland is particularly sharp in this respect, since many white students at Highland lived outside that school's district and attended that majority-black school voluntarily, because of Highland's academic reputation and because they and their parents welcomed contact with blacks.

Table 2.2 also shows the percentage of black students and of white students in each school who had to travel more than 15 minutes to get to school (as reported on our questionnaires). In all but one school, a larger proportion of blacks than whites had to travel more than 15 minutes. This was due to the fact that much larger proportions of blacks than whites came to school by bus (either school bus or city bus) in these schools. White students were more likely than blacks either to walk or to come to school by car.[3] The one school to which whites had to travel longer was Lakeview, the school to which many whites were brought by school bus and to which the majority of others rode a city bus.

Social Class of Students' Families. The average education and the average overall socioeconomic status (SES) of students' families are shown in Table 2.3, separately by race and by school. The socioeconomic status of each student's family reflects both the education of parents and the family income, as estimated from the occupations of those people helping to support the student. These data are based on the reports of a sample of students in each school. (The student samples are described later in this chapter.)

Table 2.3. Average Education of Parents and Average Socioeconomic Status of Students' Families, by School and Race[1]

School	Average Education of Parents[2]		Average Socioeconomic Status of Family[3]	
	Blacks	Whites	Blacks	Whites
Pershing	3.6	3.9	13.7	13.1
Jefferson	3.8	4.1	11.5	13.6
Eastern	3.5	4.0	10.9	13.6
Southwest	3.7	3.5	10.7	12.0
Emerson	3.8	4.4	11.9	14.5
Hillcrest	3.8	4.7	11.3	15.4
Roosevelt	3.3	3.1	10.5	10.9
John Price	3.3	3.0	10.8	11.3
Harrison	3.2	3.1	10.3	11.9
Lakeview	3.5	3.6	11.1	12.3
Highland	4.0	5.3	12.0	16.7
Carver	3.3	—	10.4	—

1. Data based on reports of students in our sample. See Appendix A for *N*s of samples in each school.
2. Scores were assigned to parent education as follows: (1) went to grade school but did not graduate; (2) finished 8th grade but did not go further; (3) went to high school but did not graduate; (4) finished high school but did not go further; (5) had some schooling after high school; (6) finished a four-year college or went beyond. Where student had two parents (or parent substitutes), scores were averaged.
3. SES score is an average of scores on parents' education and on family income, as estimated from occupation of persons helping to support student, as reported by student. Education and estimated income were each scored on 11-point scale and the two scores were summed.

In seven of the eleven biracial sites (all except Highland, Hillcrest, Emerson, and Eastern), black students and white students came from families whose average SES was not greatly different. Only at Pershing, which had a small number of blacks, did the families of black students score higher in average SES than those of whites. But the average SES scores of black and white families at most of the other schools in this set were fairly close, and in three schools (John Price, Roosevelt, and Southwest) the average educational level of black students' parents was slightly higher than that of white students' parents.

At four schools, however, the SES of white students' families was clearly higher than those of black students' families. The greatest difference was found at Highland. The parents of black students at that primarily academic school had a higher average education (completion of high school) than parents of blacks at any other school and also scored high in overall socioeconomic status. However, the white students at Highland came from families with a very high educational level (averaging almost completion of a four-year college) and the white students' families scored very high in average SES. A wide gap also existed at Hillcrest, where the families of black students were about average (for all black families) in education and overall SES, while the families of white students were almost as high in SES as those of students at Highland. Smaller, but still substantial, gaps in the average education and overall SES of the families of black and white students also were found at Emerson and at Eastern. Of course, within each racial group, at each school, there was considerable variation among individual students with respect to both family education and overall SES.

Curriculum Programs. At the time of our study, there were four programs for students in the Indianapolis high schools—academic, fine and practical arts (FPA), vocational, and general. All programs included certain basic requirements but differed in their emphases. The academic program aimed at preparing students for college and emphasized the kinds of courses (especially language, math, and science) necessary for college entrance. The fine and practical arts program taught students a variety of artistic subjects, such as creative arts, sculpture, and jewelry. The vocational program offered courses to train students in a variety of crafts, such as carpentry, auto repair, and plumbing. The general program, as its name indicates, did not provide a specific emphasis for a student's set of courses.

Beginning in the fall of 1970, phasing out of the separate curriculum programs was begun. Although students might still take different types of courses, in the future all would get the same diploma. Juniors and seniors were permitted to continue the programs in which they were enrolled. Although sophomores had already enrolled in programs, their formal status in these programs was ended. Freshmen were not asked by the schools to choose a diploma program. However, programs continued to be an informal reality for sophomores and freshmen in the sense that the great majority of these students knew whether they intended to take a college-preparatory, vocational, arts, or more general set of courses. In describing the programs which students were following, we will rely on actual program enrollment for juniors and seniors and the stated plans of freshmen and sophomores (on our questionnaire) regarding the kinds of courses they planned to take.

For students in all high schools together, about an equal proportion of blacks and whites was in the general program (see Table 2.4). Also, only a small proportion of those of both races was in the vocational program. However, over twice as large a proportion of whites as blacks (39% vs. 19%) was in the academic program. A greater representation of whites in the academic program was found in every school, without exception. On the other hand, a larger proportion of blacks than whites (24% vs. 12%) was in the fine and practical arts program. This greater representation of blacks in the FPA program also was found in every school—though the difference between the races was very slight in several schools.

In addition to these overall patterns, there was some variation among schools in the types of programs which students were following. Among black students, the proportion in the academic program was by far the highest at Highland, which had followed a selective admissions

Table 2.4. Curriculum Programs in Which Students Were Enrolled, or Type of Courses They Planned to Take, by School and by Race (Percentages)[1]

School	Academic Bl (Wh)	General Bl (Wh)	Fine and Practical Arts Bl (Wh)	Vocational Bl (Wh)
Pershing	28 (41)	28 (43)	44 (11)	0 (6)
Jefferson	11 (37)	51 (42)	15 (14)	8 (5)
Eastern	19 (40)	41 (44)	31 (12)	5 (2)
Southwest	17 (35)	44 (38)	32 (18)	5 (7)
Emerson	12 (46)	62 (37)	17 (13)	6 (2)
Hillcrest	16 (52)	51 (34)	23 (8)	8 (4)
Roosevelt	11 (26)	54 (48)	27 (19)	6 (6)
John Price	10 (18)	57 (52)	18 (11)	11 (18)
Harrison	11 (22)	62 (51)	13 (11)	12 (14)
Lakeview	21 (31)	22 (26)	39 (24)	3 (2)
Highland	54 (74)	17 (19)	19 (2)	7 (2)
Carver	27 (—)	27 (—)	32 (—)	11 (—)
All Schools	19 (39)	45 (40)	24 (12)	8 (6)

1. Data based on reports of student sample in each school. See Appendix A for *N*s.

   Juniors and seniors were enrolled in a program. Sophomores (who had enrolled in programs but were no longer formally in these) and freshmen were asked: "How would you describe the kinds of courses you plan to take during the rest of the time you are in high school?"

   Rows do not add to 100% since some students said they did not plan to be in school after the current year.

(—) Indicates too few students to percentagize.

policy.[4] The proportion of blacks in the academic programs of other schools was roughly similar (and uniformly low). The proportion of blacks in the practical and fine arts program varied somewhat more widely among schools. The vocational program was chosen by only a small proportion of blacks at each school.

Among white students, the proportion enrolled in (or planning) an academic program varied more widely than among blacks. After Highland, the "academic school," the academic program was most popular among whites at Hillcrest and Emerson. It was least popular among whites at John Price and Harrison. These latter two schools also had the largest proportion of white students—although under 20%—in the vocational program. The fine and practical arts program attracted between 10% and 20% of the whites at most schools.

School Staff and Facilities. Finally, we may describe briefly some aspects of the staff and facilities in the schools studied (see Table 2.5).

In all but three of the schools, 85% or more of the faculty was white. In five schools, over 90% of the faculty was white. The three schools with

Table 2.5. Faculty Racial Composition, Faculty–Student Ratio, Number of Security Guards, and Rated Adequacy of School Facilities, by School

School	Percent White Faculty[1]	Faculty–Student Ratio[1]	Number of Security Guards[2]	Adequacy of Facilities (Administrator Ratings)[2]
Pershing	93	1:20	0	2.7
Jefferson	94	1:19	1	3.3
Eastern	89	1:20	2	*
Southwest	94	1:20	1	3.0
Emerson	91	1:20	2.5†	4.0
Hillcrest	87	1:20	2	3.6
Roosevelt	91	1:18	1	2.1
John Price	85	1:12	1	3.1
Harrison	89	1:18	12	3.3
Lakeview	53	1:10	*	*
Highland	72	1:16	4	2.9
Carver	29	1:16	3	3.2

1. Data from records of Indianapolis Public Schools.
2. Data from administration at each school. Administrators were asked to assess the following facilities at their respective schools: classroom space, laboratory facilities, lecture hall(s), library, auditorium, gymnasium, instructional equipment, cafeteria, study hall space, shop and vocational facilities, textbooks now in use. Response categories were: (1) very inadequate, (2) somewhat inadequate, (3) just adequate, (4) good, and (5) excellent. Data shown are average ratings.

* Data not available.
† One-half guard indicates part time.

the largest proportion of black students also had the largest fraction of black teachers. One was Lakeview, where the almost 50–50 racial balance of the freshmen at this new campus was paralleled by a faculty which had an almost equal number of blacks and whites. At Highland, which had over 70% black students, the faculty was 72% white, but the proportion of black faculty was larger than at most other schools. Only at Carver, the traditionally all-black school, were whites a minority of the faculty (29%).

Two of the eleven schools had black principals. One was Carver, the all-black school.[5] The second was Hillcrest, where a black man had just become principal. At most schools where a white man was principal (all principals were men), a black man was an assistant principal.

The ratio of faculty to students was roughly the same at most schools—from about 1:18 to 1:20. Four schools—which tended to be those with the most heavily black student bodies—had more favorable faculty–student ratios. The ratio at Highland and at Carver (1:16) was slightly better than at most schools. Two schools—John Price and Lakeview—had unusually favorable faculty–student ratios, 1:12 and 1:10

respectively, probably reflecting the special academic problems at these schools.[6]

All schools—with the exception of Pershing—had at least one security guard. Differences in the number of guards at various schools generally were due to variations in school size and in the number of security problems—both those involving students and those involving outsiders entering the school—which each school had experienced. Most schools had one or two guards; Carver had three; Highland had four; and Harrison had the unusually large number of twelve. The large security force at Harrison was due partly to the fact that this school was by far the largest and occupied a number of separate buildings on the same campus. It was due also to an unusually large number of fights within the school which were serious enough to be reported to the central school administration.[7]

With respect to facilities, administrators at each school were asked to rate the quality of each of a number of facilities at their schools. These included: classroom space, laboratory facilities, lecture hall(s), library, auditorium, gymnasium, instructional equipment, cafeteria, study-hall space, shop and vocational facilities, and textbooks now in use. Each of these school facilities was rated by an administrator (usually the principal) on a scale with the following categories: (1) very inadequate, (2) somewhat inadequate, (3) just adequate, (4) good, and (5) excellent. While these ratings are subjective, and the standards used by administrators at different schools may vary, the results are of some interest.

In general, ratings of school facilities by administrators did not vary much among schools. Facilities at seven of the ten schools were rated, on the average, as about "just adequate." Facilities at one school, Roosevelt, were rated "somewhat inadequate" on the average. Facilities at two schools were rated highest; these were Emerson, where the average rating was "good," and Hillcrest, where the average rating was somewhat below "good." These latter two schools were among the newer schools, located away from the heart of the central city.

Study Procedures

Our first aim at the start of the study was to get familiar with the schools. We wanted to know what was going on at each school and what was on the minds of students and staff members.

Informal Interviews. At each of the twelve school sites, we arranged to conduct interviews with five black students, five white students, two black teachers, two white teachers, and the principal. This plan was carried out, with minor variations, in each school. In addition, in most schools we interviewed a number of other persons—such as assistant principals, guidance counselors, school social workers, and student government leaders—who could give us further information about specific topics. A total of about 170 interviews was conducted in all schools together.

In each school, interviews were conducted by one of the four project staff members and by one or more assistants hired for these interviews. For interviews with students (though not necessarily for those with teachers or administrators), each person was interviewed by someone of his or her own race. Interviewers followed guides which indicated the subjects to be covered and possible questions to be asked, but the interviews were informal and interviewers were not bound to follow a rigid format. Almost all interviews were tape recorded.

In each school, students in various school years and programs, and both boys and girls, were interviewed. They were asked about a variety of subjects, including their interracial contacts, school courses and teachers, and their aspirations for the future. Despite the fact that the students interviewed usually were selected by school administrators (our selection of representative samples came later), they did not appear reluctant to tell us about negative, as well as positive, aspects of their school experiences. They were assured, of course, that the interviews would be completely confidential.

Teachers who were interviewed also were asked about a variety of subjects, including their teaching methods; any differences in how well black students and white students did in their classes; and relationships between black students and white students. The school principal (and often other administrators as well) were asked about characteristics of the total school (facilities, programs, etc.); about characteristics of the student body (social class, percent going to college, etc.); characteristics of the faculty (experience, background, etc.); relations between the school and the community; and other matters. Members of the project staff also made informal observations in and around the schools during this preliminary period. We observed students interacting with teachers and with each other in hallways, cafeterias, classrooms, study halls, auditoriums, meetings of students organizations, and other settings.

Developing Questionnaires. This early work in the schools, particularly our interviews with students and staff, served to familiarize us with daily life in these schools and especially with interracial contact in these settings. During the same general time period (as well as earlier), we had been reviewing the literature on intergroup and interracial relations in the schools and elsewhere (see Chapter 1).

Our aim during the next phase of the study was to develop systematic data-gathering instruments which (1) would obtain information bearing on the main conceptual variables which prior theory and research had suggested to be important in intergroup contact, and (2) at the same time, would be concrete and specific enough to obtain information which was relevant and meaningful in these particular situations. In the relatively short time (about three months) which our schedule permitted, we developed questionnaires for students, teachers, and administrators which were intended to fulfill these purposes.

Student Questionnaires. Because of the large amount of information which we wished to obtain from students, two student questionnaires—to be administered at different times—were developed. The first form included questions about the student's courses (e.g., the type he was taking); his satisfaction or dissatisfaction with various aspects of school; certain school-relevant behaviors (time spent doing homework, cutting classes, etc.); school activities in which the student participated; his friends and some of their characteristics; his educational and occupational aspirations; and his perception of some aspects of the school (e.g., disciplinary strictness, willingness of administrators to heed student suggestions).

The second student questionnaire focused on the student's interracial contacts. It included questions about his interracial contacts in grade school and neighborhood; his perceptions of and feelings toward other-race students in his school; the amount and types of friendly and unfriendly contact he had with other-race schoolmates in his school; his perceptions of the relative status and relative power of black students and white students in his school; his perceptions of the norms of others (e.g., peers, teachers) concerning interracial contact; possible racial favoritism by school personnel; and information about the student's personal background (religion, parents' education and occupation, etc.).

Preliminary versions of the student questionnaires were tried out with a group of high school students (both blacks and whites) from East Chicago, Illinois. These students pointed out any instructions which were difficult to follow, wordings which were unclear, or items which did not seem meaningful or relevant. On the basis of the feedback from these students, some revisions were made and final forms of the questionnaires were prepared for use in the Indianapolis high schools. (These forms are included as an appendix in a preliminary report on the study; see Patchen and Davidson, 1973.)[8]

The first questionnaire—the one *not* focused on race relations—was identical for all students at all schools. The second questionnaire, which focused on interracial contacts in the school, also was essentially identical for black students and for white students, with the exception that the words "black" and "white" were transposed. When a black student was asked about other-race students, he was asked about white students; whites were asked about black students. In addition, special versions of questionnaire 2 were prepared for white students at Pershing; for white sophomores, juniors, and seniors at Jefferson; and for black students at Carver. As indicated by our discussion of school racial composition, these groups of students had little opportunity for contact with students of another race in their present schools. Therefore, some questions concerning present interracial contacts were omitted for these students.

Sample. In choosing a sample of students within each school, we wished to have an adequate representation of students of each race and of students from each of the different class years (freshman, sophomore, etc.). We decided to aim for a sample of 50 black students and 50 white students in each class of each school—i.e., 50 black freshmen, 50 white freshmen, etc. To compensate for an expected loss of some students selected in the initial sample (because of absence from school, etc.), this basic number was increased to 60 of each race in each class in each school.

Students were selected systematically (i.e., every nth name) from enrollment lists provided to us by the schools. When there were fewer than

60 students of one race in a given class, all of the students in this group were included in the sample. These selection procedures resulted in a total sample for all schools of 2,645 black students and 2,834 white students, or 5,479 students in all. (See Appendix A for number in sample in each school.)

The administration of questionnaires to students began during the first week of May 1971 and continued through the first week of June. The questionnaires were administered to students during school hours by members of our research staff (almost always including at least one white person and one black person). Students, as well as their parents and teachers, had been sent letters about the study shortly before the time they were asked to participate in it. Students were asked to come to a school room (e.g., a library, a large classroom) during a specified class period. To keep the groups of students gathered together at one time fairly small, as well as to avoid disruption of school operations, students were scheduled throughout the day, usually during one of their "free" periods, such as a study period.

Since there were two versions of the second questionnaire in every school—one for blacks and one for whites—these had to be distributed properly without focusing undue attention on this matter. The problem was handled by identifying each student visually as black or white (by social definition) as he or she entered the room and giving the person a form from the appropriate pile. Members of the research team had very little difficulty in making these racial identifications. A check on their accuracy was made later by comparing the student's own racial identification with that of the form given to him. Only a few discrepancies were found and these were resolved by checking school records concerning the students' race.

When a group of students was assembled, and the questionnaires distributed, our staff members explained the purpose of the study in general terms—i.e., to learn more about students' experiences and opinions. Students were asked for their cooperation and were assured that their individual answers would be confidential. Each student then filled out the questionnaire at his or her own pace. Staff members were present and answered any questions which arose.

In each school, part 1 of the questionnaire was administered during one day and part 2 was given during the second day, usually several days later. Thus, each student spent two whole class periods filling out the two questionnaires. In all but one school, where few students missed taking the questionnaire, a third visit (or more) was made to each school to administer questionnaires to those students who had missed taking one or both forms.

Despite our attempts to locate all students selected in the sample, some students did not take one or both questionnaires, primarily because of absence from school, difficulties encountered by the schools in finding time when students were free, or mix-ups in scheduling (which was done primarily by the schools). In all schools together, 77.5% of the black students and 83.9% of the white students in our original sample completed the first questionnaire; 78.1% of the black students and 83.0% of the white students completed the second questionnaire. These completion rates varied only slightly among the twelve school sites.

We did not assume that the fact that a student had filled out a questionnaire guaranteed its usefulness. While the great majority of students appeared to fill out the forms carefully and thoughtfully, a few students appeared to be "fooling around" during the administration period. Moreover, although we had tried to keep the wording of questions simple, a few students had difficulty reading and understanding the questions. We therefore carried out a careful checking process to find and eliminate invalid questionnaires. First, coders were asked to be alert for signs of invalid questionnaires—such as strange response patterns (e.g., where check marks formed zigzags or diagonals), an unusual number of unanswered questions, or inappropriate or abusive comments. Members of the research staff reviewed questionable forms and 98 questionnaires (either part 1 or part 2) were eliminated at this stage.

After the data had been put on IBM cards, computer programs searched each questionnaire for "block" answers (i.e., where a series of questions were all answered the same), for inconsistencies in answers, for students' not following directions, and for unusual responses (e.g., saying one was seven feet tall). Inconsistencies were corrected, either by checking school records or by deleting the inconsistent items. Where the number of block answers or unusual responses was small, the data were left unchanged. Where that number became moderately large, responses to particular sections of questionnaires were deleted. Questionnaires with an excessive combination of inconsistencies and/or block answers and/or unusual responses were eliminated altogether. As a result of these computer checks, we excluded an additional 156 forms (either questionnaire 1 or 2), making 256 questionnaires (or 2.9% of all completed questionnaires) eliminated at any stage of the checking process. Of those questionnaires eliminated, 162 (63.8%) came from black students and 92 (36.2%) were from white students.

As a result of this careful, rather laborious checking procedure, we felt that we could have reasonable confidence in the quality of the data to be used in our analysis. The final number and proportion of acceptable questionnaires (after elimination of invalid ones) are shown in Table 2.6. Of the total sample in all schools, 85.4% acceptably completed at least one part of the questionnaire and 71.5% acceptably completed both parts.[9]

Teacher Questionnaires. Our main source of information about students' interracial contacts was intended to be the students themselves. However, we wished also to get some information which could be obtained best from teachers. A questionnaire prepared for teachers was put in every teacher's mailbox during May 1971, with the request that he or she fill it out and mail it back to us at Purdue. An identifying number was put on each questionnaire so that we could tell which teachers had returned the forms, but teachers were assured of the confidentiality of their responses.

The teacher questionnaire included questions about procedures the teacher used in classes (e.g., method of assigning seats); about the relationships between black students and white students; and, for those who

Table 2.6. Acceptably Completed Student Questionnaires
(Number and Percent of Total Sample)

	Black Students	White Students	Total
Both part 1 and	1,769	2,146	3,915
part 2 acceptable	(66.9%)	(75.7%)	(71.5%)
Only part 1	217	201	418
acceptable	(8.2%)	(7.1%)	(7.6%)
Only part 2	200	146	346
acceptable	(7.5%)	(5.2%)	(6.3%)
Neither part	459	341	800
completed or	(17.4%)	(12.0%)	(14.6%)
acceptable			

coached, advised, or directed a school activity, a series of questions about each activity, including its racial composition.[10] (The information about each activity was matched later with student reports of the activities in which they participated).

Two follow-up letters, along with extra copies of the questionnaire, were sent, in May and June of 1971, to those teachers who did not return their forms promptly. In addition, since we were especially interested in the interracial interaction which takes place in activities, we made another attempt, in the fall of 1971, to obtain more complete information about school activities. Brief questionnaires, containing only the series of items about activities, were put in the mailboxes of teachers who advised some student activity during the previous school year. The teacher was asked to fill out and return this brief form concerning the last school year's activities, if he/she had not answered these questions in the spring.

A total of 900 faculty members in all high schools, or 61.7% of the total, returned a questionnaire by mail during the spring. In general, there was little variation in response rates among schools. In the fall, an additional 209 teachers, or 14.3% of all teachers, returned the abbreviated questionnaire about school activities.

Administration Questionnaire. Some information about the school could be obtained most easily and reliably from administrators in each school. Accordingly, we prepared a questionnaire to be filled out by the school principal and/or by members of his administrative staff knowledgeable about the topics covered. The administration questionnaire contained questions about a variety of procedures and conditions in the school, including the nature and racial composition of some student groups, such as the Student Council; the adequacy of various school facilities; disciplinary rules and problems; guidelines for assigning students to particular programs and classes; and a variety of other matters. A completed administration questionnaire was returned to us from each of the eleven schools.

Data from School Records. Some of the most vital data for the study came from school records. Copies of computer tapes at the Indianapolis Public School headquarters were made available to us and we were given access also to student records at each school. From these sources, we obtained directly, or computed, a variety of data about each student. These include the following information:

1. *IQ scores.* In almost all cases, these scores were based on tests given in grade school. The great majority (93.4%) of students in our sample took the California Test of Mental Maturity in the eighth grade. A small number of students took that test or another IQ test in the sixth grade (1.9%) or during the ninth grade (4.7%).
2. *Grades.* The grades which students had received in each of their high school courses were available from the schools. From these data we computed each student's grade average for the current semester (when our questionnaire was given) and for the student's entire high school career.
3. *Achievement test scores.* Students' scores on a battery of nationally used standardized achievement tests were obtained. Students took these tests during their sophomore year of high school. Those who were freshmen or sophomores at the time they filled out our questionnaires took the Metropolitan Achievement Tests. Those who were juniors or seniors at the time they completed our questionnaires had taken the National Educational Development Tests. (See Chapter 10 for further information about the achievement tests.)
4. *Absences.* The number of days which each student was absent from school during the spring 1971 semester was obtained.
5. *Class racial composition.* School records listed the classes which each student took during the spring 1971 semester. From these data we computed the racial composition of each class in each school. Then we computed for each student the average racial composition of the classes in which he was enrolled.

A variety of other data also was obtained from school records. Some of these data were used to verify some of the personal information (race, sex, and year in school) given by students on questionnaires. In the very few cases where discrepancies turned up, a check was made with school administrators to obtain the correct information.

Strengths and Limitations of Study

In total, the information which we obtained in these high schools on matters relevant to interracial contact is unusual in its scope and detail. In fact, they constitute what is—to our knowledge—the most rich and detailed set of data of its type which ever has been gathered. These data provide an opportunity for us to learn a great deal about the determinants and effects of interracial contact in the schools.

Some limitations of the study also should be noted. While some of our data (e.g., class racial composition, achievement scores) are based on school records, other information—including our measures of interracial behavior—is based on the reports of students. We tried to ask questions which were as factual as possible—e.g., how often students had visited the home of, or had gotten into a physical fight with, students of another race during the current semester. Despite these efforts in wording questions, the assurance of anonymity to students, and our efforts to eliminate questions which were not completed carefully (see above), there undoubtedly remains some error in responses due to faulty recall, hasty answers, or other reasons. Some error of this sort is almost inevitable in a large-scale study of this kind since, as a practical matter, much of the data gathered could not be obtained in any way other than through student reports. The magnitude of response error is reduced by the fact that almost all of our measures are based on responses to many items, rather than to only one item. Moreover, when school-level data are used, the errors of individual students (to the extent they are random) tend to cancel each other out.

Another limitation of the study which should be noted is that most of the data were gathered during a single time period (i.e., the spring 1971 semester) rather than over a longer time period. This limits somewhat the extent to which we can infer cause-and-effect relationships rather than mere associations. However, there are a number of features of the study which aid us in inferring causal directions. First, even though two pieces of data may refer to the same time period, it often is clear that one event preceded another. For example, it is clear that students were assigned to classes of a particular racial composition before they had a chance to interact with schoolmates during that semester. Second, some of our data obtained from students are reports of events which occurred at an earlier time (e.g., attendance at a grade school of a particular racial composition) or about facts which predated the current semester (e.g., the education of their parents). Third, a few important pieces of information were obtained at times prior to, or following, our collection of data about interracial contact. Most notable are scores on IQ tests, which students took in grade school, and scores on achievement tests, which some students took one year after our data on interracial contact were collected. In sum, the study is limited by not being longitudinal, but some of the data obtained do help in inferring causal relations.

Schools and Individuals: As the account above indicates, we have obtained information both about individual students and about schools as units. Our emphasis throughout will be on the experiences of, and outcomes for, individuals. This emphasis stems in part from the fact that the theoretical ideas on which we draw most heavily—e.g., contact theory—are of a social-psychological kind which apply most directly to individuals. Also, from a methodological point of view, a focus on our large sample of individual students means that we can use a variety of statistical techniques which distinguish the separate effects of each of many variables, as well as the interactions among them. Using the small number of schools as units makes it much more difficult to disentangle the effects of one characteristic of the school from that of other characteristics or to know the effects of particular combinations of characteristics. However, we will examine some results which bear on the explanation of differences among schools in race relations and in academic outcomes. Such results, though generally simple correlations with no or few controls, are interesting both in themselves and for their degree of consistency with our more extensive results at the individual level.

It may be noted also that most of the characteristics of particular schools will be reflected in variables measured at the individual level. For example, the racial composition of the total school will tend to be reflected in the average racial composition of classes attended by particular individuals; the average socioeconomic status of students of each race at a school will affect the status of individual students relative to schoolmates of the other race; and the average racial attitudes of the entire student body will affect the immediate peer pressures which are experienced by individual students.

Summary

In the early 1970s, the Indianapolis Public Schools wished to accomplish greater racial desegregation and to reduce friction between students of different races, especially in the high schools. School officials agreed to cooperate fully in a study of the determinants and effects of interracial contact in high schools. There were twelve high school sites in the school system. These varied widely in racial composition. Variations also existed among (as well as within) schools with respect to parents' socioeconomic status, proportions of students in different curriculum programs, staff racial composition, and other characteristics.

In the first stage of the study, we interviewed a small number of students, teachers, and administrators in each school in order to become familiar with school procedures and problems. More systematic data were then gathered from much larger numbers of students and teachers, as well as from administrators. A two-part questionnaire was administered to each student (on two separate days) during school hours. Of a total sample of 5,479 students of both races, in all schools, 85.4% acceptably completed at least one part of the questionnaire; 71.5% acceptably completed both parts.

Information was obtained also from mail-back questionnaires given to teachers and to administrators. Finally, important information about students was obtained or computed from school records made available to us. These included IQ scores, grades, achievement test scores, absences, and the racial composition of students' classes. The total set of data obtained provided us an opportunity to explore in unusual depth and detail the determinants and effects of interracial contact in the schools.

Before attempting to trace the determinants and effects of interracial contact, we will describe the nature of the social relationships that did occur—i.e., the attitudes and behavior of black students and of white students. In the next chapter, we consider students' interracial attitudes.

Social Relations between the Races

3 | *Interracial Attitudes*

What is the nature of the attitudes which black students and white students had toward schoolmates of the other race? To what extent did the attitudes of each change for the better during the course of their high school careers?

One reason the answers to these questions are important is that, while attitudes and behavior are not always consistent, there is a tendency for more friendly, cooperative behavior to accompany more positive attitudes (Schuman and Johnson, 1976). (In the next chapter, we will discuss the relationship between interracial attitudes and interracial behavior in these schools.) But aside from the association between attitudes and behavior in high school, interracial attitudes are important because those which form, are strengthened, or are changed in high school may be expected to affect students' behavior beyond high school—on the job, in their neighborhoods, in their support of various public programs, and in the ways they shape the racial attitudes of their own children.

Meaning of "Attitude"

Before going any further, we should make clear what we mean by the term "attitude." While a variety of definitions has been advanced, most of them include two key elements: (1) the cognitions or perceptions which the person has about some object, together with (2) the affect or feelings which the person has toward the object. Thus Newcomb, Turner, and Converse (1965, p. 40) describe attitudes as "stored cognitions that have positive or negative associations." We follow this same meaning of attitude. In discussing interracial attitudes, we will describe both the perceptions which black and white students have of other-race schoolmates and their feelings toward members of the other-race group.

37

Previous School Studies

There have been many studies of the racial attitudes of students in racially integrated schools (Carithers, 1970; St. John, 1975). However, these studies have generally limited themselves to reporting summary scores of students' attitudes—focusing, for example, on whether racial attitude scores changed following desegregation. Few studies have provided detailed descriptions of the content of such racial attitudes—i.e., what specific perceptions and feelings students have regarding their other-race schoolmates. One in-depth report about student interracial attitudes is provided in a study by Petroni et al. (1970). Their study is rich in qualitative material from a few students but does not provide quantitative, systematic information for a sample of the student body as a whole.

In the present chapter, we present a description in some detail of the racial attitudes of both black and white students in the Indianapolis high schools. This description draws on our interviews with students of both races but also presents more systematic data from our sample of the student body as a whole. These data should help us to understand the specific positive and negative perceptions and feelings which students of each race have regarding schoolmates of the other race.

Data on Attitudes

In our preliminary interviews with students (see Chapter 2), we asked each student for his impression of what other-race students in his school are like. Then, probing further, we asked in what ways the other-race students are similar to and/or different from students of his own race. We also asked students how they feel when they come into contact with students of the other race—e.g., whether they feel at ease or not; what things they like about other-race students with whom they are friendly (if any); and what things they dislike about other-race students whom they don't like too well (if any).

Drawing on the content of the interviews—as well as on past work about interracial perceptions—we included the following multipart item in the questionnaire given to a large sample of students: "Listed below are a number of words that probably fit some people of every race. In your opinion, how many of the [*other-race*] *students of your own sex* in this school seem to fit each of the descriptions listed below?"

Twenty-six brief descriptive phrases were then listed. The list included descriptions such as: are fun to be with; are loud and noisy in school; want to get good grades; don't obey school rules; are smart in school; and talk and act in a crude or coarse way. (Many of these descriptive phrases are shown in Figures 3.1 and 3.2.) For each item, the student checked one of the following answers to show how many other-race students fit this description: none; only a few; quite a few, but less than half; about half; most; all or almost all.

Figure 3.1 Black Students' Perceptions of White Schoolmates (W),
as Compared to Their Perceptions of Black Schoolmates (B)[1]
(Percentages)

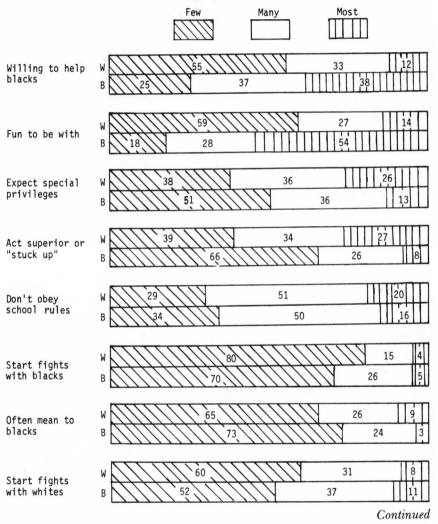

Continued

Figure 3.1 *Continued*

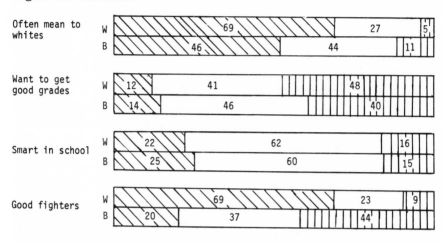

1. Perceptions shown here are selected from a larger set (see Patchen, Hofmann, and Davidson, 1976). Response categories shown here combine six original categories as follows: few = "none" or "only a few"; many = "quite a few but less than half" and "about half"; most = "most" and "all or almost all." Percentages may not add to 100% because of rounding.

Later in the questionnaire, the student was asked to respond to an almost identical set of items concerning students of his *own* race. Thus, for most items, we can compare his perceptions of schoolmates of each racial group.

We also included in the questionnaires several items concerning liking for, anger at, and fear of students of each race.

Let us examine the results, first for black students and then for white students.

Black Students' Perceptions

How did black students see their white schoolmates? Our data indicate, first, that the blacks tended to see the whites in terms of six general underlying characteristics.[1] These "dimensions of perception," and some of the specific items which appear to reflect each dimension, are the following:

1. *Friendliness to black students.* Willing to help black students; friendly to black students; fun to be with
2. *Norms violations.* Don't obey some school rules; expect special privileges for themselves in school; talk or act in a crude coarse way; are loud and noisy in school; act superior or stuck up
3. *Unfriendliness to black students.* Act bossy; start fights; often mean (to black students)

Figure 3.2. White Students' Perceptions of Black Schoolmates (B), as Compared to Their Perceptions of White Schoolmates (W)[1] (Percentages)

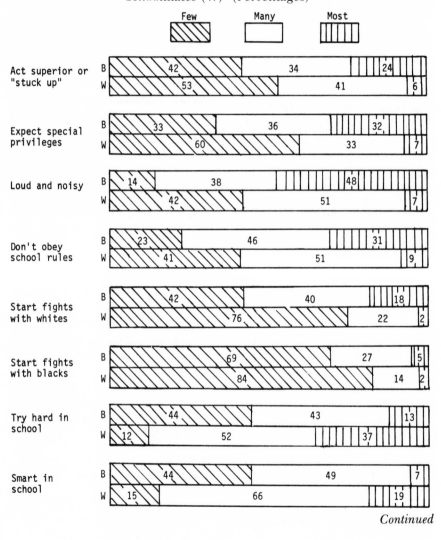

Continued

Figure 3.2 *Continued*

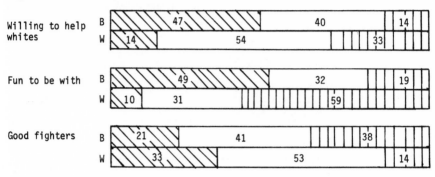

---

1. Perceptions shown here are selected from a larger set (see Patchen, Hofmann, and Davidson, 1976). Response categories shown here combine six original categories as follows: few = "none" or "only a few"; many = "quite a few but less than half" and "about half"; most = "most" or "all or almost all." Percentages may not add to 100% because of rounding.

4. *Unfriendliness to white students.* Act bossy; start fights; often mean (to white students)
5. *Academic orientation.* Try real hard to do well in school; want to get good grades; are smart in school; would like to go to college
6. *Physical toughness.* Are good fighters; are afraid of white students.[2]

To what extent, and in what ways, did black students see their white schoolmates as different from their black schoolmates with respect to these general characteristics?

First, it should be noted that many black students recognized similarities between themselves and the whites. For example, asked whether white kids and black kids are similar in any ways, a black junior girl at Southwest replied: "Yes, well in almost all ways. They're here to learn and make grades like we are."

A black junior girl at Harrison said: "Yes, I have a friend that's a white student here, and me and her, both of us, we're just almost the same. There's no difference."

But these students, and most other blacks, also saw some differences, on the average at least, between students of the two races. Many of these perceived differences, as indicated by questionnaire responses, are shown in Figure 3.1.

Friendliness toward Blacks. In general, black students saw white schoolmates as not being friendly toward blacks. They saw greater proportions of students of their own race than of whites as "willing to help black students" and as "fun to be with." Less than one-fourth of all blacks saw most whites as "friendly to black students."

Some comments of students, taken from interviews, illustrate black perceptions of a lack of friendliness on the part of whites.

A black senior girl at Emerson commented about some white class-mates: "The only time they'll really speak to you is when, like the teacher says, 'Let's have a test,' and they don't happen to have a sheet of paper, then they may lean over and ask you for a sheet of paper. That's about the only time you'll get a word or two out of them."

Another black student said: "I'd say most of them . . . don't like blacks too much . . . they don't want to be around you, you know."

Some black students explained the lack of friendliness of many whites in terms of their parents' prejudices. A senior boy at Southwest said: "Most of them are pretty friendly although . . . if you see them at night, at the shopping center or at a football game with their parents, they can't hardly say anything to you because their parents will get upset with them and ask them why they spoke to you."

Norm Violations. In their questionnaire responses, blacks also indicated that they saw larger proportions of whites than of blacks as violating certain norms of behavior. Specifically, they saw whites as more often "acting superior or stuck up," as being "two-faced or insincere" with other-race students, and as "expecting special privileges for themselves in school." These traits all seem to have in common a perceived tendency of whites to treat blacks as inferiors. In interviews with black students, the image of whites thinking they are better than blacks appeared often.

A black senior boy at Southwest said of those white schoolmates he didn't like: "They are always trying to put your color down—or trying to put you down."

A black junior girl at Southwest said of those whites she didn't like: "I don't like their attitudes. Some of them are just plain mean. They treat you like you're nothing but something you can walk on. . . . Some white people act like they're higher than everybody else."

Regarding the perceived insincerity of many whites, a black male junior at Hillcrest said of those whites he disliked: "They're the type that will grin in your face and [when] you see them with some others, they'll start talking about you."

Unfriendliness. While black students often resented what they saw as whites' aloofness and/or whites' acting superior, blacks indicated on questionnaires that they did not see most whites as overtly unfriendly. Although blacks saw a slightly larger percentage of whites than blacks as "often mean to blacks," only a small proportion of blacks (9%) thought that most whites acted in this way. Furthermore, the great majority of blacks (80%) believed that few whites started fights with blacks; indeed, blacks saw students of their own race as somewhat more likely to start fights with blacks than were whites. Comments by blacks during interviews generally were consistent with these questionnaire responses. For example, a black girl senior at Emerson, describing fighting between the races, was asked which race started the fights. She replied: "I think it's about equal between blacks and whites, but blacks may do a little more now and then."

The infrequency of unfriendly actions by whites toward blacks was sometimes seen as connected to whites' fear of blacks. Thus, a black male sophomore at Highland said: "Maybe a black guy might walk up to them and ask for some money. Some of them get scared. . . . They don't pick on anybody like some of the black people do."

Just as most black students did not see whites as overtly unfriendly to blacks, so too most black students did not see whites as unfriendly to other whites. Blacks were more likely to see students of their own race as mean to, and especially as starting fights with, whites than they were to see whites as acting in these ways.

Academic Orientation. Black students indicated on the questionnaire that they saw about the same proportion of each race as "smart in school." However, they tended to see whites as more highly motivated in several respects (e.g., wanting to get good grades, wanting to go to college).

Some illustrative comments regarding white students' motivation were made by a black male student at John Price, who said that he sometimes got help from whites in his algebra class. He explained: "Their parents, seems like they'd be pushing them. I've heard a lot of them say that, if they don't get good grades, their mother and father won't let them go out this weekend."

A black male senior at Hillcrest said: "Black students seem to put more faith in material things, more than white students do . . . things that are not going to help them out in later life. They would rather take twenty dollars and buy a suit with it than take twenty dollars and submit an application to some college, where whites do just the opposite. I was going to do something like that and I got to thinking that's why the white man's ahead of us now. They sacrifice things in order to gain more things."

Physical Toughness. Finally, black students saw themselves as much tougher physically than whites. Specifically, on questionnaires they indicated that they saw much larger proportions of blacks as "good fighters" and as not "afraid of [other-race] students." One black athlete commented about the white students in his school: "I guess they're kind of scared of you . . . if you know a lot of people and stuff, they don't want to start nothing."

Summary of Blacks' Perceptions. Overall, the picture which black students tended to have of their white classmates might be summarized as follows. There are some bad things about them: they (the whites) are not friendly and many of them act as though they're better than we are. However, in some ways they're not too bad—they don't show open hostility toward us very often. In some ways they can be admired—they aren't any smarter than we are, but they tend to be more highly motivated academically. Finally, they're less tough physically than we are.

Black Students' Feelings

Given the perceptions of whites just described, what were the feelings of black students toward white students in their schools?

In interviews and in written comments on questionnaires, some blacks told of being friendly with, and liking, some whites. However, a few black students expressed strong negative feelings about whites. For example, one black student wrote: "I feel the damn whites should straighten up. If they don't, we'll straighten the motherfuckers."

Another wrote: " ... I don't trust whitey. I feel that the whitey hasn't never ever done anything for me. Why should he now? If he did, I wouldn't go for it. Whitey can't do a *damn* thing for me. You might think my feelings are wrong, but it was wrong when whiteys down South hung up black women who were going to have babies, cut their stomach open and watch the baby fall out. ...."

How widespread were such feelings of hate and anger? Figure 3.3 shows the answers of black students on questions concerning liking for, anger at, and fear of students of each race.

Only a small percentage (11%) of all black students said that they disliked most of the white students in their school. Slightly more than one-fourth said they "don't especially like but don't dislike most of the whites"; almost half said they like most of the white students "pretty much"; and 14% said they like most of the whites "very much." However, while a majority of blacks said they like most of their white schoolmates, at least a little, blacks clearly did not indicate as much liking for whites as for fellow blacks.

With respect to anger, black students were only slightly more likely to say that "white students do things that make me angry" than that black students do such things. Thirty-nine percent said that white students made them angry often (a few times a week or more) as compared to 33% who said that other black students often did things that made them angry.

Only 13% of black students said they thought often about the possibility "that some white student[s] might hit or attack me" and almost two-thirds said they never thought about this. Black students were somewhat more likely to think about the possibility that other black students might hit them (20% thought of this often and only 41% never).

Overall, then, the expressed feelings of black students toward white schoolmates were fairly positive, in comparison to their feelings toward students of their own race. Though blacks did not indicate as much liking for whites as for other blacks, only a small minority said they disliked whites. Blacks indicated only slightly more frequent anger at whites and less frequent fear of whites, as compared to blacks.

White Students' Perceptions

Let us turn now to the interracial attitudes of white students. First, how did the whites see their black schoolmates?

Whereas black students tended to differentiate between several types of negative and positive white characteristics, white students tended to see the blacks in terms of more general clusters of negative traits and

Figure 3.3   Feelings of Black Students toward Schoolmates of Each Race[1] (Percentages)

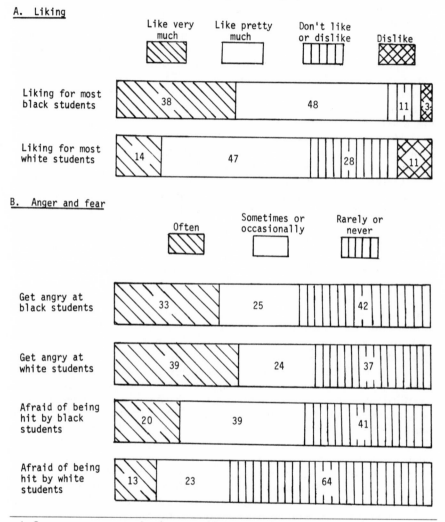

A. Liking

Like very much
Like pretty much
Don't like or dislike
Dislike

Liking for most black students
38   48   11   3

Liking for most white students
14   47   28   11

B. Anger and fear

Often
Sometimes or occasionally
Rarely or never

Get angry at black students
33   25   42

Get angry at white students
39   24   37

Afraid of being hit by black students
20   39   41

Afraid of being hit by white students
13   23   64

1. Some response categories shown combine or paraphrase original categories as follows: Liking: dislike = "dislike slightly" and "dislike very much." Don't like or dislike = "don't especially like but don't dislike." Anger: often = "almost every day" and "a few times a week"; sometimes or occasionally = "about once a week" and "once every few weeks." Fear: often = "very often" and "fairly often"; sometimes or occasionally = "sometimes but not often" and "only once in a while."

positive traits.[3] Some of the specific positive and negative items which tended to cluster together in whites' perceptions are as follows:

1. *General negative evaluation.* Talk and act in a crude or coarse way; act superior or stuck up; expect special privileges for themselves in school; are loud and noisy in school; have a chip on their shoulders (too sensitive); act bossy toward white students; start fights with white students; are often mean to white students.
2. *General positive evaluation.* Try hard to do well in school; want to get good grades; are smart in school; would like to go to college; are friendly to white students; are willing to help white students; are fun to be with; want to take part in school activities.

Note that whites tended to see items reflecting norm violations and items reflecting unfriendliness as going together, while blacks distinguished between these (see above). Similarly, whites tended to see academic orientation and friendliness as going together, while blacks distinguished between these traits.

In addition to the major dimensions of positive and negative evaluation, there are several other dimensions which appeared to underlie white perceptions of blacks. These include:

3. *Unfriendliness to black students.* Act bossy toward black students; start fights with black students; often mean to black students.
4. *Physical toughness.* Are good fighters; are afraid of white students.

How did white students see their black schoolmates with respect to these clusters of traits?

In interviews, some white students said they saw little, if any, differences between the black students and the white students at their school. Asked whether her impressions of blacks have changed any, a white junior girl at Highland replied: "No ... my parents had taught me that everyone was equal and so forth. I expected them to be just as interested in studies as I was, and they were mostly. I didn't expect any differences and I didn't see any."

Asked what the black students in his school are like, a senior boy at Southwest replied: "Well, that's hard to say. It's like saying 'What are the white students like?' There's going to be good ones and bad ones wherever you go ... when you get here, it didn't take six weeks, you say, 'They're just like I am. They're no different.'" (This student did say he thought most blacks are better athletes than whites.)

But most white students whom we interviewed did see differences between the two racial groups in their school. In some instances, whites saw blacks, more often than whites, as tending to have certain positive traits. Most notably, some whites saw black students as fun loving or fun to be with.

One white student said: "I think they have better personalities than whites ... they seem to have a good sense of humor and get along well and seem happy."

Asked what black students are like, another white student said: "Well, kids that I know are really nice. I guess they have fun and go in the cafeteria instead of class. They like to do things with you."

A white boy said: "I've come close to four of them on the football team and they strike me as, they're funny, they're always cheerful, they've always got something good to say."

However, the differences seen by most whites were unfavorable to blacks (see Figure 3.2).

Negative Evaluations. Results from our questionnaires show, first, that white students generally saw their black schoolmates as possessing (more often than whites) the whole array of traits that were negatively evaluated. First, white students tended to see their black schoolmates as more unfriendly to whites than were other whites. Thus, a majority of whites saw many or most blacks as acting bossy with whites, starting fights with whites, or as often mean to whites; in contrast, a majority of whites saw few whites as acting in these ways.

In interviews, many whites commented on what they saw as overt unfriendliness by blacks. A white male senior at Highland said: "There is a violent section of blacks that I don't like, because I've been mauled several times in my high school career. I just resent that very much, that they would have the gall to do that."

A white boy in the same school distinguished between "two cliques of blacks . . . the proud blacks and the blacks who really don't want to buckle down under the school and the blacks who work. For the most part the blacks who work are gentle and get along pretty well. [*Q.* What are the "proud blacks" like?] . . . Usually they are trying to hang together in a group, not with whites. I imagine some of them go around beating up whites outside school, but not many. Most of them in school flaunt threatening looks and malevolent stuff toward the whites. . . ."

A white sophomore boy at Hillcrest said that he gets along with about half of his black schoolmates "just like friends" but that with the other half "there is some hate in there that their parents gave to them and it's the same with white kids . . . they do stuff, like in the main hall, they'll just stand there when you want to get through . . . football games, something goes wrong and maybe they'll start a fight. They fight a little more than us. [*Q.* Is the fighting between blacks and whites?] It doesn't seem to matter; it just seems like they like to fight sometimes."

Asked if there are any differences between black and white students, a white sophomore girl at Emerson said: "They act a lot rougher than most of the white kids I know. And they usually pick more fights."

White students also saw larger proportions of blacks than of whites as norm violators in a variety of ways—i.e., as crude, loud, not obeying school rules, expecting special privileges, and acting superior or stuck up.

Some comments made by white students in interviews at a number of schools indicate the kinds of perceptions involved. A white senior boy at Southwest, who thought most blacks were pleasant, described "a few" blacks as "pushy": "When they walk down the hall, they'll be screaming and jumping and yelling. They don't hardly have any consideration, cutting in lunch lines."

Asked what the black kids generally are like, a white male senior at Emerson said: "The ones I associate with would definitely be on the top. They would be the kind that would have better grades, come from better backgrounds. However, I notice a lot that are rude, unruly at times, carrying things like transistor radios in the school or standing out in front playing these radios loudly. Some of them don't seem to have many academic concerns. They just don't seem to be concerned about education."

A sophomore boy at Hillcrest, who had said that some white kids hate the blacks, was asked what reasons such students have for these feelings. He replied: "What they [blacks] do in school—interrupting classes, sometimes coming in late, starting fights in the hall, get in the way."

Like the previous students quoted, this student saw such disruptive behavior as characteristic of those students who were less academically oriented. Explaining his perception of the differences between those black kids who "are really nice" and those who aren't, he said: "Most of the good ones get kind of decent grades, about average; the ones that seem to hate people goof off in school."

Another white student who saw several negative traits to be interrelated commented: "There is a few, I mean, they resent so much being shipped here, you know they won't even talk to you and they call you names and they say some things . . . that will make you so mad. And they won't do anything in classes and if they are good at sports they won't go out; they don't want to help the team. They just don't want to go to school . . . they just resent having to be shipped all the way across town and they are taking it out on us people here."

Positive Evaluations. Just as white students indicated on the questionnaire that they saw larger proportions of blacks than whites as having a number of negative traits, so also white students saw a smaller proportion of blacks as having a variety of positive traits. Though a majority of whites saw many blacks as trying hard in school, as smart in school, as wanting to get good grades and as wanting to go to college, whites saw larger proportions of whites as academically oriented in each of these ways.

With respect to the friendliness of black students, a majority of whites indicated that they saw many black schoolmates as willing to help whites, as friendly, and as fun to be with. However, whites saw smaller proportions of blacks, compared to their own race, as having each of these positive traits.

The perception among whites that many black students were unwilling to be friendly—a perception similar to that which blacks had of whites—is illustrated by many comments in our interviews. Asked what the black students in her school are like, a white junior girl at Emerson replied: "I have several in my class and just a few of them are really friendly. There are one or two that I really talk to. Most of them, if they're a group—like five or six in a class—they'll stay within their group.

. . . They won't be friendly or associate with you as much as they would their own kind."

In a somewhat similar vein, a white junior girl at Hillcrest commented: "I think the blacks could try a lot harder to become closer to the whites. They seem to be drifting off. They don't seem to be trying very hard to get along with us."

A white junior boy at Southwest said: "They kind of separate as a group. Some of them will talk to you and some of them just go into a group and don't talk to anybody else . . . they just ignore you, like you're nothing."

Unfriendliness to Blacks. While white students saw many blacks as unfriendly to whites, they did not see large proportions of either race as unfriendly to blacks. Whites saw somewhat larger proportions of blacks than of whites as starting fights with blacks and as acting bossy with blacks. However, whites saw a somewhat larger proportion of their own race as "often mean to blacks."

Physical Toughness. Whites tended to agree with blacks in seeing the blacks as more physically tough. Specifically, whites saw larger proportions of blacks than of whites as "good fighters" and smaller proprotions of blacks as afraid of students of the other race.

Though fighting was more frequent among boys than among girls, perceptions of toughness were not confined to black boys. For example, one white girl commented in an interview: "I have noticed the colored girls do more harassing. They are a lot stronger. They yell and try to start something."

Summary of White Perceptions. Overall, we may note that in some ways the image which whites tended to have of black schoolmates was similar to the image which blacks tended to have of the whites. Like blacks, white students tended to see other-race students (compared to their own race) as not friendly and as trying to act superior in certain ways (e.g., acting "stuck up" and expecting special privileges). However, unlike blacks, white students also tended to see the other race as more overtly unfriendly (to students of both races) and as less academically oriented. Finally, whites tended to agree with blacks in seeing the blacks as physically tougher.

White Students' Feelings

What were the feelings of white students toward the black students in their school? In interviews, some white students told us about black schoolmates with whom they were friendly and whom they liked.

One white boy said: "There are some blacks on the basketball team and I like them . . . they were nice. There are a few, you know, who are willing to talk with you and they just go out of their way to help you and you learn to do it for them."

On the other hand, in interviews and in comments written on questionnaires, a few whites expressed strong negative feelings toward black students in their school. For example, one student wrote: "I am sick and tired of hearing about black people. I hate them and, if I had the money, I'd go to an all *white* school."

Another wrote: "I hate blacks and this busing stuff. The niggers are just tearing up this school and making a mess out of our community. As far as I'm concerned the niggers should all be killed and done away with. I'm sure the world would be a lot better off without stupid niggers."

Some white students, including some who expressed no special dislike of blacks, indicated a fear of their black schoolmates.

One white girl at Harrison told an interviewer: "I hate to have to say this because I know a lot of black students and I think they're nice, but it seems like some of them are so offensive. . . . A lot of them will just sit there and eye you and . . . if you make any little slip, you're going to get on the wrong side of him and it's going to scare you, because it does me."

Asked whether he is friends with any particular blacks, a white boy at Highland answered: "No. It could be that I'm kind of scared. I am scared of blacks. I got beat up last year by some guys, out of school."

To what extent are such feelings typical? What were the feelings of the majority of white students toward their black schoolmates? Figure 3.4 shows how whites' feelings of liking for, anger at, and fear of blacks compared to similar feelings toward white schoolmates.

Although white students did not indicate quite as much liking for blacks as for their own race, their expressed feelings toward "most of the black students" were generally positive. Only a small proportion of whites (13%) said that they disliked most of their black schoolmates.

Like black students, whites were only slightly more likely to report frequent anger at other-race students than at students of their own race. However, unlike black students, who reported greater fear of their own race than of whites, white students indicated that they were afraid of being hit by blacks somewhat more often than they were afraid of being hit by other whites. Such fear is especially common among white boys (see Chapter 6). Overall, then, dislike of, or anger at, black schoolmates was not especially marked among white students, but physical fear of blacks was fairly common.

Summary Attitude Measures

By combining information about each black student's perceptions of his white schoolmates and his feelings (liking, anger, fear) toward them, we constructed a summary measure of each black student's attitude toward his white schoolmates. In the same manner, a summary measure of each white student's attitudes toward his black schoolmates was computed.[4]

We also computed, for students of each race at each school, the average score and a measure of variation among students (the standard deviation) on the overall measure of racial attitudes (see Appendix B).

In addition to substantial variation in racial attitudes within each school, there were significant average differences among schools. Both

Figure 3.4 Feelings of White Students Toward Schoolmates of Each Race[1] (Percentages)

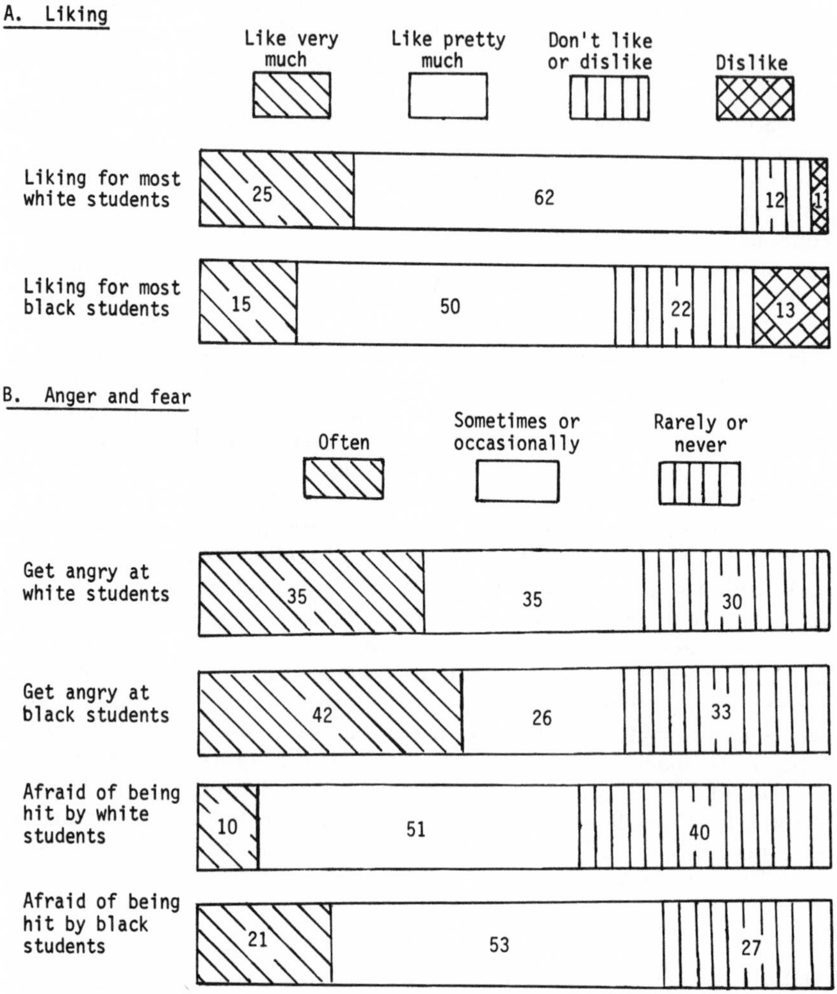

A. Liking

	Like very much	Like pretty much	Don't like or dislike	Dislike

Liking for most white students: 25 | 62 | 12 | 1

Liking for most black students: 15 | 50 | 22 | 13

B. Anger and fear

	Often	Sometimes or occasionally	Rarely or never

Get angry at white students: 35 | 35 | 30

Get angry at black students: 42 | 26 | 33

Afraid of being hit by white students: 10 | 51 | 40

Afraid of being hit by black students: 21 | 53 | 27

1. Some response categories shown combine or paraphrase original categories as follows: Liking: dislike = "dislike slightly" and "dislike very much." Don't like or dislike = "don't especially like but don't dislike." Anger: often = "almost every day" and "a few times a week"; sometimes or occasionally = "about once a week" and "once every few weeks." Fear: often = "very often" and "fairly often"; sometimes or occasionally = "sometimes but not often" and "only once in a while." Percentages may not add to 100% because of rounding.

black students and white students had by far the most positive racial attitudes at Highland, the mostly academic school (71.2% black). Racial attitudes also were relatively positive at several schools with widely different racial compositions—for both races at Eastern (13.6% black), for blacks at Pershing (1.1% black), and for blacks at Harrison (53.0% black).

The most negative average racial attitudes among black students were found at John Price (36.9% black), Emerson (26.6% black), and Southwest (13.9% black). Average white attitudes also were relatively negative at Emerson and were most negative at Hillcrest (35.5% black). It is interesting to observe that, in general, the average racial attitudes of black students in a given school were *not* related much to the average racial attitudes of whites at the same school.[5]

Change in Attitudes

So far, we have been considering the racial attitudes which students had at a single point in time during their high school careers. Now we consider the question of whether their attitudes toward people of a different race *changed*, for the better or for the worse, since coming to high school.

In the interviews, a few students commented about their own changes in attitude. Several mentioned that contact with schoolmates of another race made their racial opinions more positive.

One white student said: "I used to feel like I'm not going to associate with them [blacks] because from what you've heard, that they're mean and everything. . . . I've learned how they were alike and everything and they're just like another white person. . . . The ones I know are really great people. They really want to learn and they don't care that they have to come over here, you know, get bused over here, to do it. . . . They just seem to fit into the school like anybody else and I'd say they are not any different than we are."

However, a few students mentioned negative changes in their racial attitudes. For example, one white student wrote at the end of his questionnaire: "I have never been against black people, but these last two years I have really changed my attitude, just because it seems the higher authority in this school seems to be afraid of them and they get by with more than whites."

On the questionnaires, we asked each student: "Since coming to this school, has your opinion of most [other-race] people gotten worse, gotten better, or stayed the same?" Students could check one of five answers: gotten much better; gotten a little better; stayed the same; gotten a little worse; gotten a lot worse.[6]

Although answers to this question are subject to problems of faulty memory, it seems likely that most people can report their own changes of opinion during the past few years with reasonable accuracy. Let us examine the responses of students to this question about their changes in opinion.

Among black students, reported changes in opinions of most white people were overwhelmingly in a positive direction. For black students in all schools combined, 44% said their opinions of whites changed for the better, 41% said these opinions stayed the same, and only 14% said they became worse. There were clearly more positive changers than negative changers in opinion among blacks in every school.[7]

Among white students, the predominant opinion change was also positive, but less markedly so. For white students in all schools combined, 36% reported that their opinions of black people changed for the better, 38% said they stayed the same, and 27% said their opinions of blacks became worse.

Among white students, opinion change varied greatly among schools.[8] In eight of the eleven racially integrated schools, positive opinion change was more frequent than negative change. In one school, Jefferson, positive and negative opinion change was about equal (almost 30% going each way). In two schools, Emerson and Hillcrest, negative opinion change was about twice as frequent as positive change (half of the whites saying their opinions of blacks had become worse). It may be noted that the three schools where negative change among whites was most frequent were all relatively distant from the central city, in almost-all-white neighborhoods. All had experienced a rapid increase in black enrollment (due largely to redrawing of school lines, coupled with busing) during the few years just prior to our study. In later chapters, we will examine some of the factors which were related to change in opinion, as well as to present attitudes, focusing on the experiences of individual students.

Summary

The results examined in this chapter provide some insights concerning the images and feelings which black students and white students had with respect to the other race. There were a number of positive aspects to these interracial attitudes. Many students of both races saw only a minority of other-race students as having negative characteristics. While many students did not like most other-race schoolmates as well as those of their own race, only a small proportion indicated dislike of most of the other race. Both black and white students reported only slightly more frequent anger at students of the other race than at those of the same race. And changes in racial opinion among students of both races were mostly for the better—especially among blacks. These findings indicate that, despite the interracial friction that did exist—and that sometimes got widely publicized—the overall attitudes of most students toward their other-race schoolmates were fairly positive.

On the other hand, there clearly were some things about each race (at least as perceived) which tended to bother students of the other race. First, both blacks and whites often saw their other-race schoolmates as not friendly and/or as acting "stuck up." Thus, each group tended to see the other as having these identical negative traits. Such images of the other group as aloof and unaccepting were clearly a barrier to positive relationships between blacks and whites. Many students of each race told us, in approximately these words, "I'd be friendly if they were willing to be friendly." But so long as members of each group saw the other group as unwilling to accept them, on an equal basis, they were not likely to take friendly initiatives.

Another major problem concerned perceptions of unfriendly behavior by the other race. Although some blacks reported seeing many whites as overtly unfriendly, generally this was a matter that disturbed white students more. In large part, the question was one of physical violence. Whites saw blacks as physically tough, as often overtly unfriendly—including starting fights—and many whites were afraid of blacks. Closely tied to these images was the image of blacks as noisy and disruptive in school. This interrelated set of white perceptions and feelings, centering around the blacks as dangerous and disruptive, led many white students to try to avoid black schoolmates and to have less than friendly relationships with the blacks.

There often were wide differences in racial attitudes among students in the same school. There also were significant differences among schools. In later chapters (5 through 9), we will try to explain such differences in students' interracial attitudes, as well as in their behavior. Before such attempts at explanation, however, we need to describe students' interracial behaviors and the relationship between their attitudes and behavior. We turn to these topics in the next chapter.

4 | *Interracial Behavior*

What kinds of contacts did black students and white students actually have with each other in the high schools studied? How often did students of each race avoid contact with schoolmates of the other race? How much friendly contact was there between the races? How much unfriendly contact?

In this chapter, we will describe students' interracial behaviors. We will consider the ways in which blacks and whites, and students in different schools, differed in various types of behavior. In addition, we will consider the ways in which different kinds of interracial behavior were related to each other and to students' interracial attitudes.

Before examining our own results, let us consider briefly the work relevant to interracial interaction which has been done previously. As Schofield points out, of those studies purporting to investigate interracial behavior in schools "the large majority use variants on traditional sociometric techniques (Moreno, 1934) which involve asking people to report whom they would choose to interact with in various situations rather than actual choice behavior" (Schofield, 1978, p. 332). Studies relying on sociometric techniques have reached varying conclusions about the extent to which social integration occurs in desegregated schools. Reporting on a large-scale longitudinal study of school desegregation in Riverside, California, Gerard and his associates conclude that "little or no real integration occurred during the relatively long-term contact situation represented by Riverside's desegregation program" (Gerard et al., 1975, p. 237). However, some studies have indicated a lessening of in-group choices among children as a result of desegregated experiences in schools and other settings (e.g., Yarrow, 1958; Schofield, 1975).

A few studies have used observational techniques to assess students' interracial behavior, including the amount of interaction which occurs

56

and the seating patterns in cafeterias and other settings (e.g., Silverman and Shaw, 1973; Schofield and Sagar, 1977). Schofield notes in her summary of these studies that "the extent of racial clustering in desegregated schools varies markedly, but it appears to occur almost everywhere. In some schools, the resegregation seems almost total" (Schofield, 1978, p. 334). Petroni (1970), drawing on interviews with students in a Kansas City high school, reports that black students generally refrained from joining academically oriented clubs which were predominately white, feeling that only "Uncle Toms" would do so.

Aside from the indirect information obtained from sociometric methods (which do not measure actual behavior) and data from the small number of observational studies (which focus on racial clustering in public settings), there has been very little information gathered about the kinds of contacts which occur between black and white students in schools.

There has been almost no direct study of the amount and kinds of friendly contact which students may have with other-race schoolmates within and outside the school.[1] And despite the fact that racial fights in schools are sometimes the subject of frightening newspaper stories, and often the subject of intense gossip in a community, little or no systematic information on the extent of fighting and other unfriendly interaction in the schools has been available.

In this chapter, we present systematic evidence about interracial interaction among students in one school system which goes beyond the evidence which has been available before. Rather than asking the student to make friendship choices on the spot (which may be unrelated to his actual life), we have obtained information about who his actual friends are and about the social groups to which he belongs. Also, we obtained information about the frequency with which each student had a variety of specific friendly and unfriendly interactions with other-race schoolmates during the (then) current semester. In addition, we obtained information about the frequency with which each student attempted to avoid schoolmates of the other race in a variety of settings within and outside the school.

These data on interracial interaction are not without their limitations. The most important limitation is that they are based on student reports. Self-report data are vulnerable to several sources of possible error, including lapses in respondents' memories and efforts to answer in ways that are socially desirable.

However, the questions asked of students were quite factual and a great effort was made to phrase them in ways which would not appear to put a student in a bad light if he answered in a particular way. Moreover, asking students about their own experiences and actions was the only practical way to get the kinds of information desired concerning several thousand students of each race. Despite their limitations, these data provide us with the most extensive and detailed picture of interracial interaction in schools which is available to date. Let us look at the results.[2]

Avoidance

Most visitors to racially mixed schools are struck by the fact that black students and white students sometimes segregate themselves within the school. This is usually seen most clearly in the school cafeteria. As one white girl at Harrison put it: "The cafeteria's kind of segregated; there is white on this side, white and black in the middle, and black on the other side." (Our observations usually revealed very little, if any, of a racially mixed "middle.")

Avoidance of other-race schoolmates occurred also in other school settings. For example, a black girl at Emerson told us: "If there were too many blacks that came into the activity, the whites would want to cop out . . . like the cheerleading . . . when the white girls found out about black students were going to try to cheerlead, they just gave up all hope; they didn't want to try to cheerlead."

Black students too were sometimes seen as trying to avoid their other-race schoolmates. For example, a white girl at Emerson said of her black schoolmates: "Most of them, if they're a group, like five or six in a class, they'll stay within their own group. I mean they'll talk to you but they won't be friendly or associate with you as much as they would their own kind."

To assess systematically the extent to which students tried to avoid schoolmates of the other race, we included in the questionnaire this item: "Some [your-race] students have had bad experiences with [other-race] students or have heard about other people who have had bad experiences. They may prefer not to have too much to do with [other-race] students if they can avoid it. How often during this semester have you tried to avoid being with [other-race] students in each of the ways listed below?"

Seven types of avoidance (shown in Figure 4.1) were then listed. The student was asked to show how often he/she had engaged in each of these types of avoidance, by checking one of five categories, ranging from "more than 10 times this semester" to "never this semester." A summary of these results, for students of each race, is shown graphically in Figure 4.1.

Interracial avoidance appeared to be fairly common in everyday situations around the school. A majority of students of both races said they had avoided sitting near some other-race students at least once or twice during the current semester. About half admitted that they had avoided talking to other-race schoolmates and sizable proportions said they had avoided walking or standing near other-race schoolmates at least once or twice during the semester.

Other items concerned interracial avoidance with respect to activities outside of regular school hours. Roughly 30% of the students of each race said they didn't attend at least one or two school events because they expected many other-race students to attend. And about one-fourth of the black students, and 14% of the whites, said they had decided not to join (or drop out of) a club or activity because "too many" other-race students

Figure 4.1 Interracial Avoidance Reported by Black Students (B) and by White Students (W)[1] (Percentages)

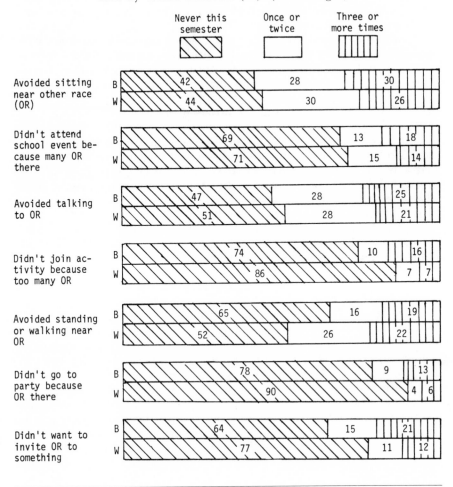

1. These questions not asked of blacks at Carver or of whites at Pershing, or of white upperclassmen at Jefferson.

were in it. Since many students participated little in school activities, regardless of their racial composition, this amount of conscious avoidance of the other race in school activities was substantial.

Differences in interracial avoidance between blacks and whites generally were small. Blacks were more likely than whites to stay out of a club because of its racial mixture. This difference probably was due mainly to the fact that clubs were more likely to be predominately white than predominately black. Blacks were also somewhat more likely than whites to indicate that they tried to avoid the other race at social events outside school. On the other hand, whites were somewhat more likely than blacks to say that they avoided walking or standing near some students of the other race. This difference probably reflects the greater fear of the other race among whites (see Chapter 3).

School Comparisons. Answers by each student on the seven items concerning avoidance of other-race students were combined into an avoidance index.[3] Also, for students of each race at each school, average scores and a measure of variation among individual students (the standard deviation) on this index were computed (see Appendix C). Within each school, there was substantial variation in interracial avoidance and there also were significant differences among schools. While there was no consistent relationship between school racial composition and avoidance, black students' avoidance of whites was lowest in the three schools which had a black majority (Harrison, Lakeview, and Highland). Avoidance among blacks was fairly similar at the other eight racially mixed schools, with avoidance of whites somewhat higher at Southwest (14% black) and at John Price (37% black) than elsewhere.

White students at various schools did not differ greatly in their avoidance of black schoolmates, with one exception. White avoidance was highest at Lakeview (53% black), where, as we have seen, whites had generally been bused to a newly desegregated school against their own and their families' wishes. Avoidance was lowest at another majority-black school, Highland (71% black). As we have seen, Highland had the special characteristics of being primarily academic and of being attended by choice by whites from families with generally liberal racial attitudes.

A comparison of black avoidance and white avoidance in each of ten schools (where scores for both races were computed) shows that the average avoidance scores were roughly equal in six schools. The average avoidance scores of blacks were appreciably higher in three schools (Jefferson, Southwest, and John Price) while that of whites was considerably higher in one (Lakeview). It is interesting to note that the average amount of avoidance by blacks in a school was essentially uncorrelated with the average level of avoidance by whites in the same school ($r = -.09$).

Friendly Interaction

How much friendly contact did black students and white students have with schoolmates of the other race? And how many students formed interracial friendships?

When asked about their relations with schoolmates of the other race, many students mentioned friendly conversations and sometimes helping each other out. Some examples—a white girl at Harrison: "I met a [black] girl the other day in study hall that is in one of my classes. We just sat there and talked. She's interested in Majorettes. She works for her grades. We get along pretty good."

A white girl at Emerson: "In the halls, I have contact with them. For instance, this morning there was a Negro girl and she's a sophomore and her locker's right next to mine. We always talk. We tease each other. We close each other's locker when we get them open."

A black boy at Harrison: "Like this one boy, we help each other out, but we don't copy off each other's paper or anything. If we have a question, we'll help each other out. He's a white boy."

In addition to friendly contacts within the school, a number of students mentioned doing things socially with schoolmates of the other race outside of school.

A white senior boy at Southwest: "One of them, he plays football for Southwest; last summer we used to go out messing around, some friends of ours, during the school year too. I don't feel any different riding around in a car with him than I would with anyone else."

A black senior girl at Emerson: "A lot of the white girls in school, we've gone out on weekends together. We don't only associate in class. All the white students here that I've associated with, they've been over to my house; we've went out together, had a real nice time."

A number of students indicated that they considered one or more schoolmates of the other race to be good friends. Asked whether any particular white student was a friend of hers, a black junior girl at Highland said: "Yes, I met her in a freshman orientation class. We've been friends ever since. She seems to have the same interests. We might party together; holding conversations."

A black sophomore boy at Hillcrest, describing his contacts with whites, said: "I have a couple of good friends. They take me home from practice sometimes . . . during the summer, they will come pick us up, we'll pick him up. We call each other, we go off to his house, or they come over to our house. Other times, he'll take us home from school. We come to the football games together. He's almost like a brother."

Friendly Contact

On the questionnaire, the main source of data about friendly (as well as unfriendly) contact came from a series of items which was introduced as follows: "Listed below are some ways in which students sometimes act toward one another. For each of these ways, please show how many times any [other-race] students have acted that way toward you this semester." This phrasing in terms of the actions of others was intended to discourage students from biasing their answers to make their own actions appear socially desirable.

A series of friendly contacts with other-race schoolmates, from the most casual ("greeted you, saying hello when you pass by") to the most intimate ("visited your home or had you over to their home"), was listed. For each item, the student checked one of six categories, from "never" to "more than 20 times," to show how often this kind of contact had occurred during the semester. A later item asked how often this semester, if ever, the student had dated a schoolmate of the other race. For two items, concerning school work and having schoolmates over to one's home, comparable questions were asked about friendly contacts with schoolmates of the *same* race. Thus, friendly contact within and across racial lines can be compared on these items.

The results, presented in Figure 4.2, show that the overwhelming majority of students of both races reported at least some friendly interracial contacts of a casual kind (greetings, friendly conversations). However, only about a third of the students reported such casual contacts frequently (more than 10 times) over the course of the semester.

As the nature of the contact in school became somewhat more intimate—i.e., walking together in hallways, sitting together, doing school work together—the frequency of friendly interaction decreased. However, a majority of students of both races reported at least some friendly contact of each of these kinds. On the school work item, about two-thirds of all blacks and over half of all whites said that they had done school work with other-race classmates at least once or twice during the semester. (This compares to about 90% of students of each race who reported ever doing homework with schoolmates of their own race.) About one student in seven of each race reported doing school work frequently (more than 10 times) with a classmate of the other race. (This compares to about one in three who said they did school work frequently with schoolmates of their own race.)

Friendly interracial contact *outside* school also was far from unusual. Almost half the students of each race said that they had done things together with other-race schoolmates outside of school at least once or twice that semester. Almost half of the blacks and over a third of whites said they had talked with a schoolmate of the other race on the telephone. Over a third of blacks and almost a third of whites reported that they visited the home of another-race schoolmate and/or had that person over to their home. (This compares to over 90% of students of each race who reported home visits with students of their own racial group.) Finally, over one in five black students, and 9% of white students, said that they had dated a schoolmate of the other race that semester.

Overall, these results indicate that, while friendly interaction was much more frequent *within* rather than *between* racial groups, a considerable amount of friendly contact between white and black students did take place. This interaction was, as would be expected, most frequent in fairly casual and perhaps superficial contacts. But the amount of friendly contact of a more intimate, sustained kind was substantial.

School Comparisons. How did the amount of friendly interracial contact vary among schools? For each student, an index score of friendly interracial contact was computed[4], then average scores (as well as standard deviations) on this index were computed for black students and for white students at each school (see Appendix C). In addition to substantial variations among students in each school, there were significant average differences among schools.

Figure 4.2 Friendly Interracial and Intraracial Contacts,
Reported by Black Students (B) and by White Students (W)[1] (Percentages)

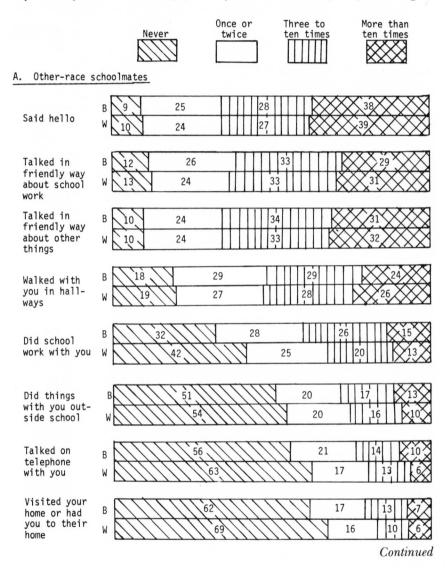

Continued

Figure 4.2 *Continued*

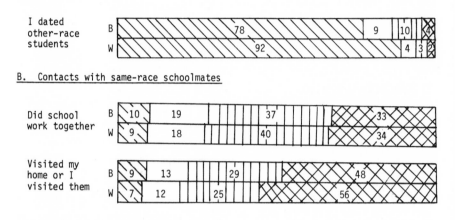

1. These questions not asked of blacks at Carver or of whites at Pershing, or of white upperclassmen at Jefferson. Percentages may not add to 100% because of rounding.

Among black students, the small number at 99%-white Pershing reported far more friendly contact with whites than did those at the other ten racially mixed schools. Differences in the average scores of blacks at other schools generally were not great.

Among whites, average scores on friendly contact were somewhat lower in schools which were predominately (about three-quarters or more) white and somewhat higher in schools with larger proportions of blacks. However, within these broad categories, there was no consistent relation between racial composition and the amount of friendly interracial contact reported by white students. At one school, Highland, friendly interracial contact reported by whites was far higher than at other schools. This probably reflects the combination of a high proportion of blacks (71%) at Highland and other special features of this school, as described in Chapter 2, which tended to promote friendly interracial contact for whites.

When we compared the amount of friendly interracial contact reported by blacks and whites at each school, we found that blacks generally had somewhat more friendly interracial contact than did whites. This was true especially in those schools where blacks were most outnumbered (i.e., in schools up to about one-third black). On the other hand, at the most heavily black school, Highland (71% black), whites reported much more friendly contact than did blacks. Thus, in schools where one race was a clear minority, the minority members had more friendly interracial contact than did members of the majority group. There was little correlation between the average amount of friendly contact reported by blacks and by whites in the same schools ($r = .23$).

Friendship Relations

In addition to learning about the various types of friendly interracial contacts which students had, we wanted to find out whether they had formed on-going relationships of friendship with schoolmates of the other race.

Several sets of questionnaire items are relevant to this matter. First, we asked each student to tell us how many other-race students in his school "are friends of yours." The student could check one of six answers, from zero to "more than 20." Ninety percent of the students of both races said that at least one or two students of the other race were friends. About two-thirds of the students of each race said that at least three to five other-race students were friends. And about one-third of the black students and one-fourth of the whites said that more than ten other-race students were friends (see Figure 4.3).

These results probably indicate that the great majority of students had some friendly interaction with, and some friendly feeling toward, at least a few schoolmates of the other race. But the question about how many other-race students "are friends of yours" is subject to varying interpretations of what "friend" means. In most cases, the student probably did not mean that the other-race persons he had in mind were close friends. To obtain information about the student's closest friends, we asked elsewhere on the questionnaire: "Now we have a few questions about your friends. First, please write down the first initials of the five people you are most friendly with." After the student had done this, he was asked to check several characteristics of each friend—including the race of that person.

The results (see Figure 4.3) show, as expected, that the great majority of students of each race—about four out of five—indicated that all their best friends were of the same race as themselves. However, one in five blacks and almost the same proportion of whites identified at least one of their best friends as being of the other race. A small, but not trivial, proportion of blacks (8%) and of whites (6%) indicated that more than one of their best friends was of the other race.

Finally, we asked students: "Is there any informal group of friends (a group without a name) with whom you hang around a lot, or with whom you do things pretty often?" If the student checked "yes," he was asked "What kind of people are in the group you spend the most time with?" Several questions were then asked about this social group, including its racial composition.

Of those students who said they did belong to an informal group[5] (and who identified the racial composition of the group), almost three out of every four students of each race said that the group was entirely of their own race. However, more than one in every four said that the informal group to which they belonged was racially mixed.

When we examine responses to the questions concerning "best friends" together with those concerning informal groups, we find that

Figure 4.3   Interracial Friendships Reported by Black Students (B)
and by White Students (W)[1] (Percentages)

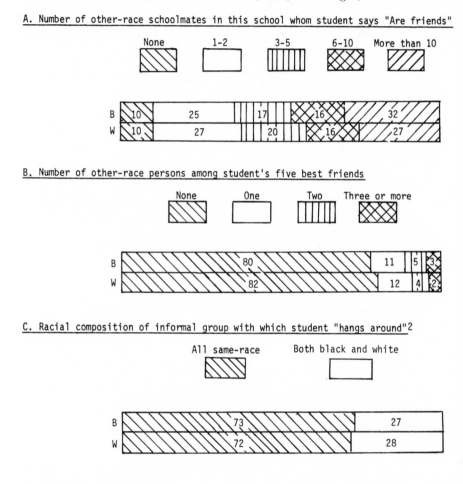

A. Number of other-race schoolmates in this school whom student says "Are friends"

B. Number of other-race persons among student's five best friends

C. Racial composition of informal group with which student "hangs around"[2]

---

1. These questions not asked of blacks at Carver or of whites at Pershing, or of white
   upperclassmen at Jefferson. Percentages may not add to 100% because of rounding.
2. Asked only of those who said there was "an informal group of friends" with whom they
   "do things pretty often".

34% of all black students and 31% of all white students either named an
other-race student as one of their best friends or said they belonged to an
informal group which was biracial.

Overall, then, the evidence indicates that a majority of students of
each race did have some friendly relationships with other-race students
but that their closest social contacts were limited to their own racial group.
However, a sizable proportion of both blacks and whites had students of
the other race in their closest social circles.

School Comparisons. On the basis of students' answers to the three items shown in Figure 4.3, we computed for each student an index of interracial friendship.[6] For students of each race in each school, an average score (and standard deviation) on this index also were computed (see Appendix C). Among black students, the average friendship score was highest for the small number of blacks at Pershing (1.1% black). However, interracial friendship for blacks was not related generally to the overall racial proportions in their schools. For white students, average friendship with blacks was slightly lower than average in the most heavily white schools. Interracial friendship was by far the greatest for whites at Highland (71.2% black). However, there was no consistent association between average interracial friendships reported by whites and the racial compositions of their schools.

Unfriendly Interaction

While many students had friendly contact with schoolmates of the other race, many (often the same persons who had friendly contacts) reported unfriendly contacts.

Some students told us in interviews that they had been insulted or called names by schoolmates of the other race. A number of black students said that racial epithets had been used against them by some white students. A black male sophomore at Emerson said: "Most of them in my classes are seniors. They call you 'nigger' and stuff."

A white junior girl at Southwest, talking of racial problems at her school, said: "A white person could call a black person a name, like 'nigger.' I've talked to a lot of people; they have heard other people call the colored people 'nigger' and they take it as they're trash."

In addition to verbal insults, many students complained about actual or threatened physical coercion by students of the other race. White students, and especially white boys, were most apt to report personal experiences of this kind. For example, a white senior boy at Harrison told us: "I've had a few problems with other students, Negro students, asking me for money. Once I was threatened. I was standing at the bus stop, waiting for a bus. One of them asked me for some money. I said I didn't have it. He said he was going to throw me off the bridge, so I gave him the money."

A white junior boy at Highland told us: "I am scared of blacks. I got beat up a couple of times last year by some guys from out of school . . . [Highland] Junior High and guys from, like, Harrison. It happened in school with me, in the halls. There's quite a problem with that last year."

Some white girls also mentioned incidents of physical attacks by black schoolmates. A white sophomore girl at Emerson recounted: "Sometimes there's fights between the different races . . . last year I was in one of them . . . some girl spilt some mayonnaise on the floor and I slipped on it; I started to laugh; she thought I got her in trouble; she kept picking on me . . . she wouldn't leave me alone. Every time I'd come up on her, she'd push me around."

Some white students saw physical attacks on them as due solely to the fact of their race, and not to any provocation on their part. Thus, when the white boy at Highland, who told of being beaten up by blacks, was asked why he thought they did this, he replied: "I was white and passing by at the wrong time." A white junior girl at Emerson, who told of blacks hitting whites, was asked whether these blacks attack someone they have a grudge against. She answered: "Normally it's someone they have a grudge against but sometimes they pick them at random. I don't know if it's because they're popular, or because they're pretty, or a lot of times if they have blonde hair. It's just because they're white."

On the other hand, some black students told of fights with whites which they said were started by insults on the part of whites. A black senior boy at Emerson recounted: "This one boy, in football practice almost two years ago. When we were leaving the stadium, he said, 'Them fucking niggers think they're so good.' We had a fight." A black senior girl at Southeast told us: "There was this girl . . . she was a white girl, she was going around yelling about how she was so much better than black people, so pretty soon everybody got tired of hearing it, so this girl beat her up. This was in lunch class."

Some black students also told of violence by whites against blacks. A black senior girl at Emerson said: "Like today they said there's supposed to be some kind of riot; it's the white boys starting this one. They were talking in the cafeteria yesterday about they were going to jump the colored boys 'cause of something they'd done in one of the games last week. . . . The majority of times when I see a black and white girl fighting, the white girl starts it most, and I have a reason to say it. Last year, I have a sister that goes here, and she got into a fight three times, and all three times the white girls hit her first."

The way in which violence sometimes escalates and spreads is illustrated by an incident described by this same black student: "In the cafeteria the other day, someone threw a carton across the cafeteria and hit a white girl in the head. She turned around and grabbed a black girl in the chest and told her she was going to fight her over this . . . so they started fighting, and a white boy started to take up with the white girl, so a black boy jumped him, and there it was, just a big mess; that's how little things get started."

The reciprocal nature of much of the violence that occurs is illustrated also by these comments by a white junior girl at Emerson: "They [the blacks] harrass them [the whites], they corner them. The blacks normally do the cornering. The white kids rebel against it. Some of them will gang up, mostly guys, will gang up against the Negroes and fight."

Our systematic data on unfriendly contacts are based on several series of questionnaire items. The first series of questions asked the student "how many times any [other-race] students have acted . . . toward you this semester" in each of a variety of unfriendly ways, from "talked to you in an unfriendly way" to "threatened to hurt you in some way." Most of these items are shown in part A of Figure 4.4. We also asked each student how often he had gotten into an argument or physical fight with students of the other race, or was forced to give money to any of these students. The items concerning fights probed how often the student had fought back when attacked and how often he "got so mad at [other-race] student(s)" that he struck first (see part B of Figure 4.4).

Finally, we asked later in the questionnaire how often the student had experienced a variety of unfriendly contacts with students of his own race. These data permit us to compare unfriendly contacts within and across racial lines on a number of items.

The results show, first, that white students were much more likely than black students to report that other-race students had said unfriendly things to them. For example, about half of all black students but almost three-quarters of whites said they had been called bad names at least once or twice by other-race students during the semester. Whites also were more likely than blacks to report that students of the other race had talked to them in an unfriendly way; had tried to force them to give money; or had threatened to hurt them in some way. On the latter item, about one out of two whites said he had been threatened by blacks at least once or twice that semester, as compared to one in six blacks who said he had been threatened by whites.

While black students were somewhat more likely than whites to report getting into verbal interracial arguments, a greater proportion of whites reported being pushed or hit by someone of the other race. In particular, white students were twice as likely as blacks (40% to 20%) to say that they had been "pushed or hit by [other-race] students but decided not to push or hit back." Consistent with these data, about one in three black students, as compared to one in seven whites, said that he "got so mad at [other-race] student(s) that I hit or pushed that person first." About equal proportions of each race (roughly one-third) said that they had been pushed or hit by other-race students and pushed or hit back.

A comparison of arguments and fights within each racial group, as compared to those across racial lines, is interesting. Black students reported unfriendly contacts (being called bad names, getting into a fight, and hitting another student first) as often or more often with students of their own race as with whites. Similarly, white students reported getting into fights slightly more often with students of their own race than with blacks. White students also were less likely to hit first at black students than at white students. Thus, the greater frequency with which whites reported physical attacks by blacks than vice versa does *not* result from the blacks directing more of their physical aggression against whites than against other black students. It appears, instead, to result from (1) the whites directing *less* of their own physical aggression against blacks than against their own racial group and (2) a slightly higher overall level of fighting by blacks than by whites.

Similarly, the greater frequency with which whites reported being called names by blacks than vice versa does not result primarily from a greater readiness of blacks to direct name-calling at whites than at their

Figure 4.4 Unfriendly Interracial and Intraracial Contacts Reported by Black Students (B) and by White Students (W)[1] (Percentages)

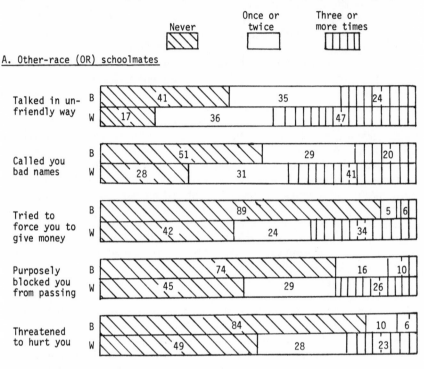

A. Other-race (OR) schoolmates

Talked in un-friendly way
B 41 / 35 / 24
W 17 / 36 / 47

Called you bad names
B 51 / 29 / 20
W 28 / 31 / 41

Tried to force you to give money
B 89 / 5 / 6
W 42 / 24 / 34

Purposely blocked you from passing
B 74 / 16 / 10
W 45 / 29 / 26

Threatened to hurt you
B 84 / 10 / 6
W 49 / 28 / 23

B. Contacts with other-race

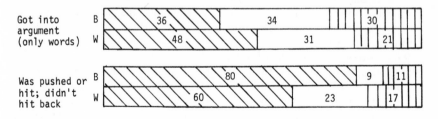

Got into argument (only words)
B 36 / 34 / 30
W 48 / 31 / 21

Was pushed or hit; didn't hit back
B 80 / 9 / 11
W 60 / 23 / 17

Figure 4.4 *Continued*

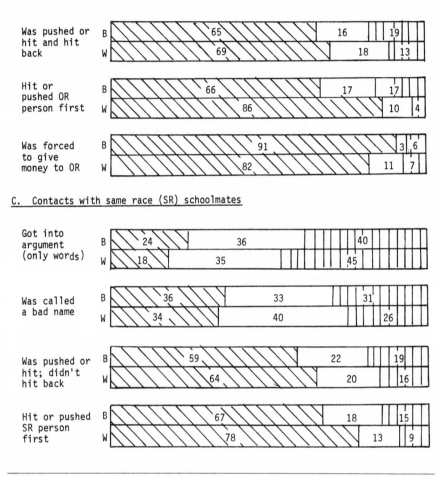

C. Contacts with same race (SR) schoolmates

1. These questions not asked of blacks at Carver or of whites at Pershing, or of white upperclassmen at Jefferson.

own racial group (although there is some difference in this direction). Rather, it results mainly from the fact that whites are *less* likely to call blacks names than they are to call other whites names.

The comparison of unfriendly behavior between and within racial groups also shows that students of both races were more likely to have verbal arguments with schoolmates of their own race than with those of the other race.

Of course, these results do not indicate that unfriendly contact among students was completely random with respect to race. Our interviews indicate that racial differences often were pertinent. Also, it is likely that the ratio of unfriendly contacts to total contacts was lower within racial groups than across racial lines. However, the amount of unfriendly contact between black and white students looms less large when seen in the context of the "normal" level of friction among schoolmates of the same race.

School Comparisons. For each student, two indices summarizing his unfriendly interactions with other-race schoolmates were computed. The first index, Total Amount of Unfriendly Experiences, includes all of the unfriendly contacts listed in parts A and B of Figure 4.4, plus two other items.[7] Most of the items in this index are concerned with unfriendly behavior by other-race students which the student reported experiencing. (He may or may not have provoked this behavior.) A second index was intended to reflect the amount of unfriendly action which the student himself initiated, or which he took an active part in sustaining. This index of Participation in Unfriendly Contact with Other-Race Students is based on the first, third, and fourth items in part B, Figure 4.4.

For black students and white students in each school, average scores and standard deviations on these two indices of unfriendly interracial contacts were computed (see Appendix D). Within each school, there were substantial variations in the extent of unfriendly experiences reported by individual students. There also were significant average differences among schools. Among black students, unfriendly contact with whites (as measured by either index) was lowest among those at Highland, the mostly academic school (71.2% black). The most unfriendly contact with whites was reported by blacks at John Price (36.9% black), a school where students of both races generally were low both in socioeconomic status and in academic orientation. Unfriendly contact with whites also was unusually high at Jefferson (8.7% black), the school to which freshman blacks had begun to be bused during the current school year.

Among white students, the average amount of active participation in unfriendly interracial contact did not vary as widely among schools as it did for blacks. However, whites at different schools varied more than blacks in the average total amount of unfriendly interracial experiences they reported. On both indices, whites at Lakeview reported an unusually large amount of unfriendly experience with black schoolmates. The reader will recall that Lakeview was the newly created facility of the previously all-black school.

White students reported a larger total amount of unfriendly interracial experiences than did blacks in all of the ten schools at which scores for both races were computed. Blacks, on the other hand, scored higher in eight of these ten schools on the index of participation in unfriendly interracial contacts. The two schools in which whites reported slightly more participation in unfriendly interracial contact were schools where whites were a minority (Lakeview and Highland). These results indicate that whites in all schools were more likely than blacks to report being the target of unfriendly behavior by other-race students, whereas, with the exception of two schools, black students were more likely to report initiating or participating in unfriendly interracial contact.

There was little association between the average amount of un-friendly interracial contact reported by blacks and by whites at the same schools.[8] Thus, for example, black students at John Price reported rela-tively frequent participation in unfriendly contact with whites but whites at that school were not unusually high on either index of unfriendly con-tact with blacks. Such an apparent anomaly may have resulted from differences in the proportion of blacks and whites in a school and from differences in the number of blacks and whites who were involved in a typical unfriendly encounter.

Relations among Different Behaviors

We have considered a variety of types of interracial behaviors in the schools—including avoidance, friendly contacts, friendship relations, and unfriendly contacts. How are these kinds of behaviors related?

Table 4.1 shows the correlations among indices of several types of interracial behavior, separately for black students and for white students.[9] These results show, first, that for students of both races, there was a small-to-moderate association between avoidance of other-race school-mates and participation in unfriendly interracial contacts. This association suggests that, while avoidance and unfriendly contact are clearly separate kinds of behavior, there is a tendency for them to go together. Probably they both reflect hostility toward other-race schoolmates. Also, unfriendly contacts at one point in time may lead to avoidance later.[10]

As might be expected, there is a moderate positive association be-tween the indices of friendly contact and friendship. Among both blacks and whites, those students who had a variety of specific friendly contacts with other-race schoolmates tended also to report interracial friendships.

What is most interesting, however, is the absence of any appreciable association between friendly contact (or friendship) and unfriendly con-tact. Among students of both races, the amount of friendly interracial contact (or friendship) which students reported was essentially unrelated to the amount of unfriendly interracial contact they reported.[11] These results are consistent with what students told us in interviews. Time after time, a student would describe a warm and friendly relationship with one schoolmate of the other race and then go on to describe a fight or argu-ment with another student of that race; or first tell of an other-race per-son he disliked and then of one he liked. These results indicate that it is unrealistic to think of a single friendly–unfriendly dimension of interra-cial behavior. Rather, it is clear that students may have little or much of both types of contact. The interviews indicate that the friendly and un-friendly contacts are likely to be with different individuals of the other race and that students can differentiate their behavior with no apparent difficulty.

Table 4.1. Pearson Correlations among Different Measures of Interracial Behavior (Blacks above Diagonal, Whites below Diagonal)[1]

	Avoidance	Unfriendly Contact[2]	Friendly Contact	Friendship
Avoidance	X	.43	−.08	−.16
Unfriendly contact	.38	X	.08	−.08
Friendly contact	−.15	.08	X	.44
Friendship	−.22	.00	.48	X

1. Average N for correlations is about 1,500 for blacks and about 1,600 for whites; N varies somewhat for each correlation, depending on number of cases with valid data. With Ns of about this size, correlations of .08 are significant at .01 level and higher correlations are significant at .001 level.
2. Index of participation in unfriendly interracial contact was used (see Chapter 4).

The data of Table 4.1 also show only small correlations, for students of both races, between the amount of avoidance of, and the amount of friendly contact with, other-race schoolmates.[12] The correlations between avoidance of, and friendships with, other-race schoolmates are a little larger, but still small. These results, too, do not necessarily indicate irrational inconsistency in students' behavior. Rather, many students made it clear in interviews that they distinguished between other-race schoolmates whom they saw to be friendly and desirable as associates and those whom they considered hostile, offensive, or dangerous. They would then go on to describe their friendly contacts with one group and their efforts to avoid the latter group.

Relation of Behavior to Attitudes

To what extent were students' interracial behaviors consistent with their interracial attitudes? Previous research has found that the association between attitudes and behavior—including interracial attitudes and behavior—often is weak (Wicker, 1969; Schuman and Johnson, 1976). However, there has been little evidence on this subject from racially mixed school situations. St. John comments: "Whether sociometric or observed behavior in the classroom corresponds with expressed attitudes toward the other race has been virtually ignored in desegregation research" (St. John, 1975, pp. 72–73).

Evidence bearing on this subject is presented in Table 4.2. These results show that there were small-to-moderate positive correlations between students' overall attitudes toward their other-race schoolmates and their behavior toward those schoolmates.

For students of both races, racial attitudes correlated most highly with interracial avoidance (the more negative the attitude, the more frequent the avoidance). The correlations between racial attitudes and the measures of friendly and unfriendly interactions were smaller than those between attitudes and avoidance, but also were in the expected direction. The more positive the students' attitudes toward other-race schoolmates, the more they had friendly contacts and friendships and the less they participated in unfriendly contacts with schoolmates of that race.

Table 4.2. Pearson Correlations between Students' Interracial Attitudes and Interracial Behaviors[1]

		Attitude toward Other-Race Schoolmates	Positive Change in Opinion of Other-Race People
Avoidance	Blacks	−.45	−.27
	Whites	−.56	−.33
Friendly contact	Blacks	.25	.13
	Whites	.37	.26
Friendships	Blacks	.28	.22
	Whites	.35	.26
Participation in unfriendly contacts	Blacks	−.35	−.13
	Whites	−.31	−.12

1. All correlations (Pearson rs) are significant at .001 level. The number (N) of students on which correlations are based vary somewhat with the number of valid scores on each pair of variables. The median N for blacks is about 1,350; the median N for whites is about 1,600.

Why should racial attitudes have been more strongly related to students' avoidance than to their friendly or unfriendly contacts? Two reasons probably account for this result. First, whether a student chooses to avoid others is almost entirely within his own control, whereas friendly or unfriendly contacts often depend in part on the attitudes and actions of schoolmates of the other race as well. Secondly, just as the attitude questions involved reactions to the entire group of other-race schoolmates at the school, interracial avoidance often involved actions toward these students as a total group (or perhaps toward some segment of the whole group). On the other hand, friendly or unfriendly contacts were with specific individuals, so that the student might distinguish between his attitudes toward other-race students as a group (or the "typical" other-race student) and particular individuals whom he especially liked or disliked.

The associations between students' interracial attitudes and behavior were not the same under all circumstances. Further analyses (not presented in detail here) show that among black students, having negative racial attitudes was associated most strongly with avoidance of whites when the racial attitudes of black peers were most negative. Among whites, positive racial attitudes were most strongly associated with friendly interracial contacts when the racial attitudes of their white peers were relatively positive. These results indicate that the extent to which students' behavior is consistent with their attitudes may depend on the extent to which there is support within their own racial group for the behavior.

Behavior and Attitude Change. Another question of interest is the relation between students' interracial behavior and their *changes* in racial attitudes. Table 4.2 shows also correlations between various interracial behaviors in high school and reported change in opinion toward other-race people during high school. While these associations are fairly small, they are in the expected direction—i.e., those students who reported more positive contacts with other-race schoolmates also reported a more positive change in opinion toward other-race people since starting high school. It is plausible to think that more friendly and pleasant interracial experiences contributed to positive opinion change while unfriendly experiences led to less positive (or negative) changes in opinion. However, it also is possible that those who changed their racial attitudes for some other reason then adjusted their interracial behavior to correspond more closely with their changed opinions. Both processes may have operated to some extent, though it is not possible from these data to tell the relative importance of each.

Overall Description of Interracial Contacts

In the previous sections of this chapter, we have examined evidence showing both positive and negative aspects of interaction between black and white students. There is evidence of much friendly interaction, but also of much contact that was unfriendly. It is of interest, therefore, to see how students of both races described their overall relationships with students of the other race.

We did not ask students for an overall evaluation of their interracial contacts during the present semester. We did, however, ask two general questions about students' overall relationships with the other race in their school. First, we asked each student: "In general, how friendly were most of your contacts with [other-race] students in this school *before this semester?*" The results (see Figure 4.5.A) show that a small majority of both races (55%) described their earlier interracial contacts in the school as

Figure 4.5 General Description of Interracial Experiences at Present High School by Black Students (B) and by White Students (W)[1] (Percentages)

A. "In general how friendly were most of your contacts with (other-race) students in this school before this semester?"

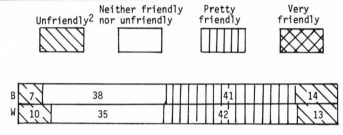

B. "Please show what kind of experiences you have usually had with (other-race) people . . .at this high school."

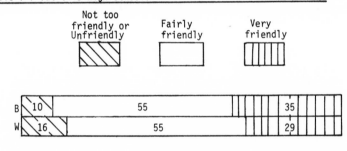

1. These questions not asked of blacks at Carver or of whites at Pershing, or of white upperclassmen at Jefferson.
2. Includes "very unfriendly" and "pretty unfriendly."

generally friendly, while a large minority (45%) said these contacts generally had been less than friendly (though not necessarily unfriendly). Only about one in seven of each race said their interracial contacts had been "very friendly" but even smaller proportions said their contacts had been actually "unfriendly."

There is reason to think that these results may show a somewhat more negative picture than was true for the second semester, to which our specific questions about avoidance, friendly contact, and unfriendly contact refer. We asked students to rate "race relations in this school," for both the first and second semesters, along a four-point scale from "very bad" to "very good." In every school (with one minor exception) students of both races described race relations in their school as better during the second semester than during the first semester.

These results are consistent with the comments of some teachers and administrators that there is often a "shakedown" period early in the school year during which students of different races learn to adjust to one another. Thus, the results of Figure 4.5A probably give a somewhat more negative view of students' overall interracial contacts than would be true for the second semester.

We also asked students a second general question, about "what kind of experiences . . . you have usually had with [other-race] people . . . at this high school." Note that whereas the first question concerned the period prior to the present semester, this second question was applicable to their entire stay at this school. Also, note that this second question refers to other-race "people" and not specifically to students.

In general, the answers to this question give a more positive overall picture of students' interracial contacts than their answers to the questions about experiences prior to this semester. Again, only a small minority of each racial group described their interracial experiences as usually unfriendly. A majority (55%) of each racial group said their experiences were usually "fairly friendly." A substantial minority (about one in three blacks and over one in four whites) described their interracial experiences in the school as "very friendly." Why the "very friendly" response is much more frequent here than in the previous question is not clear. It may be due to the difference in the time period referred to, the difference in the other-race group referred to, the difference in the set of response categories, or differences in question wording.

Overall, responses to the two general questions indicate that most students described their overall interracial contacts in moderate or mixed terms. However, a majority of students of both races appeared to see themselves as having predominately positive contacts. At the extremes, only a small minority described their overall contacts as unfriendly, while a somewhat larger minority said their overall contacts were very friendly.

While there were some variations among schools, in general, students' overall descriptions of their interracial contacts did not differ greatly across schools. In every school, only a small minority of students of either race said their interracial contacts in the school had generally been unfriendly.

Summary

Let us now summarize the results presented in this chapter.

First, the results show that both black students and white students tried fairly often to avoid at least some schoolmates of the other race. Most frequently, this involved such small but important everyday actions as not sitting near, talking to, or walking near some other-race schoolmates. In addition, substantial minorities of each race said they avoided school events that many other-race students would attend or (especially among blacks) stayed out of a club because "too many" students of the other race were in it.

While students often tried to avoid some other-race schoolmates, a good deal of friendly interaction between the races occurred. For example, during the current semester, about two-thirds of all black students and over half of the whites reported doing school work together with a schoolmate of the other race at least once or twice; about half of the students of each race said they had done things together outside of school with a schoolmate of the other race; and about one in five students of each race identified one or more of his five best friends as being of the other race. Such results indicate that some of the hoped-for social results of biracial schooling—meaningful, nonsuperficial, friendly contacts—did occur at least sometimes for a majority of the students of both races.

Although friendly contact between the races was fairly frequent, sizable proportions of both races also reported unfriendly interracial contacts. For example, about five out of ten blacks and seven out of ten whites reported being called bad names by someone of the other race; one in two whites, and one in six blacks, said that an other-race student had threatened to hurt him in some way. White students were more likely to report that black students acted in an overtly unfriendly way toward them than vice versa. Consistent with this result, blacks were more likely than whites to say that they had gotten so mad at someone of the other race that they had pushed or hit that person first.

These results were put into a better perspective when we looked also at unfriendly contact *within* racial groups. Members of each racial group reported as much unfriendly contact (name-calling, fighting) within their own racial group as across racial lines. The greater frequency with which whites reported unfriendly actions against them by blacks than vice versa resulted primarily from (1) the whites directing less of their aggression against blacks than against their own racial group and (2) a somewhat higher overall level of unfriendly actions (fighting, name-calling) by blacks than by whites.

In addition to substantial variation in the behavior of individual students within each school, there were significant differences among schools in the average amount of avoidance, friendly contact, and unfriendly contact which students of each race had with schoolmates of the other race. However, the average interracial behaviors reported by black students at a given school tended to be independent of these reported by white students at the same school.

The results showed also that the types of interracial interactions which students reported were not necessarily consistent. There was a tendency for avoidance of, and unfriendly contacts with, other-race schoolmates to go together. However, the amount of friendly contact and the amount of unfriendly interracial contact which students experienced were essentially independent of each other. These results indicate that many students had very different kinds of contacts with different schoolmates of the other race.

For both blacks and whites, behaviors toward schoolmates of the other race tended to be consistent with their attitudes toward the other-race group. But interracial attitudes were associated more strongly with avoidance than with friendly or unfriendly interactions.

Finally, while most students had both positive and negative interracial experiences, the positive ones appeared to predominate in their thinking. In every school, a large majority of the students of each race described their overall interracial experiences in that school as at least "fairly friendly."

Now that we have described students' interracial attitudes and behaviors, we will begin to try to explain the differences found. In the next chapter, we examine how students' interracial attitudes and behavior were related to their early background and experiences prior to high school.

Determinants of
Social Relations

5 | Students' Early Experiences

Students do not enter high school devoid of any racial attitudes nor, in many cases, without some previous experiences with people of another race. Their families probably have transmitted to them images of what those of another race are like and what kind of behavior toward those of another race is appropriate. Students also may have had personal experiences—either positive or negative—with other-race people in their neighborhoods, grade schools, or elsewhere in the community (Proshansky, 1966; Harding et al., 1969).

To what extent are the kinds of interracial behaviors and attitudes which students manifest in high school related to such early experiences and influences? Which specific early influences seem to be most important? How do the effects of varied influences (e.g., grade school experiences and family attitudes) combine? And what are the mechanisms through which early experiences affect later behavior? These questions are addressed in this chapter.[1]

What does previous work have to say about these issues? Psychologists of varied theoretical persuasions have argued for the importance of early experiences in shaping attitudes and behavior (e.g., Freud, 1938; McClelland, 1951). The evidence with respect to racial orientations indicates that children's preference for their own racial group increases with age until a "leveling-off" occurs at about age twelve (Proshanksy, 1966). Such research evidence, plus the common-sense notion that children are more "pliable" at younger ages, has led some to suggest that racial desegregation in schools will be most successful (socially, at least) when it is done in the earliest grades.

The available research evidence tends to support this expectation, indicating that cross-racial adjustments are less difficult when black and white children are brought together at earlier rather than later ages (Dwyer, 1958; Yarrow, 1958; Hildebrant, 1962). However, the evidence of better interracial relations at early grades is more consistent for white

83

children than for black children. For blacks, some studies have found more positive results of interracial contact for older rather than younger children (St. John, 1975, p. 77). Moreover, Herman (1967) found that white sixth graders from integrated neighborhoods showed less tolerance toward other racial groups than did whites from segregated areas. Black children living in these two types of neighborhoods did not differ in their attitudes toward whites.

Another important question is the extent to which attitudes and behavior learned in early years are "carried over" to new situations. In studies of interracial contact in job and housing situations, prior interracial contact sometimes has been found to affect the amount of current interracial contact (Deutsch and Collins, 1951; Ford, 1972). However, the more common finding is that changes in behavior and attitudes in one situation do not generalize outside the situation in which these new behaviors are learned—e.g., from the job to the community (Minard, 1952; Amir, 1969). Some researchers have pointed to the strength of social norms in the new situations to explain this lack of generalization.

With regard to the school situations, there is some evidence that white children who experienced cross-racial contacts in grade school were less likely than other whites to prefer all-white high schools (U.S. Commission on Civil Rights, 1967; O'Reilly, 1970). Several studies of white adults indicate that having attended desegregated elementary schools was associated with more positive interracial attitudes and more interracial associations as adults (Brown, 1974).

While these studies would lead us to expect a carryover from early interracial experiences and attitudes to high school, more direct evidence has been scanty. St. John (1963) related the racial composition of grade schools attended by black students to their choice by whites as friends in high school. She found that the greater the proportion of blacks in the grade schools which blacks attended, the less often they received positive choices by whites. The racial proportions of grade schools attended by blacks did not relate significantly to their own choice of whites, although there was a tendency for blacks from more heavily black grade schools to choose whites less often. No information about the racial composition of white students' grade schools was obtained in this study. However, Webster (1961) found that the friendship choices which white students gave to blacks in a newly integrated junior high school were not related to their pre-contact acceptance of blacks. Overall, the effects of early interracial attitudes and contact on later interracial behavior and attitudes have remained very much in doubt.

Important Background Factors

To try to shed additional light on these matters, we have obtained information about a variety of early interracial experiences and influences. These include data concerning grade school, neighborhood, and family. We will discuss these specific background variables next, indicating the reasons we would expect each to affect attitudes and behavior in high school and indicating also the kind of information obtained about each background variable. In later sections of the chapter, we will indicate how students' early backgrounds actually are related to their interracial behaviors and attitudes, both prior to high school and during high school.

Grade School Contacts

We would expect the amount, and more importantly, the nature of interracial contacts in grade school to have some important effects on later interracial attitudes and behavior. First, the extent to which a student has pleasant or unpleasant experiences in his contacts with schoolmates of another race is likely to affect his attitudes toward people of that group. In part, this may occur by the formation, and perhaps revision, of his perceptions of the other race. It may occur also through a process of classical conditioning (Byrne, 1971), whereby people of a certain race are associated with stimuli that evoke positive or negative feelings. Perceptions and feelings thus formed in grade school may be generalized to new other-race people in new situations (e.g., high school).

Secondly, the student may learn in grade school certain patterns of behavior—e.g., friendly horseplay, or crossing to the other side of the street, in the presence of other-race schoolmates. Such patterns of behavior may generalize to interaction with new other-race people in new situations.

It is also possible that a student will meet in high school some of the other-race students he knew in grade school. If so, a simple continuation of his learned attitudes and behaviors toward those individuals would probably occur.

The extent to which attitudes and behaviors learned in grade school will generalize to new situations will depend on a variety of circumstances. These include (1) how similar or different other-race people in the new situation are from those known earlier and (2) what the social norms of important others are, and what the sanctions are, for various behaviors in the new situation.

Among students in our Indianapolis high school sample, the amount and nature of interracial experiences which students had in grade school varied widely. Some students had frequent contacts with the other race in grade school. Others had little or no interracial contact there.

Asked during an interview whether there were white kids in her grade school, one black girl at Highland replied: "Hardly any . . . there was only about two or three. I didn't meet them."

One white girl at Harrison remarked: "I went to a completely white grade school and when I got over here, it was really different."

When students did have contact with schoolmates of another race in grade school, the nature of the contact differed considerably. Some students of both races recalled the friendly relations they had with other-race classmates. One black boy at Southwest, who said that his grade school was about half white, said: "We got along at that school, no fights, no nothing; everybody was on the football team. It was like everybody was the same color; no prejudice or nothing over there."

A white boy at Highland, who said there were just a few blacks in his grade school, was asked how the blacks got along with other kids. He replied: "Very well, I think. I think black kids may tend to get along better with white kids . . . white kids don't want to seem to be prejudiced, so they will try especially hard to get along."

However, some students of both races told us during interviews of unpleasant interracial experiences in grade school. One black girl at Emerson said that she began the fourth grade as the only black student in her class. "What made it so bad was the teacher sat me right in the middle so everybody can really get a good look at you and act surprised . . . as I got up into the seventh and eighth grades, [the school] became almost completely black. But during the whole time I was there, none of the white students associated with me."

A black boy at John Price said that his grade school was 80% white. "It was mostly hillbillys that didn't care for black. . . . All my friends fought and they fought mostly black and Mexicans against white. Almost every day there'd be a fight."

To obtain more systematic information about students' interracial experiences in their grade schools, we included a number of relevant items on the questionnaire.[2]

Racial Composition, Grade Schools. First, we asked each student to write down each grade school he had attended and the number of grades he had attended there. Then, for each school, we asked the student to check one of six boxes to show the proportions of students in his classes who were black and white. The six categories were: (1) all whites: (2) mostly whites, very few blacks; (3) mostly whites, quite a few blacks; (4) mostly blacks, quite a few whites; (5) mostly blacks, very few whites; (6) all blacks. We then combined the information about all schools the student attended (weighted by how long he attended each) into an index showing the racial composition of his grade school(s).

Friendliness of Grade School Contact. We also asked each student a series of questions concerning the "number of [other-race] people" he had "gotten to know" (none; one or two; some; or many) in each of a number of places and "the kind of experiences (if any) you have usually had with [other-race] people there" (very friendly; fairly friendly; not too friendly; unfriendly). One of the places about which these questions were asked was "at grade school." By multiplying the score for the number of other-race people known in grade school by the score for the friendliness of these contacts, we derived for each student an index score of friendly interracial contact in grade school.

Neighborhood Contact

The early experiences which students have with people of another race in their neighborhoods also may be expected to affect their later attitudes and behavior. The reasons are the same as those given above concerning interracial contacts in grade school. The pleasantness or unpleasantness of early experiences may—through a classical conditioning process—help to mold the emotional reactions which are evoked by other-race people. Perceptions of other-race people may be formed or revised. Patterns of behavior, either positive or negative, may be tried out, found to succeed, and become habitual. Such attitudes and behavior, learned with respect to particular other-race people in the neighborhood, may generalize to new people of that race or, in some cases, merely be continued with the same people in new settings.

In Indianapolis, as in most cities, many students of both races grew up in neighborhoods where few (if any) people of another race lived. However, some students mentioned having had interracial contacts in their neighborhoods.

A number of students described such contacts in a positive way. Asked about the contacts between whites and blacks on sports teams at John Price, a black boy answered: " . . . The guys that go out for those sports are like the ones that grew up together, the ones that lived on the south side all their life, white and black, so, like, they won't fight; they play with each other. They been friends for, like, eight years."

A black boy at Harrison said: "Most of the white boys around where I live, we consider each other equal; we do everything together."

A white boy at Highland said: "A lot of kids from both groups live on the North side . . . our neighborhood, a lot of the people are black. It's a beautiful neighborhood."

An illustration of both the positive and negative interracial contacts that occur in neighborhoods was provided by a black boy at Southwest, who, when asked if he had any white friends, answered: "Yes, I live in a white neighborhood. I was walking down the street and these two big boys come up and start a fight with me. I ran and this boy was friendly, his mother was friendly; they let me in and called the police. That's how I met him." This same boy went on to say of the white youths in his neighborhood: "They're friendly but . . . they'll slip and say 'nigger,' something like that, talking about black people and we'll come up there and put them down."

To obtain more systematic information about students' interracial experiences in their neighborhoods, we asked a number of relevant questions on the questionnaires.

Segregation of Neighborhood. We asked each student, "About how many [other-race] families live within two blocks of your home now?" (six response categories, from "all or almost all [other-race] families" to "no [other-race] families I know of"). Note that this question refers to the student's present neighborhood. Unfortunately, we did not obtain information specifically about the racial composition of the student's neighborhood prior to high school. However, it is very probable that most students lived in the same neighborhood just prior to high school as they did when answering our questionnaire. This assumption receives support from the substantial correlations between the reported racial composition of students' neighborhoods and their reports of how many other-race people they had "gotten to know" in their neighborhoods before high school (r = .60 for blacks, .55 for whites).

Friendliness of Neighborhood Contact. We asked each student how many (other-race) students he had "gotten to know in my neighborhood(s) before I came to high school" (none; one or two; some; many) and "what kind of experience you have usually had with [other-race] people there" (very friendly; fairly friendly; not too friendly; unfriendly). On the basis of this information, each student was assigned a score showing the amount of friendly interracial contact he had in his neighborhood prior to high school. Similar information was obtained about interracial contacts in the neighborhood during high school (see Brown, 1974), but, since we are interested here primarily in the effects of early experience, we will focus on the earlier neighborhood contacts.

Family Racial Attitudes

We would expect that the racial attitudes and behaviors which children learn will be influenced also by the racial attitudes of their families. (Research—e.g., Sartain, 1966; Hough et al., 1967—is consistent with this expectation.) Family members—especially parents—often will provide real or fictional "information" about people of another race—e.g., that they are nice or mean, lazy or industrious, intelligent or stupid. Such images transmitted by the family will help to form the students' racial perceptions and—because some of these images are emotionally charged—also will evoke certain emotional reactions (e.g., liking, disliking, fearing) in response to other-race people.

In addition to its role in shaping the child's perceptions of and feelings toward other-race people, the family also may encourage or discourage particular kinds of behavior. Parents, for example, may advise the student to avoid other-race schoolmates and praise him for doing so. On the other hand, parents may suggest inviting an other-race schoolmate home to play and/or praise him for doing so. In such ways, parents may help to shape patterns of interracial behavior at an early age. Such influences may continue into later years—as, for example, when a high school student's parents react either with understanding or with rage to the news that the student plans a date with an opposite-sex schoolmate of the other race.

Although we did not ask directly in interviews about the racial attitudes of students' families, some students mentioned the racial feelings of their parents or their parents' instructions concerning the types of contacts they should have, or should not have, with other-race children. (See Chapter 8 for further discussion of family racial attitudes.)

On the questionnaire, we asked two questions about family racial attitudes. The first asked the student how his family "feel about [other-race] people." He could choose among four response categories from "like very few [other-race] people" to "like almost all [other-race] people." The student could also check "don't know."

The second item, later in the questionnaire, asked how the student's family "feel about how friendly [your-race] students should act toward [other-race] students." Students checked whether they thought their families felt that they should (1) "act as friendly with" the other race as with their own race; (2) "act friendly, but not too friendly" with the other race; or (3) "not have much to do with" the other race. Students could also indicate that their family didn't care about this matter or that they didn't know how their family felt about this.

Students' responses to these two questions were given numerical scores and an index based on these scores was computed. Although these data are based on students' reports of their families' *present* racial attitudes, it seems reasonable to assume that the racial attitudes of most parents did not change greatly from the time the student was small until he was in high school. We have no evidence about how accurately students perceived their family's racial attitudes, but it seems likely that most parents and other family members expressed such attitudes candidly around the home. Moreover, students' perceptions of their families' racial attitudes may be more important than the actuality.

Parents' Education

It seems possible that the socioeconomic level of the students' families—especially their education level[3]—also may play a role in the racial attitudes and behavior which students develop at an early age. However, the magnitude, or even the direction, of this influence is not readily apparent.

On the one hand, the educational level of the student's parents may affect the extent to which he (and/or his parents) are similar in attitudes, behavior, and vocabulary to people of another race. Among blacks, one might expect students whose families have the least education to be most different in upbringing from the average white child and, therefore, to form friendships less easily with those of the other race. Among whites, one might expect the same to be true of students whose families have the highest education.

On the other hand, there is consistent evidence that white families of highest education have more egalitarian racial attitudes than do whites of lesser education (e.g., Campbell, 1971). For this reason, there may be a tendency for students from more highly educated families (especially whites) to form more positive racial attitudes at an early age and perhaps to act more positively in interracial situations.

While the possible overall effects of parent education were hard to predict, it seemed useful to include this variable in our analysis. Our measure of parents' education is based on students' reports about the education of each parent (or parent substitute) with whom he was living. For each such person, the student checked one of six categories, from "went to grade school but did not graduate" to "finished a four-year college or went beyond." (The student could also check "I don't know.") Where two parents were present, their education scores were averaged.

Sex

The interracial behaviors and attitudes of boys and girls often have been found to differ (St. John, 1975). Thus, it is possible that the effect of students' early backgrounds on their interracial behaviors and attitudes will differ for the two sexes. For this reason, the student's sex also was included in these analyses.

Racial Opinion prior to High School

As we have noted, one of the key ways in which early life experiences may affect later attitudes and behaviors is through their effect in molding the student's early racial attitudes.

To assess racial attitudes prior to high school, we asked each student: "In general, what was your opinion of most [other-race] people just before you came to this high school?" Response categories were: good; pretty good; not too good; not good at all; had no real opinion of them then.

Combined Effects of Early Experiences

We have discussed a variety of factors in a student's early life experiences which may affect his interracial behaviors and attitudes in high school. But each of these factors operates in the context of all the others. How are they related to each other?

Figure 5.1 shows a hypothetical model of how the various early experiences and influences may combine to affect later attitudes and behaviors. According to the model, several basic conditions of the student's early life (racial composition of grade school, family racial attitudes, etc.) may affect the amount of friendly interracial contact which he has prior to high school. The amount of friendly interracial contact, in turn, affects the racial attitude which the student has when he enters high school. This early racial attitude, in turn, affects the student's interracial behavior and attitudes while in high school.

Figure 5.1   A Hypothetical Model of the Relation of
Background Factors to Interracial Behavior
and Attitudes in High School

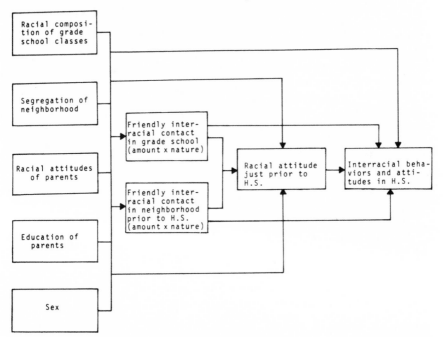

In addition to the effects which are expected to occur via this causal chain, other effects may be more direct:

1. Aspects of the student's background may have influenced his own early racial attitudes. For example, if the student's family has positive racial attitudes, they may have influenced his own early attitudes in a positive direction, regardless of the extent to which such family attitudes led to more friendly interracial contact at an early age.

2. Aspects of the student's early background may have direct effects on his behavior in high school. For example, parents with negative racial attitudes may actively discourage interracial contact (especially those which involve both sexes) during the high school years, regardless of whether they discouraged interracial contact at an earlier age or influenced the student's early racial attitudes.

3. The friendliness of interracial contacts prior to high school may have direct effects on behavior and attitudes in high school. For example, friendly interracial contacts with a few other-race students in grade school may lead to continued friendly contact with these particular students in high school, regardless of the student's general racial attitude prior to high school.

Differences by Sex and Family Background

The model shown in Figure 5.1 assumes that the causal variables, while related, are additive—i.e., that the effect of each does not depend on the level of the others. However, it is conceivable that the impact of racial mixing in grade school and neighborhood may vary for students who differ with respect to family background and sex. To check these possibilities, we examined the data to see whether the effects of grade school racial composition on (1) the friendliness of interracial contact in grade school and (2) racial attitudes prior to high school differed for students with different family characteristics and for boys versus girls. We looked also to see whether the effects of neighborhood segregation on friendly early contact varied for different groups of students.[4] These analyses were performed separately for black students and for white students.[5] The results (too extensive to present completely in detail) are summarized next.

Grade School. For black students, attending more racially mixed classes in grade school was related to more friendly contacts with whites in grade school ($r = .52$) and to more positive early opinions of whites ($r = .20$). These relations did not vary significantly when blacks from families of different educational levels were considered separately. Greater racial mixing of classes also had a positive effect on friendly interracial contacts and on early racial attitudes regardless of the racial attitudes of parents. However, as Figure 5.2 shows, the positive effect of mixed classes on the friendliness of contact with whites was stronger among blacks whose families' racial attitudes were relatively positive than it was among those whose family attitudes were most negative.

The positive effect of racially mixed classes on friendly interracial contact in grade school and on early racial opinions was found both among black boys and black girls. However the relationship with friendly grade school contact was slightly stronger among girls.[6]

Among white students, as among blacks, attending more racially mixed grade school classes was associated with more friendly interracial contacts in grade school ($r = .54$) and with more positive early racial attitudes ($r = .19$). These associations did not differ significantly for white boys as compared to white girls. However, the relationships with friendly interracial contacts in grade school (though not with early racial attitudes) did differ somewhat for white students from families with different racial attitudes and different educational levels.

Figure 5.3 shows that among white students whose families had the most positive (or even intermediate) racial attitudes, friendly contact with blacks in grade school increased steadily as the proportion of blacks in classes increased. Among white students whose families had the most negative racial attitudes, having increasing proportions of blacks in one's grade school class was associated with more friendly interracial contact there so long as blacks remained a minority; but when the proportion of blacks rose to half or more of the class, friendly contacts with blacks de-

Figure 5.2 Friendly Contact with Whites in Grade School
(Average Scores), as Related to Racial Composition of
Grade School Classes, for Black Students with Families
Having Different Racial Attitudes[1]

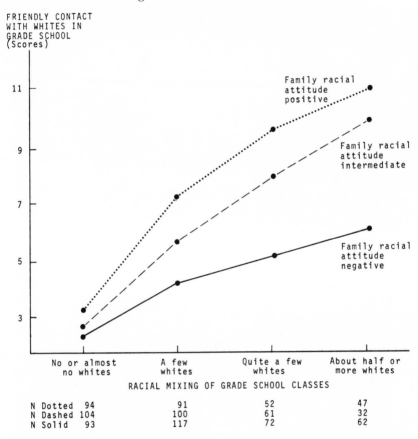

FRIENDLY CONTACT
WITH WHITES IN
GRADE SCHOOL
(Scores)

Family racial
attitude
positive

Family racial
attitude
intermediate

Family racial
attitude
negative

No or almost   A few   Quite a few   About half or
no whites   whites   whites   more whites

RACIAL MIXING OF GRADE SCHOOL CLASSES

N Dotted 94	91	52	47
N Dashed 104	100	61	32
N Solid 93	117	72	62

1. The main effects of racial composition of grade-school classes and of family racial attitudes both were significant at .001 level. The interaction between these factors was significant at the .01 level.

clined somewhat. It may be that white students who came from families with the most negative racial attitudes were able to "tolerate" some blacks but reacted negatively when the proportion of blacks became large.

The relation between racial composition and friendly interracial contact in grade school classes also differed somewhat for white students from families of different educational levels. Figure 5.4 shows that among students whose parents had the most education, having increasing proportions of blacks in one's grade school classes was accompanied by steadily increasing friendly contact with black schoolmates. This tended to be

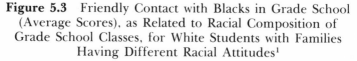

Figure 5.3 Friendly Contact with Blacks in Grade School
(Average Scores), as Related to Racial Composition of
Grade School Classes, for White Students with Families
Having Different Racial Attitudes[1]

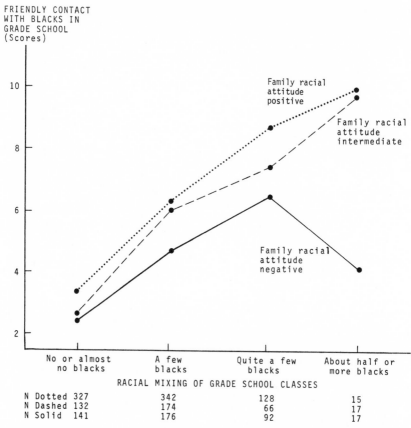

1. The main effects of grade school racial composition and of family racial attitudes both
were significant at the .001 level. The interaction between these factors was significant
at the .01 level.

true also, though not so consistently, among white students whose parents
had graduated from high school. However, among white students from
families with the least education (not completing high school), increases in
the proportion of blacks beyond a minimal representation brought little
increase in friendly contact. The difference between white students from
low-education family backgrounds and other white students is especially
noticeable for the relatively few white students who reported that their
grade school classes were half or more black. As we noted earlier, racial
attitudes tend to be most hostile among lower-class whites. It may be,

Figure 5.4 Friendly Contact with Blacks in Grade School
(Average Scores), as Related to Racial Composition
of Grade School Classes, for White Students with Parents
of Different Educational Levels[1]

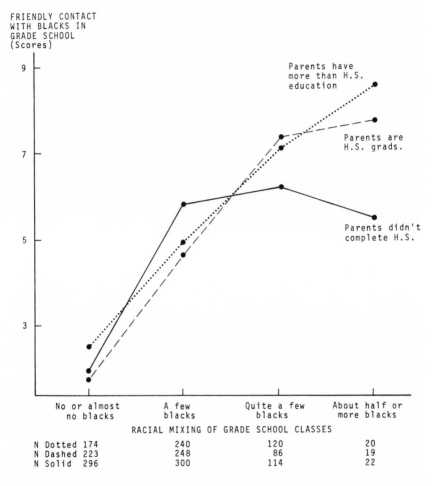

FRIENDLY CONTACT
WITH BLACKS IN
GRADE SCHOOL
(Scores)

Parents have
more than H.S.
education

Parents are
H.S. grads.

Parents didn't
complete H.S.

No or almost no blacks — A few blacks — Quite a few blacks — About half or more blacks

RACIAL MIXING OF GRADE SCHOOL CLASSES

	No or almost no blacks	A few blacks	Quite a few blacks	About half or more blacks
N Dotted	174	240	120	20
N Dashed	223	248	86	19
N Solid	296	300	114	22

1. The main effect of racial composition of grade school classes was significant at the .001 level; the main effect of parents' education was not significant; and the interaction between these two factors was significant at the .02 level.

therefore, that the relatively small increases in friendly contact which occurred for students from low-education families reflected the racial attitudes and norms of their social group.

Neighborhood. What about the effects of the racial composition of the neighborhood? Before considering whether these effects differed among subgroups of students, let us consider its effects for all students.

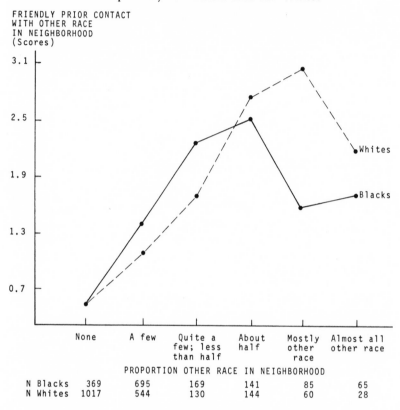

FRIENDLY PRIOR CONTACT
WITH OTHER RACE
IN NEIGHBORHOOD
(Scores)

| N Blacks | 369 | 695 | 169 | 141 | 85 | 65 |
| N Whites | 1017 | 544 | 130 | 144 | 60 | 28 |

PROPORTION OTHER RACE IN NEIGHBORHOOD

1. Differences in friendly prior contact for those who lived in different types of neighborhoods were significant both for blacks and for whites at beyond the .001 level.

Figure 5.5 shows the overall relationship between the racial composition of students' neighborhoods and the amount of friendly interracial contact they had in their neighborhoods prior to high school.[7] Among white students, there generally was a steady increase in friendly early contact with blacks as the proportion of blacks in their neighborhoods increased. Only for the small group of whites who reported living in almost all-black neighborhoods was there a moderate drop in friendly interracial contact (as compared to those in mostly black neighborhoods).

Among blacks, the pattern is clearly curvilinear. As the proportion of whites in the student's neighborhood increased from none to almost half, there was a fairly steady rise in friendly contacts with whites. However, as whites became a majority in the neighborhood, friendly contact with whites fell off.

The dip in friendly interracial contact among blacks living in mostly white neighborhoods (and among whites in almost all-black neighborhoods) may reflect social problems which arise for numerical minorities—especially small minorities. Such minorities may not be accepted by many members of the majority and may themselves feel uncomfortable about interacting with members of the majority.

Despite the drop-off in friendly interracial relations among students (especially blacks) living in neighborhoods where the other race was a majority, early opinions of other-race people were more positive among students from integrated than from segregated neighborhoods. Among students of both races, those living in completely segregated (all own-race) neighborhoods reported the most negative racial attitudes prior to high school. Among blacks, opinions of whites became slightly but steadily more positive up to the point where the neighborhood was about half white and then leveled off. Among white students, early opinions of blacks became more positive up to the point where blacks were a sizable minority and then, with minor fluctuations, leveled off too.

The associations of neighborhood racial composition with early friendly interracial contacts in the neighborhood, and with racial attitudes prior to high school, did not differ for boys as compared to girls. Nor did these associations vary for students with parents of different educational levels.

However, for white students (though not for blacks), the effect of neighborhood racial composition on friendly interracial contact depended to some extent on family racial attitudes. As Figure 5.6 shows, having more blacks in the neighborhood resulted in the greatest increase in friendly interracial contact among white students whose families had the most positive racial attitudes. However, even among those white students whose families had the most negative racial attitudes, living in more racially integrated neighborhoods did bring some increase in friendly contacts with blacks prior to high school.

Relation of Early Experiences to High School Behavior and Attitudes

So far we have examined the effects of students' early backgrounds on their racial contacts and attitudes prior to high school. Next we will consider the effects of students' early backgrounds on their relations with other-race schoolmates in high school.

We will look at the correlations between various background factors and interracial behavior and attitudes in high school. In addition, to take account of the network of relationships among the background variables,

Figure 5.6 Friendly Contact with Blacks in Neighborhood
Prior to High School (Average Scores), as Related to Proportion of
Black Families in Neighborhood, for White Students with
Families Having Different Racial Attitudes[1]

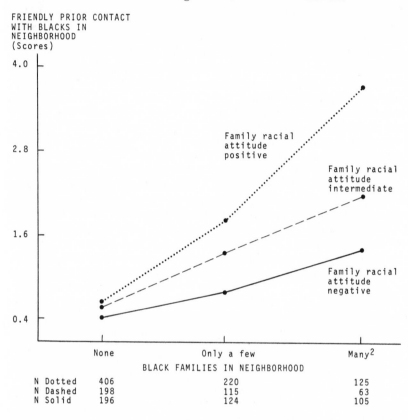

FRIENDLY PRIOR CONTACT
WITH BLACKS IN
NEIGHBORHOOD
(Scores)

N Dotted	406	220	125
N Dashed	198	115	63
N Solid	196	124	105

BLACK FAMILIES IN NEIGHBORHOOD

1. The main effects of proportion of blacks in the neighborhood and family racial attitude, and the interaction between these two factors, all are significant at the .001 level.
2. Combines "quite a few but less than half"; "about one-half"; "mostly"; and "all or almost all" black families.

we will present the results from the standpoint of the causal model shown
in Figure 5.1. To do this, we have made use of the technique of path
analysis (Namboodiri, Carter, and Blalock, 1975).

This technique permits us to see the direct effects which each background factor has on a given social outcome, separate from the effects of
other background factors. In addition, the technique of path analysis
permits us to trace the indirect effects of each background factor. For
example, we can see to what extent the racial composition of grade school
classes affects friendly behavior in high school through its effect on racial
opinion prior to high school.

Following the model shown in Figure 5.1, we performed a separate path analysis for each of six aspects of interracial behavior and attitudes: friendly contact, friendship, avoidance, unfriendly contact, attitude, and opinion change. Each analysis was done separately for black students and for white students.

Before summarizing the results of these analyses, a few technical points should be noted. In performing the path analyses, we have treated each of the variables at the extreme left of the model (neighborhood racial composition, etc.) as having effects which are independent of one another. Despite the fact that we found some significant interaction effects among these variables (see above), these effects were small compared to the independent ("main") effects of each separate variable. Also, in some cases, the interaction effects involved a very small proportion of the total sample of students. We judged that trying to build the small interaction effects into the analysis would have disadvantages which outweighed the advantages[8] and would not affect the results much in any case.

However, our analyses do take account of several instances described above in which relationships between variables were found to be markedly nonlinear. Specifically, the racial composition of black students' neighborhoods and the educational level of white students' parents are handled in ways which permit nonlinear relations to be shown.[9,10]

For the path analyses, scores on friendly interracial contact in grade school and in the neighborhood were added to form a single index of friendly interracial contact prior to high school.[11] Prior analyses had shown that these two variables were additive in their effects on racial opinion prior to high school and on interracial behavior in high school.

To present full data on all twelve path analyses would be unnecessarily lengthy and tedious. Instead, we will present in detail (graphically) only results concerning friendly contact with the other race. The results of path analyses of other interracial behaviors and attitudes are available elsewhere.[12] They will be summarized briefly here as they become relevant.

Black Students

Let us consider first the results for black students, looking at how each aspect of their early experiences affected later attitudes and behavior.[13]

Racial Composition of Grade School Classes. Did the opportunity to know more white students in grade school lead blacks to have better relationships with whites in later school years?

The racial composition of the grade school classes attended by black students had only a small positive correlation with the amount of friendly contact they had with white schoolmates in high school (see Table 5.1). Having more whites in grade school classes did contribute substantially to having more friendly contacts with whites *prior* to high school (see Figure 5.7). Such friendly early contacts, in turn, had a positive effect on opin-

ions of whites just prior to high school, which, in turn, contributed to
more friendly contacts with whites in high school. But because of the indirect nature of this connection, the overall effect of the racial composition
of grade school classes on friendly contacts with whites in high school was
quite small.[14]

Having more whites in grade school classes had a more substantial
effect on changes in black students' opinions of white people during high

Table 5.1. Early Background of Black Students, as Related to Their
Interracial Behavior and Attitudes in High School
(Pearson Correlations)[1]

	Friendly Contact	Friendship	Avoidance	Unfriendly Contact[2]	Positive Attitude	Positive Opinion Change
Proportion of whites in grade school classes	.08	.01	.01	−.01	−.03	−.25
Racial composition of neighborhoods[3]:						
Mostly white	.09	.06	.01	.06	.00	−.08
Many whites[4]	−.02	.02	−.04	−.04	.04	−.06
Few whites	−.04	−.05	.01	.02	−.04	.03
Positive family racial attitudes	.24	.30	−.32	−.16	.43	.24
Parents' education	.17	.12	−.03	.02	.11	−.02
Sex	−.06	−.04	−.06	−.19	.03	−.03
Friendly contact with whites before high school	.25	.19	−.19	−.04	.18	−.09
Positive opinion of whites before high school	.31	.26	−.36	−.25	.44	−.04

1. Correlations are based on 395 blacks for whom valid data on all variables in table were available. Correlations based on much larger Ns, for those for whom data are available for each
   pair of variables, are very similar to those shown here. For Ns of this size, correlations of .10
   are significant at .05 level and correlations of .13 are significant at .01 level.
2. Index of participation in unfriendly interracial contact used (see Chapter 4).
3. Students in each of the neighborhood categories are compared to students who reported no
   whites in their neighborhood.
4. Includes "about half white families" and "quite a few, but less than half, white families."

school (see Table 5.1). But this effect was negative; i.e., the greater the proportion of whites in their grade school classes, the *less* positive was the change in opinions of whites during high school. Path analysis shows that this was a direct effect, rather than operating through effects on interracial contact and opinions prior to high school.

It may be that changes in opinion of whites during high school (which generally were in a positive direction) were less frequent among black students who had attended integrated grade schools because their opinions of whites were more crystallized than were the initial opinions of black students who had known few whites in grade school (see also Brown, 1974, pp. 177–181). Another possibility is that blacks who had attended racially integrated grade schools tended to find their white schoolmates less friendly in high school than in grade school—perhaps because of more discriminatory white norms associated with being of dating age. If so, blacks coming from racially mixed grade schools would have changed their opinions of whites in a less positive (or more negative) direction than did blacks with less prior contact with whites.

The racial composition of black students' grade school classes had little overall relation to other aspects of their relations with whites in high school—i.e., to interracial avoidance, friendship, unfriendly contacts, or racial attitude (see Table 5.1).

Overall, these results indicate that the racial composition of their grade school classes had little effect on the relationships which black students had with whites in high school.

Racial Compositions of Neighborhoods. Did the opportunity to meet white people in their neighborhoods affect the social relations which black students had with white schoolmates in high school?

The results show, first, that the proportion of whites in black students' neighborhoods had little overall relation to the amount of friendly contact which these students had with whites in high school (see Table 5.1). Having whites in their neighborhoods (especially a substantial number) did contribute to having more friendly contacts with whites *prior* to high school (see Figure 5.7). In turn, such friendly early contacts contributed to having more friendly contacts with whites in high school. However, this indirect effect of having whites in the neighborhood on friendly contact with whites in high school was quite small, largely because the effect was weakened as it was transmitted along the causal chain. Moreover, having many whites in the neighborhood ("quite a few but less than half" or "almost half") also had an opposite negative effect, contributing directly to *less* friendly contact with whites in high school. (It may be that neighborhoods with such racial compositions were experiencing racial frictions which tended to discourage friendly contacts with whites in high school.) Overall, this network of small and opposing effects resulted in little association between neighborhood racial composition and the friendly contacts which black students had with whites in high school.

The racial composition of black students' neighborhoods also had very little association with any other interracial behaviors and attitudes in high school—i.e., with avoidance, friendships, unfriendly contacts, racial

Figure 5.7   Path Diagram Showing Effects of Early Life Situation of Black Students on Their Friendly Contact with Whites in High School[1]

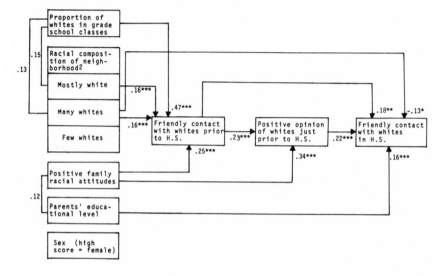

---

1. Figure shows correlations of .10 or more among exogenous variables (those on left) and shows all path coefficients which are significant at .05 level or better; one, two, and three asterisks (*) indicate significance at .05, .01, and .001 levels respectively.
2. Students in each category are compared to those living in neighborhoods which have "no whites."

attitude, and attitude change. Overall, then, among black students, the racial composition of their neighborhoods appeared to have had little effect of any kind on their attitudes toward, and interactions with, white schoolmates in high school.

Racial Attitudes of Family. While the racial composition of grade schools and neighborhoods had little overall impact on black students' relations with whites in high school, the racial attitudes of their families had a greater effect (see Table 5.1).

First, the more positive the racial attitudes of black students' families, the more friendly contacts they reported with whites in high school. This effect of family racial attitudes was indirect—operating through its impact on black students' racial experiences and opinions prior to high school (see Figure 5.7).

Positive family racial attitudes also were associated with a whole range of other behaviors and attitudes toward whites in high school—more friendships, less avoidance, more positive overall attitudes, more positive opinion change and (least strongly) fewer unfriendly contacts (see Table 5.1).

Whereas the racial attitudes of the students' families affected friendly contacts with whites in high school only indirectly (through their impact on early experiences and opinions), family racial attitudes affected friendships with whites directly as well. Probably friendships—which usually involve home visits and parental knowledge—are more likely to come under direct parental influence than the variety of friendly contacts which fall short of a friendship relation.

Positive family racial attitudes also had both direct and indirect effects in reducing avoidance of whites, improving attitudes toward white schoolmates, and changing general opinions of whites in a favorable direction. Thus, the considerable influence of families appeared to operate both through the effects they had on students' experiences and opinions prior to high school and through a continuing impact during the high school years.

Parents' Education. How about the educational level of black students' parents—did this affect their relations with white students in high school?

As the educational level of black students' parents increased, the students tended to have more friendly contacts with whites in high school (see Table 5.1). Figure 5.7 shows that this represents a direct effect, rather than operating through students' early experiences and opinions. It may be that black students from relatively well-educated families had patterns of behavior and values that facilitated friendly contact with whites in high school. The education of black students' parents also had small positive correlations with friendships with whites and with positive attitudes toward whites in high school. However, other path analyses show that parents' education did *not* have a significant direct effect on friendship, attitudes, or any other measures of black students' relations with white schoolmates in high school. Nor did it have any indirect effects on these other outcomes. Overall, then, the impact of the education of black students' parents on the students' social relations with whites in high school was slight. (Further results show that a measure of parents' socioeconomic status, based on both education and occupation, had even smaller correlations with black students' interracial behavior and attitudes than those shown for education in Table 5.1.)

Friendly Contact Prior to High School. We have seen that opportunity for contact with whites prior to high school (as indicated by the racial compositions of grade school and neighborhood) had little relation to friendly contact with whites during high school. However, the amount of *friendly contact* with whites prior to high school had a more appreciable effect (see Table 5.1).

The more that black students had friendly contact with whites in grade school and in the neighborhood prior to high school, the more friendly contact they also had in high school.[15] Figure 5.7 shows that this association was, in part, an indirect one. Friendly contact with whites prior to high school led to more positive opinions of whites just before entering high school, which, in turn, led to more friendly contact with whites during high school. In addition, friendly early contact had a direct effect on friendly contact in high school. In part, this direct effect may mean that patterns of friendly interracial behavior which were learned at an early age were generalized to new white schoolmates in high school. In addition, in some cases the whites with whom blacks were friendly in high school were the same persons with whom they had established friendly relationships in their grade school or neighborhood.

Friendly early contact with whites prior to high school also was related—though modestly—to more friendships with, less avoidance of, and more positive attitudes toward whites during high school (see Table 5.1). As in the case of friendly contact in high school, these associations reflect both direct effects and indirect effects through more positive early opinions of whites.

Friendly contact with whites prior to high school had little relation to unfriendly contacts with whites in high school or to change in opinion of white people during high school.

Overall, the more friendly contact black students had with whites prior to high school, the more positive their relationships with white schoolmates in high school.

Early Opinion of Whites. In discussing the effects of various background variables, we have touched on the role of early opinion of whites as a link in the causal chain. Focusing more specifically on this variable, we see that the correlational results (Table 5.1) show that a more positive opinion of whites prior to high school was associated with more positive interactions with, and more positive attitudes toward, whites in high school. The path analyses show that a positive prior opinion had a positive direct effect on every type of interracial behavior and on racial attitudes as well. The only social outcome not affected by prior racial opinion was change in opinion of white people after starting high school.

White Students

What about the white students? How did their early backgrounds affect their relationships with blacks in high school?

Racial Composition of Grade School Classes. Among white students, having a larger proportion of black students in grade school classes was associated with more friendly relations with blacks in high school (see Table 5.2). This effect was indirect. Figure 5.8 indicates that having more blacks in grade school classes contributed substantially to more friendly contacts with blacks prior to high school. Such friendly early contact, in turn, contributed to friendly contact with black schoolmates in high school, both directly and, to a lesser extent, through its positive effect on opinion of black people prior to high school. Because the causal chains are indirect, the overall correlation between grade school racial composition and friendly contact with blacks in high school, though positive, is small.

Among whites, having larger proportions of blacks in grade school classes also was associated positively, though slightly, with other aspects of

Table 5.2. Early Background of White Students, as Related to Their Interracial Behavior and Attitudes in High School (Pearson Correlations)[1]

	Friendly Contact	Friendship	Avoidance	Unfriendly Contact[2]	Positive Attitude	Positive Opinion Change
Proportion of blacks in grade school classes	.17	.13	−.11	.06	.13	−.02
Proportion of blacks in neighborhood	.23	.19	−.09	.04	.08	−.02
Parents' education:						
High school	−.12	−.10	.03	.01	−.02	−.02
Some post-high school	.00	−.04	−.04	−.04	−.02	−.06
College	.18	.06	.00	.02	.03	−.06
Positive family racial attitudes	.19	.23	−.30	−.13	.40	.14
Sex	−.03	.06	−.15	−.31	.16	.05
Friendly contact with blacks before high school	.39	.34	−.17	.03	.23	.05
Positive opinion of blacks before high school	.25	.27	−.29	−.16	.40	−.12

1. Correlations are based on 814 white students, for whom valid data were available on all variables in the table. Correlations for much larger samples having valid scores on each pair of variables are very close to those shown here. With Ns of this size, correlations of .08 are significant at .05 level; correlations of .10 are significant at the .01 level.
2. Index of participation in unfriendly interracial contact used (see Chapter 4).
3. Students in each category of parents' education are compared to those whose parents average less than a high school education. "High school" includes high school graduate or close to it. "College" includes college graduate or close to it.

Figure 5.8 Path Diagram Showing Effects of Early Life Situation of White Students on Their Friendly Contact with Blacks in High School[1]

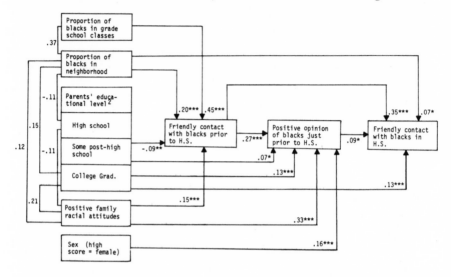

1. Figure shows correlations of .10 or more among exogenous variables (those on left) and shows all path coefficients which are significant at .05 level or better; one, two, and three asterisks (*) indicate significance at .05, .01, and .001 levels respectively.
2. Students in each category are compared to those whose parents average less than a high school education.

relations with blacks in high school—i.e., with more friendships, more positive attitudes, and less avoidance (see Table 5.2). Other path analyses show that the racial proportion of grade school classes did not have a direct positive effect on any of these outcomes in high school. Rather, its positive effects were consistently indirect—though its substantial impact on more friendly contacts with blacks prior to high school, which, in turn, affected relationships with blacks in high school directly and/or through its effect on opinions of blacks prior to high school.

There was little relation between grade school racial composition and the amount of unfriendly contact which white students had with blacks in high school. Nor was there any appreciable correlation between grade school racial composition and change in opinion of blacks during high school.

Overall, then, the more white students attended racially mixed grade school classes, the more they tended to display positive behavior and attitudes toward blacks in high school, but these associations were weak.

Racial Composition of Neighborhoods. Were the relations which white students had with black schoolmates in high school related to the racial composition of the whites' neighborhoods? The results show that having a larger proportion of blacks in the neighborhood was associated with more friendly contacts with blacks in high school (see Table 5.2).

Part of this modest association was due to a very small direct effect (see Figure 5.8). This direct effect may indicate that having friendly contact with blacks in high school was facilitated by being able to see blacks around the neighborhood. In addition, living in more racially mixed neighborhoods contributed indirectly to more friendly interracial contact in high school, by leading to more friendly contacts with blacks prior to high school. Such early friendly contacts, as we have seen, led to more friendly contact in high school, both directly and by contributing to more positive opinion of blacks prior to high school. Finally, the overall association of neighborhood racial composition with friendly contact in high school was increased by the fact that living in racially mixed neighborhoods was linked to other background characteristics—especially having many blacks in grade school classes—which also had positive associations with friendly interracial contacts during high school.

Living in more racially mixed neighborhoods also was associated with more friendships with blacks during high school. (The causal links are similar to those between neighborhood composition and overall friendly contact in high school.) However, the associations between neighborhood racial composition and other aspects of white students' relations with blacks in high school all were very small (see Table 5.2).

Overall, these results indicate that having blacks in the neighborhood did lead to somewhat more friendly interaction with blacks—both before and during high school—but that its effects on racial attitudes and on other behavior, like avoidance of blacks, were slight.

Racial Attitudes of Family. The racial attitudes of white students' families had relatively strong associations with the students' relations with blacks in high school (see Table 5.2). Positive family attitudes were associated most strongly with positive attitudes toward black schoolmates and with less avoidance of blacks in high school. More positive family racial attitudes also were associated with more friendly contact and friendships with blacks and, slightly, with fewer unfriendly contacts and more positive changes in opinions of blacks during high school.

The effect of the racial attitudes to white students' families on their friendly contacts with blacks in high school was indirect, through its impact on early interracial experiences and opinions. Family racial attitudes affected other interracial behaviors and attitudes of white students more directly as well. Positive racial attitudes by the student's family contributed directly to more positive attitudes, less avoidance, and more positive change in opinions of blacks while in high school. In addition, positive family attitudes made smaller direct contributions to more friendships with blacks and to fewer unfriendly contacts with blacks. Overall, these results indicate that the white student's family did have an immediate present influence on much of his interracial behavior and attitudes while he was in high school. These influences probably reflect the pressures which parents put on their children while in high school (e.g., concerning with whom they should associate) as well as the more subtle influences of family ideas and examples during the high school years.

In addition, the racial attitudes of white students' families exerted an indirect influence on all aspects of interracial behavior and on interracial attitudes, through their impact on students' early experiences and attitudes.

Parents' Education. The educational level of white students' parents generally had little association with the students' behavior and attitudes toward blacks in high school. (A measure of socioeconomic status, based both on parents' educations and occupations, had even smaller correlations with the interracial behavior and attitudes of white students in high school.)

White students whose parents were college educated did have somewhat more friendly contact with black schoolmates than whites whose parents had less education. (The least amount of friendly contact with blacks was found among white students whose parents completed high school but didn't go beyond.) Figure 5.8 shows that the association between having college-educated parents and friendly contact with blacks was not due primarily to the small association of parents' education with more liberal racial attitudes nor to its small positive effect on early opinions of blacks. Rather, coming from a college-educated family contributed directly—though only a little—to friendly contact with blacks in high school. It may be that norms concerning contact with blacks were more liberal in college-educated social circles, apart from the racial attitudes of the students' own parents.

The associations of parents' education with other aspects of social relations with blacks in high school were very small.

In general, then, having college-educated parents contributed somewhat to white students' having more friendly relations with blacks in high school, but parents' education did not have much effect on other aspects of their interracial relations.

Friendly Contact prior to High School. While the racial composition of their grade schools and neighborhoods had only weak effects on white students' relations with blacks in high school, the effects of *friendly contact* with blacks prior to high school were stronger. Such friendly early contacts were correlated most strongly with friendly contact, friendship and positive attitudes toward blacks during high school, and also were associated with less avoidance of black schoolmates (see Table 5.2). Figure 5.8 shows that only a small part of the effect of friendly early contact on friendly high school contact was due to the impact of such early contact in improving opinions of black people prior to high school. By far the largest portion of the association was a direct effect of friendly early contact on friendly high school contact. As in the case of black students (for whom this direct effect was also present, though weaker), this result seems to indicate that patterns of friendly behavior toward the other race, learned at an early age, were generalized to new other-race schoolmates in high school. In addition, some white students may have continued friendly relations with the same black acquaintances from their grade school or neighborhood into high school.

Other path analyses show that friendly early contact with blacks also led both directly and indirectly (through prior racial opinions) to more friendships with and more positive attitudes toward blacks in high school. With respect to negative interracial behaviors (avoidance and unfriendly contact), friendly early contact with blacks had only small indirect effects. (Friendly early contact with blacks led to more positive opinions of blacks prior to high school, which led to slightly less avoidance of, and fewer unfriendly contacts with, black schoolmates in high school.)

Finally, by contributing to a more positive opinion of blacks prior to high school, friendly early contact with blacks contributed to *less* positive changes in opinions of black people during high school. This somewhat surprising result was due to the relation between opinions of blacks prior to high school and change in such opinions during high school. The effects of prior racial opinions are considered next.

Early Opinion of Blacks. Positive early opinions of blacks were associated with positive behavior and attitudes in high school. The more positive the opinion of black people which white students had just prior to high school, the more friendly contact and friendships they had with blacks in high school, the less their avoidance of and unfriendly contacts with blacks, and (most strongly) the more positive their attitudes toward black schoolmates in high school (see Table 5.2). Path analyses show that prior racial opinion had direct effects on all of these outcomes (though sometimes small ones) which were independent of other background variables.

However, while a positive prior opinion of blacks had the positive effects just mentioned, it also was associated—though slightly (see Table 5.2)—with a *less* positive change in opinion of black people during high school. Path analysis shows that, with the effects of other background factors controlled, this negative effect of prior opinion on change in opinion of blacks becomes stronger.[16]

How can we explain this result? It may be that white students who began with relatively positive opinions of blacks had less "room" than others to move in a more positive direction (the "ceiling effect"). More important, it may be that whites with less positive initial opinions, having lower expectations of blacks, reacted favorably to the pleasant behavior of many blacks. Conversely, those with good initial opinions, having higher expectations, may have been disappointed by the behavior of some blacks of which they disapproved. Whatever the explanation, the effects of a favorable prior racial opinion were mixed; it led to positive behaviors and attitudes toward black schoolmates but to negative *change* in attitudes toward blacks.

Early Experiences and High School Situation

In discussing the effects of the student's background on his relations with other-race schoolmates in high school, we have been neglecting—for the time being—other factors which may affect relations between the races in high school. These other factors, including the racial composition of high school classes and the conditions under which interracial contact occurs in high school, will be discussed at length in later chapters.

For the moment, we wish to consider the extent to which early interracial experiences had the same or different effects in different types of high school settings. We first consider the question: Did the effects of friendly interracial contact prior to high school differ as the racial attitudes of students' high school peers differed? Analyses designed to answer this question indicate that the answer is essentially "no," both for black students and for white students. Friendly interracial contact prior to high school had almost the same relationships with interracial attitudes and behavior in high school, regardless of the average level of ethnocentrism of the student's peers.[17] Thus, it appears that the impact of early interracial experiences on the student did not vary with different types of attitudinal climates among his high school peers.

A second specific question addressed was the following: Did the effects of interracial experiences prior to high school differ among students who experienced different racial mixtures in their high school classes? Among white students, the answer is "no." Having had friendly contacts prior to high school led to more positive attitudes and behaviors toward blacks in high school, regardless of the racial composition of the students' high school classes.

Among black students, friendly early contact with whites had positive effects on most aspects of their relations with whites in high school, regardless of the racial composition of their high school classes. However, the impact of early interracial experiences on avoidance of whites in high school did vary with the racial composition of the high school setting. Among black students who had friendly contacts with whites prior to high school, there was little avoidance of whites in high school, regardless of the racial proportions of classes. However, among blacks who had little friendly contact at an earlier age, avoidance of whites was frequent only when there was a white majority in their classes (see Chapter 7 for more details). Apparently, the combination of having had little positive experience with whites prior to high school and being part of a racial minority in high school made blacks very wary of contact with whites.

Concerning other background variables, among students of both races the effect of parents' education on high school race relations did not differ as the racial composition of high school classes varied. Nor did the effects of parents' racial attitudes or of the student's sex differ as the racial composition of high school classes varied.[18] Also, the association of parents' racial attitudes with students' interracial behavior and attitudes in high school did not differ significantly as the level of ethnocentrism of high school peers varied. (See Chapter 8 for further discussion of the effects of parents' and peers' racial attitudes.)

Differences among Schools

In considering the relation between students' backgrounds and their relations with other-race schoolmates in high school, we have focused on individual students. We also may consider this matter briefly from the perspective of the total school. To what extent were differences between schools, in the types of interracial behavior that occurred, related to the average backgrounds of their student bodies?

The data (see Appendix F) show that, for blacks in eleven schools and for whites in ten schools,[19] there were rather large correlations (in the .80s and .90s) between the average racial composition of the students' neighborhoods and grade school classes and their average amount of friendly contact with schoolmates of the other race in high school. The greater the average proportion of other-race people in neighborhood and grade school, the more the average friendly interracial contact in high school.

There also were fairly large correlations, for students of both races, between the average racial attitudes of the parents of students in a school and the average amount of friendly interracial contact which students in that school reported. The more positive the average family racial attitude, the higher the average frequency of friendly contact with the other race.

However, inspection of the scatter plots for these data makes it apparent that these large correlations were due largely to the effects of two schools (one for blacks and one for whites) which were unusual in certain ways. For blacks, the overall results were greatly influenced by the black student group at Pershing, the almost totally (99%) white school in a white neighborhood. Of the small number of blacks who attended this school, an unusually large proportion came from racially mixed (or mostly white) neighborhoods and had attended grade schools with large proportions of whites. Also, the reported racial attitudes of the parents of black students in this school were far more positive than those of black parents in any other school. It was the small number of blacks in this school who reported, on the average, by far the greatest amount of friendly contact with white schoolmates.

The results for white students were greatly influenced by the unusual white student body at Highland. Highland was the primarily academic-program school, now majority (71%) black, which white students attended by choice rather than by compulsion. White students at Highland were much more likely than whites at any other school to live in racially integrated neighborhoods and to have attended grade school classes with substantial proportions of blacks. Moreover, the racial attitudes of the families of white students at Highland were far more positive than those of whites at any other school. The white student body at Highland, coming from this unusual background and also having the opportunity easily to meet blacks in their majority-black school, reported by far the largest average amount of friendly contact with black schoolmates.

The fact that the positive association between average student background and average friendly contact in high school stems largely from two school cases (one for each race) makes it impossible to draw general conclusions. However, these results do suggest that when the average background of the student body of a school is optimal, with respect to prior interracial contact and family attitudes (as they were for blacks at Pershing and whites at Highland), a high level of friendly interracial contact in high school may be expected.

Finally, the results at the school level also indicate that neither the average educational level of black students' parents nor that of white students' parents had strong associations with the average interracial behaviors of either racial group. Consistent with the results for individuals, there was a tendency for higher parental education to be associated with better race relations (especially for whites), but the associations were too small to be statistically significant for the small number of schools involved.[20]

Summary

We now summarize our findings about the effects of students' early backgrounds on their interracial behavior and attitudes.

First, we found that attending more racially mixed grade school classes led to more friendly interracial contacts and more positive racial attitudes at an early age (prior to high school). For both black students and white students, this was true regardless of the students' sex. It also generally was true regardless of the education or the racial attitudes of the students' parents. However, the positive effect of grade school contact was strongest and most consistent for those students whose parents had the most positive racial attitudes and (for white students) for those whose parents had more than a minimal education.

For students of both races (but especially blacks), the association between the racial composition of students' neighborhoods and the amount of friendly interracial contact prior to high school was curvilinear. As the proportion of other-race people increased, friendly contact first rose, but when the other race became a large majority, friendly contact in the neighborhood declined somewhat. This decline may reflect the difficulties—especially rejection by the numerical majority—which may occur where the other race is preponderant.

For both black students and white students, having greater proportions of the other race in their neighborhoods generally led to more
friendly early interracial contacts and more positive early racial opinions,
regardless of the students' sex, the education of their families, or their
families' racial attitudes. However, among whites, these effects were
strongest for those whose families had the most positive racial attitudes.

While the opportunity for interracial contact in grade schools and
neighborhood contributed substantially to friendly interracial experiences
prior to high school, it had much less effect on behavior and attitudes in
high school. This was especially true among black students. Among
blacks, the proportion of whites in their grade schools and neighborhoods
had little overall association with their relations with white schoolmates in
high school. Among white students, the overall impact of early opportunity for interracial contact was somewhat more positive. Most notably,
having a greater proportion of blacks in one's neighborhood and grade
school classes was associated with more friendly interactions with blacks in
high school. However, these associations were small.

Although proximity to the other race in grade schools and neighborhood had little effect on later relationships, the *types* of interracial experiences which students had at an early age had greater impact. First,
friendly contact in the grade school and neighborhood had some direct
effects on friendly interracial behavior in high school, indicating that
friendly patterns of behavior, and perhaps some particular friendships,
were carried over to new settings. In addition, friendly early contact had a
positive indirect effect on later behavior and attitudes, through its positive
impact on students' racial opinions prior to high school.

The impact of friendly interracial experiences prior to high school
on social relations with other-race schoolmates in high school did not vary
with a number of aspects of the high school situation. However, among
black students, the absence of friendly contact with whites prior to high
school led to avoidance of whites in high school only among those blacks
who attended majority-white classes in high school. It seems likely that
black students in majority-white classes who had little prior friendly contact with whites were most apprehensive about rejection by white peers
and therefore avoided them.

Students' interracial attitudes and behaviors in high school also were
affected by their family background. Among students of both races, those
whose parents had the most education tended to have more friendly contacts with schoolmates of the other race. However, these associations were
rather small and there was little association between parents' education
and other interracial behaviors or between parents' education and interracial attitudes. Overall, then, the impact of parents' education on relations with other-race schoolmates in high school was slight. (Other results,
using a broader measure of socioeconomic status, were very similar to
those based on parents' education.)

The racial attitudes of parents had a more substantial effect. Both
among black students and among white students, the more positive the
racial attitudes of the student's parents, the more positive his interactions

with, and his attitudes toward, other-race schoolmates in high school. In part, the influence of family racial attitudes was direct, reflecting the pressures that parents exert while the student is in high school. In addition, family racial attitudes had longer-term indirect effects on students' behavior and attitudes in high school by influencing the amount of friendly interracial contact which they had, and their racial attitudes, prior to high school.

In this chapter we have considered some aspects of students' early experiences and family background which may affect their race relations in high school. In the next chapter we will consider a number of other, more personal, and generally more contemporaneous, characteristics of students which also may affect their relations with schoolmates of another race.

6 | *Student Characteristics*

To what extent do the social outcomes of interracial contact depend on the personal characteristics of students involved in that contact? For example:

Do boys of different races get along better than do girls?

Are those students who are generally aggressive or generally frustrated in their lives especially hostile toward schoolmates of another race?

How about academic ability and motivation? Do these have an effect on how well black students, or white students, get along with other-race schoolmates?

In this chapter we will explore these and related questions concerning the relationships between students' personal characteristics and their interracial behavior and attitudes. Let us consider first the relation of interracial behaviors and attitudes to students' physical characteristics. We will consider two—sex and physical size.

Sex

One might expect the social effects of interracial contact on boys and on girls to differ for several reasons. Boys are more likely than girls to be physically aggressive, and usually direct their aggression at other boys (Maccoby and Jacklin, 1974). Thus, boys of either race are more likely than girls to initiate physical attack upon, and to experience it from, the other race. However, black boys and white boys may find they share some interests (especially sports) in which they can participate as equals. Relationships among girls, on the other hand, may center more often on their interests in social activities and their related concern about "popularity." Since social activities often are heterosexual, they are more likely to be limited to those of one race. Also, the criteria of social acceptance and popularity are such things as dress, physical beauty, and poise, with respect to which the standards of blacks and whites may differ, or—to the extent black girls accept the standards of the dominant white culture—blacks are at a disadvantage. For these reasons, interracial contact might be expected to be more frequent among boys than among girls.

Previous studies—though not always consistent—have generally suggested that black girls are more aloof from whites than are black boys, with respect to either sociometric choice or attitudes (Carithers, 1970; St. John, 1975). On the other hand, there is some evidence suggesting that, among whites, boys tend to be more hostile to blacks and more in-group in their sociometric choices (St. John, 1975; Chadwick, 1972). Our own results provide some unique evidence on this question—by comparing the sexes with respect to several types of behavior, as well as with respect to interracial attitudes.

Let us first compare black girls and black boys. Like most other school studies, we find that black girls had somewhat less friendly contact with whites than did black boys (see Table 6.1). But while black girls had somewhat less friendly interracial contact, they also had less unfriendly contact and tended to avoid white schoolmates less often. Attitudes toward white schoolmates, and change in opinion toward white people during high school, differed little between black boys and black girls. (With all other factors held constant, black boys and black girls differed significantly only with respect to the amount of unfriendly contact they had with white schoolmates [see Table 9.1].) Overall, our results suggest that the emphasis which sometimes has been placed on the difficulties black girls face in integrated situations, as compared to black boys, may have been exaggerated. While black girls interacted less with whites than did black boys, this does not indicate greater unfriendliness or greater hostility. In fact, it was the black boys who had more unfriendly contact with white schoolmates.

Among white students, both interracial behavior and attitudes appeared more favorable among girls than among boys (see Table 6.2). White boys and white girls did not differ much in friendly contact, or friendship relations, with black schoolmates. However, white boys were more likely to report avoidance of, and unfriendly contact with, blacks. In addition to these behavioral differences, white boys had less positive attitudes toward black schoolmates. White boys and white girls differed significantly in these respects even when other relevant factors were held constant (see Table 9.2). Thus, while white boys had as much positive contact with blacks as did white girls, they had more negative contacts and more negative attitudes.

For students of both races, the differences between boys and girls did not vary significantly for those with parents of differing educational levels; nor for those at different IQ levels; nor for those with school classes of differing racial compositions.

Are the differences between boys and girls due only to the fact that boys are more physically aggressive? It is true that being male and being aggressive (fighting with students of one's own race) were positively corre-

Table 6.1. Personal Characteristics of Black Students, as Related to Their Interracial Behaviors and Attitudes (Pearson Correlations)[1]

	Avoidance	Friendly Contact	Friendship	Unfriendly Contact[2]	Positive Attitude	Positive Opinion Change
Sex female	−.11	−.11	−.06	−.20	.00	−.05
IQ	−.11	.12	.07	−.09	.19	−.02
Aggressiveness	.29	.08	−.01	.37	−.19	−.02
Educational aspirations	−.07	.15	.16	−.05	.11	.05
Academic effort	−.10	.07	.12	−.10	.13	.07
General life satisfaction	−.07	.12	.07	.04	.23	.19
Religious activity	−.02	.00	.05	−.03	.03	.03
Height:						
Male	.01	.06	.03	−.02	−.03	−.07
Female	.08	.03	−.01	.02	−.01	.04

1. *N*s on which correlations are based vary somewhat, depending on the number of valid scores for each variable. The average *N* is about 1,550. With *N*s of this size, correlations of .06 are significant at .05 level; correlations of .08 are significant at .01 level, and .09 at the .001 level.
2. Index of participation in unfriendly interracial contact was used (see Chapter 4).

lated (.26 for blacks, .34 for whites). However, even when we control roughly for general aggressiveness, boys still report more negative interracial behavior. Figure 6.1 shows, separately for boys and for girls, the amount of unfriendly contact with black students which was reported by white students, as related to the amount of unfriendly contact they had with students of their own race (our measure of aggressiveness). For each level of fighting within one's own racial group, boys were more likely than girls to report interracial fighting. A combination of being male and fighting a lot within one's own white group seemed to lead to an especially high frequency of interracial fighting. Similar results are found when we look at the joint effects of sex and aggressiveness on interracial avoidance. Among black students, too, boys reported more unfriendly interaction with the other race (and also more avoidance) than did girls, even when the level of within-race aggressive behavior was controlled.[1]

Why did boys have more interracial fights and arguments than girls, avoid the other race more, and (in the case of whites) have more negative

Table 6.2. Personal Characteristics of White Students, as Related to Their Interracial Behaviors and Attitudes (Pearson Correlations)[1]

	Avoidance	Friendly Contact	Friendship	Unfriendly Contact[2]	Positive Attitude	Positive Opinion Change
Sex female	−.20	−.03	.03	−.31	.16	.05
IQ	−.05	.12	.03	−.09	.02	−.10
Aggressiveness	.21	.14	.08	.45	−.11	.04
Educational aspirations	−.06	.14	.06	−.07	.01	−.05
Academic effort	−.14	.03	.04	−.18	.07	.00
General life satisfaction	−.08	.03	.01	−.11	.13	.05
Religious activity	−.04	.04	.03	−.08	.02	−.02
Height:						
Male	−.06	.01	.01	.00	.02	.01
Female	.04	.02	.01	.03	.04	−.01

1. *N*s on which correlations are based vary somewhat, depending on the number of valid scores for each variable. The average *N* is about 1,750. With *N*s of this size, correlations of .06 are significant at .05 level; correlations of .08 significant at .01 level, .09 at the .001 level.
2. Index of participation in unfriendly interracial contact was used (see Chapter 4).

attitudes toward the other race—even when personal aggressiveness is controlled?

The sexes did not differ appreciably in their opportunity for interracial contact in classes or in activities—though black girls tended to participate somewhat less in activities ($r = .10$). Nor was there any strong association between sex and initial racial attitude—though white girls tended to report more positive prior attitudes ($r = .16$).

One reason which seems to be important in accounting for the negative reactions of boys is that boys were far more likely than girls to experience aggressive actions by students (usually boys) of the other race. Boys of both races—especially white boys—were much more likely than girls of the same race to report that other-race students had acted in unfriendly ways (insults, threats, blows, etc.) during the semester ($p < .001$ within each racial group). Thus, even though a boy might himself be unaggressive, he was much more likely than a girl to be the target of overtly unfriendly actions—including especially violence and the threat of vio-

Figure 6.1 Unfriendly Contact with Black Schoolmates
(Average Scores), for White Students with Varying
Levels of Unfriendly Contact with Own Race,
Separately for Each Sex[1]

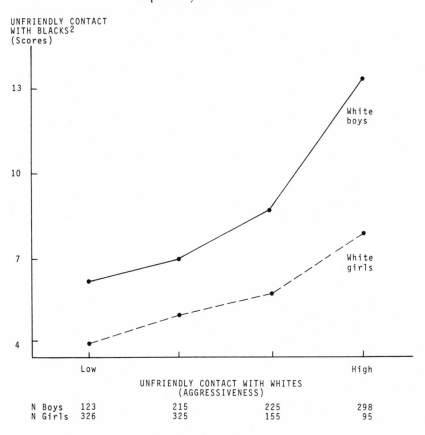

UNFRIENDLY CONTACT
WITH BLACKS[2]
(Scores)

White boys

White girls

Low   High

UNFRIENDLY CONTACT WITH WHITES
(AGGRESSIVENESS)

N Boys	123	215	225	298
N Girls	326	325	155	95

1. Analysis of variance shows the main effects of sex and of unfriendly contact to be significant at .001 level; the interaction between these two factors is significant at .002 level.
2. Measure is index of participation in unfriendly contact, rather than of total unfriendly experiences.

lence. Such experiences may have been responsible for the more frequent avoidance, unfriendly contacts, and negative attitudes which boys reported.

Height

In considering determinants of interracial behavior and attitudes, common experience suggests that physical size may have an effect. The smaller student—especially the smaller boy—may experience more attacks from other-race schoolmates (as well as those of his own race) who think him a safe target. His experiences with the other race therefore may be less pleasant than those of his bigger peers. The smaller person also may be more fearful of other-race schoolmates and, therefore, often may try to avoid them.

Our results show that, for girls of both races, physical size (i.e., height, as reported by the student) had little effect on behavior or attitudes toward schoolmates of the other race (see Tables 6.1 and 6.2).[2] Among boys, the correlations between size and relations with other-race schoolmates also are very small. However, a closer examination of the data shows that, among boys, size did have some impact on behavior. Among white boys, those who were smallest (i.e., 5 feet, 6 inches, or under) were more likely to try to avoid blacks than were boys of medium or tall height (see Figure 6.2). Additional results suggest that this was due to the smallest boys being more fearful of blacks than were bigger white boys ($p < .01$).

While small white boys tended to avoid trouble with some blacks by keeping out of their way, they were no more successful than taller boys in avoiding fights. It may be that the small boys tended to be the target of aggressors, which would cancel out their own attempts at avoidance. Height also was not a determinant of the frequency with which white boys had friendly contact with black schoolmates.

Among black boys, physical size was not related to frequency of avoiding whites, nor to fear of whites. Other results indicate that this may be because black students were less likely to be hit first by whites than vice versa, were less fearful of whites than vice versa, and were seen by both races as better fighters than whites (see Chapters 3 and 4). Thus, even small black boys probably felt relatively unconcerned about the possibility of physical attack by whites.

However, while small black boys (5 ft., 6 in., and under) were not especially apt to avoid whites, they were less likely than medium height or tall blacks to report friendly contact with whites ($p < .01$). Among white boys, there was a similar tendency for smaller boys to report less friendly interracial contact, but this difference was much less marked and not statistically significant. It may be that the smallest boys were less self-confident and outgoing and thus initiated fewer friendly contacts with others. Also, the small black boys may have been chosen less often as teammates of whites in athletic activities. Athletic and other physical prowess may have been more important among black boys than among white boys both in promoting self-confidence and in making the student attractive to others.

Aggressiveness and Dissatisfaction

Some writers have suggested that hostility toward out-groups is the result of displaced aggression, stemming from various frustrations which

Figure 6.2   Avoidance of Other-Race Schoolmates (Average Scores), as Related to Height, for Black Boys and for White Boys[1]

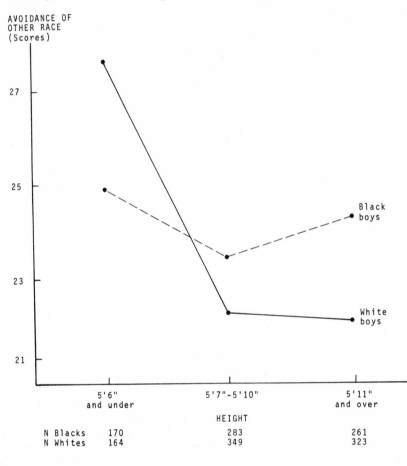

1. Differences between mean avoidance scores are significant at .01 level for whites but are not significant for blacks, with opportunity for interracial contact in classes held constant.

people experience in their lives (e.g., Allport, 1958). According to this hypothesis, students who generally are more satisfied should get along better with schoolmates of another race than those who are generally dissatisfied and frustrated. While there is some evidence linking aggressive behavior to frustration (Feshback, 1970), there has been little evidence to date concerning whether student dissatisfaction contributes to interracial friction in the schools.

In addition to hostility which may stem from situational frustrations, hostility and aggression also may reflect the individual's personality. Some previous research has indicated that youths who have aggressive personalities are most likely to be prejudiced against racial minorities with whom they have contact (Mussen, 1950; Chadwick, Bahr, and Day, 1971). There is less evidence concerning the relation of aggressive personality to interracial behavior. However, it seems quite possible that people with aggressive personalities (i.e., those whose behavior patterns are generally aggressive) will behave aggressively toward people of other racial groups just as they do toward people of their own race.

In examining our own results bearing on these issues, we will consider first the effect of general satisfaction and then consider that of aggressiveness.

Satisfaction. To assess each student's general satisfaction (and thus the possible frustration of his desires), we asked him (or her) on the questionnaire: "How satisfied are you, in general, with each of the following?" Nine items were listed. Three of these concerned things at school: the courses I am taking now; the grades I am getting in school; the teachers I have this semester. Six items concerned things not specifically connected with school: the amount of fun I have away from school; the amount of money I have to spend; how I get along with other kids; my chances for getting to be "someone" in life; the way things are at home; how popular I am with the opposite sex.

For each aspect of his life, the student checked one of four choices, from "very satisfied" to "not satisfied at all." On the basis of these answers, an index of general life satisfaction was computed for each student. To what extent was students' general satisfaction related to their interracial behaviors and attitudes?

Tables 6.1 and 6.2 show that among students of both races, and especially among blacks, the more generally satisfied a student was, the more positive were his expressed attitudes toward other-race schoolmates. Among black students, greater satisfaction also was associated with a more positive change in opinion of white people. Although these associations are fairly small, they remain significant even when other variables affecting interracial attitudes are controlled (see Tables 9.1 and 9.2). The associations between satisfaction and positive racial attitudes may indicate that those who are less frustrated are therefore less hostile and less likely to displace hostility onto an out-group.

However, the results also indicate that, while general satisfaction may have affected attitudes toward other-race schoolmates, it did *not* substantially affect students' *behavior* toward these schoolmates. Among both blacks and whites, satisfaction had only slight associations with the frequency of unfriendly interracial contact, friendly contact, or avoidance. Also, these associations are no longer statistically significant when other relevant variables are controlled (with the exception of a very small remaining association between satisfaction and friendly interracial contact among blacks).

Why does satisfaction (or, conversely, frustration) appear to have so little effect on interracial behavior, including aggressive behavior? As several writers have pointed out, there are a variety of possible behavioral reactions to frustration, of which overt aggression against out-groups is only one (Bandura, 1973). The individual may react to frustration with attitudinal hostility against out-groups, but not with hostile behavior— perhaps because he fears the consequences. Or he may react with aggression against the actual source of his frustration—e.g., his parents or teachers—rather than by displacing aggression against out-groups. Or he may react in other ways, such as by satisfaction of his needs in fantasy, or by constructive attempts to overcome obstacles to fulfilling his needs. The particular behavioral reaction shown may depend on such things as previous success with each type of behavior and the possible penalties associated with each. Internal reactions of hostility, which risk little penalty, are probably more easily learned than is overt hostility as a response to frustration. In these high school situations, at least, overt aggression against an out-group does not seem to have been a frequent reaction to frustration.

Aggressiveness. To assess the general aggressiveness of each student, we relied on his reports about the frequency with which he had each of three types of unfriendly contacts with students of his *own* race during the current semester: (1) "I got so mad at a [same-race] student that I pushed or hit that person first"; (2) "I was pushed or hit by [same-race] student(s) and pushed or hit back"; (3) "I got into an argument with [same-race] student(s), using only words." Although such unfriendly actions sometimes may be in response to the unfriendly actions of others, we assume that, over an entire semester, variations in the frequency of such contacts depend mostly on the individual's own traits.[3]

To what extent were interracial behaviors and attitudes related to aggressiveness? We will examine first the results for individual students and then look briefly at those for total schools.

Individuals. Our results show first that students who were generally aggressive acted much more negatively toward the other race than did those who were less aggressive (see Tables 6.1 and 6.2). Specifically, among both blacks and whites, students who reported more fighting (physical and verbal) with students of their *own* race also fought much more often with *other*-race students. In addition, they tried to avoid other-race students more often. These associations remain strong even when the effects of a variety of other factors which may affect interracial behavior are controlled (see Tables 9.1 and 9.2). In fact, among students of both races, general aggressiveness is by far the best predictor of unfriendly interracial contact and one of the best predictors of interracial avoidance.

Somewhat surprisingly, more aggressiveness also tended to be associated with more friendly interracial contact, especially among whites. Although small, this association may reflect the tendency, shown in previous research (Patterson, Littman, and Bricker, 1967), for aggressiveness to be accompanied by a high general level of activity. However, the frequent interracial fighting of the more aggressive students does not mean that they were merely high spirited and active. The results (Tables 6.1 and 6.2) also show that greater aggressiveness was associated with more negative attitudes toward the other race, especially among black students. More detailed results on attitudes (not presented) show that the more aggressive students were especially likely to express anger toward other-race students. (There was little association between aggressiveness and opinion change.)

Why did generally aggressive students exhibit more negative reactions toward the other race? The results indicate that it was not because they had more negative racial attitudes prior to high school, or less opportunity for interracial contact, or more negative racial attitudes among their families and peers. (Controlling on these and other variables does not substantially reduce the associations between aggressiveness and negative interracial behaviors.)

Interracial fighting is probably, in part at least, simply a generalization of patterns of behavior learned primarily within one's own group. Some people seem to fight often with others, regardless of the race of the others.

The negative racial attitudes of the generally aggressive student—especially the anger, which is especially marked—probably also reflect a high general level of inner hostility. In addition, by virtue of his behavior, the aggressive student is likely to evoke hostile and unpleasant reactions from other-race students. Such reactive behavior by the other race would tend to strengthen the negative attitudes of the aggressive student. Having negative attitudes toward the other race, he would tend to avoid them often—though, when interaction did occur, the possibility of it being unfriendly would be high.

While the responses of generally aggressive students may stem from their personalities, we may wonder whether the interracial behavior of generally aggressive students will differ in different situations. First, are aggressive persons more likely to act with hostility toward other-race schoolmates when they have the support of family and/or peers? To try to answer this question, we classified students according to (1) aggressiveness, (2) the actual ethnocentrism of same-race peers, and (3) the racial attitudes of the student's family, as reported by the student. Analyses of variance (not presented here) show that, for both blacks and whites, the associations between aggressiveness and interracial behaviors did not change substantially regardless of the level of peer ethnocentrism, family racial attitudes, or any combination of these two social influences.

Among white students, the effect of aggressiveness also did not vary much for students whose classes differed in racial composition. However, among black students, those who were high in aggressiveness were much more likely to get into fights and arguments with white schoolmates when the proportion of whites in their classes was substantial (up to about half) than when whites were a minority (see Figure 7.8). In part, this may reflect the simple fact that opportunities for contact of any kind with whites are fewer when whites are a minority. In addition, however, it may be that black students felt more secure, and/or that whites behaved in less provoking ways, in majority-black settings. If so, black students would feel less anger at white schoolmates and this would be reflected most strongly by a drop in unfriendly behavior among the most aggressive blacks.

Schools. While we have focused on aggressiveness as a characteristic of individual students, we may wonder also whether differences in race relations among schools were related to the average aggressiveness of the students of each race. Our results (see Appendix F) show that there was a tendency for a higher average level of within-group aggressiveness by each race to be associated with greater avoidance of the other race and with more unfriendly contact with the other race. These relationships are consistent with those found for individual students.

Contrary to the results for individuals, a higher average level of aggressiveness among black students was associated strongly ($r = -.80$) with less friendly contact with white schoolmates. (A similar relationship was not found for whites.) A scatter plot of the data for blacks shows that the size of this correlation was due mainly to the small group of black students at Pershing. This group of blacks was by far the lowest in aggressiveness and by far the most friendly with white schoolmates. However, in the rest of the schools as well, a lower level of aggressiveness tended to be associated with a larger amount of friendly contact with whites.

The results indicate that, while aggressive black individuals may be friendly with some whites, a high general level of aggressiveness among blacks tends to inhibit friendly contact with whites in the school as a whole. It may be that where there is a lot of fighting within the black student group, this group also tends to discourage conventional school behavior (including friendly contact with whites) and/or that the whites are "put off" by an aggressive black group and therefore are unreceptive to friendly contact.

Academic Ability

What effect, if any, does the academic ability of the student have on his relationships with schoolmates of another race? By placing him in a position of relative superiority or inferiority in the competition for grades, academic ability might affect the pleasantness of interracial contact. It could make the student resentful of those who do better than himself or contemptuous of those who do worse. Ability in school also might affect the reactions of schoolmates to the student; there is evidence that students who do better in school are more popular (e.g., Thorpe, 1955). Also, it is possible that those who differ in cognitive ability differ in their understanding of the actions of schoolmates of the other race.

Past studies have provided only a little relevant evidence. Lombardi (1963) found that the IQ scores of white high school students were not related to their change in attitudes toward blacks. However, Singer (1967) found that a combination of high IQ and high interracial contact was related to favorable change in white students' attitudes toward blacks. Gerard et al. (1975) found that high-achievement minority children were more likely than low-achievement children to receive sociometric choices from the majority.

In this section, we investigate further the relation between academic ability and race relations. The measure of ability used is the student's IQ score. These scores, obtained from school records, were based on tests given to students in grade school, usually the eighth grade.[4] Students' IQ scores were highly correlated with their scores on standardized achievement tests taken during high school and moderately correlated with high school grades (see Chapter 10). Thus, the student's IQ score generally reflects his academically related abilities, both prior to high school and during high school. We prefer to use IQ scores rather than grades or achievement scores as the measure of ability. This is because the IQ test scores preceded social relations in high school and therefore may be reasonably seen as a cause, rather than an effect, of such social relations.

We will look first at how the IQ of individual students was related to their interracial behaviors and attitudes and then consider briefly how the average IQ of each race in a school was related to race relations there.

Blacks. Among blacks, those with higher IQ scores tended to have more positive attitudes toward their white schoolmates. Associations between IQ scores and behavior toward whites were quite weak; however, the higher the black students' IQs, the more they tended to report friendly contact with whites, less avoidance of whites, and less unfriendly contact with whites. When the effects of all other factors affecting interracial behavior and attitudes are controlled, only the association between blacks' IQ scores and positive attitudes toward whites remains statistically significant (see Table 9.1).[5]

We may wonder whether the small associations of IQ with interracial behavior and attitudes are uniform throughout the IQ range or are due only to the influence of those with especially low or especially high IQs. Detailed inspection of the relationships shows that interracial attitudes and behavior tended to become more positive over the entire range of IQ scores. This is shown in Figure 6.3, which presents the average scores on attitudes toward whites for black students at four different levels of IQ. These data show that there was a steady increase in positive attitudes as IQ scores increased.

Other analyses show also that the relationships between IQ and interracial attitudes and behavior varied little for black students with different levels of family education; for black boys versus black girls; for those with various combinations of family education and sex; or for those in classes of varying racial compositions.[6]

Why did blacks with higher IQs tend to get along well with whites—especially, having positive attitudes toward whites? First, it may be that their intellectual abilities led them to see the world in a nonsimplistic fashion and therefore to be less ready than others to accept stereotypes and prejudices. In addition, higher-IQ blacks probably were affected somewhat differently than other black students by the school situation. They participated more than other blacks in activities ($r = .32$) and therefore may have had more contact with whites under conditions of common interest and common goals. High-ability black students also may have less reason to feel resentful and defensive about their academic

Figure 6.3 Attitude toward Other-Race Schoolmates
(Average Scores), as Related to IQ, Separately for
Blacks and for Whites[1]

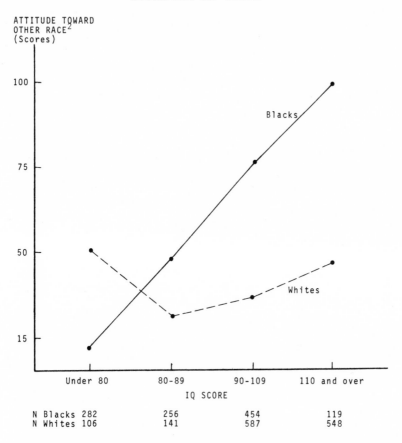

1. Differences among mean attitude scores for those with different IQ levels are significant for blacks (p. < .001) but not for whites.
2. Higher score indicates more positive attitude. Scores for whites and blacks are not strictly comparable since scores were computed relative to those of same race (see Chapter 3). All scores were multiplied by 100 and a constant of 50 added.

position than those blacks of lower academic ability. In addition, because high-ability blacks tended also to be more academically oriented than other blacks, they may have found contact with the relatively high-achievement whites to be more satisfying. In turn, white students may have respected and liked high-ability blacks more than other blacks and been more friendly toward them.

Whites. What about the impact of IQ among white students? Our results for whites (see Table 6.2) show generally little association between

IQ scores and interracial behavior and attitudes. However, there was a tendency for higher IQ to be associated with more friendly contacts. More detailed analysis of these data shows that the relation between white students' IQs and the frequency of their friendly contacts with blacks was not a linear one. Rather, a substantial increase in friendly contacts with blacks occurred only among those in the highest IQ category (see Figure 6.4).

However, white students with higher IQs also tended to change their opinions of blacks in a *less* positive direction. When other factors affecting interracial behavior and attitudes were controlled, higher IQ still

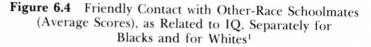

Figure 6.4 Friendly Contact with Other-Race Schoolmates (Average Scores), as Related to IQ, Separately for Blacks and for Whites[1]

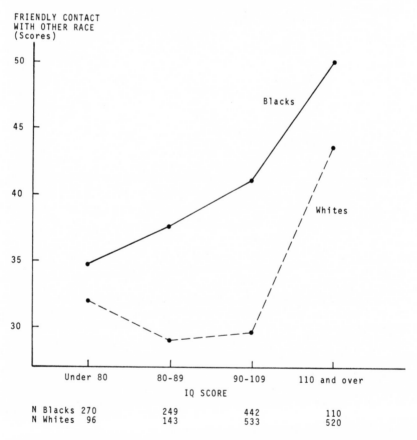

1. Differences among mean scores are significant for blacks (p=.005) and for whites (p=.001), with opportunity for interracial contact in classes held constant.

had a significant, though small, negative effect on change in opinion of black people (see Table 9.2).

The associations between IQ and interracial behavior and attitudes did not vary much for white students with different levels of parental education, or for boys as compared to girls. However, higher IQ did lead to friendly contact with blacks somewhat more often among those whites who had a substantial proportion of blacks (over 40%) in their classes than among those whose classes were predominately white. This tended to be true even when the effects of peer racial attitudes were controlled.[7]

Why did high IQ among white students tend to lead to more friendly contact with black schoolmates but also to a less positive change in opinion of black people? The relatively frequent friendly contact which high-IQ whites had with black schoolmates may have been the result of a high general level of activity and interaction among these brightest white students. Thus, the higher the IQ of white students, the more likely they were to participate in school activities ($r = .42$), where they could have friendly contact with students of both races. (Such activity would have been especially likely to result in some friendly interracial contact when the proportion of blacks was high.)

However, high-IQ white students also differed most from the majority of their black schoolmates in school performance and may have differed most in some other ways (e.g., in musical tastes) as well. In addition, high-IQ whites probably were most interested in school and therefore would have been most offended by what many whites saw as disruptive behavior by some blacks (see Chapter 3). These characteristics of high-IQ whites may have led to somewhat less positive change in opinions of black people than occurred for other white students.[8]

Overall, the results indicate that, among blacks, those with higher IQs tended to have more positive relations with their white schoolmates. Among whites, high IQ also tended to be associated with more friendly relationships with black schoolmates but contributed slightly to *less* positive change in opinions of black people.

Schools. Let us now consider results concerning students' abilities for the school as a whole (see Appendix F). Did the average ability of students of each race in a school have an effect on their relationships with the other racial group?

A higher average IQ score for blacks in a school was correlated with lower average levels of unfriendly contact with, and avoidance of, white schoolmates. However, these correlations are due almost entirely to two very different schools, John Price and Highland. At John Price, the average IQ for black students was by far the lowest among all schools and negative behavior (avoidance and unfriendly contact) with whites was unusually high. At Highland, the average black IQ was by far the highest among all schools and negative behaviors toward whites were the least frequent. Though the school-level correlations are due mainly to these two schools, they are consistent with the results for individuals, showing that higher-IQ blacks tended to get along with white schoolmates.

Among white students too, a higher average IQ in a school tended to be associated with more positive interracial contact—i.e., with lower average levels of avoidance and unfriendly contact and a higher average level of friendly contact. However, a higher average IQ among whites also tended to be associated with *less* positive average change in opinion of black people. All of these associations—though modest in size—are consistent with the results for individual white students which we have already discussed.[9]

Academic Orientation

Although those students who were high in academic ability also tended to be more academically motivated than others, these traits do not always go together.[10] It is useful, therefore, to look separately at whether students' academic orientation (i.e., their concern with doing well in school) had an impact on their relationships with schoolmates of another race.

For black students, it might be expected that those who are most academically oriented will have most in common with white schoolmates, who (more than blacks) tended to be in college-preparatory programs and to get high grades in school. Comments by some students and teachers were consistent with this expectation. Many believed that black students who were serious about their schoolwork got along better with whites than did black students who didn't care much about school. However, little systematic evidence on this matter is available from previous research.

What about the academic orientation of white students? Will the less academically oriented whites get along relatively well with blacks, with whom they might tend to have more in common (such as low grades) than do other whites? Or would low academic interest among whites tend to lead these students to get into trouble—including interracial fighting—in school? Again, little systematic evidence has been available.

To throw some light on these questions, we rely here on two indicators of the student's academic orientation. The first is his (her) educational aspirations. To assess such aspirations, we asked on the questionnaire: "How far would you like to go in school?" Each student was asked to check one of six choices, from "leave high school before finishing" to "go to graduate or professional school after finishing college."

The second indicator of the student's academic orientation is a measure of the effort he devoted to his school work. This measure was computed by first making an estimate of the total time the student spent doing homework during the semester (based on his report of time spent on an average day), and then subtracting an estimate of the amount of time he lost from school work due to such reasons as being late to class, being absent from school, and missing a class without permission (also based on the student's own reports). Our measures of academic orientation—aspirations and effort—have positive but small correlations with each other (.18 for blacks, .27 for whites).

How was the academic orientation of students related to the ways in which they got along with other-race schoolmates? Again we will focus first on results for individual students and then look briefly at results for total schools.

Blacks. For black students, the higher the student's educational aspirations and the greater his academic effort, the more he tended to report good relations—especially friendly contact and friendships—with whites (see Table 6.1). When other relevant variables—including IQ—are controlled, small but significant associations with interracial friendships remain (see Table 9.1).

Closer examination of the data indicates that friendships with whites did not increase much as black students increased their aspiration from the lowest level (finishing high school or less) to a moderate level (limited schooling beyond high school). Only those blacks who wanted to go to a four-year college or beyond reported appreciably more friendships with whites (see Figure 6.5). Similarly, friendships with whites did not increase as black students went from low to moderate in school effort, but only among those blacks whose school effort was in the highest category. (On the other hand, the relation of effort to avoidance and to unfriendly interracial contact was approximately linear.)

The positive effects of high educational aspirations and effort on friendship with whites did not differ for black students of different IQ levels. Thus, black students who were academically oriented tended to be friendly with white schoolmates regardless of the blacks' academic ability.

Why did more academically oriented blacks get along better with whites? One possibility is that being academically oriented was a cause of being friendly with whites. Since academically oriented blacks—especially those with higher aspirations—participated more in school activities,[11] this may have given these blacks a chance to meet whites under favorable circumstances. Also, academically oriented blacks probably found the company of white students more pleasant than did other blacks. More than other blacks, they were likely to value the academic help and stimulation which whites might offer. Since their grades were higher than those of other blacks (see Chapter 10), they also may have felt less defensive about their performance in school. Furthermore, academically oriented blacks may have met with greater friendliness from their white schoolmates—first, because whites generally saw academic orientation as positive (see Chapter 3) and, secondly, because academically oriented blacks were more likely than others to be in the academic program, where white students tended to be more high status and thus to hold more liberal racial attitudes.

An alternative explanation is that the causal process may have operated in the other direction—that is, forming friendships with white students may have led black students to become more academically oriented. The assumption here would be that, by virtue of such interracial friendships, black students accepted the academic values of whites who, in deed though not in words, tended to be more strongly academically oriented than blacks (see Chapter 10). However, results presented later (in Chapter

Figure 6.5 Interracial Friendship (Average Scores), as
Related to Educational Aspirations, Separately for Blacks and for Whites[1]

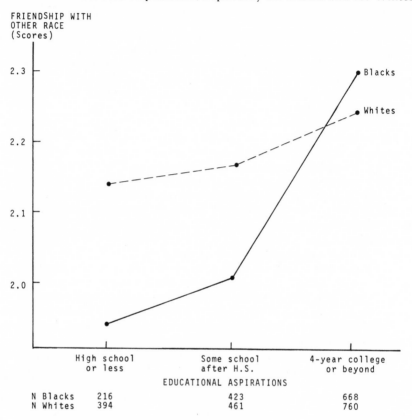

FRIENDSHIP WITH
OTHER RACE
(Scores)

	High school or less	Some school after H.S.	4-year college or beyond
N Blacks	216	423	668
N Whites	394	461	760

EDUCATIONAL ASPIRATIONS

1. The difference among mean interracial friendship scores for students with differing
   educational aspirations is significant for blacks (p < .001) but is not significant for
   whites. In both cases, opportunity for interracial contact in classes was held constant.

11) do *not* support the hypothesis that black students who were friends
with whites tried harder or aspired higher because they were influenced
by white students' values. Therefore, it seems probable that the first general type of explanation has more validity—i.e., that, in general, greater
academic orientation led black students to become friends with white
schoolmates, rather than the reverse.

Whites. Let us now consider the association between the academic
orientation of white students and their behavior and attitudes toward
black students (see Table 6.2). First, the results generally show only very
small associations between the educational aspirations of white students
and their behavior and attitudes toward blacks. There is, however, a small

positive correlation between the educational aspirations of white students and the frequency of their friendly contacts with blacks. Closer examination of these data (see Figure 6.6) indicates that friendly contacts with blacks did not differ between those with the lowest educational aspirations (finish high school or less) and those with moderate aspirations (limited education beyond high school). However, those whites who wanted to go to a four-year college or beyond were more likely than others to report friendly contact with blacks.

Figure 6.6 Friendly Contact with Other-Race Schoolmates (Average Scores), as Related to Educational Aspirations, Separately for Blacks and for Whites[1]

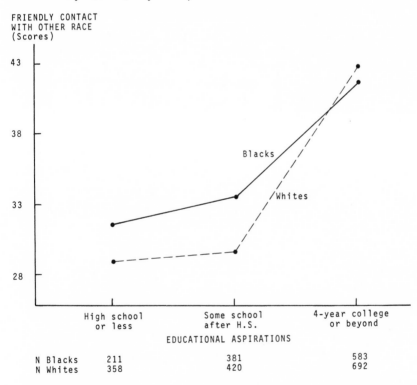

FRIENDLY CONTACT
WITH OTHER RACE
(Scores)

| N Blacks | 211 | 381 | 583 |
| N Whites | 358 | 420 | 692 |

1. The difference among mean friendly contact scores for students with different educational aspirations is significant for blacks (p < .01) and for whites (p < .001). In both cases, opportunity for interracial contact in classes was held constant.

With regard to academic effort, the results show that the less the academic effort of white students, the more likely they were to avoid black schoolmates and the more likely they were to report unfriendly contacts with blacks. While medium-effort white students reported somewhat

more interracial fighting than high-effort white students, the greatest increase in friction with blacks came among those whites with the lowest
level of academic effort (see Figure 6.7).

The positive relationship which academically oriented white students had with black schoolmates was not due to the ability level of these
whites; with white students' IQ scores held constant, high aspirations and

Figure 6.7   Unfriendly Contact with Other-Race Schoomates
(Average Scores), as Related to Academic Effort,
Separately for Blacks and for Whites[1]

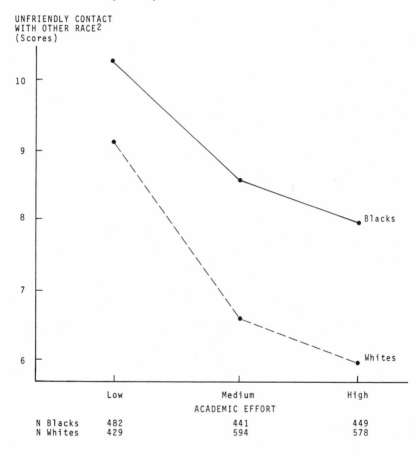

1. The difference among mean unfriendly contact scores for students with different levels
of academic effort is significant for blacks (p < .01) and for whites (p < .001), based on
analysis of variance in which opportunity for interracial contact in classes was held
constant.
2. Measure is index of participation in unfriendly contact, rather than of total unfriendly
experiences.

effort were still associated significantly with good relations with black schoolmates.

However, these associations may have been due to other characteristics of white students with high academic orientation. White students who were academically oriented also tended to participate more in activities, to come from better-educated families with liberal racial attitudes, to be less generally aggressive, and to be more often in the academic program, where they were in contact with the most academically oriented black students. When these and variables were held constant (Table 9.2), white students' aspirations and effort no longer had significant effects on their behaviors and attitudes toward black schoolmates. Thus, while the academic orientation of white students may have played some part in their behavior toward black schoolmates,[12] the results suggest that it did not have a substantial independent effect.

Schools. Our discussion thus far has focused on how the orientations of individual students were related to their relations with schoolmates of another race. We may consider also the results at a school level. Was the average degree of academic orientation among students of each race related to the types of interracial contact they generally had?

The results (see Appendix F) show, first, that the higher the average effort of black students in a school, the better they tended to get along with their white schoolmates (though their opinions of white people did not change more positively). Also, the higher the average educational aspirations of black students in a school, the less their average amount of unfriendly contact with whites (though there was little relation to their other interracial behaviors or to opinion change).[13] Generally, these results are consistent with those for individual black students, which showed that more academically oriented blacks tended to get along better with their white schoolmates.

For white student bodies, the associations between academic orientation and race relations are less consistent than for blacks. As the average effort of whites in a school increased, the average level of friendly contact with blacks tended to decrease. However, as the average educational aspirations of whites rose, friendly contact with blacks tended to increase. For both indicators of academic orientation (effort and aspirations), the higher the average academic orientation of whites, the less positive the change in their opinion of black people tended to be. Overall, the weak and somewhat inconsistent school-level results indicate little association between the academic orientation of the white student body and their relationships with black schoolmates.

Religious Involvement

Since one aspect of our major religions is their emphasis on brotherly love and "doing unto others as we would have them do unto us," one might expect more religious students to have better relationships across racial lines. On the other hand, there is some evidence that more institutionally religious persons tend to be more prejudiced against minorities (Winter, 1977).

We asked each student whether or not he belongs to a church and, if "yes," how active he is in that church (from "not active at all" to "very active"). For students of both races, our results (see Tables 6.1 and 6.2) show essentially no association between church activity and students' interracial attitudes. Nor is church activity related to any kind of positive or negative interracial behavior. This lack of association remains true regardless of the level of opportunity for interracial contact. It also remains true when other factors affecting interracial behavior and attitudes are held constant.

These results are similar to those of Campbell (1971), who—in a national survey of white attitudes toward black people—found that frequency of church attendance was essentially unrelated to attitudes on racial issues. It may be that most American churches today are not addressing themselves to racial issues and that, therefore, their influence on relevant attitudes and behavior is minimal.

Summary

We have found that the interracial behavior and attitudes of students were related to a number of their personal characteristics.

First, interracial behavior and attitudes were related to two physical characteristics of students—their sex and their height. Previous studies, which have focused on sociometric choices as the criterion of interracial relations, have generally indicated that boys—especially black boys—get along better with students of the other race than do girls. However, the present results indicate that the tendency toward more friendly contact among boys is more than counterbalanced by a higher frequency of fighting and (especially among white boys) of avoidance. Among whites, boys also had more negative racial attitudes than girls. The results indicate, further, that one of the reasons that boys reported more negative interracial behavior and attitudes is that they were more often the target of aggressive behavior by male students of the other race.

Another characteristic which may make a person a target of possible aggression, and more fearful about attack, is small physical size. We found, in particular, that the smallest white boys were more likely than other white boys to be fearful of being hit by blacks and to avoid blacks.

Among students of both races, greater general satisfaction (less frustration) contributed to more positive attitudes toward students of the other race, but had little effect on behavior toward these schoolmates. Interracial behavior was much more strongly related to the students' general patterns of aggressive behavior. Those students who fought most (physically and verbally) with students of their own race also fought most with students of the other race, as well as trying to avoid them and displaying negative racial attitudes. Among blacks, the most aggressive students were especially likely to fight with white schoolmates when the blacks were *not* a majority in classes. This probably was due not only to the presence of more whites but also to the greater racial tensions in such settings.

The findings concerning sex, height, and general aggressiveness all focus our attention on the role of aggression in the relations between the races. They indicate that students' relationships with schoolmates of another race are affected both by their vulnerability to attack by the other group and by their own disposition to use violence (and other aggressive means) in their relationships with others.

We also examined the ways in which students' academic ability and academic orientation were related to their interracial attitudes and behaviors. Among black students, those with higher ability on entering high school (as measured by IQ) tended to have more friendly interaction with whites and, especially, more positive attitudes toward white schoolmates. In addition, black students who were most academically oriented—i.e., had high educational aspirations and tried hard in school—were most likely to have white friends. (These effects of high aspirations and effort were independent of ability level and of other control variables). Overall, these results indicate that black students who had the greatest academic ability and the strongest involvement in school got along better with white schoolmates than did other black students. Probably black students with the highest ability and greatest interest in school found white schoolmates (who generally did well academically) to be attractive and the white students, in turn, found such black students attractive.

Among white students, academic ability and orientations generally had little effect on their relations with black schoolmates. There was a tendency for those whites with high IQs, those with high educational aspirations, and those who tried hard in school to have the most positive relations with their black schoolmates. This may have been due to the liberal family backgrounds and the high participation in school activities of these "elite" white students. However, white students with high IQs also changed their opinions of black students in a slightly *less* positive way than did other whites. This may have resulted, at least in part, from a strong commitment to school among high-IQ whites and a consequent disapproval of the nonconventional school behavior which white students perceived among some blacks.

Finally, for students of both races, interracial behaviors and attitudes were *not* related to their amount of church activity.

In this chapter and the previous one we have considered the ways in which the backgrounds and characteristics which students bring to the school affect their relationships with schoolmates of another race. In the next two chapters, we consider how the school situation affects these relationships. The next chapter focuses on students' opportunity for interracial contact in school.

7 | *Opportunity for Interracial Contact*

Many people have believed that the key to reducing hostility between people of different racial or ethnic groups lies in bringing members of the groups into closer contact. If only each person has the opportunity to get to know better members of the other group—the suggestion goes—then he will understand better and appreciate more the members of the other group. Reduced prejudice and improved interpersonal relations will follow. Drake and Cayton (1962, p. 281) made the observation, still relevant today, that "almost mystical faith in getting to know one another as a solvent of racial tension is very widespread." Amir (1976, pp. 245–246) comments that many national and international programs—including student exchanges, housing plans, and school integration policies—are based at least partly on this viewpoint. How valid is it?

There are a number of reasons to expect students' interracial attitudes and behavior to be affected by their proximity to schoolmates of another race. Greater proximity may lead to frequent stimuli for friendly behavior (e.g., friendly overtures by the other group), to acquiring positive information about the other group, to pleasant experiences which increase liking, and to being rewarded for friendly behavior. On the other hand, greater proximity may have the opposite effects—leading to stimuli for unfriendly behavior (e.g., insults from the other group), to acquiring negative impressions about the other group, to having unpleasant experiences which bring dislike, and to getting rewards for negative behavior (e.g., approval by peers for avoidance and/or aggression).

Differences in the racial composition of schools and classes obviously affect the likelihood that students will come into close physical proximity and interact with students of another race. Such proximity may lead to either the positive or the negative consequences just mentioned. In addition, racial composition may have effects on interracial behavior and attitudes because it determines whether students of each race are part of a numerical majority or minority group.

138

What does evidence from previous research show about the actual effect of opportunity for interracial contact in schools? In general, consistent with our discussion of the varied consequences which may result from contact opportunity, the evidence has been mixed and inconsistent. Some researchers, including several using data from the massive Equal Educational Opportunity Survey, have found that as the proportion of other-race students in classes increases, preference for students of the other race as friends also increases (McPartland, 1968; U.S. Commission on Civil Rights, 1967; Fox, 1966; Justman, 1968). This result has been found most often for black students. However, some studies do not show such positive social effects to accompany greater interracial mixing (Kaplan and Matkom, 1967; Lewis, 1971; Schmuck and Luzski, 1969). Also, the results of studies which compare the racial attitudes of students in racially integrated versus those in racially segregated schools have been inconsistent.

After a thorough reivew of this body of work, St. John (1975, p. 80) concludes: "In sum, comparative studies of the racial attitudes of segregated and desegregated school children are inconclusive. Findings are inconsistent and mixed regardless of whether students' racial attitudes or friendship choice was the object of study, regardless of whether desegregation was by neighborhood or busing, voluntary or mandatory, and regardless of whether the study design was cross-sectional or longitudinal."

Previous studies bearing on opportunity for interracial contact in school have had some important limitations. First, as we noted in Chapter 1, they have focused almost exclusively on attitudinal outcomes. In our own investigation of this subject, we will examine the effects of opportunity for contact on interracial behaviors as well as on interracial attitudes.

Secondly, the measures of opportunity for interracial contact in school usually have been limited. Sometimes students have been categorized simply as either in racially segregated or desegregated settings. Even when finer graduations of racial composition have been considered, these rarely have covered the full range of possible racial proportions. As St. John (1975, pp. 99–100) has noted: "The effect of black–white ratios on race relations has been the object of more theoretical speculation than systematic study." Furthermore, measures of interracial proximity within classes and opportunity for contact with other-race faculty have rarely been used.

In the present study, we have available measures of (1) the racial composition of each student's classes, over the full range from 100% black to 100% white;[1] (2) the student's proximity to other-race students in his classes; (3) the racial composition of school activities in which students participated; and (4) the student's opportunity for contact with black faculty members.

The most important limitation of previous research is that the effects of opportunity for interracial contact in school rarely have been examined under varying circumstances. In the present chapter, we look not only at the overall effects of opportunity for contact but also at the ways in which these effects may vary for students with different backgrounds and different personal characteristics, and for those in different school situations.

The plan of the chapter is as follows: First, we will consider how students' interracial behaviors and attitudes were related generally to their opportunities for interracial contact in schools and classes. Secondly, we will see whether these effects of opportunity for contact differed under a variety of conditions. Third, we will consider briefly the effects of opportunity for interracial contact in school activities and for contact with black faculty members. Finally, the results will be summarized.

Racial Proportions

Schools

Students' opportunity for interracial contact may be affected by the proportion of blacks and whites in the total school. To see the association between racial composition and race relations in our set of schools, we related the percentage of blacks in each school to the average interracial behaviors and opinion change of students in that school. (Average scores were computed for blacks in eleven of the twelve schools and for whites in ten of the twelve schools, where there were enough students of the other race to make interracial contact feasible.) Our results (see Appendix F) show some moderate correlations between school racial composition and the average interracial behaviors and opinion change of black students. However, when the data are plotted graphically, no consistent associations are found. For example, the correlation between a higher percentage of blacks and less unfriendly behavior by blacks is due almost entirely to the unusually low level of fighting at heavily black Highland. And the correlation between a low percentage of blacks and more friendly contact with whites is due entirely to an unusually high level of friendly interracial contact among blacks at predominately white Pershing.[2]

For white students, there was only one sizable school-level correlation: the higher the proportion of blacks in a school, the higher the average amount of friendly contact with blacks. Although there was a general tendency for friendly contact with blacks to increase as the proportion of blacks rose, the size of the correlation was increased greatly by the single case of Highland (71% black and by far the most friendly interracial contact among whites). Other interracial behaviors by white students (avoidance and unfriendly contact) and average opinion change among white students were essentially uncorrelated with the racial composition of the school.

Overall, then, the racial proportions of the school as a whole had little consistent association with the race relations experienced by either blacks or whites in that school.[3] Several facts may help to explain this general lack of association. First, the racial proportion in the total school was not a good indicator of many students' opportunities for interracial contact. Blacks and whites entered different academic programs in different proportions and were differentially assigned to high- and low-ability groups. Moreover, in some schools, there were substantial variations between classes (e.g., freshmen versus sophomore) in their racial proportions. Thus, students of the two races were not evenly distributed within a school.

Secondly, particular schools had special problems or conditions which may have countered whatever "normal" effect a given racial proportion tended to exert. Thus, for example, in two schools which had similar racial proportions (about 50% black and 50% white), the level of avoidance by whites differed widely. This was undoubtedly related to the fact that one of the schools (Harrison) had been "naturally" integrated for many years, while in the second school (Lakeview) white students were being bused to a previously all-black school in an atmosphere of resentment and protest in their segment of the white community (see Chapter 2).

Classes

A better indication of the effect of racial composition appears to come from data concerning the racial proportions of students' classes. Class racial composition is a more accurate indicator of each students' opportunity for interracial contact than is the racial composition of the entire school. Also, since the data on class racial composition are based on students from all schools pooled together, use of these data reduces the influences which are unique to particular schools. This pooling of data does not mask any major differences in the effects of class racial composition in different schools. We found no significant differences in this respect among schools.[4]

What, then, was the impact of class racial composition on students' relations with schoolmates of another race? In Figures 7.1 to 7.5, students' interracial behaviors and attitudes are plotted against average racial composition of their classes.[5] These figures show that as the proportion of students of another race increased, friendly contact with the other-race students generally increased too. (This pattern was more consistent for white students than for black students.) However, the relationships between class racial composition and negative interracial behaviors, and between class racial composition and interracial attitudes, generally were curvilinear.[6] The total set of results may be summarized by contrasting three types of situations with the following racial proportions: (1) a small minority (under 10%) of blacks, (2) a large minority of blacks, and (3) a black majority.

Small Minority of Blacks. In settings where they were a small minority, black students reported an unusually high level of friendly contact with white schoolmates. This probably was due largely to the sheer availability of whites as potential interaction partners, as compared to the shortage of other blacks.

Figure 7.1 Avoidance of Other-Race Schoolmates (Average
Scores), as Related to Racial Composition of Students'
Classes, Separately for Blacks and for Whites[1]

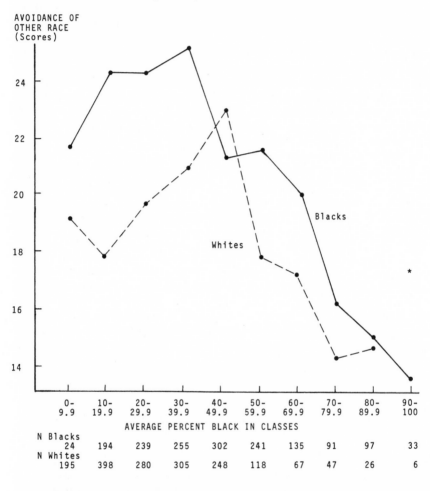

1. Differences in average avoidance among students whose classes had different racial
compositions are significant for blacks (p < .001) and for whites (p < .05). The relationship between class racial composition and avoidance deviates significantly from
linearity for whites (p < .01) but not for blacks.

* Indicates average score of six whites; curve not connected to point because of small *N*.

However, despite their relatively frequent friendly contact with
whites, blacks in these settings avoided some white schoolmates moderately often. Such avoidance probably reflected the blacks' insecurity at
being a small minority and their recognition of hostility from many
whites. Black students who were a small minority also had a moderate
amount of unfriendly contact with whites, probably due both to white

Figure 7.2 Unfriendly Contact with Other-Race Schoolmates (Average Scores), as Related to Racial Composition of Student Classes, Separately for Blacks and for Whites[1]

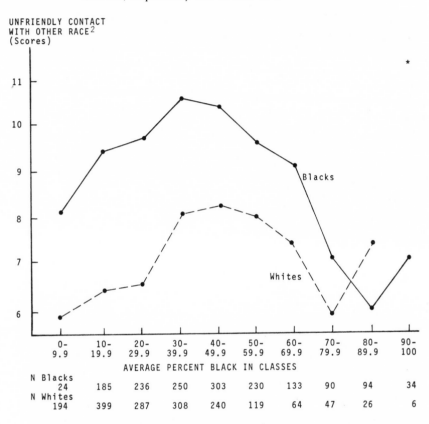

UNFRIENDLY CONTACT
WITH OTHER RACE[2]
(Scores)

AVERAGE PERCENT BLACK IN CLASSES

	0–9.9	10–19.9	20–29.9	30–39.9	40–49.9	50–59.9	60–69.9	70–79.9	80–89.9	90–100
N Blacks	24	185	236	250	303	230	133	90	94	34
N Whites	194	399	287	308	240	119	64	47	26	6

1. Differences in average unfriendly interracial contact among student whose classes had different racial compositions are significant for blacks (p < .01) and for whites (p < .001). The relationship between class racial composition and unfriendly contact deviates significantly from linearity for whites (p < .05) but falls slightly short of significance (p=.06) for blacks.
2. Measure is index of participation in unfriendly contact, rather than of total unfriendly experiences.
* Indicates average score of six whites; curve not connected to point because of small *N*.

hostility and to blacks' sensitivity to possible prejudice. Consistent with this somewhat mixed pattern of relationships with whites, the blacks' attitudes toward their white schoolmates were only moderately positive (relative to blacks in settings with other racial compositions) and their opinions of white people became only slightly more positive.

The average white student who had only a very small black minority in his classes had few contacts of any sort—friendly or unfriendly—with

Figure 7.3 Friendly Contact with Other-Race Schoolmates
(Average Scores), as Related to Racial Composition of
Students' Classes, Separately for Blacks and for Whites[1]

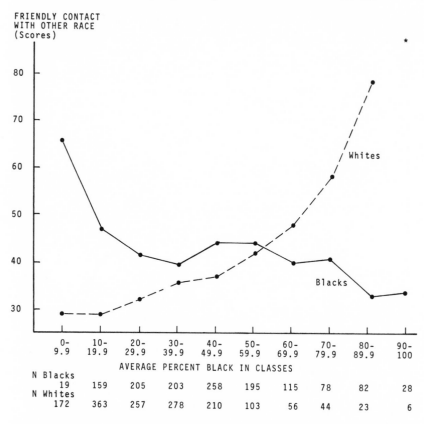

FRIENDLY CONTACT
WITH OTHER RACE
(Scores)

AVERAGE PERCENT BLACK IN CLASSES

	0–9.9	10–19.9	20–29.9	30–39.9	40–49.9	50–59.9	60–69.9	70–79.9	80–89.9	90–100
N Blacks	19	159	205	203	258	195	115	78	82	28
N Whites	172	363	257	278	210	103	56	44	23	6

---

1. Differences in average friendly interracial contact among students whose classes had different racial compositions are significant for whites (p < .001) but not for blacks (p = .07). The relation between class composition and friendly contact deviates significantly from linearity for whites (p < .01) but not for blacks.

* Indicates average score for six whites; curve not connected to point because of small *N*.

---

blacks. Undoubtedly, these results reflect mainly the sheer paucity of opportunity for contact in these settings. Despite the scarcity of blacks in their classes, these whites also reported trying to avoid blacks moderately often. Their attitudes toward black schoolmates were more negative than average and they reported that their opinions of black people had *not* changed for the better during high school. In light of their limited contact with blacks in high school, their negative attitudes towards, and avoidance of, blacks probably reflected primarily the racial prejudices which these whites had brought to high school.

Figure 7.4 Attitude toward Other-Race Schoolmates (Average Scores), as Related to Racial Composition of Students' Classes, Separately for Blacks and for Whites[1]

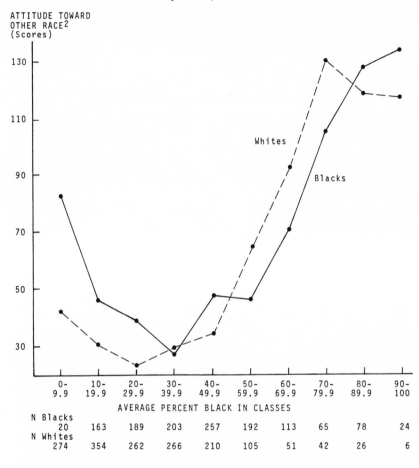

ATTITUDE TOWARD OTHER RACE[2] (Scores)

AVERAGE PERCENT BLACK IN CLASSES

	0- 9.9	10- 19.9	20- 29.9	30- 39.9	40- 49.9	50- 59.9	60- 69.9	70- 79.9	80- 89.9	90- 100
N Blacks	20	163	189	203	257	192	113	65	78	24
N Whites	274	354	262	266	210	105	51	42	26	6

1. Differences in attitudes among students in classes with different racial composition are significant for blacks ($p < .001$) and for whites ($p < .001$). The relation between racial composition and attitudes deviates significantly from linearity for both blacks ($p < .003$) and for whites ($p < .004$).
2. Higher score indicates more positive attitude. Scores were multiplied by 100 and a constant of 50 added. Scores for whites and blacks are not strictly comparable since scores were computed relative to those of same race (see Chapter 3).

Larger Minorities of Blacks. As the average proportion of blacks in classes went from 10% to about 50%, relationships between the races generally worsened. Both blacks and whites reported both interracial avoidance and unfriendly interracial contacts with increasing frequency. At the same time, friendly interracial contact reported by blacks tended to decrease, although such friendly contact increased among whites. Consis-

Figure 7.5 Change in Opinion of Other-Race People
(Average Scores), as Related to Racial Composition of
Students' Classes, Separately for Blacks and for Whites[1]

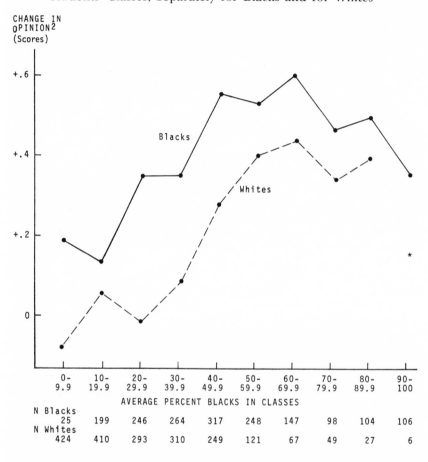

CHANGE IN
OPINION[2]
(Scores)

AVERAGE PERCENT BLACKS IN CLASSES

	0-9.9	10-19.9	20-29.9	30-39.9	40-49.9	50-59.9	60-69.9	70-79.9	80-89.9	90-100
N Blacks	25	199	246	264	317	248	147	98	104	106
N Whites	424	410	293	310	249	121	67	49	27	6

1. Differences in opinion change among those in classes with different racial proportions are significant for blacks ($p < .001$) and for whites ($p < .001$). The relation between racial composition and opinion change deviates from linearity significantly for blacks ($p < .003$) but not for whites.
2. Score of zero indicates no opinion change; positive scores indicate positive change; negative scores indicate negative change.
* Indicates position of six whites in this category.

tent with the increased amount of negative interracial behavior in this range of racial proportions, attitudes toward other-race schoolmates were relatively negative compared to settings in which blacks were either a tiny minority or a majority. Changes in opinion of other-race people were less positive than they were in majority-black settings.

Why were relationships between blacks and whites generally most negative in settings where there was a substantial black minority? From the standpoint of black students, these were settings in which they often felt disliked and unwelcome by the white student majority (and sometimes by the school staff as well). At the same time, the proportion of blacks was sizable enough so that they could form a separate "black society" which permitted them to avoid whites and feel more at ease within their own social circles. The sizable number of blacks also permitted blacks to mount some effective challenges to white dominance—through protests and sometimes through physical violence.

From the viewpoint of many white students, a substantial (and usually a growing) black minority represented a threat. Many whites saw their school environment changing in ways they didn't like. They saw a large, growing black minority as a threat to their physical security, to the academic standards of the school, and to their control over a variety of school activities (dances, cheerleading squads, entertainments, student council, etc.). Their reactions were negative attitudes toward, avoidance of, and sometimes open hostility to the blacks.

Majority Black. Relationships between the races were best among students who attended majority-black classes. Once blacks had become a majority in the average class, interracial avoidance among students of both races fell off rapidly. Likewise, once blacks were in the majority, unfriendly interracial contacts decreased greatly among students of both races. At the same time, the amount of friendly interracial contact reported by white students rose rapidly. Friendly interracial contact for blacks stayed at about the same level as in most majority-white settings, declining only when classes were over 80% black (probably reflecting reduced chances for contact with whites). Consistent with the generally positive interaction between the races, interracial attitudes of both black students and white students were most positive and reported changes in racial opinions were most positive in majority-black settings.

Why were relations between black students and white students generally best in majority-black settings? As members of a majority, black students probably did not feel defensive and resentful about possible rejection or domination by whites, as they did in majority-white situations. Moreoever, for a variety of reasons—including their greater vulnerability—white schoolmates probably were much less likely to show open hostility toward blacks in these majority-black situations. For these reasons, most black students probably felt less need to avoid whites and less hostility toward whites than in situations where blacks were a minority.

Whites in majority-black situations no longer had reason to struggle against a black "takeover." That battle, if it had been fought, was over. But it is noteworthy that whites who were in the numerical minority did not react to this status in the same way as blacks did—e.g., with avoidance and hostility to the majority group. In part, this may be because whites in a numerical minority generally did not meet the same degree of social rejection as did blacks in a numerical minority. In addition, it may be that because whites are a majority in the total society and historically have not been rejected as "inferiors," they may be less sensitive than blacks to signs of possible rebuff by a numerical majority.

It is possible too that those whites who attended majority-black classes were a somewhat selective group, less prejudiced than most other white students. Such selectivity cannot account completely for the results, since being in classes with a large proportion of blacks contributed to friendly interracial contact for whites even when a variety of other relevant factors (parents' racial attitudes, friendly grade school contact, etc.) were controlled (see Table 9.2). However, as we shall see in a later section of this chapter, whites who were in heavily black classes had a high level of friendly contact with black schoolmates only under certain conditions.

Interracial Proximity

While the racial composition of a student's classes appears to be important, it also may be important to know his proximity to other-race students in classes. Previous studies have shown that students are more likely to become friendly with classmates who are seated close to them than with those who are in the same room but more distant (Byrne, 1961; Byrne and Buehler, 1955; Maisonneuve, et al., 1952).

Comments by students whom we interviewed also suggested that physical proximity in classes may be important. For example, when asked whether he had much contact with blacks in classes, a white senior boy replied: "No, not much. If a guy's sitting next to me and he's black, sure I'll talk to him, ask what's going on in class or something." A white sophomore girl at another school told us: "I met this one colored girl in one of my classes, she's real nice and we get along real well. There's a couple of them . . . if I didn't understand the assignment, if they sit next to me, I'd ask them and they'd help me."

To obtain more extensive information about interracial proximity in classes, we asked each student: "In how many of your classes this semester do you have a seat or work place right next to one or more [other-race] students?" A similar question was asked about home room and study hall.

Combining information from these questions, we computed an index score of proximity to other-race students in classes. This index correlates moderately (.60 for blacks and .40 for whites) with the average percentage of other-race students in students' classes.

A possible problem with the proximity index should be noted at this point. It is possible that more prejudiced students might choose seats or work places away from classmates of the other race. If so, it would be incorrect to consider proximity as a cause of interracial behavior. Both might be effects of racial attitudes. However, we know from teachers' questionnaires that of those classes in which students were assigned regular places (87% of all classes), places were assigned by teachers, usually alphabetically, in 65% of the classes. Moreover, students' scores on the proximity measure were related only negligibly to their general avoidance of students of the other race.[7] Thus, while some prejudiced students may have purposely chosen a place away from other-race students, the overall effect of such prejudiced choices on interracial proximity in classes appears to have been slight.

How, then, was nearness to other-race students in classes related to students' interracial behavior and attitudes? We will not present all the relevant results in detail but will summarize them.

Avoidance. Among blacks, the relationship between avoidance and proximity, though not a smooth curve, was generally similar to that found between avoidance and the proportion of whites in classes. That is, black avoidance of whites first increased, as there was some increase in opportunity for contact with whites in classes, but then generally decreased again as such opportunity rose even further.

Among whites also, the relationship between avoidance and proximity was generally similar to that between avoidance and the racial proportion of classes. (The similarities include an upturn in white avoidance at the highest extreme of proximity to black classmates.) The most notable difference between the two measures of contact opportunity was found where opportunity for contact with blacks was least. While avoidance was fairly frequent among whites whose classes were less than 10% black, it reached a particularly high level among whites who were not near blacks in any of their classes. It may be that nearness to even one black classmate "breaks the ice" and leads to less general avoidance of blacks.

Friendly Interaction. What about the relation of proximity to friendly interracial contact? Among white students, this relationship (see Figure 7.6) was very similar to that which we found between friendly contact and the percentage of blacks in classes. By either measure of opportunity for contact, more contact opportunity in classes generally brought a substantial and accelerating increase in friendly contact with black schoolmates. Increases in proximity to black schoolmates also brought steady increases in friendship with blacks.

Among black students, greater proximity to whites in classes also was associated with more friendly interracial contacts (see Figure 7.6). This relationship was much stronger than the relation between friendly contact and the percent of whites in classes. Also, among blacks, friendship with whites was much more strongly associated with proximity to whites in classes than with the percent of whites in classes.

Unfriendly Interaction. If being near other-race classmates facilities friendly interaction, how is such closeness related to unfriendly contacts? The results indicate that proximity to the other race in classes was less clearly related to unfriendly contacts than was the racial proportion of classes. While there was a tendency—particularly among black students—for a curvilinear relation between unfriendly contact and proximity, similar to that between unfriendly contact and the racial proportions of classes, the patterns were irregular. Thus, it appears that being seated near other-race students in classes did not have consistent consequences for unfriendly interaction.

Figure 7.6 Friendly Contact with Other-Race Schoolmates
(Average Scores), as Related to Proximity to Other Race
In Classes, Separately for Blacks and for Whites[1]

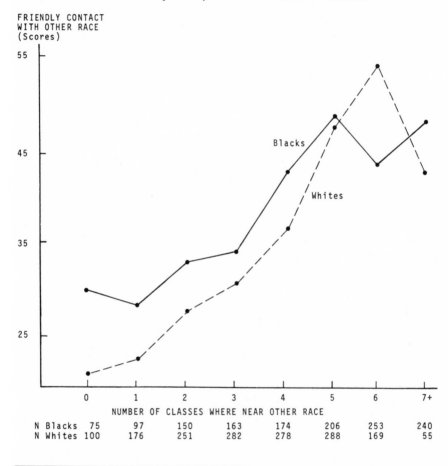

FRIENDLY CONTACT
WITH OTHER RACE
(Scores)

	N Blacks	N Whites
0	75	100
1	97	176
2	150	251
3	163	282
4	174	278
5	206	288
6	253	169
7+	240	55

NUMBER OF CLASSES WHERE NEAR OTHER RACE

1. Average friendly interracial contact differs significantly among black students with
varying interracial proximity (p < .001) and for white students with varying interracial
proximity (p < .001).

Racial Attitudes. Interracial proximity in classes was not related
consistently to the racial attitudes of black students toward their white
schoolmates. Nor was proximity to whites in classes related to the changes
in racial opinions which were reported by blacks.

However, for white students, the more classes in which they were
seated "right next to" any blacks, the more positive their attitudes toward
black schoolmates in general and the more positive their change in opinion of black people. Racial attitudes among whites seemed to respond
more quickly to proximity to particular black schoolmates than to an
overall increase in the proportion of blacks in classes.

To summarize, the results concerning the effects of proximity to other-race classmates generally are consistent with those concerning the effects of class racial proportions. The main difference is the greater effect of proximity, as compared to class racial composition, on friendly interracial interaction among black students. These results indicate that, for blacks at least, being in racially mixed classes is not sufficient for friendly contact with white schoolmates to occur. Being close enough within the class for informal, spontaneous conversation to take place seems necessary as well. That proximity appears more necessary for blacks than for whites (at least with respect to friendly contact) may be the result of a greater caution among blacks concerning interracial interaction, based on the fear of lack of acceptance by the other race.

Impact of Opportunity for Contact under Varying Conditions

In examining the effects of opportunity for interracial contact on students' interracial behaviors and attitudes, we have not distinguished between different groups of students. Now we face these important complexities. Do the effects of opportunity for contact differ for students of different backgrounds? For those with different personal characteristics? For those in different kinds of school situations?

In probing these issues, we will use the racial composition of classes as the measure of students' opportunity for interracial contact. These data are more objective than those concerning interracial proximity in classes and are less subject to the possibility of opportunity for contact being the result of prior racial attitudes.

Class Racial Composition and Students' Backgrounds

To what extent did the impact of differing racial proportions in the classroom differ for students with different backgrounds?

Parents' Education. Among black students, the relation of classroom racial composition to interracial behaviors and attitudes did not differ significantly for students whose parents had differing levels of education. Among white students, too, class racial compositions had similar effects on interracial behaviors and on opinion change, regardless of the education of the students' parents. However, among white students, the association between class racial composition and attitudes toward black schoolmates did differ significantly for those with parents of differing education. Attitudes toward black schoolmates were most positive among white students whose classes were (on the average) majority black and whose parents had more than a high school education. Many of these students were at Highland, where other conditions (such as academically able black students and positive racial attitudes among white families) also favored good race relations. Thus, it may have been such special conditions, rather than the combination of coming from well-educated families and being in majority-black classes, that led to positive racial attitudes among white students.[8]

Prior Contact. Another aspect of the students' background which might condition the impact of interracial contact in high school is interracial contact prior to high school. Did the effect of classroom racial composition differ for students who had varying types of interracial contact prior to high school? To answer this question, we computed for each student an overall score of friendly interracial contact prior to high school. This score was based on (1) the amount of interracial friendly contact he had in grade school, plus (2) the amount of friendly interracial contact he had in the neighborhood prior to high school.

Among black students, the effect of classroom racial composition on behavior toward white schoolmates in high school differed somewhat for those with differing interracial experiences prior to high school. Figure 7.7 shows the results with respect to avoidance of whites. These data show that, among black students who had early friendly contact with whites, avoidance of white schoolmates in high school remained at a fairly low level, regardless of the racial composition of their high school classes. However, among blacks who had no friendly contact with whites prior to high school, avoidance of white schoolmates increased markedly as the average proportion of whites in their classes increased. Avoidance of whites was particularly high among those black students who had little prior friendly contact with whites but who found themselves in classes with a clear (60% and over) white majority. It appears that black students in such circumstances felt particularly uneasy in the presence of whites. Being in a minority and having no positive past experiences to reassure them, these students may have been especially wary of rebuffs from the white majority.

The results for friendship with whites—though not as clear as those for avoidance—also indicate significant interaction effects between racial composition of classes and early experiences with whites. Friendships with white schoolmates in high school tended to be most frequent among blacks who had experienced a high level of friendly contact with whites prior to high school and who were now in majority-white classes. The results for friendly contacts with whites—though marginally significant—also followed a similar pattern.

While the effects of classroom racial composition on black students' interracial behavior in high school depended on their earlier interracial experiences, the same was *not* true of white students. Among white students, friendly interracial experiences prior to high school and greater proportions of blacks in high school classes both contributed to more friendly contacts with black schoolmates; but the effect of each of these factors was independent of the other.

Figure 7.7 Avoidance of White Schoolmates, by Black
Students in Classes of Differing Racial Compositions,
Separately for Those with No and Some Friendly Interracial
Contact Prior to High School[1,2]

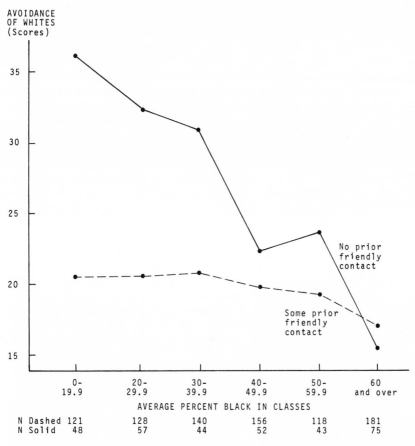

1. The main effect of class racial composition is significant (p < .001) as is the main effect
   of prior friendly contact (p < .001). The interaction also is significant (p < .02).
2. Four categories used in analysis are collapsed for graphic presentation into (a) those
   with no or unfriendly contacts and (b) others.

Class Racial Composition and Personal Characteristics

Did the impact of opportunity for interracial contact in schools depend on the personal characteristics of the students?

Sex. We looked, first, at whether the relation between classroom racial composition and relations with other-race schoolmates differed for

the two sexes. Both among black students and among white students, the effect of classroom racial composition on interracial behavior and attitudes did *not* differ for boys as compared to girls.

Aggressiveness. Since we have found personal aggressiveness to affect negative interracial behaviors (see Chapter 6), we looked also to see whether the effect of classroom racial composition on negative behaviors might differ for students with different amounts of aggressiveness. The results of these analyses indicate that, for white students, the effects of class racial composition on negative behavior toward the other race did *not* differ much as the level of personal aggressiveness varied.

Among black students, however, the effects of the racial composition of classes varied for students who differed in general aggressiveness (see Figure 7.8). Among black students who were low or medium in aggressiveness, unfriendly contact with white classmates did not differ much as the proportion of whites in classes varied. But among black students who were high in general aggressiveness, unfriendly contact with whites was much lower for those whose classes were predominately black than for those whose classes were predominately white or rather balanced racially (30–60% black). (A similar pattern was found even when the average ethnocentrism of white schoolmates was held constant.) In part, these results may be due to the fact that there are fewer whites with whom to fight in majority-black settings. However, the fact that unfriendly contact with whites did not decline between the predominately white and racially "balanced" settings indicates that more than the sheer availability of whites was involved. It may be that black students felt more psychologically secure in the majority-black situation and/or that whites behaved in less irritating ways in such settings. This would lead to lower hostility among blacks, which would be reflected most in the behavior of the most aggressive students.

Ability. Another student characteristic which we have found related to interracial attitudes and behavior is academic ability, as measured by grade school IQ (see Chapter 6). Did the social effects of classroom racial composition differ for students at different IQ levels? Among black students, the overall evidence indicates that this was *not* the case. The effects of classroom racial composition on our measures of interracial *behavior* did not differ for black students of different IQ levels. The relation of class composition to attitudes toward white schoolmates did differ for blacks of different IQ levels: attitudes toward whites were most positive among black students at the highest IQ levels in majority-black classes. However, since this category of black students was composed primarily of those at Highland, we wondered whether their positive attitudes toward white schoolmates might be due to the fact that the whites at this school had especially liberal racial attitudes. Further analyses showed that, with the racial ethnocentrism of white schoolmates controlled, there no longer was a significant joint effect of class racial composition and blacks' IQ.

Among white students, increases in the average proportion of blacks in their classes led to more friendly contact with black schoolmates, regardless of the whites' IQ levels. However, this relationship was strongest among white students at the highest IQ level.[9] Also, attitudes toward black

Figure 7.8 Unfriendly Contact with White Schoolmates (Average Scores), for Black Students in Classes with Differing Racial Compositions, Separately for Those Differing in Personal Aggressiveness[1]

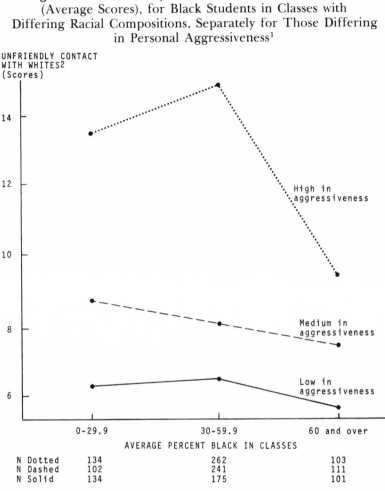

UNFRIENDLY CONTACT WITH WHITES[2] (Scores)

High in aggressiveness

Medium in aggressiveness

Low in aggressiveness

AVERAGE PERCENT BLACK IN CLASSES

	0-29.9	30-59.9	60 and over
N Dotted	134	262	103
N Dashed	102	241	111
N Solid	134	175	101

1. There are significant main effects for class composition ($p < .001$) and for aggressiveness ($p < .001$) and a significant interaction between these variables ($p < .001$). (From three-way ANOVA in which other-race peers' ethnocentrism is the third variable.)
2. Measure is index of participation in unfriendly contact, rather than of total unfriendly experiences.

schoolmates were especially positive among white students at the highest IQ levels in majority-black classes. Since most high-IQ white students in majority-black classes were found at Highland, the question again arises whether these results reflect special conditions at that school.

One possibility is that the positive interracial behaviors and attitudes of high-IQ whites in majority-black classes were a result of the liberal racial attitudes among whites at Highland. However, further analyses show that high-IQ white students in majority-black classes had especially positive relations with black schoolmates regardless of their own racial attitudes prior to high school and regardless of the racial attitudes of their peers.[10]

Just why whites who had a high IQ and also were in classes with a high proportion of blacks should have had especially positive race relations must remain a matter of speculation. It may have been due to other special circumstances present for these students, such as the generally high academic motivation of their black schoolmates at Highland.

Class Racial Composition and School Situation

Does the effect of class racial composition on behavior and attitudes toward other-race schoolmates depend on other aspects of the school situation? In considering this question, we will focus primarily on aspects of the school situation that we can measure fairly objectively—the racial attitudes of the student's peers, the similarity of the student to schoolmates of the other race, and the extent to which the student took part in groups where he had a chance to work cooperatively with other-race students.

Peer Attitudes. First, let us consider whether the impact of class racial composition varied with the racial attitudes of students' peers. Since the effect of peer attitudes may depend on family racial attitudes, reported family attitudes also were included in this analysis. We considered the possible joint effects of the racial composition of the student's classes, the racial attitudes of his peers,[11] and the racial attitudes of his family.

The results of these analyses show that, for black students, the effects of classroom racial composition on interracial behaviors and attitudes were the same regardless of the favorability of peer racial attitudes, or family racial attitudes, or any combination of these factors.

While the effect of class racial composition on black students' attitudes did not vary with the racial attitudes of their same-race (black) peers, its effect on blacks' racial attitudes did vary with the racial ethnocentrism of their *white* peers (see Figure 7.9). Most notably, the improvement in black students' attitudes toward white schoolmates which occurred when classes became over 40% black was limited to those black students whose white peers were relatively low in racial prejudice (ethnocentrism).[12]

The effect of class racial composition on unfriendly interracial contacts reported by black students also varied significantly with the level of white ethnocentrism. The change from being in minority-black classrooms to those with a larger proportion (over 45%) of blacks was accompanied by a substantial reduction in unfriendly contacts with whites only where the ethnocentrism of white schoolmates was lowest. When white ethnocentrism was medium, there was only a slight reduction, and where white

Figure 7.9 Attitude toward White Schoolmates (Average Scores), for Black Students in Classes of Differing Racial Compositions, Separately for Those Whose White Peers Were High or Lower in Racial Ethnocentrism[1]

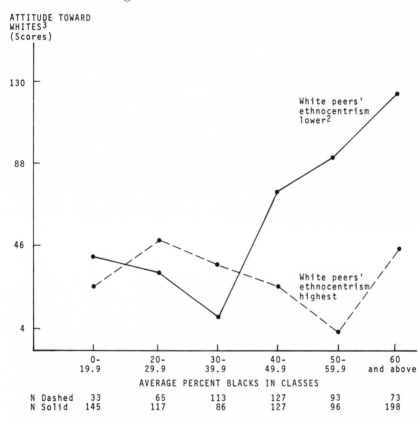

ATTITUDE TOWARD
WHITES[3]
(Scores)

130 —

88 —

46 —

4 —

White peers'
ethnocentrism
lower[2]

White peers'
ethnocentrism
highest

	0- 19.9	20- 29.9	30- 39.9	40- 49.9	50- 59.9	60 and above
AVERAGE PERCENT BLACKS IN CLASSES						
N Dashed	33	65	113	127	93	73
N Solid	145	117	86	127	96	198

1. There is a significant main effect for class composition (p < .001), a marginal main effect for white peer ethnocentrism (p=.06) and a significant interaction between these variables (p=.002). (From three-way ANOVA in which black peers' ethnocentrism was third factor.)

2. Analysis used three categories of white peer ethnocentrism. Results for those whose white peers were medium or high in ethnocentrism are similar and are collapsed for graphic presentation.

3. High score indicates more positive attitude. Scores were multiplied by 100 and a constant of 50 added.

ethnocentrism was highest, there actually was a very slight increase in unfriendly contacts with whites when blacks were no longer a minority.[13]

These results indicate that the overall tendency for black students to get along better with whites in majority-black settings was true primarily when the whites' racial attitudes were not ethnocentric. When white schoolmates were highly ethnocentric, then blacks in majority-black situations may have been self-confident enough to exhibit little avoidance of whites and even to be friendly with some whites. But their attitudes and some of their behavior toward whites were rather negative in these circumstances.

How about white students? Did the effect of class racial composition on white students' interracial behavior and attitudes vary among those whose peers' racial attitudes differed? Figure 7.10 shows that among those white students whose peers' racial attitudes were relatively negative, increases in the proportion of blacks in classes brought only a small and inconsistent increase in friendly contact with blacks. However, among the smaller number of white students whose white peers had especially positive racial attitudes, an increase in the proportion of blacks in classes to above 40% brought a large increase in friendly contact with black schoolmates. This combined effect was found even when the racial ethnocentrism of other-race (black) students was held constant.

It should be noted that, even where peer racial attitudes were favorable, there was no consistent increase in friendly contact with blacks as the proportion of blacks in classes rose from 0–10% to 30–40%. It may be that, even where peer racial attitudes were relatively positive, it was not fully acceptable among whites to be friendly with blacks so long as blacks were in the minority. When blacks achieved parity or superiority in numbers, it may have become more acceptable to relate to blacks as full equals (given also the presence of positive racial attitudes by same-race peers).

The effect of class racial composition on friendly contact with blacks did *not* vary as the racial attitudes of the student's family varied. Nor did they vary appreciably as the racial ethnocentrism of other-race (black) peers varied.[14]

Similarity of Other-Race Students. Does the effect of class racial composition also depend on the similarity of other-race students to the student whose behavior and attitudes we assess? The results show clearly that it does not, at least with respect to similarity in academic ability and in socioeconomic status (SES). Both among black students and among white students, the effects of class racial composition did not vary with the extent to which other-race students in their school and class (e.g., sophomore) were similar to them in IQ. Nor did the effects of class racial composition vary with the similarity of other-race students in SES.

Interracial Task Group. Do the effects of class racial composition depend on the extent to which students participate in task groups with other-race schoolmates? We found that the racial mix of students' classes had essentially the same relations to their interracial attitudes and behavior, regardless of the extent to which they reported participating in interracial subgroups within these classes. Participation in such subgroups was related to interracial behavior and attitudes (see Chapter 8), but these relations were independent of class racial composition.

To summarize, our analyses show that, among blacks, being in a numerical minority led to the most negative interracial relations among those who had little friendly contact with whites prior to high school and among those who were most generally aggressive. Being in classes with a

Figure 7.10 Friendly Contact with Black Schoolmates (Average Scores), as Related to Racial Composition of Students' Classes, Separately for White Students Whose White Peers Were Low or Higher in Ethnocentrism[1]

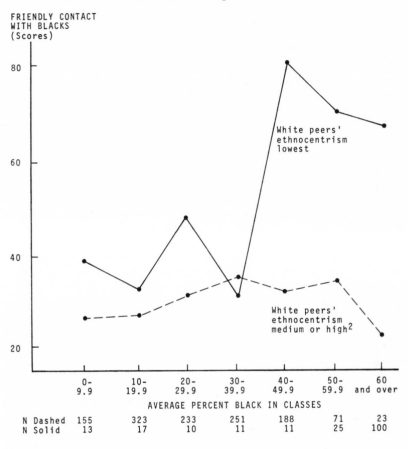

	0- 9.9	10- 19.9	20- 29.9	30- 39.9	40- 49.9	50- 59.9	60 and over
N Dashed	155	323	233	251	188	71	23
N Solid	13	17	10	11	11	25	100

1. There were significant main effects for class composition (p < .001) and for white peers' ethnocentrism (p < .001) and a significant interaction between these variables (p < .001). Results taken from three-way analysis of variance with black peers' ethnocentrism as third variable.
2. Three categories of white peers' ethnocentrism were used in analysis. Curves for medium and high are similar and are combined for graphic presentation.

large proportion of blacks led to more positive interracial contacts only among blacks whose white schoolmates had positive racial attitudes.

Among white students, being in majority-black classes was associated with the most positive race relations for those who came from the best-educated families and who had high IQs. These results may reflect the special conditions at the majority-black but "academic" school, Highland. A more general finding is that whites who were in classes with a substantial (over 40%) proportion of blacks got along best with black schoolmates only when the racial attitudes of their white peers were positive.

School Activities

So far we have focused on the classroom as a setting in which black students and white students have the opportunity to interact with each other. But opportunity for interracial contact also occurs outside of the classroom. School activities—sports, clubs, musical groups, publications, etc.—seem particularly important as places where black students and white students can get to know each other.

Among students of both races, the more students participated in school activities, the more friendly contact they had with schoolmates of another race (see Chapter 8). However, it was not clear whether these associations were due to greater opportunity for interracial contact which the activities provided or to some other reason (e.g., that those who participated in activities were more outgoing people). To try to shed additional light on this question, we can see whether the interracial contacts and attitudes of students varied with the racial composition of the activities in which they participated.

Teacher advisors of activities were asked (as part of a series of questions) to give the number of black students and of white students taking part in the activities for which they had responsibility. From this information, we were able to compute, for a portion of students in our sample, the average racial proportion of activities in which they participated during the current semester.[15]

For black students who participated in one or more activities, there was little relation between the average racial proportions in these activities and their overall relations with white schoolmates. Having a larger proportion of whites in activities was associated slightly with less unfriendly contact with whites ($r = -.12$, $p < .05$). But there were no significant associations with the frequency of avoidance, friendly contact, friendship, attitudes, or opinion change. Since the great majority of activities had a substantial proportion of whites, it may be that almost all activities had a sufficient number of whites to provide partners for friendly interracial contacts.

Among white students who participated in activities, there was more of an association between the racial composition of these activities and their overall relations with black schoolmates. Most notably, the greater the average proportion of black students in their activities, the more friendships they had with black students ($r = .20$, $p < .001$). These results suggest that when white students did have greater opportunity for contact with black schoolmates in activities, such opportunity contributed to their forming friendships with blacks.

Of course, the likelihood that participation in activities will lead to friendly relations depends on more than the mere racial composition of the activities. The extent to which the activity requires cooperation versus competition, and the extent to which it brings together people with similar interests and values, also affect the outcome of participation in activities. This subject is discussed further in Chapter 8.

Opportunity for Contact with Black Faculty

So far we have considered the associations between students' interracial behavior and attitudes and opportunity for contact with *students* of another race. We may wonder also whether students' behavior and attitudes may be affected by opportunity for contact with *teachers* of another race.

All of the schools covered in our study had a substantial proportion of white teachers. Therefore, students did not vary much with regard to opportunity for contact with white teachers. However, many of the schools had only a small number of black teachers. Thus, students did vary in their opportunity for contact with black teachers (see Chapter 2).

One might suspect that contact with black teachers would tend to shatter the "lower-class" stereotypes which whites tend to have of black people. If so, this also might improve white students' relations with their black schoolmates. For black students, the possible consequences of contact with black teachers seem less clear, perhaps depending on the kinds of racial attitudes which black teachers show.

On the questionnaire, we asked each student: "How many teachers that you've had in high school have been black?" (response categories from "none" to "more than 10"). We asked also: "Have you had any other black person as a counselor, coach, or sponsor of a high school group you belonged to?" ("none" to "more than 5"). We combined each student's answer to these questions into an index of opportunity for contact with black faculty.

What is the relation between contact with black faculty and interracial behavior and attitudes? For white students, the amount of opportunity for contact with black faculty had essentially no impact on changes in their opinions of black people.[16] Why this was the case is not completely clear. It may be that, although black teachers do not fit traditional negative images of blacks, the relationship between a teacher and a student tends to inhibit positive attitude change. The teacher (of any race) has authority over the student, may pressure the student for greater effort, and may penalize the student at times. Given this type of (frequently unpleasant) contact with a teacher, white students may not have developed positive feelings toward black teachers any more than they did toward most white teachers. Thus, they would not have developed a more positive feeling toward black people in general, even though their perceptions of blacks may have changed somewhat.

Opportunity for contact with black faculty also had little impact on the behavior and attitudes of students toward schoolmates of the other race. Both among white students and black students, opportunity for contact with black faculty had almost no association with interracial avoidance, unfriendly interracial interaction, or attitudes toward other-race schoolmates. Among white students, there were small positive correlations between opportunity for contact with black faculty and friendly interactions with black schoolmates; but these associations were reduced to nonsignificant levels when other factors affecting friendly interaction were controlled.

We may note, however, that while sheer opportunity for contact with faculty of a given race may not affect behavior, the racial attitudes and norms of the faculty members may make a difference. The subject of teachers' racial attitudes is discussed in Chapter 8.

Summary

Our results indicate that the social effects of opportunity for interracial contact differed for different social outcomes. In general, as the proportion of other-race schoolmates in their classes increased, students—especially whites—had more friendly interracial contact. But the relations between class racial composition and other social outcomes (avoidance, unfriendly contact, and attitudes) were generally curvilinear.

As the proportion of blacks increased from that of a very small minority to a larger minority, both avoidance and unfriendly contact increased and attitudes became more negative among students of both races. Then, when blacks became a majority, negative interracial behavior decreased sharply and attitudes became much more positive among both blacks and whites. Thus, relationships between black students and white students generally were worst when blacks were a substantial minority and were best when blacks were a majority.

These general patterns did not hold under all circumstances. The poorer race relations which tended to occur in situations with a large black minority depended in part on students' earlier racial experiences. For black students in particular, being in a minority was associated with avoidance of, and lack of friendly interaction with, white schoolmates only among those who had little friendly contact with whites prior to high school. These results suggest that the interracial strains that are likely to occur when there is a large black minority—in particular, apprehension among blacks that they are unwelcome in a "white school"—are most likely to occur when students of each race are most alien to each other.

The positive social relations between blacks and whites, generally found in majority-black settings, depended especially on the racial attitudes of white students. Among blacks, the improvement in attitudes and behavior toward whites that occurred when blacks were no longer a minority was found only when their other-race (white) peers had relatively positive racial attitudes. For blacks, the combination of being in a majority and having white schoolmates who were relatively unprejudiced apparently made contact with whites unusually pleasant. Among whites, an increase in the proportion of blacks brought an increase in friendly interracial contacts only among those students whose (white) peers had positive racial attitudes. Apparently, being in a majority-black setting and having support for friendly interracial contact from white peers made such contact especially attractive for whites.

Positive social outcomes in the majority-black situation also were found more among students with certain personal and background characteristics. Most notably, among blacks, the decline in unfriendly contacts with whites in majority-black situations was greatest among the most aggressive blacks. It may be that, as resentment toward whites was reduced in majority-black settings, this was reflected most among those most prone to expressing hostility overtly.

In addition to investigating the effects of the racial composition of students' classes, we examined the effects of several other factors affecting opportunity for interracial contact. Within classes, whether students were seated near those of another race affected their relations with schoolmates of that group. For black students especially, their proximity to other-race schoolmates in classes contributed more strongly to friendly interracial contacts than did the racial composition of their classes.

Participation in school activities also provided an opportunity for interracial contact. Our results provide some evidence—for white students specifically—that greater opportunity for interracial contact in school activities was associated with more friendship with schoolmates of another race.

Finally, the results indicate that, for white students, greater opportunity for contact with black *faculty* had little effect either on relationships with black schoolmates or on changes in opinion of black people in general. The authority relation between teacher and student probably acts, in most cases, to prevent the development of close relations between people in the two roles. Thus, the results suggest that we need to look more to the relations between black and white peers, rather than to those between students and other-race teachers, for the development of positive interracial behavior and attitudes.

In this chapter, we have focused on students' opportunity for interracial contact and have touched only briefly on other aspects of the school situation in which such contact occurs. In the next chapter, we consider the school situation in much greater depth.

8 | *School Situation*

Attempts to understand the effects of intergroup contact on attitudes and behavior often have focused on the nature of the contact situation. Such aspects of the situation as the relative status of the groups coming into contact, the norms of relevant groups concerning such contact, and the presence of either competition or common goals often have been mentioned as important. However, evidence concerning the impact of such situational factors, singly and in combination, on students' interracial attitudes and behavior in schools has been very limited.

In this chapter we examine the ways in which various aspects of the school situation may affect the relationships between black and white students. We will focus especially on three general aspects of the situation. These are: (1) the racial attitudes of important others (peers, parents, and teachers); (2) similarities and differences between the races (in socioeconomic status, in status within the school, etc.); (3) the presence of shared goals in classes and school activities. We will examine the extent to which each of these aspects of the situation seems to have effects on students' interracial behavior and attitudes. We will consider also the effect of various *combinations* of these situational conditions—a matter on which little or no evidence exists.

In addition, we will consider how several other aspects of the school situation are related to students' interracial contacts. These are the strictness of discipline, the relative power of black students and white students, racial favoritism by school staff, and the extent to which student grievances are handled effectively.

In examining most aspects of the school situation, we will make use both of objective information and of students' perceptions. However, in considering racial favoritism by school staff and handling of student grievances, we will have to rely entirely on student perceptions.

In each section to follow, we will review briefly relevant work on that aspect of the school situation and then look at what our own data show. At the end of the chapter, we will summarize the findings.

164

Racial Attitudes of Others

Many discussions of the effects of intergroup contact have emphasized that the behavior of members of each group may be affected strongly by the attitudes of important others in the contact situation. There are a number of reasons why this may be so. First, peers or teachers or parents may provide direct stimuli for behavior in the form of orders or suggestions. For example, a group of friends may say: "Let's sit far away from those blacks." A teacher may say: "Why don't you and Johnny see if you can work out that problem together."

Important others also may influence the perceptions which individuals form about other-race schoolmates. For example, if a student is not sure how to interpret a funny remark by an other-race classmate, he may be told by same-race friends either "He probably was trying to be friendly" or "He was making fun of you."

Most important, perhaps, peers, teachers, and parents may reward or punish specific kinds of interracial behavior. Some white students may win approval from "liberal minded" friends for being friendly with blacks while other whites may risk being ostracized by peers for being a "nigger lover." Similarly, a black student who is friendly with whites may, in various circumstances, be admired by fellow blacks, ignored on this count, or condemned as an "Uncle Tom." Also, teachers can overtly—or in subtle ways—indicate approval of, disapproval of, or indifference to friendships between blacks and whites.

Research in school settings has provided some evidence that students' racial attitudes tend to be consistent with those held (or perceived to be held) by parents and friends (e.g., Sartain, 1966; Whitmore, 1957; Chadwick et al., 1971; Bullock, 1976) and by school staff (Forehand et al., 1976; N.O.R.C., 1973). There is evidence also that social pressures, especially from peers, are related to white students' avoidance of blacks (Chadwick, 1972).

However, school studies bearing on social influences have been limited in that (1) usually only student perceptions of others' racial attitudes, rather than objective measures of others' attitudes, have been used;[1] (2) the racial attitudes of others usually have been related to student racial attitudes but not to their behavior;[2] (3) the effect of social norms often has not been separated from the possible effect of other variables; (4) the effect of various possible *combinations* of norms held by different relevant groups has not been investigated (For example, what is the effect on interracial behavior if parents' racial attitudes are prejudiced but peers' racial attitudes favor equal treatment?); (5) there has been no investigation of the combined effect of racial norms and other presumably important situational conditions—especially the relative status of the groups, the presence of common goals, and the racial composition of classes. In this study, we have attempted to overcome all of the above limitations—at least to some extent.

In presenting our results concerning others' racial attitudes, we will consider first the effects on students' interracial behavior and attitudes of the *actual* racial attitudes of schoolmates of their own race and of school-mates of the other race. Then we will consider the effects of students' *perceptions* of the attitudes of their schoolmates, as well as those of their families and their teachers.

Actual Racial Attitudes of Schoolmates

What effect did the racial attitudes of students' peers have on their relations with other-race students?

Ethnocentrism of Same Race. To measure the actual racial attitudes of each student's same-race schoolmates, we computed the average racial ethnocentrism score of his same-race peers (defined as those in the same school and same year). This measure of ethnocentrism, based on six questionnaire items, assesses beliefs in the desirability of keeping apart from other-race people, in the moral superiority of one's own race, and in a militant position toward the other race.

Examples of items from the index of white ethnocentrism are: (1) white people shouldn't try to be friendly with black people until black people prove they want to be friendly with us; (2) compared to black people, white people have a better feeling for what is right and what is wrong; (3) white people have given in too many times to the pressures put on them by black people.

Items included in the index of black ethnocentrism, while not all identical to those used for whites, were generally of a similar type. Thus, the three items above—with only the words "black" and "white" transposed—were used in the index of black ethnocentrism as well as in the index of white ethnocentrism.

To what extent were students' interracial behaviors and attitudes related to the ethnocentrism of peers of their own race?

Let us look first at the results for black students (see Table 8.1).[3] These results show that, as the ethnocentrism of same-race (black) peers increased, avoidance of white schoolmates tended to increase too. Greater ethnocentrism among black peers also was associated with less positive attitudes toward white schoolmates and, slightly, with less positive changes of opinion toward white people. The relationships of peer ethnocentrism to avoidance and to negative attitudes remain significant, though small, when other factors which may affect race relations are controlled (see Table 9.1). However, among blacks, peer ethnocentrism was *not* related significantly to the frequency of either friendly interactions or unfriendly interactions with white schoolmates. Thus, having ethnocentric peers appeared to make black students somewhat less receptive to contact with whites, but did not appear to affect the actual frequency and types of contact that developed.

Among white students, the effects of ethnocentrism among same-race peers appear to have been greater than for blacks (see Table 8.1). As was the case with black students, greater ethnocentrism among same-race peers was associated—though modestly—with greater avoidance of, less positive attitudes toward, and less positive change in opinion of the other race. These relations remain significant when other relevant variables affecting intergroup relations are controlled (see Table 9.2). In addition, among white students, greater ethnocentrism among peers was associated substantially with more friendly interactions with black schoolmates. This was particularly true with respect to friendly contact. Also, while peer ethnocentrism has only a tiny positive correlation with unfriendly contacts with blacks, it has a significant—though still quite small—relation to unfriendly contact when other relevant factors are controlled. Thus, among white students, the level of peer ethnocentrism appears to have affected not only students' receptivity to contact with blacks, but also the kinds of interracial contact which they had.[4]

Table 8.1. Racial Ethnocentrism of Schoolmates, as Related to Students' Interracial Behaviors and Attitudes (Pearson Correlations)[1]

		Average Ethnocentrism of:	
		Same-Race Peers	**Other-Race Peers**
Avoidance	Blacks	.15	.11
	Whites	.14	.01
Friendly contact	Blacks	−.02	−.06
	Whites	−.35	−.05
Friendship	Blacks	−.05	−.06
	Whites	−.21	−.08
Unfriendly contact[2]	Blacks	.02	.11
	Whites	.04	.00
Positive attitude	Blacks	−.21	−.28
	Whites	−.24	.01
Positive opinion change	Blacks	−.10	.00
	Whites	−.12	−.01

1. *N*s for correlations average about 1,500 for blacks and about 1,700 for whites. With *N*s of about this size, correlations of .06 are significant at .05 level, correlations of .08 are significant at .01 level, and correlations of .09 are significant at .001 level.
2. Index of participation in unfriendly interracial contact was used (see Chapter 4).

Ethnocentrism of the Other Race. If behavior toward schoolmates of another race is affected by the ethnocentrism of same-race peers, perhaps such behavior is affected also by the ethnocentrism of schoolmates of the other race. Perhaps students react positively when they encounter friendly, nonracist attitudes by other-race schoolmates and react with negative behavior when they encounter hostile, racist attitudes.

To assess the racial attitudes of each student's other-race school-mates, we computed the average racial ethnocentrism scores of his other-race peers—that is, those in the same school and same year. To what extent were the interracial behaviors and attitudes of students of each race related to the ethnocentrism of schoolmates of the other race?

Among black students, attitudes toward white schoolmates became more negative as the ethnocentrism of the whites increased (see Table 8.1). When other factors affecting relations with whites are controlled (Table 9.1), this effect on attitudes becomes smaller and not quite significant statistically. Avoidance of and unfriendly contacts with whites also tended to increase as white schoolmates became more ethnocentric. However, these relations are quite small and become insignificant when other factors affecting race relations are controlled. Overall, these results suggest that the racial attitudes of black students tended to be more negative when their white schoolmates were more ethnocentric, but that their behavior toward whites was affected very little by the degree of white ethnocentrism.

Among white students, the ethnocentrism of other-race schoolmates appeared to have even less effect. Correlations between the average ethnocentrism of black classmates and white students' own interracial behavior and attitudes were close to zero (see Table 8.1).[5] (With other relevant factors held constant [Table 9.2], this is still essentially true.)[6] It is clear that white students' relationships with black classmates were linked much more to the racial attitudes of schoolmates of their *own* race than to those of the *other* race.

It may be that, while students often would hear expressions of racial attitudes from schoolmates of their own race, they seldom would hear the racial attitudes of the other race expressed. Moreover, there may have been only a weak relation between the very general racial attitudes of the other racial group (as expressed on our ethnocentrism measure) and their overt behavior.

So far in this section we have looked at the separate effects of the average ethnocentrism of same-race and other-race peers. But it is possible that the attitudes of *both* racial groups must be relatively positive in order for friendly interracial behavior and attitudes to occur. It may be, also, that the effects of peers' racial attitudes differ in situations of varying racial compositions. To check on these possibilities, we examined the combined (interaction) effects of (1) the average ethnocentrism of students' *same*-race peers, (2) the average ethnocentrism of their *other*-race peers, and (3) the racial composition of their classes. Results of these analyses (not presented in detail) indicate that, for both races, the effects of same-race ethnocentrism and other-race ethnocentrism were largely independent of each other.[7] The ethnocentrism of *same*-race peers was consistently more important.

Among white students, low ethnocentrism among same-race peers was associated with friendly interracial contact most strongly among those whose classes had more than 40% blacks (see Chapter 7). Apparently, the combination of support for friendly interracial contact among peers and a high degree of opportunity for such contact led whites to have relatively frequent friendly contact with blacks.

Among black students, there was no parallel interaction between the ethnocentrism of same-race peers and the racial composition of classes. However, among black students, being in classes with a large proportion (over 40%) of blacks and also having *white* peers who were low in ethnocentrism was associated with the most positive racial attitudes (see Chapter 7).

For both races, there were no substantial or interpretable three-way interactions among same-race ethnocentrism, other-race ethnocentrism, and class racial composition.

Additional analyses show that the effects of peer ethnocentrism on students' attitudes and behavior did not depend on the kinds of interracial experiences which students had prior to high school. The racial attitudes of peers tended to influence racial attitudes and behavior about as much among students who had a relatively large amount of friendly interracial contact prior to high school as among those with less friendly early contact.

Nor did the effect of peers' racial attitudes on students' own behavior and attitudes vary with the students' socioeconomic status or with their academic status (grades), relative to schoolmates of the other race. However, among whites, positive racial attitudes among peers (i.e., low ethnocentrism) appeared to contribute to interracial friendships only among those students who participated in interracial subgroups within classes (see Figure 8.1). These results are consistent with those mentioned above, which show that, for whites, a combination of low peer ethnocentrism and a high proportion of blacks in classes led to much friendly interaction. Apparently, positive racial attitudes among peers had their greatest effect when the opportunity for interracial contact in classes was high and/or there was a chance to work closely with blacks in classes.

Perceptions of Others' Racial Attitudes

We have seen that students' interracial behavior and attitudes were related to the actual racial attitudes of schoolmates—especially those of their own race. Now we consider how these social outcomes of interracial contact were related to students' *perceptions* of the racial attitudes of those around them.

In interviews, we asked students how friends of their own race would react if they were friendly with students of the other race. Some students of each race did not think there would be any problem.

Asked if his white friends would get upset if he had black friends, a white male sophomore at Harrison said: "No, too many white people have colored friends. They just don't think nothing about it."

Similarly, a black sophomore girl at Hillcrest said: "All my friends here got white friends . . . they're not just sticking to blacks."

Figure 8.1   Friendship with Blacks Reported by White
Students (Average Scores), as Related to Average Ethnocentrism
of White Peers, Separately for Those with Varying
Participation in Interracial Class Subgroups[1]

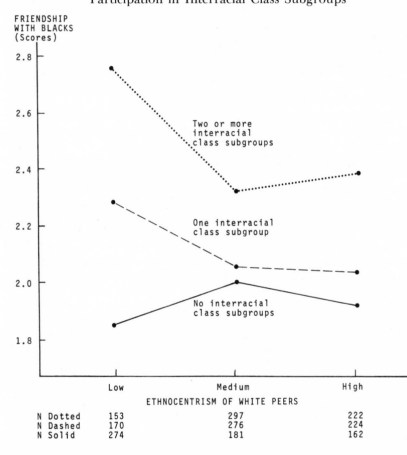

FRIENDSHIP
WITH BLACKS
(Scores)

Two or more
interracial
class subgroups

One interracial
class subgroup

No interracial
class subgroups

Low   Medium   High
ETHNOCENTRISM OF WHITE PEERS

	Low	Medium	High
N Dotted	153	297	222
N Dashed	170	276	224
N Solid	274	181	162

1. There are significant main effects for participation in interracial subgroups ($p < .001$)
and for peer ethnocentrism ($p < .005$) and a significant interaction between these variables ($p < .002$). (Taken from three-way analysis of variance, with other-race ethnocentrism as third variable.)

However, many students of both races were not so sanguine about the possible reaction of their same-race friends. Asked how his friends would act if he became friendly with a black, a white freshman boy at Hillcrest replied: "They probably wouldn't play with me anymore. They're always talking about them. They said they hate them. They [the blacks] keep asking them for money."

On the other side of the racial line, many blacks reported similar social pressures. After telling about a friendship with a white boy, a black sophomore boy at Southwest said of his black friends: "They don't like it. Some of them call you a 'Tom.' But I don't pay no attention to them."

We did not ask students about the racial attitudes of their families, but many students mentioned this subject. A black senior girl at Southwest, who was generally hostile to whites, commented: "You get a lot of influence from your parents. . . . Now my mother, for instance, since we've been living in an all-white neighborhood, she is like me. We don't get along too good with white folks. We don't talk to them unless they talk to us. . . . My mother has some white friends, but she don't like all white people."

A white junior girl at Hillcrest told of a friendship with a black boy, saying: "I haven't gone out [with blacks] on any occasion except once. We were so close . . . we would just go out and talk. . . . But my parents are really against me going out with blacks."

Another white junior girl at Emerson told us: "My Dad is very prejudiced. If he for once saw me talking to Negroes, like I do, he would be very upset. . . . When your parents are prejudiced, it's hard for yourself not to be."

In addition to awareness by students of the racial attitudes of peers and parents, many students commented about the racial attitudes of teachers. Some students—usually blacks—described their teachers as showing prejudice by their actions. For example, one black junior girl at Southwest said: "When I first came over here, we couldn't wear coulotts and the teachers would say your dresses were too short. It seems like, well, mostly in women's classes, if a white girl wore short dresses, she wouldn't send them to the office, but the day a black girl came in with one, seems like she'd go straight to the office."

On the other hand, some students saw teachers as fair and unbiased with respect to race. A black junior girl at Emerson said of her teachers: "I've liked every one of them, especially my English teacher, Mrs. F_____; she was really sweet. There wasn't anything that she would do for a white student that she wouldn't do for a black student. And I happen to know that she had invited black students to her home for dinner."

In addition to perceptions about the racial attitudes of peers, parents, and teachers, many students had formed impressions of the racial attitudes of students of the other race. (See Chapter 3.)

While comments of students in interviews provided some good insights, student responses on questionnaires provided systematic information on the perceptions of a much larger number of students. We asked each student on the questionnaire: "How do the people you know seem to feel about [other-race] people?" Three groups were then listed: most (same-race) students I know at school; the (same-race) students I'm most friendly with; my family. For each of these groups, the student could check one of four answers: (1) like very few (other-race) people; (2) like some, but not most . . . ; (3) like most . . . ; (4) like almost all . . . ." The students also could check that he/she didn't know how the group felt about people of the other race.

Much later in the questionnaire, students were asked this question: "Listed below are some people you know. In your opinion, how does each of these groups feel about how friendly [same-race] students should act toward [other-race] students?" Among the groups listed were: (1) the (same-race) students I am most friendly with; (2) most (same-race) students in this school; (3) most (other-race) students I know; (4) most (same race) teachers I know; and (5) my family.

For each of these groups, the student indicated his perception of whether they felt that students of his own race should: (1) act "as friendly with" the other race as with their own racial group; (2) act "friendly, but not too friendly," with the other race; or (3) "not have to much to do with" the other race. (The student also could indicate that this group didn't care about the matter or that he didn't know how they felt about it.)

On the basis of answers to both questions just described, scores were assigned to each student reflecting his perception of the racial attitudes of same-race peers and of his family. Scores reflecting perceptions of the racial attitudes of other-race peers and of teachers were based on students' answers to the second question.[8]

To what extent were students' interracial behaviors and attitudes related to their perceptions of the racial attitudes of these important others?

The results (see Table 8.2) show that, among students of both races (but especially among whites), the more students perceived their same-race peers to have positive racial attitudes, the more positive were their own behaviors and attitudes toward schoolmates of the other race. The same was true with respect to perceptions of family racial attitudes. For both black students and white students, the more positive the students saw their families' racial attitudes to be, the more positive were their own interracial behaviors and attitudes. Generally, these correlations were small to moderate in size.

Students' perceptions of teachers' attitudes on matters of race also were related to their own attitudes and behaviors. However, student perceptions that teachers supported friendly interracial contact were related more to an absence of negative interracial behavior (avoidance or unfriendly contact) than to friendly interaction with other-race schoolmates. It may be that teachers tended to be more active in rebuking undesirable actions between the races than in encouraging positive actions.

Finally, for students of both races, perceptions of the racial attitudes of schoolmates of the other race had only very small correlations with their behaviors toward members of that group. There were somewhat stronger associations between students' perceptions of the racial attitudes of schoolmates of the other race and their own attitudes toward that group.[9]

Combined Effects of Others' Racial Attitudes. We have seen thus far that students' interracial behavior was related to their perceptions of the racial attitudes of their family, their peers, and—to some extent— their teachers. But the racial attitudes of one group do not exist in isolation from those of other groups. The attitudes of important others may be consistent or they may clash. What is the effect on interracial behavior

Table 8.2. Students' Perceptions of Racial Attitudes of Other Groups, as Related to Their Interracial Behavior and Attitudes (Pearson Correlations)[1]

		Perception of Positive Racial Attitudes of:			
		Same-Race Peers	Other-Race Peers	Same-Race Teachers	Family
Avoidance	Blacks	−.22	−.10	−.22	−.34
	Whites	−.26	−.14	−.25	−.29
Friendly contact	Blacks	.17	.08	.02	.20
	Whites	.35	.18	.07	.21
Friendship	Blacks	.21	.09	.09	.28
	Whites	.37	.18	.11	.24
Unfriendly contact[2]	Blacks	−.14	−.03	−.20	−.20
	Whites	−.14	−.03	−.19	−.12
Positive attitude	Blacks	.37	.24	.19	.38
	Whites	.58	.33	.21	.40
Positive opinion change	Blacks	.30	.11	.11	.25
	Whites	.37	.15	.10	.15

1. Ns for correlations average about 1,300 for blacks and about 1,400 for whites. With Ns of this size, correlations of .06 are significant at the .05 level, correlations of .08 are significant at .01 level, and correlations of .09 are significant at .001 level.
2. Index of participation in unfriendly interracial contact was used (see Chapter 4).

of various *combinations* of perceived racial attitudes of those groups important to students?

To shed light on this matter, we examined (using three-way analyses of variance) the combined effects of the perceived racial attitudes of family, teachers, and same-race peers. The results, which are too extensive to present in detail, may be summarized as follows:

For black students, the effects of the racial attitudes of peers, parents, and teachers were essentially additive. The association between the perceived attitudes of any of these groups and the student's own behavior and attitudes did not depend on his perceptions of the attitudes of either of the other groups. In general, as the black student perceived more of his potential reference groups—peers, family, and teachers—to have positive racial attitudes, his own interracial behaviors and attitudes were more positive.

For white students, the picture is a little different. The effect of perceived teacher attitudes was the same regardless of perceived family and peer attitudes. However, the effects of peer attitudes depended to some extent on family attitudes and vice versa. Figure 8.2 shows the

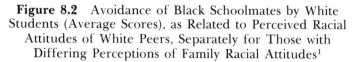

Figure 8.2 Avoidance of Black Schoolmates by White
Students (Average Scores), as Related to Perceived Racial
Attitudes of White Peers, Separately for Those with
Differing Perceptions of Family Racial Attitudes[1]

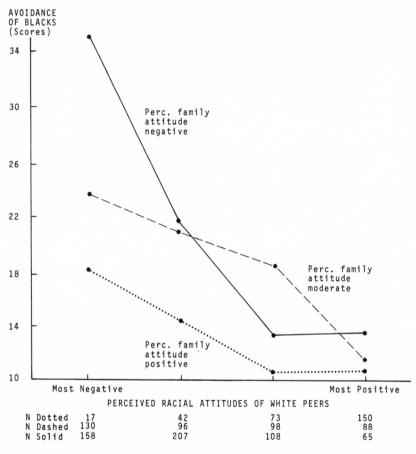

1. There were significant main effects both for peer racial attitudes ($p < .001$) and for
family racial attitudes ($p < .005$), and a significant interaction between these variables
($p < .002$). (Taken from three-way analysis of variance which included perceived racial
attitudes of teachers as third factor.)

combined effect of perceived peer attitudes and perceived family attitudes
on white students' avoidance of black schoolmates. Seeing family racial
attitudes to be negative was associated most strongly with avoidance of
blacks when peer attitudes also were seen to be most negative. Conversely,
seeing peer attitudes as negative led most strongly to avoidance of blacks
when family racial attitudes also were seen to be negative. In other words,
a combination of seeing *both* family racial attitudes and peer racial atti-

tudes as negative was associated with a particularly high frequency of avoiding blacks.

The same general pattern is found with respect to white students' attitudes toward black schoolmates and white students' change in opinion about black people since coming to high school. When white students saw both family and peers as having negative attitudes toward blacks, their own attitudes (and attitude change) were even more negative than would be expected from the simple sum of these two influences.

Overall, these results suggest that while the perceived racial attitudes of either family or peers is important, each has a magnified effect (especially when negative) when it is consistent with the attitudes of the other group.

Similarities and Differences between the Races

Status Similarity

One of the most widespread ideas concerning intergroup contact is that such contact is likely to have positive effects when the two groups are of equal status. Allport made the first influential statement of this idea in his classic book *The Nature of Prejudice* (1958). In the years following, the notion has been often repeated that equality of status between groups is necessary for contact to have beneficial effects (e.g., Pettigrew, 1969; Ford, 1972). In this tradition, St. John (1975, p. 108) has hypothesized that racial desegregation in the schools may reduce students' racial prejudice, provided that (along with several other conditions) students are equal in status.

There has been some disagreement in the literature about the application of the equal-status concept—e.g., whether it refers to a person's general position (and related prestige) in society or to his position in the immediate situation (e.g., Pettigrew et al., 1973) and whether two groups objectively equal in status may be considered equal if members of one or both groups perceive or expect them to be unequal (e.g., Robinson and Preston, 1976).

Moreover, despite frequent repetition of the supposed importance of equal status, two recent reviewers of relevant studies have pointed out that the supporting evidence is quite limited and inconsistent (Amir, 1976; Riordan, 1975). Hunt and Walker (1974, p. 46) also have questioned the general applicability of the equal-status hypothesis, noting that "competition and contact on the basis of equal-status may accentuate bitterness."

In school settings, several studies have indicated that black children of higher social or academic status get along somewhat better with whites than do blacks of lower status (St. John and Lewis, cited by St. John, 1975,

p. 78; Willie, 1973; Gerard et al., 1975). However, these studies bear only indirectly on the question of whether black students' status *relative* to that of white schoolmates is important. In a study dealing more directly with this issue, Forehand et al. (1976) found that greater differences between black students and white students with respect to SES and achievement were related to negative racial attitudes. However, the meaning of their measure of racial attitudes is ambiguous.[10]

There also is little evidence concerning (1) the effects of relative status when other relevant variables are controlled; (2) the effects of different kinds of status—e.g., SES versus academic status; (3) the impact of objective versus perceived differences in status; and (4) the relation of status differentials to a variety of different social outcomes, e.g., to friendship versus opinion change. In this section, we will present evidence bearing on all of these matters.

Other Similarities

While the literature on intergroup contact has focused on similarity of *status* as a key determinant of interpersonal attraction, many social psychologists—primarily in experimental studies—have investigated the relationship of interpersonal attraction to other types of similarity. Many studies have shown that attraction toward strangers—including those of another race—increases as the similarity of attitudes on various social issues increases (Byrne, 1971; Rokeach and Mezei, 1966; Newcomb, 1963). In addition, several laboratory studies have shown that attraction toward a stranger is affected by the similarity of their known intellectual abilities (London, 1967; Reagor and Clore, 1970). Still other studies have indicated that similarity of behavior contributes to interpersonal attraction (Huffman, 1969). We might expect also that certain other similarities—e.g., of interests—would be mutually rewarding and would therefore contribute to interpersonal attraction. However, little evidence has been available about how various similarities and differences between black and white students may affect the social relationships between them.

In this study, we do not have measures of all the many kinds of possible similarity or dissimilarity between the races. We do, however, have some data bearing on similarities in intellectual abilities, in attitudes and aspirations, and in behavior. We can, therefore, see whether similarities in these respects affect the relationship between black students and white students.

Comments by Students

In interviews, students told us their impressions of the similarities and differences between their black and white classmates. Students of both races were aware, among other things, of a difference in economic status between the races.

A black senior girl at Southwest commented: " . . . There are some rich, rich honkeys running around here, like the ones getting $50 a week allowances. Now you know that's rich."

A black freshman boy at John Price remarked: "In the lunch room, most of the white people have the most money. But they don't buy as much as we do."

Many students of both races also were aware of a difference in academic status (e.g., grades, ability group) between blacks and whites in their schools.

A white sophomore boy at Hillcrest said: "I think more blacks get bad grades than whites. They try less."

A black junior boy at the same school commented: "They say they put more of the blacks in the S classes, slower classes. Some of the blacks are just as smart as the whites and they still put them in the slow classes."

In addition to perceptions of differences in economic and academic status, students sometimes commented on the underrepresentation of blacks in certain prestigeful positions. For example, a white junior girl at Hillcrest told us: "There was a conflict last year. There were tryouts for cheerleaders. Four black girls tried out and none of them made it. All the blacks got real mad because they wanted a black cheerleader to represent the black athletes."

To what extent were students' interracial attitudes and behavior related to the differences in status which existed between the races? To answer this question, we will first consider the impact of *objective* differences in status, as well as of other objective differences between students and their other-race schoolmates. Then we will consider the effect of students' *perceptions* of the differences in status between blacks and whites in their school.

Objective Measures of Similarity

Relative SES. We computed several measures of each student's objective status, relative to schoolmates of the other race. The first is his socioeconomic status (SES) — based on parents' educations and occupations — as compared to the average SES of other-race schoolmates in the same year of the same school (e.g., freshmen at Jefferson). Since the SES of black students tended to be lower than that of whites (see Chapter 2), higher relative SES scores usually meant more similarity to the other race for blacks and less similarity to the other race for whites.

What were the effects of students' socioeconomic status relative to schoolmates of the other race? For both blacks and whites, students' relative SES had little association with their behavior or attitudes toward schoolmates of the other race (see Table 8.3). When other variables affecting relations with other-race schoolmates were controlled (Tables 9.1 and 9.2), relative SES had no significant effects on the interracial behaviors or attitudes of black students. For white students, with other relevant variables controlled, higher SES relative to black schoolmates contributed slightly to less positive racial attitudes and less positive change in opinion of blacks, but did not affect behavior toward blacks significantly. Thus, overall, relative SES had almost no impact on the interracial relations of blacks and only a slight impact on those of whites, which was limited to their racial attitudes.

Further analyses show that, for students of both races, relative SES had little relationship to interracial behavior regardless of varying levels of ethnocentrism among peers (of either race), relative grades, or relative IQ. Nor did the effect of relative SES vary for students who attended classes with varying racial compositions or for those with different amounts of participation in interracial subgroups within classes.

Table 8.3. Status of Students, Relative to Schoolmates of Other Race, as Related to Interracial Behaviors and Attitudes (Pearson Correlations)[1]

		Relative SES[2]	Relative Grades[2]	Relative IQ[2]
Avoidance	Blacks	.06	−.11	−.05
	Whites	−.02	−.11	−.02
Friendly contact	Blacks	.04	.05	.06
	Whites	.12	.05	.02
Friendship	Blacks	−.01	.06	.02
	Whites	.09	.00	.00
Unfriendly contact[3]	Blacks	.07	−.11	−.01
	Whites	−.03	−.20	−.06
Positive attitude	Blacks	−.08	.08	.10
	Whites	.01	.05	−.03
Positive opinion change	Blacks	−.03	.03	−.03
	Whites	−.07	−.08	−.11

1. Ns for correlations average about 1,200 for blacks and about 1,400 for whites. With Ns of about this size, correlations of .06 are significant at the .05 level, correlations of .08 at the .01 level, and correlations of .09 are significant at the .001 level.
2. Higher score indicates student scored higher relative to average score of other-race schoolmates in his school and grade.
3. Index of participation in unfriendly interracial contact was used (see Chapter 4).

We also conducted a supplementary set of analyses to explore further the effects of relative status. In these analyses, we limited the category of other-race students with whom each student was compared to those with whom the student was most likely to be in daily contact (rather than all those in his school year). For freshmen and sophomores, other-race peers were defined as those in his school and year who also were in the same ability grouping.[11] For juniors and seniors, other-race peers were defined as those who also were upperclassmen and who were in the same curriculum program in the same school.

Students of each race were categorized according to whether the average parental education of their other-race peers was high, medium, or low. Students also were categorized according to their own parents' education (high, medium, or low). Using the technique of analysis of covariance, we then investigated whether students' interracial behavior and attitudes were related to the education of their own parents, to the average education of parents of other-race peers, and to the combination (interaction) of these two factors. (The main other variables affecting each type of interracial behavior and interracial attitudes were controlled in these analyses.)

The result which is most interesting for our present discussion is that, for students of both races, there were *no* combined (interaction) effects of the students' own parents' education and the education of parents of other-race peers, as these factors related to any interracial behaviors or attitudes. Thus, these results are consistent with those from our other analyses in indicating that students' socioeconomic status, relative to that of schoolmates of the other race, had little impact on their social relationships with students of that race. (The effect of parents' education is discussed more fully in Chapter 5.)

Relative Grades. How about relative status in the school situation? From one point of view, all students are of equal status in their role as students. However, students differ in prestige or status within the school. One dimension of status is academic, as reflected especially by the student's grades. Our measure of the student's *relative* grades is the difference between the student's grade average (for his entire high school career) and the mean grade average for other-race students in his year at his school. Since the grades of black students generally were lower than those of their white schoolmates (see Chapter 10), higher relative grades for blacks generally meant greater similarity to whites, while lower relative grades for whites generally meant greater similarity to blacks.

The results (see Table 8.3) show that, for students of both races, there were only small associations between their grades, relative to schoolmates of the other race, and their interracial behavior and attitudes. There was, for both blacks and whites, a tendency for those with higher relative grades to report less negative interracial behavior (avoidance and unfriendly contact). However, these associations tended to disappear when other factors affecting negative behavior were held constant (Tables 9.1 and 9.2); an exception was that, for black students, higher relative grades contributed significantly, though slightly, to fewer unfriendly contacts with whites.

For students of both races, relative grades had little association with interracial behaviors and attitudes regardless of the level of ethnocentrism of students' peers (of either race), regardless of the students' relative socioeconomic status, and regardless of the frequency with which students participated in interracial groups within the classroom. Overall, these results indicate that, both for whites and for blacks, students' relative academic status had little effect on their relationships with schoolmates of the other race.

Relative IQ. A third indicator of objective similarity is the difference between each student's IQ score (usually obtained in grade school) and the average IQ score of the other-race students in his school and year. As in the case of grades, higher relative IQ scores for blacks and lower relative IQ scores for whites usually meant greater similarity to the other race (see Chapter 10).

Since students did not know the IQ scores of their schoolmates, this is not a measure of relative prestige or status. But IQ tests reflect knowledge, interests, and abilities (e.g., vocabulary) which may affect social relationships.

Our data indicate, however, that students' IQ scores, relative to schoolmates of the other race, generally had little effect on their relationships with other-race students (see Table 8.3). Both for blacks and for whites, relative IQ had very little association with interracial avoidance, unfriendly interracial contacts, or friendly interaction with other-race schoolmates. Higher relative IQ tended to be associated with more positive racial attitudes among blacks and with less positive change in racial opinions among whites, but these associations were quite small. (They are, however, consistent with the effects of IQ reported in Chapter 6.)

Relative IQ had consistently little effect on interracial behavior and attitudes even when we examined separately students who differed with respect to: their relative SES, the ethnocentrism of their peers (of either race), and the racial composition of their classes.

Overall, then, these results indicate that the difference between a student and his other-race schoolmates with respect to general cognitive abilities (as indicated by IQ) was not an important determinant of his social relationships with members of that group.

To explore this issue further, we also computed, for each student, the average IQ score of those schoolmates of the other race with whom he was in closest daily contact (see above), rather than for all those in the same school year. Each student was categorized according to the average IQ level of these other-race peers (high, medium, or low) and according to his own IQ score (high, medium, or low). Analyses of covariance were then run to see the separate and combined effects of the student's own IQ and the average IQ of his other-race peers on his social relations with students of the other race. For the analysis involving each type of behavior or attitude, the effects of other important determinants of that outcome were controlled.

The result from these analyses which is most pertinent to our present discussion is that, for both blacks and whites, there were *no* significant interaction effects between students' own IQs and the average IQ of their other-race peers. The relation of students' own IQs to their interracial behaviors and attitudes did not depend on whether the average IQ of other-race peers was higher, lower, or about the same as their own. These results are consistent with those reported above, which used a different definition of other-race peers and were derived from different methods of analysis. Both indicate that similarity of cognitive ability (as developed at that time) had very little effect on social relations between students from different racial groups.

Average Racial Differences in Schools. So far we have looked at several ways in which individual students were objectively similar to, or different from, schoolmates of the other race. It is also of interest to look at the differences between the total black student body and the total white student body in each of ten schools.[12] Were greater average differences between blacks and whites in a school—with respect to socioeconomic status, academic status, aspirations, values, and school behavior— associated with more negative race relations in the school?[13]

First, the results of school-level analyses (see Appendix F) do *not* indicate that differences in socioeconomic status between blacks and whites contributed to worse race relations. To the contrary, a greater average difference in the education of black parents and white parents was correlated with more friendly interracial contact for white students and with less avoidance and less unfriendly contact among students of both races. However, inspection of the scatter plots indicates that there was little association between differences in parental education and student race relations in the total set of schools. The correlations found are due primarily to the case of Highland, where—despite a relatively high level of education among black parents—the racial difference in parents' education was greatest and race relations were generally good.

With respect to the relative *academic* status of the races, the results show that average differences between the races were not associated much with average differences in interracial behavior. White students reported more friendly interracial contacts and black students reported fewer unfriendly interracial contacts in schools where greater proportions of both races were in the academic program. But it was the absolute proportion of each race in the academic program and not the relative proportions that was most important. Nor did average differences between blacks and whites in grades, in IQ scores, or in proportion on the honor roll, have sizable associations with interracial behavior.

However, academic differences between the races appeared to have a more substantial effect on opinion change among white students. The greater the difference in the proportion of blacks and whites in the academic program, the smaller the proportion of whites who changed their opinions of black people in a favorable way ($r = -.76$). Also, the greater the average difference between the IQ scores of black students and white students in a school, the less positive the opinion change among white students ($r = -.78$). Inspection of the scatter plots for these associations indicates that the large negative correlations were due primarily to two schools (Emerson and Hillcrest). In those schools, there were the largest differences between blacks and whites in IQ scores and in the proportion of each race in the academic program. At the same time, opinion change among white students was most negative. While the academic differences between the races probably contributed to the negative opinion change in these two schools, other factors—e.g., a rapid increase in the proportions of black students, problems caused by the busing of large numbers of blacks to these schools (see Chapter 2)—probably also were contributors.

With regard to differences in expressed values and aspirations of blacks and whites, we have data concerning: (1) students' educational aspirations, (2) students' occupational aspirations, and (3) acceptance of conventional norms concerning school behavior (e.g., "Obey all school rules whether they agree with them or not"). In general, there were not large differences in the expressed aspirations and values of black and white students in each school (see Chapter 10). The size of the average differences which did exist generally had only small associations with the interracial behavior of students of either race. There was, however, a sizable correlation between the average black–white difference in occupational aspirations and the average change in racial opinions among white students. The larger the difference in aspirations, the less positive the whites' opinion change.

Finally, we related the average interracial behavior and attitudes of students in each school to average differences between the races with respect to school behavior. The first type of behavior was effort toward school goals, as measured by an index based on time reported spent on homework and on reported frequencies of lateness, cutting classes, absences, and several other effort-relevant behaviors. The second type of behavior was aggressiveness, as measured by several questions concerning the frequency of fighting and arguing with schoolmates of one's own race. The results show that the average interracial behaviors of white students in a school had little relation to the behavioral differences between the races in their school. For blacks, there were two sizable correlations: the more the difference between blacks and whites with respect to school effort, and with respect to unfriendly interaction within their own racial group, the more likely the blacks were to report unfriendly contact with whites. The scatter plots for these associations indicate that they were due primarily to the effect of two schools—Jefferson and John Price. In these schools, fighting among blacks was more frequent, and school effort among blacks was lower, than in any other schools. Blacks in these schools also were considerably different from whites in their schools in these respects (especially effort) and had a greater amount of fighting with whites than in other schools. Thus, in these two schools, unusually nonconformist, nonschool-oriented behavior among blacks was associated with conflict with white schoolmates as well.

Overall, the results for the total black and white student bodies in a school agree with those for individuals. Both indicate that greater differences between the races in SES, academic ability, or academic success were *not* associated generally with less favorable race relations. The school-level results also provide some evidence that greater differences between the races in aspirations and in behavior may contribute to less favorable race relations.

Perceived Similarity of Status

We have examined the ways in which objective differences between black students and white students were related to relationships between these groups. But how about students' *perceptions* of the relative status of the races? To what extent did students' interracial behaviors and attitudes vary with their perceptions of the relative status of blacks and whites with respect to economic position, academic position, and position in school activities?

Perceptions of the relative status of blacks and whites are difficult to measure directly. To obtain relevant information from students in terms that were meaningful to them, we first asked each student the following question: "As far as you know, how many black students and how many white students are in each of the groups listed below?" Ten "groups" were then listed. The first was "the whole student body at this school." Three were groups which reflected varying academic ability: students in advanced classes, students in slow classes, students who get very good grades. The remaining six groups were ones which enjoy nonacademic prestige — e.g., members of school athletic teams, school and class officers, leaders of clubs and other activities.

For each group listed, the student was asked to check one of seven categories, ranging from "all whites" to "all blacks," which reflected his perception of the proportion of blacks and whites in that group. The perceived proportion of blacks and whites in each (high or low status) group was then compared to the proportion of blacks and whites the student judged to attend the school. This indicated how much (if at all) he perceived members of one race to be overrepresented in the particular group.

On the basis of this information, each student was assigned scores indicating his perception of (1) the relative *academic* status of blacks and whites in his school and (2) the relative *nonacademic* status of blacks and whites in his school.

To assess students' perceptions of the relative status of the races outside the school, we made use of two pieces of information obtained from other questions. The first is the proportion of other-race students in their school (ranging from "none" to "all or almost all") whom the student judged "are from low income families." The second is the identical question asked about students of his own race. The difference between the proportion of each race judged to come from low-income families is our measure of perceived relative economic status.

What do the data show about the relationship of perceived differences in status to interracial behavior?

Blacks. For black students, views of the relative statuses of blacks and whites in their school generally were not related very much to their behavior and attitudes toward whites (see Table 8.4). However, the higher that black students saw the academic status of their own race to be, the more they tended to act negatively (avoidance, unfriendly contact) toward white schoolmates and to have less positive attitudes toward the whites. More detailed inspection of the data indicates that those who saw blacks as higher than, or close to, whites in academic status reported more negative behavior and attitudes toward whites than those blacks who saw whites as higher than blacks academically. It may be that those blacks who were more hostile to whites tended to distort their perception of the relative academic standing of the two races to be consistent with their own racial pride. In any case, the data for blacks do *not* show perceptions of more equal status to be associated with more positive relationships with whites.

Table 8.4. Students' Perceptions of Relative Statuses of Blacks and Whites in Their School, as Related to Their Interracial Behavior and Attitudes (Pearson Correlations)[1]

		Family Income	Academics	Non-academics
Avoidance	Blacks	.06	.13	.07
	Whites	−.24	−.09	.00
Friendly contact	Blacks	−.04	−.01	.03
	Whites	.07	−.12	−.08
Friendship	Blacks	−.03	−.02	.00
	Whites	.14	−.08	−.04
Unfriendly contact[2]	Blacks	.03	.10	.09
	Whites	−.07	−.08	−.01
Positive attitude	Blacks	−.11	−.18	−.09
	Whites	.29	.15	.04
Positive opinion change	Blacks	.00	.00	.06
	Whites	.17	.13	.04

(The table is headed by the spanning label: **Perception of Relative Status of Blacks Regarding:**)

1. *N*s for correlations average about 1,500 for blacks and about 1,700 for whites. With *N*s of this size, correlations of .06 are significant at .05 level, correlations of .08 are significant at .01 level, and correlations of .09 are significant at .001 level.
2. Index of participation in unfriendly interracial contact was used (see Chapter 4).

Further analyses (not reported in detail here) indicate that the effects of black students' perceptions of the relative academic status of the races did not depend on the extent to which they perceived whites as facilitating or impeding their goal attainment, or on the extent to which they saw the school staff as showing favoritism to whites. Nor did black students' perceptions of their group's relative status on each of the three status dimensions (economic, academic, and nonacademic) have any combined (interaction) effects on their relations with white schoolmates.

Whites. Among white students, interracial behavior and attitudes had some relation to perceptions of the income of black students relative to that of whites (see Table 8.4). In particular, the less that white students saw their black schoolmates as coming from relatively poor families, the less likely they were to avoid the blacks, the more positive their attitudes were toward the blacks, and (less markedly) the more frequently they reported friendship with, and positive opinion change toward, the blacks. Further inspection of these data shows that negative reactions among whites occurred only when a substantially larger proportion of black than white schoolmates was seen as coming from low-income families.

The association between whites' perceptions that their black classmates came from relatively poor families and their avoidance of blacks did not vary significantly for groups of whites who differed with respect to their perceptions of the relative academic status of the races, their perceptions of the racial attitudes of their peers, or their perceptions of the extent to which black students facilitated or impeded their goal attainment.

Why should whites have tended to avoid and otherwise react negatively to black students whom they saw as coming from lower-income families? An important clue comes from other analyses of the interracial perceptions of these students (see Patchen, Davidson, and Hofmann, 1976). These analyses show that a perception of blacks as coming from low-income families often was part of a cluster of negative perceptions, including seeing blacks as noisy, not obeying school rules, starting fights with whites, etc. Thus, negative reactions to blacks seen as low in SES may have been due less to the matter of status than to the fact that, in the minds of many whites, low-income background went together with a variety of traits which the whites found unpleasant.

White students' perceptions of the relative status of blacks and whites within the school generally had less impact than did their perceptions of the relative economic status of the two races (see Table 8.4). There was a tendency for whites who saw black schoolmates as relatively high in academic status to have more positive attitudes toward the blacks and to change their opinions of black people more positively; however, they also tended to have less friendly contact with blacks.

The (weak) associations between white students' perceptions of relative academic status and their interracial behavior and attitudes remain fairly constant when a number of other aspects of the school situation (as perceived by the student) are varied. These include the relative economic status of the races, favoritism to black students, and the extent to which black schoolmates facilitate or impede goal attainment.

However, the association of perceived academic status and friendly contact with blacks did differ among white students who perceived the racial attitudes of their peers in different ways. The greatest frequency of friendly contact with blacks was reported by white students who perceived their own race as higher than blacks academically but who also perceived the racial attitudes of their peers as most positive. This result suggests the possibility of a norm of "noblesse oblige" among "liberal" whites toward the black schoolmates whom they saw as lower in academic status. Whatever the explanation, these results clearly do not support the hypothesis that friendly contact is facilitated by perceived equal status.

Overall, the results bearing on differences between blacks and whites (actual and perceived) provide little support for the proposition that equality of either socioeconomic status or academic status is an important condition for good social relations between the races to occur in schools. Interviews with students (see Chapter 3) and some of the other findings in this section suggest that racial differences in status *per se* may be less important than whether students of each race behave in ways that members of the other group find agreeable. Relevant behaviors (e.g., school effort and fighting) may be related only slightly to differences in socioeconomic and academic status.[14]

Cooperative and Competitive Situations

Another element of Allport's well-known "contact hypothesis" is that contact between majority and minority groups will lead to reduced prejudice when that contact is "in the pursuit of common goals."

There is considerable evidence from both experimental and historical studies that cooperation is more likely when individuals' goals are compatible and that people will like better those who facilitate, rather than interfere with, their goal attainment (e.g., Deutsch, 1949; Sherif and Sherif, 1953; Wilson and Miller, 1961; Rudwick, 1964).

In school settings, a number of studies focusing on common goals have been done. Witte (1972), DeVries and Edwards (1972), and Aronson et al. (1975) all found that involving blacks and whites in cooperative classroom task groups increased interracial friendliness and/or liking. Forehand et al. (1976) found that interracial team activities had a strong positive influence on students' racial attitudes. Chadwick and his associates (Chadwick et al., 1971; Chadwick, 1972) reported that, in the high schools they studied, students who expressed concern about interracial competition in later life were more likely to avoid and discriminate against the other race in high school.

A few studies have reported no positive effects of cooperative intergroup activities or mixed effects. Kupferer (1954) found that participation in interracial class sports did not improve the sociometric status of blacks among white schoolmates. Weigel et al. (1975) found that white students who attended classes which stressed cooperative classroom activities showed more positive attitudes toward Mexican-American classmates than did their peers in control classrooms. However, the cooperative classroom experiences did not appear to influence white students' attitudes toward, or their sociometric choices of, blacks. Nor did this type of experience influence the attitudes and sociometric choices of blacks or Mexican-Americans toward out-group classmates.

Overall, then, most of the available evidence indicates that relationships between two groups will tend to be harmonious when the situation requires them to work together toward common goals. However, as Schofield (1978) notes, the fact that results are not completely consistent suggests the need for further exploration of this subject. In particular, we need to know more about the ways in which the effect of common or competitive goals may vary with other aspects of the contact situation.

Our own data on this topic are not as extensive as we might like, but we do have some relevant information.

Class Subgroups

First, we tried to get an indication of the extent to which students were placed in situations where they had common academic goals with other-race schoolmates. We asked each student: "In how many of your classes this semester (including gym) have students ever been divided into teams or small groups of students working together?" (categories from "no class" to "three or more classes").

For those students who indicated at least one class of this type, the student was then asked: "In how many of these classes have any [other-race] students been in the same group as you?" ("no class" to "three or more classes").

On the basis of this information, a score was given to each student showing the extent to which he had participated in cooperative interracial groups in his classes. Over 57% of all students indicated they had participated in at least one cooperative interracial group during the current semester.

The results show that, among both races, participation in interracial class groups had little relation to negative interracial behavior (avoidance or unfriendly contacts), to racial attitudes, or to opinion change (see Table 8.5). However, participation in interracial class groups had a somewhat stronger association with friendly interactions between the races. Participation in such groups was related not only to our measure of more friendly contacts but also to our measure of interracial friendship. This measure reflects general bonds of friendship which would extend beyond the immediate situation of the classroom group.

These associations, while modest ones for students of both races, remain significant among black students when other factors affecting friendly relations are held constant (see Table 9.1). Among the other factors held constant is the racial composition of classes. Thus, it is apparently participation in group activities, and not only the presence of other-race students, which leads to more friendly interaction.[15]

For students of both races, the associations between participation in interracial subgroups in classes and interracial behavior did not vary

Table 8.5. Being in Situations Requiring Cooperation, as Related to Inter-racial Behaviors and Attitudes (Pearson Correlations)[1]

		Division of Classes into Interracial Subgroups	Participation in School Activities
Avoidance	Blacks	−.09	−.04
	Whites	−.06	−.04
Friendly contact	Blacks	.17	.31
	Whites	.13	.25
Friendship	Blacks	.15	.17
	Whites	.22	.10
Unfriendly contact[2]	Blacks	−.03	−.01
	Whites	.01	−.05
Positive attitude	Blacks	.07	.13
	Whites	.10	.03
Positive opinion change	Blacks	.08	.08
	Whites	.08	−.06

1. Ns for correlations average about 1,500 for blacks and about 1,700 for whites. For Ns of this size, correlations of .06 are significant at .05 level, correlations of .08 are significant at .01 level, and correlations of .09 are significant at .001 level.
2. Index of participation in unfriendly interracial contact was used (see Chapter 4).

significantly among students of differing levels of SES or grades, relative to the other race. Nor did the associations vary for students whose classes differed in racial composition.

However, the relation between participation in interracial class subgroups and interracial friendship did appear to depend on the racial attitudes of peers. Among black students, greater participation in class interracial subgroups was related most strongly to friendships with whites when their white peers were least ethnocentric ($p < .05$). The impact of participation in interracial class groups on blacks' interracial friendships did not vary significantly with the ethnocentrism of their own-race (black) peers.

For white students, the association between participation in interracial class subgroups and friendship with blacks depended on the racial attitudes of the student's same-race (white) peers. Figure 8.3 shows that when the same-race peers of whites were high in ethnocentrism, working with blacks in class subgroups was *not* associated with an increase in friendships with blacks. However, when the racial attitudes of white peers were least ethnocentric, working with blacks in class subgroups was asso-

Figure 8.3 Friendship with Blacks (Average Scores)
Reported by White Students, as Related to Participation
in Interracial Class Subgroups, Separately for Those
Whose White Peers Had Differing Levels of Ethnocentrism[1]

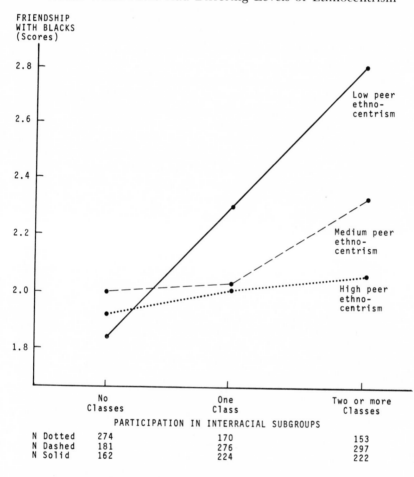

1. There were significant main effects for participation in interracial subgroups (p < .001)
   and for peer ethnocentrism (p < .005) and a significant interaction between these variables (p < .002). (Taken from three-way analysis of variance, with other-race ethnocentrism as the third factor.)

ciated with more interracial friendship. (When peers were medium in
ethnocentrism, the association between subgroup participation and interracial friendship was intermediate.) Thus, for whites, working cooperatively with blacks appeared to result in interracial friendship only when
peer norms approved such friendships.

Participation in Activities

In addition to cooperating in class activities, blacks and whites may work cooperatively toward common goals in extracurricular sports teams and in other school activities. In interviews, many students of both races told us that interracial contacts of this sort were especially apt to overcome any initial wariness or even hostility and to result in friendly relationships between those of different races.

A black senior boy at Emerson commented on black–white relations in his school as follows: "If they know each other, it's all right, but they don't want to come in no contact with each other—not unless they have to. It's all right if you're in the activities, like the football team, basketball. They can get along like that, but that's as far as it goes."

We asked a black senior boy at Hillcrest whether there were any times that blacks and whites get along really well. He answered: "If you're involved in some kind of club—like singers. After each show put on, we have a cast party. There are only three blacks in Golden Singers. We get along pretty good together. Last year we had this skit. Our cast was half black and half white. We had cast parties, dual rehearsals. Everybody dug each other . . . black guys started taking out white girls, white dudes started taking out black girls. . . . We did everything together, real nice."

Other students of both races mentioned other school activities—the Band, Y teams, etc.—as settings in which blacks and whites got along well together.

On the questionnaire, we asked each student a series of questions concerning his participation in any athletic teams, musical groups, school publications, or any other club, team, activity, or group. From this information, we computed a measure of the number of extracurricular activities in which each student participated.

We also asked teachers who advised or coached an extracurricular activity to answer a series of questions about that activity. Teachers provided data about a total of 377 activities, in all schools together. These data indicate that the great majority of activities were racially integrated to some degree. Only 12% were either all white or all black. Only 17% of the activities had less than 5% of one race.

Teacher advisors also were asked to indicate the frequencies with which students in their activities "cooperate with others in this group in some specific task or activity" and "compete against others in this group." In general, advisors indicated that cooperative activity was more frequent (averaging between "often" and "very often") than was competition (averaging between "sometimes" and "often") in these groups. Thus, the data from the advisors of activities indicate that, in general, these were racially integrated settings in which black students and white students worked cooperatively more than they competed.

How is participation in school activities related to interracial behavior and attitudes? Our results (see Table 8.5) show that for students of both races, participation in extracurricular activites was not related much either to interracial avoidance or to the frequency of unfriendly contacts with other-race schoolmates. However, greater extracurricular participation is one of the very best predictors of more friendly contact with other-race schoolmates. For students of both races, this is especially true when other factors affecting friendly interaction are held constant (see Tables 9.1 and 9.2). Also, among both blacks and whites, more participation in extracurricular activities was associated with more interracial friendship. These associations also remain significant when other factors are held constant.

The strength of the association between participation in activities and friendly interracial contacts did not differ for students in classes of varying racial compositions. Thus, the apparent effect of school activities did not depend on the amount of opportunity which students had for interracial contact in the classroom.

The association between participation and friendly interracial contact also tended to hold for the total school, as well as for individuals. The higher the average level of student participation in activities (both among blacks and whites), the greater the average amount of friendly interracial contact reported by students—especially by white students (see Appendix F).

How can we explain the relationship between participation in activities and friendly interracial contact? First, it may be that students who participate a good deal in activities differ in their personal characteristics from other students—e.g., they may be more sociable and outgoing—and that these characteristics lead to more friendly interracial contacts. Secondly, participation in activities—like attending racially mixed classes—is likely to provide an opportunity for friendly contact to occur. Third, beyond the sheer opportunity for interaction, the fact that most activities involve shared effort toward common goals might be assumed to have considerable importance.

To provide some evidence relevant to this latter supposition, we computed the correlations between friendly interracial interactions and each of two indices. The first reflected the total opportunity for interracial contact which the student had in activities during the current semester. The second reflected this total opportunity for contact, weighted by advisors' ratings of the cooperative versus competitive nature of the activities.

For white students, scores on the second index (weighted for cooperation) did not have a higher correlation with friendly interracial contact than did scores on the first index; for black students, scores on the second index had only a slightly higher correlation with friendly contact than did scores on the first index (.26 compared to .20). Thus, these results provide little evidence that the cooperative nature of activities contributed to friendly contact. However, since almost all activities involved a good deal of cooperation among their members, the small amount of variation may have masked the importance of the cooperative aspect of activities.

In addition, there are other aspects of activities which probably helped to promote friendly contact between blacks and whites. These include the fact that activities offer an opportunity for more intimate acquaintance than usually is possible in the classroom and the fact that participants are likely to become quickly aware of similar interests and values.

Perception of Goal Facilitation

In addition to information about objective aspects of the school situation which promote cooperation or competition between the races, we obtained information about relevant student perceptions. In particular, we were interested in the extent to which students of each race saw those of the other race as helpful or as impeding them in some way.

In interviews, both blacks and whites told us of ways in which students of the other race had been helpful to them. For example, a black sophomore boy at Hillcrest described a white boy he liked in this way: "He did favors for me and I returned them. Like he would loan me money, I'd loan him money. We eat at the same lunch table. He wasn't scared to eat on the black side; I eat on his side. He carried my trays for me, I carried his tray. He took me home, that's the one I really appreciated; I didn't have no ride."

On the other hand, some black students told of ways in which they thought white schoolmates made things more difficult for them. A black junior boy at Hillcrest described whites he didn't like partly in this way: "They're the kind that gets you in trouble a lot, kicked out of school."

Some white students mentioned ways in which they had been helped by blacks. But many whites were angered by what they saw to be disruptive and inconsiderate behavior by some blacks. A white male senior at Southwest said of some of his black classmates: "When they walk down the hall, they'll be screaming and jumping and yelling. They don't hardly have any consideration for other people, cutting in lunch lines."

Asked why some of the white kids don't like their black schoolmates, a white sophomore boy at Hillcrest replied: "What they do in school; interrupting classes, sometimes coming in late, starting fights, in the halls, get in the way."

To get relevant and systematic information from our large sample of students, we included in the questionnaire this item: "Listed below are some things which students often want. For each of these, first show how important this is to you. Then tell us whether [other-race] students at this school usually make this thing harder to get, make it easier to get, or don't affect this."

Ten goals were listed. Three were academic goals (my getting good grades, my getting a good education, by being able to go to a college); seven were nonacademic goals (e.g., having good school teams; electing the school or class officers I'd like; my getting on, or playing on, a school team; having good school activities and entertainment). The student first rated each goal as (1) very important to me, (2) fairly important to me, (3) not too important to me. He then checked whether (1) (other-race) students usually make this harder, (2) usually make this easier, (3) usually do not affect this. On the basis of this information, each student was given a score showing the extent to which he saw students of the other race as helpful for, versus hindering, the attainment of his personal goals.

To what extent are students' perceptions of goal-helpfulness by schoolmates of the other race related to their behavior toward the other-race students? The results (see Table 8.6) show a considerable amount of association, especially among whites. The more that students saw other-race schoolmates as helping the achievement of their goals, the less often they avoided the other race, the more friendly interracial contact they had, and the more positive their interracial attitudes and attitude change.[16]

The associations between interracial behaviors and attitudes, on the one hand, and perception of helpfulness by students of the other race, on the other hand, do not change when we look separately at students who differ in their perceptions of the relative academic or socioeconomic status of the two races,[17] or in their perceptions of favoritism shown by

Table 8.6. Other Perceived Aspects of School Situation, as Related to Students' Interracial Behaviors and Attitudes (Pearson Correlations)[1]

		Extent Other-Race Students Facilitate Reaching Own Goals	Favoritism of School Personnel toward Other Race	Disciplinary Strictness of School	Amount of Problem-solving Activities in School
Avoidance	Blacks	−.16	.12	.10	−.19
	Whites	−.34	.07	−.03	−.15
Friendly	Blacks	.11	−.07	−.04	.04
contact	Whites	.23	−.10	−.01	.10
Friendship	Blacks	.10	−.11	−.06	.05
	Whites	.21	−.07	−.03	.11
Unfriendly	Blacks	−.06	.05	.03	−.11
contact[2]	Whites	−.14	.10	.08	−.10
Positive	Blacks	.23	−.30	−.23	.28
attitude	Whites	.47	−.15	.03	.26
Positive opinion	Blacks	.16	−.12	−.03	.20
change	Whites	.30	−.04	.10	.19

1. *N*s for correlations are about 1,400 for blacks and about 1,600 for whites. With *N*s of about this size, correlations of .06 are significant at .01 level, correlations of .08 at the .01 level, and correlations of .09 at the .001 level.
2. Index of participation in unfriendly interracial contact was used (see Chapter 4).

school staff to students of the other race. However, the relation of inter-racial avoidance to perceptions of the helpfulness of other-race students appeared to depend in part on the racial attitudes of the student's same-race peers. Figure 8.4 shows that avoidance of other-race schoolmates was especially frequent among students who saw the other race as hindering their goal attainment and also saw their same-race peers as having nega-tive racial attitudes. This effect was similar for both black students and for white students. These results suggest that a combination of personal re-sentment against the other race (based on perceptions of their making it harder to reach one's goals) and social support for discrimination against the other race leads to frequent interracial avoidance.

Figure 8.4 Avoidance of Other-Race Schoolmates (Average Scores), As Related to Perceptions of Other-Race Schoolmates as Impeding or Helping in Reaching One's Own Goals, Separately for Those with Differing Perceptions of Racial Attitudes of Same-Race Peers[1]

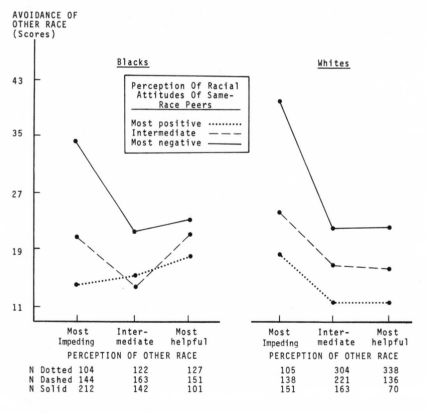

---

1. For both whites and blacks, the main effects of both perceptions of the goal facilitation by other-race students and perceptions of the racial attitudes of same-race peers, and the interaction between these variables, are significant at the .001 level.

Overall, the results—both those based on objective indicators of cooperative school situations and those based on student perceptions—provide some support for the proposition that people of different groups will get along better when members of each group help those of the other group to attain their goals. This effect appears to occur regardless of the relative status (actual or perceived) of the members of each group, and regardless of the relative size of the two groups. However, both the objective and perceptual data suggest that the positive effects of being in a cooperative situation depends on there being positive racial attitudes among peers of one's own race.

Disciplinary Strictness

Some people have argued that interracial conflict in the schools—at least in its overt forms—could be reduced if administrators were less permissive. They have urged strict penalties against students who break school rules, fight, or are otherwise disruptive. However, there has been little evidence about the extent to which variations in discipline affect either the amount of interracial fighting in school or other types of interracial behavior and attitudes.

One source of evidence about discipline in the schools we studied was the school principals. We asked each principal, on the administration questionnaire, about "policies governing the suspension or dismissal of students from school." We presented each principal with a list of eleven fairly serious offenses by students (e.g., attempted extortion, seriously disrupting class, fighting in school, striking a teacher, vandalism in school) and asked him to rate "how likely is this offense to result in suspension or dismissal from this school." (The likelihood of each penalty was judged separately on a five-point scale, from "never" to "always.") On the basis of this information, we computed an overall index of disciplinary strictness, as reported by the principals.

For eleven schools, this measure of strictness had only negligible correlations with the average frequency of unfriendly interracial contact reported by students of each race, as well as with other measures of interracial behavior (see Appendix F). These results indicate, then, that disciplinary strictness, as reported by principals, had little relation to interracial behavior.

We also asked students about how strict they saw their school to be. The questionnaire item was: "How strict would you say this school is in each of the following ways: (1) the kinds of rules it has; (2) trying to catch students who break rules; (3) the punishments given to students who break rules." For each of these aspects of discipline, the student checked whether he thought his school was: strict, pretty strict, not strict but not lenient, pretty lenient or easy, very lenient or easy. Each student was then given a summary score indicating his perception of the overall strictness of the school.

When student perceptions of strictness were related to their interracial behavior, there was very little association for students of each race (see Table 8.6). These results include those concerning unfriendly interracial contact. It will be recalled that two of the three items comprising the measure of unfriendly contact concern physical fighting (the other concerns verbal arguments). Neither the frequency of such unfriendly interaction, nor other types of interracial behavior, seems to have been affected, for better or worse, by students' perceptions of disciplinary strictness in their school. This remains true when other factors which may have affected interracial behavior are held constant.

The only outcome related to perceptions of school strictness was the interracial attitudes of black students. The more strict blacks saw their school, the less favorable their attitude toward white schoolmates. A similar result was *not* found for whites. It may be that blacks tended to see greater strictness as directed more against blacks.

On the whole, however, the evidence from both student perceptions and from principals' reports of disciplinary strictness are consistent. Strictness had little association with the types of interaction which occurred between black and white students.

These results do not necessarily mean that disciplinary strictness has no importance in a school. Results presented earlier (especially in Chapters 3 and 6) suggest that students' fear of violence may inhibit them from associating with schoolmates of another race. Moreover, it may be that school discipline and the amount of fighting have a relationship over time which is not revealed by the data examined in this section. Disciplinary strictness may reduce gradually the frequency of fighting and, once this happens, discipline may then become gradually less strict in the calmer situation. Data obtained at essentially one point in time, as ours were, may not catch this type of process, if it occurs.

However, despite these qualifications, our results are interesting. They indicate that, at any given point in time, the nature of race relations in a school may be affected very little by the discipline then in effect at that school.

Relative Power

Some theorists have viewed the relationships between different racial and ethnic groups from the perspective of their relative power positions (Blalock, 1967; Schermerhorn, 1970; Lieberson, 1961; Kriesberg, 1973). They have pointed out that one group frequently has been in a position of dominance and that the relationships between the groups have reflected this situation: the dominant group attempting to maintain its control and the subordinate group resentful of its lack of power. Kriesberg states: "The weaker one side is, the more reason its members have to complain" (1973, p. 92).

In some Indianapolis schools, black students expressed discontent about students of their race not being represented sufficiently in student offices.

A black sophomore boy at Emerson commented: "I think the white people get to do more than the colored people. Every time the white people get elected, most of the time white people get elected . . . there are more of them and they get most of the votes."

Black complaints about underrepresentation in offices sometimes appeared to reflect a concern about a more general underrepresentation in high-status positions, rather than with political power as such.

Thus, one black girl, a senior at Southwest, said: "Another thing I don't like about this school, there aren't any black class officers, none of them have ever been Prom Kings or Queens or anything."

While some blacks were disturbed about a white dominance of influential or prestigeful positions, whites in some schools were disturbed at what they saw as a physical dominance by blacks. For example, one white junior girl at Hillcrest said: "They seem to think that they can own the hallways, block off the lines, be as slow and just loiter in the hallways, while the whites want to get to their classes."

Other students told us that it was much more frequent for a black to hit a white without retaliation than for the reverse to happen.

Students of each race also sometimes voiced discontent about what they saw as disproportionate influence granted to the other race by teachers and by school administrators.

Student Council Representation

We do not have objective information about every way in which black students and white students enjoyed influence in each school. However, we did obtain information from each school principal about the makeup of the Student Council in the school. While the actual influence of these groups probably varied from school to school, their usual function was, in the words of one principal, "service to pupils; liaison between students and administrators; making known wants and needs of pupils." To assess the representation of each racial group, we computed the proportion of blacks and of whites on each school's student council, in relation to the proportion of each race in the total student body of that school.

For black students, there was a substantial correlation between greater Student Council representation and a greater average amount of friendly contact with white schoolmates (see Appendix F). However, this association is due to the situation at Pershing, where the small number of blacks was far "overrepresented" on the Student Council (having one member) and, also, had an unusually high average amount of friendly contact with whites.

Among white students, greater Student Council representation was correlated with more friendly contact with, less avoidance of, and less unfriendly contact with black schoolmates. Again, however, these associations were not general for the total set of schools but were due to two schools. At Highland, whites were considerably overrepresented in the Student Council and had an unusually high level of friendly contact with blacks. At Lakeview, whites were underrepresented on the Student Council and their behavior toward black schoolmates was unusually negative. Since there were other unusual factors which might affect race relations at these schools (see Chapter 2), it is doubtful that Student Council representation had a major effect on these relations.

Perceptions of Power

We also assessed student *perceptions* of the relative power of blacks and whites in their school. The following item was included in the questionnaire: "Listed below are a number of ways in which students may be able to affect what goes on at this school. For each of these, do you think that white students are more able to do this, black students are more able to do this, both are equally able to do this, or neither is able to do this very much?"

Seven types of influence were listed. Two items concerned influence on the school administration—e.g., "get the school to sponsor things (like speakers, concerts, dances, etc.)"; two items concerned students' offices (e.g., "get students they like elected"); two items concerned physical dominance (e.g., "push students of the other race without the other race fighting back"); and a final item was "get teachers to do things in a different way."

On the basis of his answers regarding the relative influence of each race in each matter, every student was given a score indicating his perception of the relative power of blacks and whites in his school.

Interestingly, among both races, students who saw a discrepancy in influence were more likely to see those of the other race as having greater overall influence than students of their own race (see Ns in Figure 8.5). More detailed results (not presented) show that black students were especially likely to see whites as influential with the principal, with teachers, with the Student Council, and in elections. On the other hand, blacks saw their own race as dominant physically—e.g., being more able than whites to push students of the other race without the others fighting back.

White students, on the whole, saw relatively little difference between the races with respect to their influence on the principal and teachers, and in student politics. However, like the blacks, they tended to see the blacks as dominant physically.

To what extent were students' overall perceptions of the relative power of the races in their schools related to their interracial behavior and attitudes?

Inspection of the results shows that these relations were generally curvilinear. Figure 8.5 shows the relation between students' perceptions of relative power and one type of interracial behavior: their avoidance of other-race students. The curves for blacks and for whites are almost identical. For students of both races, avoidance was least among those who saw blacks and whites as equal in influence within the school. The more students saw either race as having greater power than the other, the more apt they were to avoid students of the other race.

Similar relationships are found, for students of both races, between

Figure 8.5 Avoidance of Other-Race Schoolmates (Average Scores), as Related to Students' Perception of the Relative Power of Blacks and Whites in Their School, Separately for Blacks and for Whites[1]

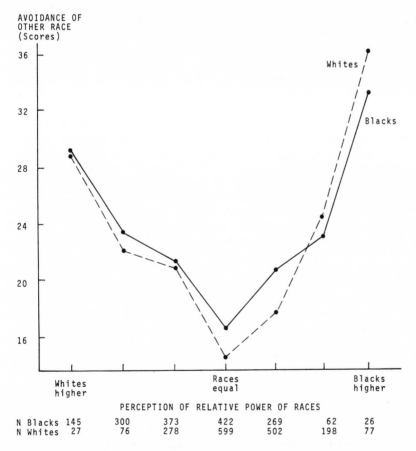

	Whites higher			Races equal			Blacks higher
PERCEPTION OF RELATIVE POWER OF RACES							
N Blacks	145	300	373	422	269	62	26
N Whites	27	76	278	599	502	198	77

---

1. Differences among means are significant for blacks (p < .001) and for whites (p < .001). Relationships for both races deviate significantly from linearity (p < .001). Analyses were performed using measure of perceived relative power which had thirteen points; scale has been collapsed for presentation in graph.

perceptions of relative power and (1) interracial friendship, (2) unfriendly interracial contacts, and (3) attitudes toward other-race schoolmates. In each case, the most positive behavior or attitude was found among those who perceived little or no difference in the power of the two races within the school. Students who saw one race (either their own or the other) as having more power were more negative toward the other race. (The differences cited are all statistically significant, though more strongly so among whites, and all of these relationships deviate significantly from linearity.)

When other factors which affect race relations are controlled, perceptions of the relative power of the races in school still have significant associations with interracial behavior and attitudes (see Tables 9.1 and 9.2). These relationships are stronger among white students than among blacks. Among whites, those who saw blacks as having more power were especially likely to react negatively to blacks. However, those whites who saw their own race as having more power than blacks also were more likely to display negative attitudes and behavior than were those who saw power as equal. Among blacks, those who saw either race as more powerful than the other tended to have negative attitudes toward whites, but those who saw their own race as more powerful reported the most negative behavior toward whites.

How can we explain the generally curvilinear relationships found between perceptions of relative power and interracial behavior and attitudes? The relatively negative reaction among those who saw the other race as more powerful than their own race is not too surprising. Such perceptions may result in resentment of the other race and, therefore, in less friendly behavior and attitudes. Alternatively, those who were hostile toward the other race for other reasons may have been especially sensitive to possible signs of undue power enjoyed by the other race.

The relatively negative reactions among those who saw their own race as more influential than the other seem to require a different explanation. One possibility is that those who saw the other race as less influential in the school tended to look down on and avoid members of that group just because they saw them as less powerful. Alternatively, some of those who already were hostile to the other race may have tended to glorify the power of their own race in a kind of jingoistic reaction.

Clearly, our explanations of these results must be very tentative. It is not possible to tell from these data—collected at a single point in time—the extent to which students' perceptions of relative power affected their reactions to the other race and the extent to which the opposite process occurred.

We also are faced with the fact that our results do not show generally better race relations in schools where the Student Council representation of the two races was more nearly equal. The differences between these data and those on student perceptions of power may arise for many reasons, including the fact that the perceptual measure includes more aspects of influence, and possible differences in the effects of the objective situation and those of students' perceptions of the situation.

Overall, then, we can draw no firm conclusions about the effect of power differences on race relations in the schools. However, the curvilinear associations found between perceptions of relative power and relationships between the races are intriguing. The facts that similar curvilinear relations occurred for several kinds of interracial attitudes and behavior and that these results were similar for blacks and whites—despite the types of power differences seen by each race—indicate that the relationships found probably are meaningful. They suggest that we should explore further the hypothesis that those of different races will get along better when their relative power is and/or is seen as being about equal.

Favoritism by Staff

The extent to which authorities favor one group over the other—or are perceived to do so—can have an impact on the feelings and actions of each group toward the other. In communities, blacks and other minorities have long been bitter about officially sanctioned or permitted discrimination against them. In more recent years, some whites have become angry at what they see to be favored treatment given to blacks and other minorities by various governmental agencies. In the schools, the racial attitudes of black high school students have been found to be affected strongly by their perceptions of the fairness of the school administration (Forehand et al., 1976).

In the high schools of Indianapolis, some black students and some white students complained about actions by teachers and school administrators which, the students believed, favored those of the other race.

Many blacks complained that some white teachers discriminated against them because of their race. For example, when asked whether he thought white teachers treat black kids differently from whites, a senior boy at John Price replied: "Yes, especially, like, Biology—especially him. . . . I'd do everything he'd say and turn it in and this Japanese girl would do everything he said and turn it in, and this white girl would do everything he said and turn it in. But they were getting A's and B's and I was getting C's . . . I couldn't figure it out. Seems to me it was just prejudice or something."

While white students complained only rarely about racial hostility from teachers, some whites complained that some teachers let black students "get away with" disruptive or rule-violating behavior that they would not tolerate from white students. For example, a freshman girl at Emerson was disturbed by what she called a "double set of rules" which some teachers have. She illustrated this by describing the actions of one white teacher. "He lets some kids do this and, like, most white kids, they can't do it. . . . I've seen him being real nice to some of the black kids. Then he'll just turn around and be a different person to the white kids."

We do not know the extent to which favoritism by staff toward one race over the other actually occurred in these schools. However, we did obtain information concerning students' perceptions of favoritism. We asked this question: "As far as you know, how many teachers, administrators, or security guards at this school show any favoritism toward either white students or black students?" Each student rated separately: white teachers, black teachers, school administrators, and security guards. For each category he could check: "none that I know of favor whites," "one or two favor whites," or "quite a few favor whites." Identical categories were provided regarding favoritism to blacks. Then each student was given overall scores showing his perceptions about the amount of (1) staff favoring of whites and (2) staff favoring of blacks.[18]

Among black students, there was a substantial correlation between perceptions of staff favoritism toward white students and negative attitudes toward whites (see Table 8.6). The association remains fairly strong when other factors affecting racial attitudes are controlled (see Table 9.1). Associations between black students' perceptions of favoritism and their interracial behaviors are much weaker. Greater perceptions of favoritism tended to be associated with greater avoidance of white students, less friendship with whites, and less positive change in opinion of whites. These correlations are quite small, though those with friendship and opinion change remain significant when other determinants of interracial contacts are held constant.

The association between black students' perceptions of racial favoritism by staff and negative attitudes toward white schoolmates is difficult to interpret. Perceptions of favoritism toward white students may lead to negative feelings toward the white students. Or those with negative feelings toward whites may tend to see more favoritism toward whites. Or both perceptions may reflect an overall negative feeling toward the school. Whatever the causal dynamics, these results suggest that black students' attitudes toward white schoolmates were intertwined with the issue of favoritism. On the other hand, perceptions of favoritism by staff do not appear to have a major influence on black students' behavior toward whites.

Among white students, perceptions of racial favoritism appeared to be less important than for blacks (see Table 8.6). While those who saw more favoritism toward blacks tended to have less friendly contact with, and less positive attitudes toward, blacks, these associations are small and become nonsignificant when other factors affecting race relations are held constant.

The lesser importance of perceived favoritism among whites than among blacks may reflect the fact that black students were more likely than whites to see discrimination by school staff members against their race.[19] It may be also that while white students sometimes became annoyed at what they saw to be favoritism toward blacks, the issue of discrimination did not arouse their feelings to the same extent it did among blacks. Blacks are, of course, aware of and sensitive about a long, painful history of discrimination.

Problem-solving Mechanisms

Aggression by members of a given racial group, especially a minority, has sometimes been viewed as occurring when legitimate channels for the solution of grievances have been blocked (e.g., Laue, 1971; Kriesberg, 1973). In such a situation, where mechanisms for solving or even for communicating problems may be inadequate, frustration and anger may boil over into aggressive action.

In the high schools studied, students sometimes organized to try to air grievances or get changes of one sort or another. Issues concerned such matters as dress codes, new courses, getting a certain kind of entertainment, and having more blacks represented as cheerleaders. One possible channel through which students may have grievances handled is the school administration (principal, vice-principals, etc.). We found that many students had definite opinions about the extent to which particular administrators were responsive to student complaints or ideas.

A black senior girl at Southwest had this to say about her school's administration: "None of them in the administration office are very good because all of them's for white folks and they surely let you know it. . . . I remember [a group] was sponsoring this committee about last month and they called it the Congress of Black Students. They took a paper over to him [school administrator], their constitution, what they was standing up for, and he just threw it in the waste basket. That gives you an idea of how they feel around here."

However, other students, including black students in schools with a black principal or vice-principal, felt more able to voice their complaints to school administrators. For example, a black male senior at Emerson said: "This year is kind of better, because we have a black person in the administration office. It was kind of hard to go down and voice your complaints . . . to an all-white faculty."

Another possible channel for handling student problems is the Student Council. Such a group was found in every school, although its effectiveness apparently varied considerably from school to school. In a few schools, there was also a student Human Relations Council, which aimed specifically to promote improved communication about and solutions to racial problems. However, most of the high schools did not have such a group.

We asked students in all schools these questions: (1) "If students like yourself have a suggestion about changing something in this school, how often does the school (principal, vice-principal, etc.) try to do something about the suggestion?" (five response categories, from "always" to "rarely or never"); (2) "How much does the student council or other student groups do to solve any problems that come up between white and black students in this school?" (four categories, from "a lot" to "hardly anything at all").

Each student was given a score, based on his answers to these questions, showing how much problem-solving activity he perceived to be going on at his school.

Among both black students and white students, the more that students saw problem-solving activity at their school, the more positive their attitudes toward schoolmates of the other race and the more they reported favorable change in their opinion of the other race (see Table 8.6). These associations remain significant when other factors affecting racial attitudes are held constant (see Tables 9.1 and 9.2).

Associations between perceptions of problem-solving and interracial behavior were small. However, for students of both races, those who saw more problem solving in the school tended to avoid other-race schoolmates less often; this association remains significant for blacks but not for whites when other factors are held constant.

We do not know why there is some association between perception of problem solving in the school and positive interracial attitudes. The perception that something is being done about problems (especially interracial problems), and perhaps actual solution of some problems in the school, may lead students to react more positively to their other-race schoolmates. On the other hand, those with positive attitudes toward schoolmates may tend to see problem-solving efforts in a more rosy light. Or both processes may operate to some extent. Whatever the causal direction of the relation, it appears that racial attitudes are linked to perceptions that something is being done to solve relevant problems. On the other hand, there is little evidence that such perceptions are related much to interracial behavior.

This is not to say that mechanisms for solving problems which arise between the races may not affect interracial behavior at times, especially for specific groups of students who are directly involved in these problems or their solution. By virtue of the cooperative interaction and improved communication occurring in problem-solving groups, the racial norms of student groups may move in a more positive direction. In addition, actual changes which are made in school policies or procedures may remove or reduce grievances. To the extent that reducing grievances encourages students (perhaps especially the minority) to participate fully in school activities, this would lead to more friendly interaction between the races.

Summary

We have looked in this chapter at the ways in which students' interracial behavior and attitudes were related to various aspects of the school situation.

First, we considered the impact of the racial attitudes of significant others. We found that students' own interracial behavior and attitudes tended to be consistent with both the actual and the perceived racial attitudes of peers of their same race. This was especially true of white students but also was true of black students.

For both races, students' interracial behavior appeared to be affected much more by the racial attitudes of schoolmates of their own race than by those of the other race. For whites, positive racial attitudes among peers were associated with friendly interracial contacts most strongly when students had considerable opportunity to be with blacks, or to work together with blacks, in the classroom.

The racial attitudes of students' families also appeared to have impacts on the students' interracial attitudes and behavior. The more positive the racial attitudes of students' families, the more positive their own relations with schoolmates of the other race. Among white students, the racial attitudes of families and of peers had a combined (interaction) effect on students' reactions to other-race schoolmates. Those white students who saw both their families and their peers as having negative racial attitudes were especially likely to avoid black schoolmates and to have negative attitudes themselves toward the blacks.

The racial attitudes of teachers also were related to students' interracial attitudes and behavior. However, these associations generally were smaller than those for peers and for family. Also, teachers' attitudes appeared to play more of a role in discouraging negative interracial behavior than in promoting friendly behavior.

A second major aspect of the school situation which we considered is the extent of similarity between blacks and whites. First, differences in socioeconomic status (SES) generally had little or no negative effect on interracial behavior and attitudes. Among white students, those with higher SES, relative to black schoolmates, did have slightly more negative attitudes toward blacks. However, relative socioeconomic status had no significant effects (other things equal) on the interracial behavior of students of either race. Moreover, at the school level, a greater average difference in education between black parents and white parents had no negative effects on how students of the two races got along.

Differences between black students and white students with respect to academic ability and status also had little overall impact on interracial attitudes and behavior. The grades of individual students, and their IQs, relative to those of schoolmates of the other race, had little effect on their relationships with the other group. (A minor exception is that, for blacks, lower grades, relative to white schoolmates, contributed slightly to more unfriendly contacts with whites.) At the school level, average differences in IQ and academic attainment between blacks and whites generally had only weak associations with race relations. Also, students' perceptions of differences between blacks and whites in their school with respect to both academic and nonacademic status were not related substantially to their behavior and attitudes toward the other race.

Overall, while status differences were not totally without effect, the results do not support the proposition that equal status is an important prerequisite for intergroup contact to have positive results. Nor do the results indicate that equal abilities are important for good social relations.

The third major aspect of the school situation considered in this chapter is the extent to which students were involved in activities which call for working with other-race students toward common goals. We found that—especially for blacks—the more often students participated in interracial subgroups in classes, the more they tended to report interracial friendships extending outside of class. Also, for students of both races, the more students participated in school activities, the more likely they were to have friendly contacts with schoolmates of the other race.

Results concerning students' perceptions of common goals also are consistent with the proposition that compatibility with respect to goals is important. They indicate that the more that students—especially white students—saw other-race schoolmates as helping, rather than hindering, them in reaching their own goals, the more likely they were to get along with the other race.

Our results indicate, further, that the positive effects of working cooperatively with students of another race did not depend on the students' status, relative to those of other race, nor on the racial composition of their classes. However, the effect of cooperative activity did appear to depend to some extent on the racial attitudes of same-race peers. White students who participated in interracial class subgroups were especially likely to form interracial friendships when the racial attitudes of their peers were positive. And when students (of either race) saw schoolmates of the other race as helpful in reaching their goals, and also saw the racial attitude of their peers as positive, their behavior toward the other race was especially positive. Thus, a combination of cooperative activities and positive racial norms among peers seems to produce the most friendly contact between the races.

We also considered (more briefly) several other aspects of the school situation which might be thought to affect students' behavior and attitudes toward those of the other race. There was little association between the strictness of school discipline and interracial behavior. Neither the stringency of the rules and penalties reported by the school administration, nor students' perceptions of the likelihood and severity of punishment for rule breaking, were related much to the frequency of fighting between the races or to other interracial behavior.

Concerning the relative power of blacks and whites within the school, the extent to which either race was represented on the student councils was not related consistently to the average interracial behavior of students in that school. However, among both black students and white students, those who saw the two races as generally equal in power got along better with other-race schoolmates than those who saw a disparity of power favoring either race. These results suggest that equality of power between the races may contribute to more harmonious relationships.

Finally, we considered briefly students' perceptions of racial favoritism by the staff and of the extent to which administrators and student groups were trying to solve student problems, including racial grievances. While student perceptions concerning these matters were not related much to their interracial behavior, black students who saw the school staff to favor whites and who saw little effort in the school to handle their problems also tended to have negative attitudes toward white schoolmates. In addition, black students who saw the school as more strict also were more likely than other blacks to have negative attitudes toward their white schoolmates. These results indicate that black students' attitudes toward their white schoolmates were linked to, and may have been affected by, their attitudes toward the school as a whole.

9 | *What Counts Most for Each Social Outcome?*

We have examined, in previous chapters, the ways in which students' relations with schoolmates of another race are affected by various aspects of (1) their backgrounds, (2) their personal characteristics, (3) their opportunities for interracial contact in high school, and (4) the high school situation. Now we consider all of these factors together and ask: Which factors have the greatest impact on interracial behaviors and attitudes? Are the factors which have the greatest effect on one social outcome (e.g., interracial avoidance) the same ones which are most important for other outcomes (e.g., interracial attitudes)? And are the factors which appear to have the greatest effect on the interracial behaviors and attitudes of black students also the same ones which are most important for white students?

Previous research on these issues has been very limited. As Carithers (1970, pp. 31–32) pointed out, almost all single studies of school desegregation up to 1970 dealt with only a small number of factors which may affect social relations between the races, in isolation from other causal factors.

More recently, a few researchers have used multivariate methods to try to assess the relative importance of various factors which may affect relations between black and white students (Chadwick et al., 1971; NORC, 1973; Forehand et al., 1976; Bullock, 1976). However, these recent efforts have focused almost entirely on students' racial attitudes and have given little attention to their interracial behaviors.

In this chapter, we provide information about the relative impact of a variety of factors (including aspects of students' backgrounds, students' personal traits, and the school situation) on six different social outcomes. These outcomes include: (1) avoidance, (2) unfriendly contacts, (3) friendly contacts, (4) friendships, (5) racial attitudes, and (6) change in racial opinions. For each of these outcomes, we compare the determinants of black students' reactions with those of white students. The analyses in

208

this chapter are limited to individual students, since the large number of individuals permits us to use multivariate methods. These methods show the unique effect of each variable on interracial behavior and attitudes, while holding constant the effects of other variables.

A Note on Methods

Before we summarize the results, it should be helpful to say a few things about our methods. (The reader who is not interested in the more technical aspects of the study may wish to skip to the next section.)

To try to answer the questions posed above, we have relied on the statistical technique of multiple regression analysis.[1] This technique permits us to see how well each of a number of possible variables (i.e., aspects of students' background, school situation, etc.) can predict a particular student behavior or attitude (e.g., avoidance of other-race schoolmates). The size of the relationship between the outcome to be explained and each specific predictor is assessed independently of the effect of all other predictors. For example, if interracial avoidance is the outcome and we have three possible predictors—parents' education, family racial attitudes, and peers' racial attitudes—we would look first at the effect of parents' education on avoidance, while removing statistically the effects of family and peer racial attitudes; then we would look at the effect of family racial attitudes on avoidance, removing the effect of parents' education and peers' racial attitudes, and so on.

Importance of Predictors. The size of the relationship between each predictor variable and the outcome to be explained is indicated by a number called the "partial beta coefficient" ("partial beta," for short). The partial beta indicates the amount of change in the outcome which is associated with each unit of change in a particular predictor. If, for example, in predicting white students' avoidance of blacks, the partial beta of family racial attitudes is −.25, this indicates that for each unit of change in positive family racial attitudes, there is a decrease of .25 of a unit of avoidance.[2] The rank order of a group of partial betas (e.g., those in each column of Table 9.1) reflects their relative importance as predictors of the outcome in which we are interested. (The sign of each partial beta does not affect its importance.)

Linearity and Additivity. The technique of multiple regression assumes that the relationship between each predictor and the outcome variable is linear. We have examined, separately for each race, the shape of the relation between each predictor and each outcome variable. As previous chapters have shown, some relations are not linear or even monotonic. For example, as the proportion of black students in classes rises, interracial avoidance by white students rises, up to the point of about 50% black. Then, as the proportion of blacks increases still further, avoidance by whites decreases. In such cases, the predictor variable has been treated as a set of categories called "dummy variables" so that this nonlinearity could be taken into account and not distort the results.[3]

Multiple regression analysis also assumes that the effects of the various predictor variables on the outcome variable are additive—i.e., that the effect of predictor A does not change as the value of predictor B changes. For example, if class racial composition and sex are possible predictors of unfriendly interracial contact, it would be assumed that the effect of class racial composition does not differ for boys as compared to girls. We have examined the combined effects of a large number of pairs and trios (and occasionally larger sets) of predictors. As reported in previous chapters, in some cases the combined effects of two predictors were not additive. Instead, they had a combined effect which was different from the sum of the two effects operating separately. For example, among blacks the effect of being in minority-black classes on interracial avoidance depends on whether the student has friendly contacts with whites prior to high school. Where such combined (interaction) effects were substantial with respect to a given outcome, we have constructed a new variable representing this combined effect. These new variables also are handled as "dummy variables"—i.e., a set of categories reflecting particular combinations of the component variables on which they are based.

By taking account of both nonlinearity and nonadditivity in the relationships, our analysis is relatively free of the distortions which frequently occur when multiple regression is performed without attention to these aspects of the relationships.

Causal Interpretations. Though these analyses tell us how well each given variable predicts the behavior or attitude in which we are interested, they do not tell us anything about the direction of causation. Some of our predictors (e.g., grade school racial composition, sex, grade school IQ) are clearly prior in time to high school race relations and so can be causes but not effects of such relations. In other instances, while a predictor is not prior in time to an outcome, it seems logical or more consistent with common knowledge that it is a cause rather than an effect of race relations. For example, it seems much more likely that the socioeconomic status of a student's family might affect, rather than be affected by, his relationships with students of another race.

In still other cases, the direction of causation, if any, is less clear on temporal or logical grounds. We will sometimes interpret such associations as reflecting a particular causal direction because this seems more plausible theoretically or because there is other evidence, from this study or from previous studies, which tends to support such a causal interpretation.

Order of Entering Predictors. For each of the social outcomes studied, most of the possible predictors of this outcome were entered into the regression equation simultaneously. This was done in order to see the independent effect of each with all other possible relevant variables held constant.

However, there are a number of variables which were judged to be less clearly determinants of relations between the races than were the other variables used as predictors. For example, while an association between students' sex and their racial attitudes is clearly due to the effect of sex on attitudes, it is much less clear how an association between interracial attitudes and perceptions of racial favoritism should be interpreted. Perception of favoritism might affect racial attitudes but it may, in turn, be affected by such racial attitudes. If sex and perceptions of favoritism were both entered together into a regression analysis to predict racial attitudes, the effect of sex might be artificially reduced because its effect would be controlled for one of the possible results (perceptions of favoritism) of the outcome it is predicting.

For this reason, it was deemed advisable to enter the possible predictor variables into each regression equation in two successive blocs. The first and larger bloc included those variables which were judged to be exclusively or predominantly causes rather than effects of interracial attitudes and behavior. The partial coefficients for those variables, shown without section (§) marks in Tables 9.1 and 9.2, are those computed prior to the introduction of the second bloc of variables.

The second, relatively small, bloc of variables is composed of those which were judged as likely to be affected by, as well as affecting, interracial attitudes and/or behavior. They are identified by section (§) marks in Tables 9.1 and 9.2. Despite the fact that their associations with interracial behavior and attitudes may not reflect causation running in one direction only, this second bloc of variables concerns aspects of student characteristics and the school situation which may have important impacts on social relations between the races.

With these methodological points set forth, let us turn now to the results of the summary analyses.

Avoidance

One of the key aims of most racial integration plans is to permit students of different races to get to know one another. But black students and white students often try to stay separate from, and avoid contact with, schoolmates of the other race. What factors contribute most to such interracial avoidance?

First, the results (see Tables 9.1 and 9.2) indicate that negative racial attitudes by those persons closest to the students were among the strongest determinants of interracial avoidance. Among students of both races, the single best predictor of avoidance was a negative racial attitude by the student's family (as reported by the student). Negative racial attitudes by same-race peers (as measured by us) also contributed to avoidance of other-race schoolmates. The contribution of peer attitudes to avoidance was greater among whites than among blacks but was significant for blacks as well. Among white students, the racial attitudes of same-race teachers (as perceived by students) also affected avoidance. The more that white teachers were seen as favoring friendly contact across racial lines, the less often white students avoided black schoolmates.

The associations between interracial avoidance and the racial attitudes of others may be due to several factors. First, students may tend to perceive the attitudes of their family and teachers as consistent with their own attitudes and behavior. (This consideration does not apply to peer attitudes, which we measured independently.) However, from all we know about the strong effects of social norms on behavior (e.g., Kiesler and Kiesler, 1969), it is likely also that the actual attitudes of family and teachers, as well as those of peers, were affecting avoidance. These social influences would operate in several ways. First, the attitudes of important others would help to define for students just what students of the other race were like (e.g., whether helpful and trustworthy) and how pleasant or unpleasant contact with them would be. Second, the racial attitudes of others often would lead them to convey, explicitly or subtly, social pressures either to avoid other-race peers or not to do so. Third, the racial attitudes of others sometimes would lead them to provide stimuli for avoidance behavior—e.g., a students' peers suggesting that they all sit far away from schoolmates of the other race.

Next in important to the racial attitudes of others in determining avoidance were the personal traits of students. However, the particular traits involved differed somewhat for black students as compared to white students.

Among blacks, the student's aggressiveness (as indicated by fighting and arguing with students of one's own race) was one of the strongest contributors to avoidance of whites. Avoidance of whites was probably one

Table 9.1. Summary of Significant Predictors of Interracial Behaviors and Attitudes among Black Students (Partial Beta Coefficients)[1]

	Avoid-ance	Friendly Contact	Friend-ship	Un-friendly Contact[2]	Positive Attitude	Positive Opinion Change
A. Background						
No early friendly contact with whites; high school classes < 40% black	.13***	—	—	—	—	—
Much friendly contact with whites in grade school	—	.12*	–	–	–	–
Amount of friendly neighborhood contact with whites prior to high school	—	—	–	–	.08*	–
Much friendly contact with whites in neigh-						

Continued

Table 9.1 *Continued*

	Avoid-ance	Friendly Contact	Friend-ship	Un-friendly Contact²	Positive Attitude	Positive Opinion Change
borhood prior to high school	—	.15***	—	—	—	—
Positive family racial attitudes	−.25***	.16***	.24***	−.14***	.29***	.25***
B. Student Characteristics						
Aggressiveness	.24***	.09**	–	.32***	−.13***	–
Sex female	–	–	–	−.12**	–	–
Educational aspirations §	–	–	.08*	–	–	–
IQ	–	–	–	–	.11**	–
General life satisfaction	–	.08*	–	–	.19***	.18***
High effort §	–	–	.11**	–	–	–
C. Opportunity for Interracial Contact in High School						
Classes < 40% black; no early friendly contact with whites (see A also)	.13***	—	—	—	—	—
Classes 80% black or more	—	−.09*	—	—	—	—
Classes 40–90% black	—	—	—	—	—	.17***
Participation in activities	–	.27***	.14***	–	–	–
D. High School Situation						
Ethnocentrism of same-race peers	.09*	–	–	–	−.12***	–
Participation in interracial sub-groups in classes	−.07*	.10**	.10**	–	–	–
Grades, relative to white school-mates	−,+	–	–	−.08*	–	–
Power of blacks perceived much greater §	.07*	–	–	.08*	−.07*	–

Continued

Table 9.1 *Continued*

	Avoid-ance	Friendly Contact	Friend-ship	Un-friendly Contact[2]	Positive Attitude	Positive Opinion Change
Power of blacks perceived a little greater [§]	.10*	–	–.12**	–	–	–
Power of whites perceived a little greater [§]	–	–	–	–	–.08*	–
Power of whites perceived much greater [§]	–	–	–	–	–.08*	–
Perception of school trying to solve problems [§]	–.09*	–	–	–	.11**	.10*
Perception of favoritism toward whites [§]	–	–	–.14*	–	–.24***	–.14*
Perception of school strictness	–,+	–	–	–	–.12***	–
Proportion of variance ex-plained (R^2)	.25	.24	.18	.21	.39	.15

1. Results from multiple regression analyses with pairwise treatment of missing data. Ns for correlations on which analyses were based averaged about 1,500. Other variables included in the regression analysis, which did not have significant effects, were: church activity; height; SES, relative to white schoolmates; ethnocentrism of other-race schoolmates; opportunity for contact with black faculty; perceived favoritism by staff toward own race; perceived attitudes of same-race teachers concerning interracial contact.
2. Index of participation in unfriendly interracial contact used (see Chapter 4).

* Significant at .05 level; ** significant at .01 level; *** significant at .001 level; – partial beta not significant; — this variable not used to predict the dependent variable; + dummy variables used as predictors.
§ Variable was among those judged to be less clearly a cause, rather than effect, of interracial attitudes or behavior. These variables were entered as a second bloc into the regression analysis. (Perception of school strictness was in second bloc only when unfriendly contact was dependent variable.) Partial beta coefficients for other variables were computed prior to inclusion of second bloc of variables.

of the several ways in which generally aggressive black students expressed their relatively hostile attitudes toward whites. In addition, since aggressive students were more likely than others to get into interracial fights, they undoubtedly found many such contacts unpleasant and thus would tend to avoid contact with some whites.

Among whites, the student's sex, in combination with aggressiveness, had a substantial effect on interracial avoidance. Boys—especially the more aggressive boys but also unaggressive boys—were more likely than girls to avoid black schoolmates. Data reported in Chapter 6 suggest that this result reflects a greater physical fear of blacks among white boys than among white girls. The fact that more aggressive white boys were somewhat more likely than other boys to avoid blacks probably is due to the fact that the more aggressive boys were more likely to get into fights with blacks than were other white boys; having more unpleasant experiences of this type may have led them to increased avoidance of blacks.

While interracial avoidance seemed to be affected most strongly by the racial attitudes of important others and by the personal characteristics of students, past and present interracial experiences also played a part. Among black students, those who had no friendly contact with white people prior to high school and who attended primarily (60% or more) white classes were most apt to avoid white schoolmates. It seems likely that black students with this particular combination of background and present situation would have been especially wary of rebuff by white schoolmates. Their past had given them no experience of friendly contact with whites and may have led them, instead, to expect contacts with whites to be unpleasant. Being in a minority, they were subject also to the insecurities of minority status and to greater hostilities from white students than was true in situations where blacks were not a minority. However, participation with whites in class subgroups tended to reduce avoidance of white schoolmates slightly.

Among white students, as among blacks, those who had no friendly interracial experience prior to high school were more likely than others to avoid schoolmates of the other race. Like blacks without prior friendly contact, these whites probably were apprehensive that interracial contact might be unpleasant. However, among whites, those with no friendly prior contact avoided blacks more than did others regardless of the racial composition of their classes.

The racial composition of classes did have a small effect of its own on avoidance among whites. Those white students whose classes averaged 30 to 50% black were slightly more likely than other whites to avoid black schoolmates. This result appears to be part of the general pattern of greater friction between the races when there was a large black minority (see Chapter 7). This pattern may stem, at least in part, from resentment and fear among whites that a growing proportion of blacks was "taking over our school," and a corresponding hostility by blacks in response to that of the whites.

We have pointed out that, for students of both races, the nature of interracial experiences prior to high school affected interracial avoidance in high school. One would expect that the kinds of interracial experience students have in high school also would affect the likelihood of their trying to avoid other-race schoolmates. Additional results (not reported in Tables 9.1 and 9.2) show that the more often students reported unfriendly actions toward themselves by other-race schoolmates in high school, the more likely they were to avoid the other race. (Correlations are .42 for blacks and .44 for whites.) These associations may not have been due entirely to the effects of unfriendly actions by the other race on stu-

dents' own avoidance.[4] But they are consistent with the associations between students' interracial experiences prior to high school and their
avoidance of other-race schoolmates in high school. Both results suggest
that previous unpleasant interracial experiences (or at least a lack of
pleasant experiences) contribute to interracial avoidance.

Finally, some student perceptions of the school situation were related to interracial avoidance. The strongest of these associations is the
following: White students who perceived blacks as having much more
power than whites were considerably more likely than other whites to
avoid black schoolmates. This association may be another indication of the
importance of fears of physical violence in contributing to white
avoidance. When whites saw blacks as having greater power, this perception usually concerned physical power (e.g., "push students of the other
race without the other race fighting back"). Thus, many whites who perceived blacks as having such physical power over whites probably were
afraid of some blacks and tried to avoid them for this reason.

However, interracial avoidance was not associated only with perceptions of students' of the other race having more power than those of one's
own race. Among whites, those who saw their own race as having slightly
more overall power than blacks (usually reflecting greater white control
over offices and activities) were somewhat more likely to avoid blacks than
were those who saw the two races as equal in power in the school. Similarly, among blacks, those who saw their own race as having more power
than whites were more likely than others to avoid whites. These latter
results are hard to interpret, especially since perceptions of relative power
may have been affected by the same factors (e.g., racial attitudes) that
affect avoidance. Whatever the causal connections, those students who
saw a discrepancy in power between the races (in either direction) were
more likely to avoid schoolmates of the other race than were those who
saw the power of the two groups as equal.

A number of other factors did *not* have an independent effect on
avoidance, among either black or white students. These include students'
grades and socioeconomic status, relative to schoolmates of the other race;
the average ethnocentrism of other-race schoolmates; and opportunity for
contact with black faculty. Additional variables which were not significant
predictors of avoidance are indicated in the body and footnotes of Tables
9.1 and 9.2.

Overall, the results suggest that interracial avoidance is determined
primarily by those factors which affect the extent to which students anticipate that contact with schoolmates of the other race will be unpleasant
and/or that social disapproval will follow such contact.

Friendly Interactions

When interaction does occur between black and white students,
when are these contacts friendly ones? And what contributes to friendships between students of each race?

Friendly Contact. As in the case of avoidance, the amount of friendly contact which students had with other-race schoolmates was affected by the racial attitudes of their families (see Tables 9.1 and 9.2). This association was especially marked among black students.

Table 9.2. Summary of Significant Predictors of Interracial Behaviors and Attitudes among White Students (Partial Beta Coefficients)[1]

	Avoidance	Friendly Contact	Friendship	Unfriendly Contact[2]	Positive Attitude	Positive Opinion Change
A. Student Background						
Unfriendly neighborhood contact with blacks prior to high school	.09**	–	–	.15***	–	–
Some friendly neighborhood contact with blacks prior to high school	–	–	.09**	–	–	–
Much friendly neighborhood contact with blacks prior to high school	–	.29***	.15***	.09**	.09**	–
Amount of friendly contact with blacks in grade school	–	.09**	.11**	–	.11***	–
Positive family racial attitudes	-.24***	.10***	.15***	-.08*	.33***	.14***
B. Student Characteristics						
Male, aggressive, and short	.15***	—	—	—	—	—
Male, aggressive, and tall	.17***	—	—	—	—	—
Male and unaggressive	.11**	—	—	—	—	—
Female	—	–	–	-.13**	.14***	.07*
Aggressiveness	—	.11***	.07*	.37***	–	–
IQ	-,+	–	–	–	–	-.09*

Continued

Table 9.2 *Continued*

	Avoid-ance	Friendly Contact	Friend-ship	Un-friendly Contact[2]	Positive Attitude	Positive Opinion Change
General life satisfaction	–	–	–	–	.11***	–
C. Opportunity for Interracial Contact in High School						
Classes 30–50% black	.08*	—	—	—	—	—
Percent black in classes	—	—	.15***	–,+	–,+	–,+
Classes 20–60% black and same-race peers high in ethnocentrism	—	.09*	—	—	—	—
Classes > 40% black and same-race peers low in ethnocentrism	—	.21***	—	—	—	—
Participation in activities	–	.22***	.11*	–	–	–
D. High School Situation						
Ethnocentrism of same-race peers	.15***	—	—	.09*	–.25***	–.15***
Ethnocentrism of same-race peers high and much partic. in interracial class subgroups	—	—	.07*	—	—	—
Ethnocentrism of other-race peers	–	–,+	–	–	.09**	–
SES, relative to black schoolmates	–	–	–,+	–	–.08**	–.08*
Perception of positive teacher racial attitudes§	–.11***	–	–	–.08*	.07*	–
Power of whites perceived much greater§	–	–	–	–	–.09***	–

Continued

Table 9.2   *Continued*

	Avoid-ance	Friendly Contact	Friend-ship	Un-friendly Contact[2]	Positive Attitude	Positive Opinion Change
Power of whites perceived a little greater§	.12***	–	–.07*	.08*	–.10**	–
Power of blacks perceived a little greater§	–	–	–.08*	–	–.18***	–.12***
Power of blacks perceived much greater§	.23***	–.08*	–.10**	.12**	–.26***	–.19***
Perception of problem solving in school§	–	–,+	–	–	.12***	.11***
Proportion of variance ex-plained (R^2)	.25	.32	.21	.31	.39	.15

1. Results from multiple regression analyses, with pairwise treatment of missing data. Ns for correlations on which analyses were based averaged about 1,600. Other variables included in the regression analyses, which did not have significant effects, were: religious activity; height; school effort; educational aspirations; opportunity for contact with black faculty; grades, relative to black schoolmates; perception of school strictness; perception of favoritism by staff toward own race.
2. Index of participation in unfriendly interracial contact was used (see Chapter 4).

* Indicates significant at .05 level; ** indicates significant at .01 level; *** indicates significant at .001 level; – indicates partial beta not significant; — indicates this variable not used to predict the dependent variable; + indicates that dummy variables used as predictor.
§ Indicates variable was among those judged to be less clearly a cause, rather than effect, of interracial attitudes or behavior. These variables were entered as a second bloc into the regression analysis. Partial beta coefficients for other variables were computed prior to inclusion of second bloc of variables.

However, for students of both races, the best predictors of friendly interracial contact in high school were the opportunities for, and circumstances of, students' own interracial experiences, both prior to and during high school. First, friendly interracial contact in the neighborhood prior to high school and in grade school contributed to more friendly interracial contact in high school. Among whites, the effect of friendly neighborhood contact was especially strong and was, in fact, the single strongest predictor of friendly high school contact.

For both races, the combined effect of friendly contact in the neighborhood and in grade school was substantial. As evidence presented in Chapter 5 shows, the positive effect of friendly early contacts on later behavior was due in part (but not entirely) to their positive impact on the racial attitudes that students brought to high school. In addition, it seems likely that those students who learned to engage in friendly interracial contacts, and found these satisfying, transferred these patterns of friendly behavior to the high school situation.

A number of aspects of the high school situation also appeared to have contributed to friendly interracial contact. For both blacks and whites, more participation in school activities had a relatively strong association with friendly interracial contacts. The reasons for this association are not completely clear. Those who participate in activities may tend to be those who are most sociable. However, the evidence (see Chapter 7) indicates that participation in school activities contributes to friendly interracial contact in part because it provides an opportunity for interracial contact outside the classroom. The fact that contact in such settings usually involves cooperation toward common goals among students with similar interests undoubtedly makes it more rewarding. Also, for many students—especially members of a racial minority—participation in activities may contribute to a feeling of belonging in the school and thus indirectly to friendly interaction with other-race schoolmates.

Opportunity for interracial contact in classes—in combination with other school conditions—also had an impact on friendly contact. Among white students, those whose classes averaged 40% or more black and whose white peers had positive racial attitudes were especially likely to have friendly contacts with black schoolmates. Apparently, the combination of high opportunity for interracial contact, plus peer support for friendly contact, produced this positive result.

Among black students, the effect of class racial composition on friendly interracial contact was smaller. However, blacks in classes which had more than 20% whites had more friendly contact with whites than those in classes with smaller proportions of whites. Among black students, participation in interracial subgroups within classes also contributed to friendly contacts with whites. Like school activities outside the classroom, working cooperatively toward common goals in class activities or projects probably helped to make these contacts pleasant and thus led to friendly interaction both within and outside the classroom.

Whereas personal characteristics of students (especially their sex and aggressiveness) played a big part in determining interracial avoidance, personal traits had only small effects on friendly interracial contact. Among both blacks and whites, aggressive students had slightly *more* friendly interracial contacts than less aggressive students. Though this result may seem surprising—especially in light of the strong association between aggressiveness and negative interracial behavior—it is consistent with evidence from other research that aggressive children are more active in a variety of ways (Patterson, Littman, and Bricker, 1967). Among black students, greater satisfaction with life also contributed slightly to friendly contact with whites. Perhaps happier students were more outgoing and more fun to be with.

Finally, a number of factors did *not* have a significant effect, among either blacks or whites, on the amount of friendly interracial contact students had, when other relevant factors were held constant. These nonsignificant factors include the student's sex; the level of ethnocentrism of other-race schoolmates; students' grades and socioeconomic status, relative to other-race schoolmates; and students' perceptions of teachers' attitudes concerning interracial contact. Additional factors which did not have signifcant independent effects on interracial behaviors or attitudes are indicated in the body and footnotes of Tables 9.1 and 9.2.

Overall, friendly contact with other-race schoolmates appears to be determined by those factors which lead students to experience and to expect rewarding interracial contact, and which lead them to anticipate social approval for friendly contact.

Friendships. The predictors of interracial friendships were similar to those of friendly interracial contacts (see Tables 9.1 and 9.2) but several differences are worth noting. For both races, family racial attitudes had stronger effects on interracial friendships than on friendly contacts. In fact, for blacks, family racial attitude was the largest single determinant of interracial friendships. It seems likely that families are more likely to be aware of, and concerned about, friendships than about the more intermittent and often more casual contacts that are included in the measure of friendly contacts.

On the other hand, among blacks, personal interracial experiences prior to high school were not significant predictors of interracial friendships, though they did contribute to friendly contact. It may be that friendly early experiences were sufficient to encourage blacks to have similar contacts in high school but generally were not intimate or intense enough to lead blacks to enter the more intimate and long-term relationship of friendship.

Among black students, several indicators of involvement in school work—high academic effort and high educational aspirations—also were related significantly to friendship with whites. It may be that black students who were most dedicated to academic goals saw themselves, and were seen by whites, as having most in common with their white schoolmates. Such compatibility may have led to friendships in many cases. (See also Chapter 11 for a more extensive discussion of the relation between interracial friendship and academic values and performance.)

Unfriendly Contact

Like interracial avoidance, unfriendly contact with other-race schoolmates was affected most by students' personal characteristics and by their backgrounds (see Tables 9.1 and 9.2). Among both blacks and whites, by far the strongest predictor of unfriendly contact was the student's general aggressiveness. Put another way, those students who fought and argued most with schoolmates of their own race also fought and argued most with students of the other race.

A second personal characteristic which had a substantial, though lesser, impact on unfriendly interracial contact was the student's sex. Boys of both races reported getting into interracial fights and arguments more often than did girls. This result undoubtedly reflects the general cultural, and perhaps biological, pattern for boys to fight physically more than do girls. (The questions about unfriendly contact concerned mainly "pushing" and "hitting.") Thus, the results concerning the impact of aggressiveness and of being male on unfriendly interracial contacts indicate that, to a considerable extent, such fighting is a reflection of general patterns of behavior which are not specifically interracial.

While unfriendly actions toward other-race schoolmates appear to be affected strongly by general patterns of interpersonal behavior, they may be triggered by negative interracial attitudes or, once started, they may involve such attitudes. Other factors, directly relevant to interracial attitudes and experiences, also affected the frequency of unfriendly interracial contacts. Among white students, the most important of these other factors was unfriendly experience with blacks in the neighborhood prior to high school. Whites who had such unfriendly early contacts were more likely than those without prior interracial neighborhood contacts to have unfriendly contacts with blacks in high school. Since this result occurs with the effect of aggressiveness in high school controlled, it does not appear to be due to personal traits of the students. It seems likely, rather, that students who had previous unfriendly contacts with blacks brought hostile attitudes toward blacks to high school. These attitudes would have affected both their reactions to black schoolmates and the reactions of the blacks to them, leading in some cases to interracial fights. Also, those white students who learned earlier to respond to frictions with blacks by fighting may have transferred such patterns of behavior to the high school setting.

While unfriendly neighborhood contacts prior to high school contributed to whites' having more unfriendly contacts in high school, friendly prior contacts did not lead to less fighting in high school. In fact, those whites who had the most friendly early contacts with blacks in their neighborhood had slightly more unfriendly contact with blacks in high school than did those whites with no early contact with blacks. This result must be seen in the context of the much larger contribution which friendly early contact made to friendly interracial contact in high school. In other words, friendly contact with neighborhood blacks prior to high school led to more interaction of every kind with blacks in high school. This was primarily friendly contact but there also was slightly more unfriendly contact, as compared to those with no prior neighborhood contact with blacks.

The racial attitudes of other persons also affected the frequency of unfriendly interracial contacts. Among students of both races, the more positive the racial attitudes of the student's family (as he reported them), the less unfriendly contact he had with schoolmates of the other race. This effect was stronger among blacks than among whites. Among white students, high ethnocentrism among peers of their own race and perceptions of lack of support for racial integration among same-race teachers also contributed slightly to more unfriendly contacts with blacks. These associations were not significant for blacks, with other variables controlled. Overall, the results indicate that unfriendly contact was somewhat more frequent when important others provided (or were perceived to provide) some support for such behavior.

Finally, several other factors had small effects on the frequency of unfriendly interracial contacts. Among blacks, having lower grades, relative to white schoolmates, contributed slightly to unfriendly contacts. It may be that some blacks who were getting low grades were resentful of whites' getting higher grades and this resentment sometimes contributed to fights.

Among blacks, those who saw their own race as having more power than whites in their school and, among whites, those who saw either race as having more power than the other, reported slightly more unfriendly interracial contacts than those who saw the races as equal in power. While we cannot be sure that perception of unequal power actually was a cause of unfriendly interaction, it may be that those who saw their group as inferior in power were resentful about this while those who saw their group as superior in power tended to act arrogantly toward members of the other group. Both types of reactions may have contributed to unfriendly contacts.

Finally, there are a number of factors which did *not* have significant effects (when other relevant variables were held constant) on the amount of unfriendly interracial contact reported by students of either race. These nonsignificant factors include: class racial proportions; students' socioeconomic status, relative to other-race schoolmates; participation in activities involving common goals; and the level of ethnocentrism of other-race schoolmates. Additional variables which did not have significant independent effects on unfriendly interracial contacts are indicated in the body and footnotes of Tables 9.1 and 9.2.

Overall, unfriendly contact with schoolmates of the other race appears to be affected most strongly by students' personal characteristics which lead them to react to interpersonal frictions by fighting. In addition, unfriendly contact is affected by factors which affect social approval or disapproval for fighting and which affect students' interracial hostility.

Attitudes

Students' attitudes toward schoolmates of the other race appear to have been affected most strongly by the racial attitudes of other persons who are important to them. For both blacks and whites, the best single predictor of a student's racial attitudes was the racial attitudes of his family (as reported by the student). The racial attitudes of peers (as measured independently) also had a substantial impact on students' attitudes, especially among white students; the greater the level of ethnocentrism among his schoolmates of the same race, the more negative the student's attitudes toward schoolmates of the other race. Among white students, the perceived racial attitudes of teachers also contributed slightly to their own attitudes toward black schoolmates. Overall, these results are consistent with those of other studies which show the racial attitudes of family, peers, and teachers to be among the most important correlates of students' own interracial attitudes (Chadwick et al., 1971; Bullock, 1976).

These associations may not be due entirely to the effects of others' attitudes on those of the student. As we have noted, students may distort their perceptions of the attitudes of family and teachers to match their own attitudes (although our objective measure of peer attitudes is not subject to such distortion). Also, the attitudes of the individual student and those of persons important to him may be affected by the same circumstances (social-class background, school events, etc.). However, despite these caveats, evidence about the effects of group norms on attitudes suggests that attitudes of significant others are likely to exert a powerful influence on those of each individual (Cohen, 1964; Kiesler and Kiesler, 1969). The student's view of what other-race persons are like will be strongly influenced by these others. Moreover, his expression of the "right" attitudes will be rewarded by approval and expression of the "wrong" attitudes will be punished by disapproval.

Personal characteristics of students also had a substantial impact on their racial attitudes. Specifically, greater satisfaction with life (for both races) and low general aggressiveness (for blacks) contributed to positive racial attitudes. The latter result is consistent with previous findings that personal traits reflecting general hostility were among the largest contributors to black students' racial attitudes (Chadwick et al., 1971; Bullock, 1976). Together, these results suggest that negative attitudes toward other-race schoolmates may be determined in part by general feelings of hostility which are either extended or displaced to an out-group. Conversely, positive racial attitudes may reflect, in part, positive feelings toward people in general.

Several other personal characteristics also affected attitudes toward other-race schoolmates. Among blacks, those with higher IQs had more positive attitudes toward whites. This may reflect a greater sense of shared interests and abilities with whites among higher-IQ than among lower-IQ blacks. Such similarities would make whites seem more attractive.

Among whites, being female contributed to more positive attitudes toward blacks. This was due, in part, to the lesser fear of blacks which white girls expressed. (Fear is one component of the attitude index.) In addition, the more positive attitudes of white girls may have been due to the fact that white girls had fewer unfriendly (and thus unpleasant) contacts with black schoolmates than did white boys.

While students' racial attitudes were related most strongly to those of other people they knew, and to their personal traits, the kind of racial experiences they had prior to high school also had some effect on their attitudes. Both among blacks and among whites, friendly contact with other-race people in their neighborhood prior to high school contributed slightly to more positive attitudes towards other-race schoolmates in high school. Among white students, friendly contact with blacks in grade school also contributed to positive racial attitudes in high school.

Opportunity for interracial contact in high school (as indicated especially by the racial composition of classes) did *not* contribute significantly to students' racial attitudes. Nor did participation in school activities or in interracial subgroups within classes affect racial attitudes. The reader will recall that it was these variables—especially class racial composition and participation in school activities—which had substantial impacts on friendly interaction between the races. Thus, it appears that opportunity for contact with other-race schoolmates contributed to friendly contacts with specific other-race schoolmates rather than to attitudes about the entire group of other-race schoolmates in the school.

While racial attitudes had little relation to opportunity for interracial contact in the school, attitudes were related to students' perceptions about some other aspects of the school situation. Among blacks, perceptions of the supportiveness of the school staff appeared especially important. The more that black students saw the staff as favoring whites over blacks, saw administrators (as well as student groups) as not trying to solve their problems, and saw the school as strict, the more negative their attitudes toward white schoolmates. These results are consistent with those of another, large-scale study which found acceptance of interracial interaction among black students to be determined primarily by their perceptions of the fairness of the school administration (Forehand et al., 1976).

It may be that resentment of the staff (usually mostly white) was generalized to white students (especially since white students were seen as the beneficiaries of staff favoritism). Another possibility is that attitudes toward staff and students may form part of a general set of positive or negative attitudes toward the school as a whole. In any case, the attitudes of black students toward school staff and toward white peers seem to be linked.

Among white students, perception of greater efforts by the school administration (as well as student groups) to solve racial and other problems also contributed to positive attitudes toward black schoolmates. But the aspect of the school situation which appeared to have the greatest impact on white attitudes was their perception of the relative power of blacks and whites in the school. White students who saw black schoolmates as having more power than whites had the most negative attitudes toward the blacks. Since greater perceived power for blacks usually meant that blacks had the power to physically dominate whites, this result may reflect resentment by many whites at potential and/or actual physical coercion of whites by some blacks.

The status of students, relative to those of the other race, generally did not have a substantial effect on their racial attitudes. For students of both races, relative grades did not affect racial attitudes. The only indication that the relative status of the other-race group made some difference was the fact that, among whites, those of high socioeconomic status, relative to black schoolmates, had slightly more negative attitudes toward the blacks. This latter finding may reflect a tendency for whites who were much higher in status than their black schoolmates to react negatively to the behavioral "style" of many blacks, which may have been quite different from that of middle-class whites. (It should be noted, however, that greater differences in socioeconomic status did *not* lead to a reduction in friendly interracial contact with particular other-race schoolmates—probably those who were most compatible.)

Attitudes were *not* more negative when schoolmates of the other race were more ethnocentric. (Among whites, in fact, attitudes toward black schoolmates were slightly more positive where black schoolmates, on the average, were more ethnocentric.) It may be that the racial ideology of students, as reflected on the ethnocentrism measure, had little effect on their overt behavior which was visible to those of the other race.

Finally, a number of factors did *not* have significant effects on the attitudes of either black or white students toward their other-race schoolmates. Some of these—e.g., the racial composition of students' classes and participation in school activities—already have been mentioned. Additional nonsignificant variables are indicated in the body and footnotes of Tables 9.1 and 9.2.

Overall, interracial attitudes appear to be affected most by those factors which lead to social approval for given attitudes, to positive or negative feelings toward people in general, to making personal interaction with the other race more or less pleasant, and to resentment about the way in which one's own racial group is treated in the school.

Opinion Change

The factors which were related to change in opinion of other-race people are relatively few (see Tables 9.1 and 9.2). Among blacks, positive racial attitudes by the family (as reported by students) was the best predictor of positive change in the students' racial attitudes during high school. Family racial attitudes also helped to predict opinion change among white students, but more weakly. On the other hand, among whites, but not among blacks, greater ethnocentrism among peers contributed to less positive change in opinions of the other race.

It appears, thus, that racial attitudes of students change in the direction of the attitudes of their important reference groups. This may be, in part, because they interpret the actions of other-race people in terms of the preconceptions of their reference groups. It also may reflect the effect over time of continual rewards for expressing the "right" opinions.

Personal characteristics of students also affected opinion change. Among blacks, general satisfaction with life, which was one of the best predictors of attitudes toward white schoolmates, also had a relatively strong effect on change in opinions of whites. Those who were generally more satisfied with their life circumstances reported more positive change in their opinions of whites. Thus, among black students, opinion change—like racial attitudes—seems to be influenced by individuals' general affective moods.

Among whites, general satisfaction did not contribute to change in racial opinions. However, several other personal characteristics did have significant—though quite small—effects. White girls reported slightly more positive changes in opinions of blacks than did white boys. This may be due to the greater incidence of unfriendly interracial contacts among white boys. Also, whites of higher IQ and whites of high socioeconomic status, relative to black schoolmates, reported slightly *less* positive changes in opinions of blacks. It may be that the brighter and the more high-status whites were most serious about school and therefore were most disappointed by what many white students saw to be playful or disruptive behavior by some blacks.

The racial composition of classes affected opinion change among black students. Blacks whose classes had a substantial proportion of blacks (40 to 90%) changed their opinion of white people more positively than those whose classes were more heavily white. It may be that black students felt more comfortable when they were not a minority and therefore enjoyed association with whites more in those circumstances. Perhaps more importantly, white students were less aloof from blacks when blacks were a majority (see Chapter 7). More friendly, equalitarian behavior by whites in the majority-black settings—perhaps beyond many blacks' initial expectations—probably contributed to a positive shift in the racial opinions of the blacks. However, the racial composition of classes did not have a significant effect on opinion change among white students.

These results indicate that, despite the fact that greater opportunity for interracial contact leads to more friendly interracial contacts, it does not necessarily bring more positive opinion change. Also, somewhat surprisingly, participation in school activities, which contributed strongly to friendly interracial contact, had no significant effect on opinion change among students of either race. Nor did participation in interracial task subgroups in classes have a significant effect on change in racial opinions.

Why did greater opportunity for interracial contact, which led to more friendly interracial contact, not lead also to positive change in opinion of other-race people? It may be that the friendly interracial contacts which students have in activities and classes often lead them to form positive attitudes only toward the particular schoolmates with whom they interact. Such favorable attitudes may be generalized very little to the entire group of other-race students in that school, and still less to "most (other-race) people," about whom the opinion-change question asks. Such a restriction of attitude change to the immediate situation has been found in a number of studies of interracial contact in work and neighborhood settings (e.g., Minard, 1952; Meer and Freedman, 1966).

However, additional results (not presented in Tables 9.1 and 9.2) show that students who had more friendly interracial contact (and less unfriendly contact) did tend to change their opinions of other-race people for the better.[5]

Thus, greater opportunity for interracial contact probably has an indirect effect on opinion change by contributing to more friendly contact.[6] But, partly because of its indirect nature, the net effect of opportunity for contact on opinion change is small and nonsignificant.

Another set of variables which did appear to have an impact on opinion change were students' perceptions of the school situation. The perceptions which were related to racial attitudes generally were related also to change in racial opinions, though somewhat less strongly. Perceptions of favoritism by school staff (among blacks), perceptions of greater power by blacks than by whites (among whites), and perceptions of inadequate attention to student problems by school authorities (among both blacks and whites) were associated with less positive change in attitudes toward other-race people. These results suggest again that contentment or resentment about the way the school is run, particularly with regard to handling of racial problems, may affect students' broader racial attitudes. Students who feel they are treated unfairly, especially vis-à-vis the other race, may come to dislike not only the authorities but members of the other race as well.

Finally, we may note some additional factors which had *no* significant effect on opinion change among students of either race (when other relevant factors were controlled). These include the amount of opportunity for contact with black teachers; the level of ethnocentrism of other-race schoolmates; and students' grades, relative to those of other-race schoolmates. Other variables which had no significant effects on opinion change are indicated in the body and footnotes of Tables 9.1 and 9.2.

Overall, change in opinions of other-race people during high school appears to be determined most by those factors which (1) provide social approval for positive or negative opinion change; (2) make the behavior of students and staff of the other race more pleasant (or unpleasant) than expected; and (3) affect students' general moods of satisfaction or dissatisfaction.

Variance Accounted For

For how much of the total variance in interracial behaviors and attitudes have we been able to account? The proportions of variance explained statistically (see Tables 9.1 and 9.2) are modest. Among black students, our analyses account for about one-fifth to one-fourth of the variance in different interracial behaviors. Among white students, a little more of the variance in the different behaviors—from about one-fifth to almost one-third—is accounted for. For students of both races, our analyses account for 39% of the variance in attitudes toward other-race schoolmates, but only 15% of the variance in reported change in opinion of other-race people in general.

Why do our analyses not account for larger proportions of the total variance? First, there is undoubtedly a good deal of measurement error in these data, as there is in most data of this type. For example, while we tried to measure the amount of friendly interracial interaction with care, problems of covering different types of friendly contact, wording of questions, weighting of items, respondent carelessness in answering, etc., mean that the score we gave each student is only an approximation of the amount of friendly interaction he/she actually had during the semester.

Since our data are for individuals, rather than group averages, the measurement errors among individuals do not "average out."

Secondly, our statistical procedures do not fit the results with precision. While we have attempted to take account of major instances of nonlinearity and interactions in relationships (see above), undoubtedly there remains some nonlinearity and some interaction among predictors which our statistical techniques do not capture.

Third, although we have included in these analyses a fairly large number of possible determinants of interracial attitudes and behaviors, we have (sometimes intentionally) not included all possible determinants. Certain omissions, in particular, deserve attention.

Since these analyses focused on individuals, characteristics of schools as units—e.g., rapidity of change in racial proportions—were not included as predictors. We assumed that such school-level characteristics would have their impact on individual students through their impact on the personal experiences and perceptions which we did include. For example, amount of change in racial proportions might affect the level of peer ethnocentrism or perceptions of relative power, which in turn might affect behaviors or attitudes. However, some of the impact of school-level variables may not have been "caught" in these analyses. (Information about the effects of school-level variables is included in Chapters 5 through 8.)

In addition, although these analyses include a measure of the ethnocentrism of other-race schoolmates, they do not include any measure of the behavior of other-race students toward each respondent. We had each student's reports of a variety of unfriendly actions by the other race—e.g., threats, insults (see Chapter 4)—but we could not be sure to what extent such actions by other-race schoolmates might have been a reaction to the student's own interracial attitudes and behavior. Thus, to avoid confounding cause and effect, we omitted this measure of actions by the other race as a predictor of students' own interracial attitudes and behavior.

We also did not include some of the social outcomes we were studying as predictors of other social outcomes. For example, although unfriendly contact with other-race schoolmates is correlated with avoidance of these schoolmates, we did not include unfriendly contact among the predictors of avoidance. Similarly, friendly interracial contact and unfriendly interracial contact were not included among the predictors of change in opinion of other-race people, although each is correlated with opinion change. Nor were attitudes toward other-race schoolmates included as predictors of behavior toward other-race schoolmates, despite the fact that attitudes and behavior are substantially related.

The reason for these intentional omissions is simply that we could not have any confidence that one social outcome was a cause of another, rather than being an effect of it, or both being effects of third factors. For example, unfriendly contacts with other-race schoolmates may be a consequence of negative attitudes toward the other race or may lead to negative attitudes. To take another example, while friendly contact may produce positive opinion change, the reverse equally can be true.

We preferred to focus on predictors which appear to be, more clearly, causes of students' interracial attitudes and behaviors. However, it would be desirable for future studies—especially those of a longitudinal or experimental nature—to attempt to trace the causal relations among the various interracial attitudes and behavior. In addition to its intrinsic interest, such research should help to increase the amount of explained variance in such outcomes.

What we have said in this section should give the reader an appreciation of some of the limitations of the present study, which may help to account for the limited power of our analyses to explain all the variation in students' interracial behavior and attitudes. At the same time, we would suggest that these limitations should not lead the reader to overlook the strengths of these analyses. While we have not included all possible determinants of social relations between the races, nor measured them all perfectly, these analyses do provide information about the relative importance of many aspects of students' backgrounds, personal characteristics, and the school situation. They also provide what is perhaps the first research information about the relative importance of these varied predictors for a variety of *behavioral* as well as attitudinal outcomes. Moreover, despite the limited amount of variance explained, the patterns of association found appear quite meaningful and have important policy implications. The implications are considered in the concluding chapter of the book.

Summary

In this chapter we have considered the relative impact of many situational and personal factors on students' relationships with schoolmates of another race. We found that those factors which had the greatest impact differed for different social outcomes.

Avoidance of other-race schoolmates was affected most by (1) negative racial attitudes of important others; (2) personal characteristics of students—especially being generally aggressive and being male; (3) unfriendly (or no) previous experience with the other race; and (4) being in a minority (for blacks) and seeing the other race as more powerful (for whites). (For blacks, the combination of a lack of friendly early experiences and being a minority in classes was especially apt to lead to avoidance.)

These factors probably led to interracial avoidance mainly because they led students to anticipate that contact with schoolmates of the other race would be unpleasant. Some of these factors seemed to be related especially to blacks' expectations of rejection by whites and to whites' expectations of physical attack by blacks. In addition, these factors (especially negative attitudes by others) probably led students to anticipate that contact with the other race would bring social disapproval.

Friendly contact with schoolmates of another race was affected most strongly by (1) friendly prior contact, in grade school and neighborhood; (2) positive racial attitudes by the student's family; (3) more opportunity for interracial contact in high school, combined (for whites) with positive racial attitudes among peers; and (4) participation in classroom and extracurricular activities in which students cooperate toward common goals. For blacks, high effort in school and high educational aspirations also contributed to friendship with whites.

These factors probably help promote friendly interaction between the races because they help provide students with interracial experiences which are rewarding to them and lead them to expect further friendly contacts to be rewarding. In addition, these factors help students to learn friendly patterns of behavior and lead them to expect that friendly contacts will be approved by others.

Unfriendly contact with other-race schoolmates was affected most strongly by the personal characteristics of students. Males and those who were most generally aggressive were most likely to have unfriendly interracial contacts. These results suggest that, while interracial fighting often may have a racial aspect, those who are most involved are those who fight most often generally.

However, negative racial attitudes by students' families and (for whites) by peers and teachers also contributed to unfriendly interracial contact. The racial attitudes of others probably affected especially the extent to which students expected approval or disapproval for fighting with those of the other race.

In addition, among whites, unfriendly neighborhood contact with blacks prior to high school contributed to more contact, and especially unfriendly contact, with blacks in high school. Such unfriendly early contact may have made whites more hostile to the blacks they met in high school and perhaps taught them unfriendly types of behavior.

Attitudes toward schoolmates of the other race were affected most strongly by (1) the racial attitudes of important others—especially family and peers; (2) characteristics of students (general satisfaction and aggressiveness) which appear to affect students' general feelings toward other people; (3) characteristics of students (IQ among blacks, sex among whites) which appear to affect the pleasantness of interaction with the other race; and (4) aspects of the school situation which bear on whether students of one's own race are seen to be receiving fair treatment (by the staff or by the other racial group). Among blacks, the degree of perceived supportiveness by school staff, especially racial favoritism, affected attitudes toward white students. Among whites, perceptions of the relative power of blacks in the school affected attitudes toward black schoolmates. In both cases, perceptions by those of one racial group that it was not receiving proper treatment apparently led to resentment of the other group.

Finally, *change in opinion of other-race people* was affected by several student characteristics and several aspects of the school situation. Among blacks, being in classes which were *not* predominately white and seeing the school staff as supportive in a number of ways contributed to positive change in opinion of white people. Blacks in these circumstances probably saw the behavior of whites as being more positive than they expected.

Among whites, having a high IQ and a high SES, relative to blacks, both contributed to having less positive opinions of black people. These "elite" whites may have been most serious about their school work and may have been disappointed by the unconventional school behavior of some blacks.

Among whites, males and those who saw blacks as more powerful than whites in the school also tended to change their opinions of blacks in a negative way. These whites probably found blacks threatening and their actual or anticipated contacts with blacks more unpleasant than they had expected.

This chapter concludes the third major section, which has considered the determinants of interracial behavior and attitudes in the schools. In the final chapter of the book, we will summarize the findings presented in this section and will draw a number of policy implications from them. Before doing so, however, we will consider the other major topic of our investigation—academic outcomes for students and the effects of interracial contact on such outcomes. In the next chapter, we consider the ways in which academic outcomes differed for blacks as compared to whites.

Interracial Contact and Academic Outcomes

10 | *Race and Academic Performance*

Studies extending over several decades have found fairly consistently that the average black student and the average white student differs on measures of academic achievement. White students, on the average, do better than black students and the differences found usually have been substantial (Coleman et al., 1966; St. John, 1975; Weinberg, 1977).

In this chapter, we will describe the academic performance of black students and of white students in the Indianapolis high schools. In doing so, we will examine the extent of differences between the two racial groups and the variations within each group.

We will also compare black students and white students, as well as students within each racial group, with respect to psychological variables which often have been thought to be closely related to academic performance. These include prior cognitive abilities (IQ), values, expectancies of success, educational and occupational aspirations, effort, and feelings toward peers and teachers. In addition to describing between-race and within-race differences on these subjective variables, we will examine the extent of their associations with academic performance.

The primarily descriptive results presented in this chapter will provide a context for the analyses to be presented in the next two chapters.[1] There we will consider the issue of how interracial contact in the school affects academic performance and how interracial contact affects some of the variables related to performance (e.g., values and effort) described in this chapter.

Academic Performance

We have two types of measures of students' academic performance—standardized achievement tests and grades. Students' grades tended to be consistent with their scores on achievement tests, but this association was far from perfect.[2]

Both achievement test scores and grades have advantages as measures of academic performance. Standardized achievement scores have the important advantage of being comparable among students throughout a school system and comparable also among students throughout the country. However, achievement tests reflect performance at one particular point in time, may be affected by differences in test-taking ability and motivation, and may not always test the material taught in particular schools and classes.

In contrast, a student's grades are based on performance over an extended period of time, often are based on several kinds of performance (e.g., class recitation, homework papers, and tests), and are tied more directly to the material taught in the student's own classes. On the other hand, since the material taught and standards of grading may differ, grades of students with different teachers, those in different schools, and those in different school systems may not be strictly comparable.

Achievement Tests. Let us consider first the results on standardized achievement tests. Both national and local studies have shown that black students, on the average, score consistently far below the average for white students throughout the United States. The average score for blacks usually is about one standard deviation below those of whites. This means that about 85% of black students (as compared to 50% of white students) score below the white average (e.g., Sewell, 1967).

How about the students in the Indianapolis high schools? How did the achievement scores of black students and of white students compare? To answer this question, we used scores obtained by students on standardized achievement tests given nationally. Most students in our sample took such achievement tests during their sophomore year of high school. Students who were seniors or juniors at the time of our study had taken previously the National Educational Development Tests (NEDT). Students who were sophomores or freshmen at the time of our study took the Metropolitan Achievement Tests (MAT) (the sophomores during that same year and the freshman during the next year).

The National Educational Development Tests include five tests: (1) English Usage, (2) Mathematics Usage, (3) Social Studies Reading, (4) Natural Sciences Reading, and (5) Word Usage. According to the test manual, "The questions tend not to ask for specific recall of information; instead they probe the student's capability for understanding the kinds of material he might encounter later in his education" (Science Research Associates, 1969, p. 8). A composite score, which is the average of the five test scores, and which "can be viewed as an index of total educational development" (S.R.A., 1969, p. 3), was computed by the testers. The composite NEDT score for each student is expressed in percentile terms, indicating how well he did in comparison to other students at his grade level throughout the nation.

The Metropolitan Achievement Tests, taken by freshmen and sophomores, include eleven tests, which fall into four major divisions: (1)

Language Arts: Reading, Spelling, Language (word usage, punctuation, etc.); Language Study Skills (use of dictionary, etc.); (2) *Social Studies:* Social Studies Study Skills (reading of maps, tables, etc.); Social Studies Vocabulary; Social Studies Information; (3) *Mathematics:* Mathematical Computation and Concepts; Mathematical Analysis and Problem-Solving; and (4) *Science:* Scientific Concepts and Understandings; Science Information. The authors of the tests say that they have striven to develop tests "that measure what students have actually been taught. The tests are based on thorough-going analyses of current textbooks, courses of study, and expert formulations of the goals of instruction in the various subject areas" (Durost et al., 1964, p. 3).

The MAT scores were obtained from the schools in percentile form, indicating how well each student did on each of the eleven tests in comparison to other students at his grade level throughout the nation. Using the percentile score for each of the eleven tests, we computed a composite MAT achievement score for each student. To compute this composite MAT score, we first converted each percentile score to a stanine score, in order to make the scores for different tests more comparable.[3] Next, an average stanine score in each of the four major subject areas (language, social studies, mathematics, and science) was computed. Finally, an average stanine score for all four subject areas was computed for each student. These final scores are the composite MAT scores for freshmen and sophomores.

A summary of the composite scores of black students and of white students in our sample on these achievement tests is shown in Table 10.1.A and 10.1.B. These data show that the distribution of scores among both black upperclassmen (NEDT tests) and black lowerclassmen (MAT tests) was considerably different than the distribution of scores among their white classmates. Much larger proportions of black students scored below the national average, many being far below average. Relatively small proportions of black students scored above the national average.

Table 10.1. Academic Performance of Students, by Race[1]

	Blacks	Whites
A. Metropolitan Achievement Tests, Average Stanine Score (Freshmen and Sophomores)[2]		
1.00 to 2.99 (far below average)	43.2%	14.6%
3.00 to 4.49 (below average)	35.8	28.7
4.50 to 5.49 (average)	13.2	20.6
5.50 to 6.99 (above average)	7.4	24.6
7.00 to 9.0 (far above average)	0.3	11.5
Mean Score	3.4	4.9
(*N*)	(685)	(829)

Continued

Table 10.1 *Continued*

	Blacks	**Whites**
B. National Educational Development Tests, Composite Percentile Score (Juniors and Seniors)		
0–19.99 (far below average)	36.5%	11.9%
20.00–39.99 (below average)	32.5	19.3
40.00–59.99 (average)	16.6	20.2
60.00–79.99 (above average)	8.4	19.1
80.00–100.00 (far above average)	6.0	29.5
Mean Score	32.6	56.8
(*N*)	(665)	(885)
C. Current Semester Grade Average[3]		
2.99 or less (D or less)	35.1%	20.2%
3.00–3.99 (C−)	20.6	15.3
4.00–4.99 (C+)	22.0	23.4
5.00–5.99 (B−)	12.3	17.1
6.00–6.99 (B+)	7.4	14.2
7.00 or more (A)	2.6	9.8
Mean Score	3.60	4.45
(*N*)	(2,247)	(2,529)
D. Cumulative High School Grade Average[3]		
3.00 or less (D or less)	36.4%	17.4%
3.01–3.99 (C−)	24.7	19.8
4.00–4.99 (C+)	22.1	24.4
5.00–5.99 (B−)	11.2	17.6
6.00–6.99 (B+)	4.3	13.0
7.00–8.00 (A)	1.3	7.8
Mean Score	3.6	4.6
(*N*)	(1,914)	(2,200)

1. Percentages may not add to exactly 100% because of rounding.
2. A stanine is a value on a simple nine-point scale of normalized standard scores. Conversion to stanine scores when averaging MAT test results is recommended by test authors.
3. Grades were assigned scores as follows: A = 8, B = 6, C = 4, D = 2, F = 0.

The average black upperclassman (junior or senior) scored at about the 33rd percentile on the NEDT tests; that is, about 33% of American students in the same grade scored lower than, and about 67% scored higher than, the average black in our sample. White juniors and seniors, on the average, scored about 24 percentile points higher than the average black in their grades. The average white upperclassman scored at about the 57th percentile nationally—i.e., above the national average.

The average MAT stanine score for black lowerclassmen (freshmen and sophomores) was 3.4, which was above about 30%, and below about 70%, of the scores of all American students in their grades. The average white lowerclassman had a stanine score of 4.9 on the MAT tests, which was just a shade below the average national score of 5.

Thus, the results from two different batteries of standardized achievement tests—one taken by lowerclassmen and one by upperclassmen—are consistent in showing a large average difference in academic achievement between black students and white students in the Indianapolis high schools. When the results were looked at separately for each school, the differences in achievement scores between blacks and whites were highly significant in every school.

While there was a large average difference between blacks and whites, there also was considerable variation in achievement scores within each racial group. Among black upperclassmen, about one student out of six scored close to the national average and about one student in seven scored above the national average. Among black lowerclassmen, about one student in five scored in about the average range or above.

Achievement scores also varied significantly among students in different schools (see Appendix E). On the MAT tests (on which we will focus our later analysis), average stanine scores for blacks ranged from 4.4 at Highland to 2.4 at John Price. White students' average MAT scores ranged from 6.3 at Highland to 3.3 at John Price. Within each racial group at each school, variation in MAT scores also was considerable. Typically, the standard deviation was over one stanine unit among blacks in each school and about one and a half stanine units among whites in each school.

Grades. Next we look at variations in students' grades (see Table 10.1.C and 10.1.D). As in the case of achievement test scores, the grade distribution of black students differed substantially from that of their white schoolmates. Larger proportions of blacks than of whites had grade averages at the low end of the scale (about D or C−) while larger proportions of whites had relatively high grade averages (about B+ and A). The average current and cumulative grades for black students (about C−) were significantly lower than the average grades for whites (about C+). More detailed data (not presented here) show that the average grades of blacks were significantly lower than those of their white schoolmates in every school—with the exception of Pershing, where there was a very small number of blacks.[4]

While the grades of black students were consistently lower than those of whites in the same school, there also was significant variation in the average grade of each racial group at the various schools (see Appendix E). For blacks, average current grades ranged from 3.0 (between C and D) at Harrison to 4.5 (above C) at Lakeview. For whites, average current grades ranged from 3.8 (below C) at Harrison to 5.0 (between C and B) at Lakeview and at Highland.

Variations in grades for individual students also were substantial, both within each school and for the total samples. For students in all schools combined, 35% of all blacks had grade averages of D or less for the current semester but 22% had averages of B− or higher. For all whites combined, 41% had grade averages of B− or higher, but 20% had averages of D or less.

Cognitive Abilities prior to High School (IQ)

The academic performance of students in high school may be influenced by the cognitive abilities—e.g., language concepts, mathematical concepts, logical reasoning, memory—which they have developed prior to high school. As a measure of students' cognitive development prior to high school, we make use of their scores on IQ tests. While IQ scores were developed as a measure of intelligence (the letters are an abbreviation for "Intelligence Quotient"), it is incorrect to think of them as primarily a measure of "native" intellectual ability. Rather, IQ tests measure important cognitive abilities which may be affected by a variety of influences (Honzik, 1973; Leohlin et al., 1975). These include innate learning ability (which is unlikely to differ among racial or ethnic groups), nutritional adequacy, early stimulation of language in the home, and the quality of early learning experiences in school. The abilities measured by IQ tests are not identical to those measured by standardized achievement tests but they require some of the same basic language and mathematical abilities.

A large majority of students in our sample took an IQ test, called the California Test of Mental Maturity, when they were in the eighth grade.[5] We view these scores as a standardized measure of students' general cognitive abilities shortly before they entered high school.

How did black students and white students compare in the general skills measured by IQ tests, just prior to entering high school? Table 10.2 shows that, consistent with studies in other schools and regions (Shuey, 1966), there was a large difference in the distribution of IQ scores between the races. Much larger proportions of blacks were below the overall population average and much larger proportions of whites were above the overall population average. The average IQ score for blacks was 88.7 and the average score for whites was 102.5, a different of almost one standard deviation for each group. This large difference in average IQ scores between the races parallels the large differences in achievement scores and in grades which we saw earlier. This parallel suggests that the average racial differences in achievement in high school probably are, to a large extent, due to a difference in the level of cognitive skills which students had at the time they entered high school.

There also was a good deal of variation in IQ scores within each racial group. Among blacks, the modal IQ score was in the 70–85 range and 11% of all blacks scored under 70. However, about a third of all black students had IQ scores at about the national average (96–105) or higher and about 4% of all blacks scored above 115.

Among whites, there was no clear modal tendency. Almost seven out of ten whites scored at about the national average or higher and 24%

Table 10.2. Distribution of IQ Scores, by Race[1]

IQ Score	Blacks	Whites
Under 70	11.0%	3.9%
70–85	32.3	11.9
86–95	24.5	15.3
96–105	18.1	22.8
106–115	10.3	22.2
Over 115	3.8	23.9
Mean	88.7	102.5
(N)	(1,867)	(2,134)

1. See note 5 of text for description of IQ tests taken.

scored over 115. At the other extreme, about 4% of all white students had IQ scores below 70.

To what extent were IQ scores related to academic performance in high school? Table 10.7 shows that, among freshmen and sophomores of each racial group, there was a strong relationship between a student's IQ score and his score on the standardized achievement test (MAT) taken as a sophomore in high school. For blacks, the correlation of IQs with achievement test scores was .74. For whites, the correlation was .83. These results mean that over half of the differences in achievement scores among blacks, and about two-thirds of the differences among whites, can be accounted for by the level of cognitive skills (IQ) which students had acquired prior to high school. Correlations between IQ scores and NEDT achievement scores among juniors and seniors (not shown) are very similar to those shown for the lowerclassmen.[6] Correlations between IQ scores and current high school grades (shown in Table 10.7) were much smaller but also were substantial, especially among whites. The associations between students' IQ scores and these measures of their academic performance are changed only very slightly when we control for student's current effort in high school. The associations between IQ and performance measures also remain substantial, though somewhat reduced, when a variety of other factors concerning home background, personal characteristics, the school situation, and interracial contact were held constant (see Chapters 11 and 12). Thus, prior cognitive abilities had a marked effect on academic performance in high school even when other variables which may affect performance are taken into account.

The strong association between IQ scores and achievement test scores probably reflects the fact that both kinds of tests tend to measure the same kinds of general attitudes—e.g., English-language abilities, mathematical abilities. In addition, the kinds of general abilities measured by IQ tests undoubtedly help the student to master some of the more specific skills measured by achievement tests. General cognitive abilities also would help some students to get better grades.

Values and Aspirations

Students' performance in school may be affected also by the extent to which they value doing well in school. Some writers have suggested that low academic performance among black students may be due in part to their not sharing the white middle-class values of success in school (e.g., Pettigrew, 1969; Spady, 1976).

To assess the extent to which students valued academic success, each student was asked to rate (on a three-point scale) how important each of a number of outcomes was to him. These included: (1) my getting good grades, (2) my getting a good education, and (3) my being able to go to college. Table 10.3.I shows that these academic goals were rated as very important by a majority of students of both races. On each of the three items, black students were somewhat more likely than white students to rate the academic goal as very important to them.

Related to students' academic values are their aspirations regarding further education and the type of occupation they would like to enter.[7]

Table 10.3. Academic Values and Aspirations, by Race (Percentages)[1]

	Blacks	Whites
I. **Stated Importance of:**		
A. Getting good grades		
Very important to me	74%	61%
Fairly important to me	22	33
Not too important to me	4	6
B. My getting a good education		
Very important to me	84%	75%
Fairly important to me	13	22
Not too important to me	4	3
C. My being able to go to college		
Very important to me	65%	53%
Fairly important to me	22	23
Not too important to me	14	24
II. **Highest Schooling** **Student Would Like**		
Leave high school before finishing	1%	2%
Finish high school	18	23
Vocational, technical, or business school	26	24
Junior or community college	8	5
Four-year college	36	32
Graduate or professional school	12	14

Continued

Table 10.3. *Continued*

III. Occupation Which Student Would Like to Enter (1st Choice)

Highest prestige	22%	26%
(Professional; business exec.)		
Second-level prestige	32	28
(e.g., semiprofessional; technician; own business; business manager)		
Third-level prestige	38	33
(e.g., office or clerical; skilled trade; salesman; athletics)		
Fourth-level prestige	6	7
(e.g., semiskilled or unskilled; salesclerk)		
Prestige not determinable	3	6

1. Percentages for each item may not add to exactly 100 percent because of rounding. *N*s are about 1,800 for blacks and about 2,200 for whites; exact *N* varies with number of cases with missing data for each item.

With respect to education, we asked students: "How far would you *like* to go in school?" The answers of black students and of white students were similar, with blacks wanting slightly more schooling than whites (see Table 10.3.II). Only 19% of blacks and 25% of whites wanted no more schooling beyond high school. Forty-eight percent of blacks and 46% of whites said they would like to go to a four-year college or beyond. (The rest wanted more limited schooling after high school.)

We also asked students: "How clear an idea do you have right now of what kind of work you would *really like* to do in your later life?" For those who had at least some idea about this, we asked: "What kind(s) of work do you have in mind?" Occupations mentioned were grouped into four prestige categories on the basis of the prestige accorded them by the general American population (Hodge, Siegel, and Rossi, 1966).

The data (see Table 10.3.III) show that, just as the educational aspirations of black students and white students were very similar, so too were their occupational aspirations. Twenty-six percent of whites and 22% of blacks said they would like to go into an occupation in the highest prestige category. Almost all of these students named a professional occupation. Thirty-two percent of all black students and 28 percent of all whites mentioned an occupation at the second prestige level. Semiprofessional occupations (e.g., nurse, interior decorator, newspaper reporter) and technician jobs (e.g., draftsman, X-ray technician, and computer programmer) were the type of jobs at this second prestige level which were most often mentioned by students of both races.

One-third of all white students and somewhat over one-third of all black students said they would like to go into jobs classified at the third level of prestige. Occupations in this grouping which were most often mentioned by students of both races were office or clerical work and skilled trades. Some black students also chose athletics, modeling, or fashion work.

Only a small percentage of blacks and of whites (6% and 7% respectively) mentioned any of the semiskilled or unskilled jobs which were classified at the lowest level of occupational prestige. Finally, a small percentage of both races mentioned other activities (e.g., housewife, armed forces, with rank unspecified) which could not be classified with respect to occupational prestige.

The similiarity of blacks and whites with respect to values and aspirations indicates that the large racial differences in achievement scores and grades cannot be accounted by differences on these variables. However, within each racial group, variations in values and aspirations were related to variations in academic performance. Table 10.7 shows these relationships.

Among students of both races, the higher the student's academic values and aspirations, the higher his achievement scores and the higher his grades. It seems likely that the more important academic success is to a student, the harder he will try in school, which will tend to raise his performance.[8] The causal process may operate in the other direction as well. Those students who do better in school may come to value further success more and develop higher educational and occupational goals. A third possibility is that certain student characteristics (e.g., higher social class) will tend to lead directly both to valuing academic success and to higher academic performance. Probably all three processes play a part in producing the positive associations between students' academic values and aspirations and their academic performance.

Table 10.7 also shows that values and aspirations were more closely related to grades and to achievement test scores among whites than among blacks. This may indicate that whites adjusted their aspirations to fit their academic performance more readily than did blacks. Also, whites may have been more successful than blacks in achieving the level of academic performance that was consistent with their aspirations. The wide gap between aspirations and performance found often among blacks may lead to serious problems for these students. They may find that their grades and standardized test scores do not permit them to go to college and eventually to get the kind of jobs they would like.

Expectancy of Success

While motivation and effort depend in part on the value which a student places on doing well in school, it also may be affected by his expectancy of being able to succeed (Katz, 1968; O'Connor, Atkinson, and Horner, 1966; Rotter, Chance, and Phares, 1972).

Unfortunately, we did not ask students about their expectancy of being able to get good grades if they tried. However, we did ask students how likely they thought it was that they could fulfill the educational and occupational desires they had indicated.

With respect to education, the question was as follows: "Sometimes there are problems that prevent people from going as far in school as they would like. How good would you say your chances are to go as far in school as you would like?" The student was asked to check one of five choices, from "my chances are very good" to "I'm pretty sure I won't be able to go as far as I'd like."

The answers to this question for black students and for white students are shown in Table 10.4.A. Whites were slightly more optimistic about their educational chances, but the differences between the races were slight. A substantial majority of each racial group thought their chances to go as far in school as they'd like were "very good" or "pretty good." Only about one in eight of each racial group judged his chances to be "not very good" or very poor.

Table 10.4. Expectancies of Success, by Race[1]

	Blacks	Whites
A. Perceived Chances to Go as Far in School as Would Like		
Very good	25%	30%
Pretty good	34	35
About 50-50	31	23
Not very good	7	9
Pretty sure that won't be able to go as far as would like	5	3
B. Perceived Chance to Get the Kind of Job Student Would Like		
Pretty sure	34%	39%
Probably	34	35
Chances are not good, but some chance	17	13
Very little chance	2	2
Don't know	13	11

1. Percentages for each item may not add to exactly 100% because of rounding. *N*s are about 1,800 for blacks and about 2,200 for whites; exact *N* varies with number of cases with missing data for each item.

With respect to students' occupational choice, after the student had written in the kind(s) of work he would like to do, he was asked: "What do you think your chances are of getting the kind of job you mentioned (as first choice)?" The student could check one of four categories, from "I am pretty sure I can get this kind of job" to "I have very little chance of getting it." He also could check "I don't know what my chances are."

Students' answers to this question, separately for blacks and for whites, are shown in Table 10.4.B. As in the case of expectancies for reaching educational goals, white students were more optimistic about their chances, but the racial differences were slight. Large majorities of both blacks and whites said they were "pretty sure" to or "can probably" get the kind of job they had chosen. Fewer than one in five of each racial group said their chances were not good. Overall, the expectancies of blacks about being able to fulfill both their educational and occupational desires were only slightly less optimistic than those of their white schoolmates.

Were the generally optimistic expectations of black students justified? We have noted already the sizable racial differences in grades and achievement scores. In addition, whites were much more likely to be taking courses which prepared them for college. In all schools combined, 39% of the white students, but only 19% of the black students, were enrolled in the academic program or (for lowerclassmen) planned to take "academic-type courses." Thus, while blacks and whites had similar educational and occupational desires, and similar expectancies of fulfilling these desires, realistically the chances for white students actually to go to college and to enter high-prestige, high-income occupations were much greater.

We also may consider the extent to which differences *within* each racial group with respect to expectancies of success were related to differences in academic performance. To examine this issue, we divided students of each race into two categories with respect to their educational aspirations—those who wanted to go to a four-year college (or beyond) and those who wanted less education. We also separated for analysis those students who aspired to a higher-prestige occupation (categories 1 or 2) and those who aspired to a lower-prestige occupation.

The results (see Table 10.7) show that among students of both races who wanted to go to college (and for whom achievement in high school was, therefore, important), the better chance the student saw for fulfilling this wish, the higher his current grades and his achievement scores tended to be. The correlations are small but—especially for grades—not trivial. Among students who did not want to go to a four-year college, the associations between expectations of fulfilling one's educational aspirations and academic performance were positive but weaker than for those who aspired to college.

The results concerning expectations of fulfilling occupational aspirations are similar. Among students of both races who aspired to a higher-prestige occupation, the greater the student's expectancy of being able to enter his chosen occupation, the higher his grades and achievement scores tended to be. Among students whose occupational aspirations were lower, students' expectations about being able to fulfill their aspirations had less association with academic performance. Generally, academic performance was correlated somewhat less strongly with expectations of occupational success than with expectations of educational success.

It is not possible to know from these results what the causal direction of the associations was. Students who see a good chance to reach their goals may try harder and therefore get better grades and do better on achievement tests.[9] Conversely, the better a student finds he is doing in school, the better he may believe his chances are to go to college and to enter a high-prestige occupation. Probably there is a two-way relationship between these variables. Also, both expectations of success and academic performance may be affected directly by the student's background or school situation (e.g., his social class and his school program).

Effort

Having looked at several subjective factors (values, aspirations, and expectancies) which may affect the amount of effort students devote to their school work, we now consider some more direct evidence concerning student motivation and effort. As an indicator of students' interest in their school work, we asked: "In how many of your classes this semester does time seem to drag for you?" (five response categories, from "in all my classes" to "in none of my classes"). Evidence from a previous study indicates that the extent to which people feel that time "drags" is a reliable and valid indicator of motivation on the job (Patchen, 1965). It seems reasonable that a similar question may be an indicator of student motivation.

A summary of the responses to this question is shown in Table 10.5.I. Almost two-thirds of all students said that time seemed to drag in less than half of their classes. The responses of black students and of white students did not indicate any substantial difference in interest. Answers to another item concerning what proportion of teachers "make class interesting" also show little difference between the races (data not shown).

With respect to effort, we have a number of indicators. These include: time spent on homework, completing homework, absence from school, being late to class, and missing class without permission. Our data on these matters were obtained from the questionnaires given to the students, with the exception of absence data, which were obtained both from student reports and from school records.

A summary of the data on student effort, separately for blacks and whites, is shown in Table 10.5.II. These data show considerable variation among students of each race with respect to time spent on homework, frequency of not completing one's homework, absence from school, and frequency of being late to class. The great majority of students rarely, if ever, missed a class without permission.

Black students and white students differed substantially only with respect to lateness. Black students reported being late for class much more frequently than did white students. Blacks also tended to report spending less time on homework (though they reported completing their homework just as often); tended to be absent from school more often; and tended to report missing a class without permission more often than whites. However, all of these differences between the races—with the exception of the lateness item—were quite small.

Table 10.5. Indicators of Student Interest and Effort, by Race[1]

	Blacks	Whites
I. Interest		
Number of Classes in Which		
"Time Seems to Drag"		
All or most	25%	21%
About half	12	15
One or two or none	63	64
II. Effort		
A. Number of Recorded Absences		
during Current Semester		
0–2	23%	27%
3–5	22	22
6–10	22	21
11–15	13	13
16–20	7	6
over 20	13	11
B. Time Spent per Day on Homework[2]		
One-half hour or less	38%	32%
About one hour	23	25
One and a half hours or more	39	42
C. Being Late to Class[2]		
Once or twice a week or more	45%	24%
Once every few weeks	16	14
Once a month or less often	38	63
D. Missing a Class without Permission[2]		
Once or twice a week or more	12%	8%
Once every few weeks	7	6
Once a month or less often	82	87
E. Not Getting All Homework Done[2]		
Once or twice a week or more	40%	40%
Once every few weeks	18	21
Once a month or less often	41	39

1. Percentages for each item may not add to exactly 100% because of rounding. *N*s are about 1,950 for blacks and about 2,300 for whites; exact *N*s vary slightly with number of cases with missing data for each item.
2. Student report.

To assess students' overall effort, an index score for each student was computed. This effort index was intended to reflect the net amount of time devoted to school work. The index score was derived from (1) an estimate of the amount of time the student spent on homework during the semester (based on his own report of the average amount of time spent on homework each day) minus (2) an estimate of the amount of time he lost from academic work during the semester as a result of (a) being absent from school, (b) being late to class, (c) missing a class without permission, (d) not getting all his homework done, or (e) being told [by a teacher] to come for a conference "because [he] supposedly did something wrong."[10]

The average score for all black students on the effort index was slightly lower than the average score for all white students. Although this difference was statistically significant for our large samples, the size of the difference is trivial. Moreover, when we compared the average effort of blacks and whites in each school separately, we found the difference to be *not* significant statistically in seven of eleven schools. Also, in one of the four schools where the effort difference was statistically significant, average black students' effort was greater than that of whites (see Patchen, 1975, chapter 2).

Overall, then, the data relevant to student effort indicate that white students, on the average, were more diligent than blacks in their school work. But on the whole, the difference between the races was slight and even this slight difference was not consistent across schools. Thus, the differences in effort between the races do not appear large enough to explain much of the large and consistent racial differences in both grades and achievement scores.

What about the variations in student interest and effort *within* each racial group? To what extent were these associated with differences in academic performance?

The results (see Table 10.7) show first that, for both blacks and whites, students' interest in their classes had very little association with their achievement test scores and only small positive associations with their grades. The effort index had more substantial, low to moderate correlations with grades, among students of both races. Effort also had a fairly substantial correlation with MAT achievement scores among black lowerclassmen. The association between effort and achievement scores was much smaller among whites. Associations between students' effort and the measures of academic performance were reduced slightly when IQ was held constant.

These results suggest, not unexpectedly, that greater effort by students within each racial group does result in somewhat higher academic performance, especially with respect to grades. It is possible also that those students who do well in school are encouraged to put forth greater effort.

Feelings toward Peers

In addition to the academic skills which students bring to high school, and the amount of effort they put forth, it is possible that academic performance may be affected by students' feelings toward their schoolmates. In particular, it has been suggested that black students may feel anxious or fearful as a result of hostility from white peers and that such feelings may interfere with their intellectual functioning (Katz, 1968; St. John, 1975).

We asked students several questions concerning their anger at, and fear of, other students—both those of their own race and those of the other race. The question asked and the results have been described already in Chapter 3. These results showed that the overall frequency of anger at schoolmates reported by black students and by white students was very similar. There was a tendency for students of each race to get angry at schoolmates of the other race more often than at those of their own race. However, these differences are small; both blacks and whites were almost as likely to get angry at schoolmates of their own race as at those of the other race.

While black students and white students reported getting angry at schoolmates about equally often, whites were somewhat more likely to be fearful of schoolmates (this was particularly true of white boys). Moreover, black students were somewhat more fearful of schoolmates of their own race (blacks) than of those of the other race, while white students were somewhat more fearful of the other race (blacks) than of their own race.

Overall, these results indicate that the differences in academic performance between black students and white students cannot be accounted for, even in part, by greater emotional upset among blacks resulting from relations with school peers. On the whole, black students appeared no more angry at, and somewhat less fearful of, peers than did white students.

Of course, it is possible that, within each racial group, students' anger at or fear of schoolmates will affect their academic performance. However, results presented in Table 10.7 show that, among students of both races, neither grades nor achievement scores were related much to the frequency of anger at schoolmates—either those of the other race or those of one's own race. Fear of schoolmates did tend to be associated with lower academic performance, especially for black students, but these correlations were very small for students of both races.

The small associations between fear of schoolmates and low academic performance may indicate that such fear tends to distract students' attention from their school work. Another possibility is that the small associations between fear of schoolmates and measures of academic performance are spurious—i.e., that they may be due to some third variable(s), like frequency of fighting, that is related to both. Whatever the reasons for the associations found, the total set of results indicates only a very weak link between students' feelings toward schoolmates and their academic performance.

Attitudes toward Teachers

Students' academic performance may be related also to their attitudes toward their teachers. Like negative feelings evoked by schoolmates, negative feelings toward teachers may interfere with intellectual functioning. In addition, negative attitudes toward teachers may reduce students' motivation to try hard, while positive attitudes toward teachers may contribute to motivation and effort. (Of course, teachers also may affect students' learning in other ways—especially by their skill in communicating information—but we are not concerned here with these types of teacher effects.)

We do not have data concerning students' feelings of anger at or fear of teachers or about students' anxiety in the classroom. However, we do have several measures of students' more general attitudes toward their teachers. The questions asked included:

1. "How well do you like each of the following people in this school?" Items included (a) "most of the black teachers I know" and (b) "most of the white teachers I know." (For each item, five response categories, from "like very much" to "dislike very much" were provided.)

2. "How satisfied are you, in general, with each of the following?" One item was "the teachers I have this semester." (Five response categories, from "very satisfied" to "not satisfied at all," were provided.)

Students also were asked what proportion of the teachers they had in this school fitted each of thirteen short descriptions. Most of these descriptive items concerned the relationship of the teachers to the students (e.g., "don't treat me with respect," "are often mean to students like me," "have shown an interest in me"). Additional items concerned the teacher's pedagogical ability (e.g., "explain things so they are clear to me") or their classroom management (e.g., "are too strict in class"). On the basis of answers to this series of questions, each student was given a score on an index of evaluation of teachers.

Table 10.6 shows that a large majority of students of both races said they were "very satisfied" or "satisfied" with their current teachers. More whites than blacks were satisfied but the differences were quite small. Results for the index of evaluation of teachers are similar. On the average, white students evaluated their teachers more highly than did blacks, but the difference between the races is so small as to be trivial.

Black students and white students also expressed similar amounts of liking for most black teachers, with the vast majority of both groups saying they liked most black teachers in their school either very much or pretty much. The only item concerning feelings toward teachers on which students of the races differed somewhat was that concerning liking for

Table 10.6. Attitudes toward Teachers, by Race[1]

	Blacks	**Whites**
A. Satisfaction with "the Teachers I Have This Semester"		
Very satisfied	14%	16%
Satisfied	53	58
Not too satisfied	27	22
Not satisfied at all	7	4
B. Liking for Most Black Teachers		
Like very much	35%	31%
Like pretty much	46	53
Don't especially like but don't dislike	15	12
Dislike slightly or dislike very much	5	4
C. Liking for Most White Teachers		
Like very much	14%	22%
Like pretty much	49	61
Don't especially like but don't dislike	26	15
Dislike slightly or dislike very much	11	2
D. Index of Evaluation of Teachers[2]		
(Mean score)	54.2	56.5

1. Percentages for each item may not add to exactly 100 % because of rounding. Average *N*s are about 1,800 for blacks and about 2,200 for whites; exact *N* varies with number of cases with missing data for each item.
2. Based on 13 items concerning specific actions or qualities of teachers.

white teachers. Compared to white students, black students expressed somewhat less liking for most white teachers they knew. (As Chapter 2 indicates, a large majority of teachers in most schools were white.) However, only about one black student in nine said he disliked most of the white teachers in the school. Overall, the results concerning feelings toward teachers indicate that white students felt slightly more positively toward their teachers, but they show no widespread hostility toward teachers among black students.

There is, of course (as Table 10.6 shows), variation in attitudes toward teachers among students of each racial group. To what extent were such attitudes related to students' grades and achievement scores?[11]

Among both black and white students, the more highly the student evaluated his teachers and the more satisfied he was with his teachers, the higher his academic performance tended to be. These correlations are small, though they are more substantial for grades than for achievement scores (see Table 10.7).

Table 10.7. Pearson Correlations between Academic Performance and Various Psychological Characteristics of Students[1]
(Results for Blacks outside Parentheses, for Whites inside Parentheses)[1]

	Achievement Test Score (MAT)		Current Grades	
IQ score	.74	(.83)	.28	(.47)
Academic values (index)	.15	(.23)	.26	(.35)
Educational aspirations	.31	(.53)	.27	(.42)
Occupational aspirations	.13	(.42)	.12	(.33)
Expectancy of fulfilling educational aspirations:				
College aspirers	.20	(.15)	.27	(.30)
Noncollege aspirers	.10	(.11)	.19	(.19)
Expectancy of fulfilling occupational aspirations:				
Aspirers to higher-status occupations	.18	(.19)	.20	(.23)
Aspirers to lower-status occupations	.12	(.08)	.06	(.11)
Interest in classes (index)	.10	(.06)	.16	(.21)
Effort (index)	.33	(.12)	.34	(.41)
Anger at:				
Other-race schoolmates	.01	(.01)	−.03	(.02)
Same-race schoolmates	.04	(.07)	−.02	(.03)
Fear of:				
Other-race schoolmates	−.16	(−.10)	−.13	(−.01)
Same-race schoolmates	−.11	(−.12)	−.09	(−.10)
Satisfaction with teachers	.09	(.12)	.22	(.20)
Evaluation of teachers (index)	.16	(.19)	.26	(.34)

1. Average *N*s for correlations of grades with other variables are about 1,500 for blacks and about 1,700 for whites. With *N*s of this size, correlations of .06 are significant at .05 level and correlations of .08 are significant at .01 level. Average *N*s for achievement score correlations are about 600 for blacks and about 650 for whites. With *N*s of this size, correlations of .09 are significant at .05 level and correlations of .12 are significant at .01 level.

We cannot be sure of the reason for these associations. More positive feelings toward the teacher may lead to better academic performance, by reducing the students' anxiety and/or increasing the students' motivation. Conversely, students who do better academically may, as a result, come to like their teachers better. This is more likely to be true for grades than for achievement scores, since teachers award grades but not achievement scores.

Whatever the reasons for the associations between academic performance and student attitudes toward teachers, these associations do not appear to be spurious. Additional analyses show that, even when a variety of student characteristics and aspects of the school situation are held constant, significant associations remain between students' evaluations of their teachers and their academic performance (see Chapters 11 and 12).

Summary

In this chapter, we have described variations between and within racial groups with respect to students' academic performance. We also examined variations in some relevant psychological factors and considered their associations with academic performance.

We found that achievement scores and grades varied widely within each racial group. However, on the average, the achievement scores and grades of black students were substantially lower than those of their white schoolmates.

These wide average differences in academic performance between blacks and whites, which are fairly typical of results throughout the country, present a problem of the greatest importance. It will be very difficult to achieve full equality for blacks, and for other minorities in American society, so long as a large proportion of these groups do not acquire in school the skills which can help them to achieve higher education, skilled occupations, and high incomes.

We also examined differences between and within racial groups with respect to a number of psychological factors which may affect academic performance. We found first that the large racial difference in academic performance in high school was paralleled by a similarly large difference in the cognitive abilities which blacks and whites possessed upon entering high school (as indicated by IQ scores). Also, within each racial group, prior cognitive development (IQ) accounted for a large part of the variation in high school achievement scores and a substantial part of the variation in high school grades. These results indicate the great importance of abilities acquired prior to high school as determinants of academic performance in high school. (In the next chapters, we will consider the impact of interracial contact in grade school on early IQ scores, as well as on later school performance.)

We found that black students and white students were very similar in their academic values—i.e., the importance they assigned to getting good grades, getting a good education, and being able to go to college. Blacks and whites also differed little in how far they would like to go in school and the prestige level of the occupations they would like to enter. In addition, black students saw only slightly poorer chances of fulfilling their desires regarding education and jobs. However, the relatively optimistic expectations of black students may have been unrealistic in many cases, in view of the markedly lower grades and achievement scores of blacks and the fact that a relatively small proportion of blacks were taking a college-preparatory program of courses.

Consistent with the small racial differences with respect to values, aspirations, and expectancies, differences in effort between the races also appeared generally to have been small. While white students tended to be more diligent in some ways, the small differences in effort cannot account for much of the large difference in academic performance between the races.

However, within each racial group, those who scored higher on our index of effort also scored higher on academic performance—especially grades. Within each racial group, higher achievement scores and grades also were associated with higher educational and occupational aspirations, with valuing academic achievement more, and with a higher expectancy of reaching one's educational goals. Thus, within each racial group, academic performance was higher among those who were more highly motivated and who tried harder. Although the causal connections among these variables probably are complex, these results indicate the importance of learning more about the factors which lead to higher motivation and effort among students. (In the next chapter, we will look at some of the features of the school situation—especially those relevant to interracial contact—which may affect students' effort.)

The associations between values, aspirations, and expectancies on the one hand, and the academic performance measures on the other hand, were consistently higher among whites than among blacks. These results indicate an inconsistency between the aspirations of many black students and the school performance which would permit them to realize these aspirations. To the extent that a gap exists between blacks' expectations and reality, this may cause frustration, disillusion, and anger to result for them eventually.

We examined also differences between and within each racial group with respect to feelings toward peers and toward teachers. Since some writers have suggested that "social threat" from white peers may produce emotional upset that interferes with learning by blacks, we considered students' reports of anger at, and fear of, schoolmates. Black students and white students reported anger at schoolmates of the other race (and those of their own race) about equally often. White students were somewhat more likely than blacks to report fear of schoolmates—especially those of the other race.

Within each racial group, variations in frequency of anger at schoolmates were not associated with variations in academic performance.

Fear of schoolmates did tend to be associated with poorer academic performance but these correlations were quite small. Overall, the results indicate that negative feelings aroused by schoolmates did not have a substantial impact on students' academic performance.

Finally, we considered students' feelings toward their teachers. Although black students expressed somewhat less liking for white teachers than did their white schoolmates, there was little overall difference between blacks and whites in satisfaction with their teachers and in evaluation of their teachers. Within each racial group, however, those who had more positive attitudes toward teachers tended to have higher grades and higher achievement scores.

In this chapter we have not considered variations in the school situation and in students' backgrounds which may affect academic performance. In the next chapter we turn to this subject. We will give special attention to the effects of interracial contact in the school on academic performance, as well as its effects on some of the psychological factors related to performance which we considered in this chapter.

11 | Contact and Academic Outcomes: Black Students

One of the basic reasons for promoting greater interracial and interethnic contact in schools is the hope that such contact may improve learning among minority students. In Chapter 1, we discussed the fact that evidence for such a beneficial academic effect has been inconsistent. We suggested that the key issue to be addressed is: Under what conditions will interracial contact have the most beneficial results on academic outcomes? We also discussed some of the conditions which have been hypothesized to be important in determining the impact of interracial mixing on school achievement and reviewed the evidence (mostly very sparse) bearing on these hypotheses.

Now we consider these issues in more detail and look at our own evidence concerning the relation between interracial contact and academic outcomes for black students. (Results for white students are presented in the next chapter.) We will examine first the effect on black students of contact with whites in grade school and then consider in greater depth the effects of contact with whites in high school.

In addition to looking at the overall relationships between interracial contact and academic outcomes, we will consider these associations under varying conditions. We will see whether the relation of class racial composition to academic outcomes for black students in high school depends on their own characteristics, on characteristics of their white peers, and on aspects of the school situation.

Finally, we will consider briefly the impact of interracial contact on academic outcomes for black students in comparison to the impact of other relevant factors.

Interracial Contact in Grade School

It might be expected that contact with white schoolmates will have the most beneficial academic effects on black students when such contact occurs at an early age. Any academic deficiencies related to segregated schools would not have had much chance to develop and students' motivation and work habits probably would be more pliable when they are young than at a later age.

Reviews of the relevant evidence tend to find support for the proposition that more positive academic effects of desegregation occur at earlier ages (St. John, 1975; Weinberg, 1977; Crain and Mahard, 1977). But the findings are far from uniform or conclusive. St. John (1975, p. 37) has said that there is "some indication that younger children, especially those of kindergarten age, tend to benefit more than older children from desegregation." Crain and Mahard's review indicates that when desegregation occurred by grades 1 or 2, black students usually showed gains in achievement, and that such gains were less usual when desegregation first occurred in later grades (especially grades 3 to 4). However, Crain and Mahard also note that most studies they reviewed did not report the racial composition of the schools, either before or after desegregation.

A few large-scale surveys have obtained data on the racial composition of grade schools and have related this variable to black students' achievement. Their results have not been consistent. Black students' achievement has been found to be highest when the proportions of whites was highest (Armor, 1972a; Crain and Mahard, 1977) and when there were between half and three-fourths white students (Jencks and Brown, 1975); lowest for black boys when the percentage of whites was above 70%; and, for black girls, unrelated to the racial composition of classes (Narot, 1973).

To provide further evidence on this matter, we wished to examine the relation between the achievement of black students in our sample and the racial composition of their grade school classes. In addition, we wished to see whether the friendliness of interracial contacts in grade school was related to academic outcomes. Evidence on this latter relationship has been almost completely lacking.

From a questionnaire which each student filled out, we obtained information about (1) the racial composition of the classes he attended in grade school(s) and (2) the amount of friendly (or unfriendly) contact which the student had with the other race in grade school. (See Chapter 5 for a description of these measures.)

We do not have data on students' grades or their scores on achievement tests in grade school. We do, however, have students' scores on IQ tests, which a large majority of students took in the eighth grade (see Chapter 10). IQ scores are highly correlated with achievement test scores and, like achievement test scores, they may be interpreted as measures of a number of basic skills (vocabulary, math, concept formation, etc.). While the development of such cognitive skills may be influenced by a variety of factors, learning experiences in grade school may be expected to have a major impact. Thus, if interracial contact in grade school affects students' learning, this should be reflected in their IQ scores.

Our results (see Table 11.1) show, however, that there were almost no associations between our measures of interracial contact in grade school and black students' IQ scores toward the end of grade school. The correlation between blacks' IQ scores and the proportion of white students in their grade school classes was close to zero. Similarly, there was a close-to-zero correlation between blacks' IQ scores and the amount of friendly contact they had with whites in grade school.

Table 11.1. Contact with White Classmates in Grade School as Related to Academic Outcomes for Black Students in Grade School and High School (Pearson Correlations)[1]

	Average Proportion Whites in Grade School Classes		Friendly Contact with Whites in Grade School	
	r	*(N)*	*r*	*(N)*
IQ scores[2]	−.03	(1322)	−.03	(1320)
Effort index score, high school	.01	(1448)	.04	(1442)
Current grades, high school	−.09***	(1557)	−.01	(1557)
Tenth Grade Achievement Scores, Freshmen and Sophomores				
MAT, total scores	−.09**	(703)	−.05	(691)
MAT, English language subscore	−.10**	(827)	−.05	(812)
MAT, math subscore	−.06*	(793)	−.03	(773)
Tenth Grade Achievement Scores, Juniors and Seniors				
NEDT, total scores	−.14***	(675)	−.15***	(645)
NEDT, English usage subtest	−.16***	(675)	−.14***	(645)
NEDT, math usage subtest	−.13***	(675)	−.13***	(645)

1. Correlations are changed hardly at all by controls on parents' education and sex.
2. IQ scores for 93.4% of all students were based on California Test of Mental Maturity, taken in eighth grade. Other students took this or another IQ test during sixth grade (1.9%) or during ninth grade (4.7%).

* Significant at .05 level; ** significant at .01 level; *** significant at .001 level.

Further analyses show that, even with parents' education held constant, there were no significant associations between IQ scores and the racial composition of grade school classes, or between IQ and friendly contact in grade school. Also, the associations between IQ scores and interracial contact in grade school did not differ significantly for black students who came from families of different educational levels.

Finally, we investigated whether there might be some nonlinear relations between interracial contact and IQ which were not revealed by the correlational analyses. The results showed no significant associations between the IQ scores of black students and the measures of their contact with whites in grade school.

The results reported so far indicate that the amount of interracial contact which blacks had in grade school had little effect on their academic achievement in grade school—at least as indicated by their IQ scores toward the end of the grade school years. But did contact with whites in grade school affect the academic effort or achievement of black students in high school?

Our results (see Table 11.1) show, first, that the amount of effort which black students displayed in high school was *not* related significantly to the racial composition of their grade school classes. There was, however, a tendency for attendance in grade school classes with *larger* proportions of whites to be associated with both lower grades and lower achievement scores in high school.[1] The relationship between a larger proportion of whites in grade school classes and lower achievement scores in high school—though quite small in size—is found consistently both for lowerclassmen and for upperclassmen (who took different achievement tests) and for English-language scores, math scores, and total achievement test scores. These small but significant negative correlations remain essentially the same when controlled for the effects of parents' education.

The amount of friendly contact with whites in grade school generally had less association with academic outcomes in high school than did the racial composition of grade school classes (see Table 11.1). Both effort and grades in high school were essentially unrelated to friendly contact with whites in grade school. Among black upperclassmen, more friendly contact with whites in grade school was associated with lower achievement scores (English language, math, and total) in high school. However, no significant relation between friendly interracial contact in grade school and achievement scores was found among black lowerclassmen. When the correlations between friendly contact with whites in grade school and academic outcomes in high school are controlled for the effects of parents' education and the student's sex, these correlations remain essentially the same.

Overall, these results do not provide any support for the proposition that attending more racially mixed grade schools will improve academic outcomes for black students. There was, in fact, a tendency in the opposite direction—i.e., for blacks who attended more racially mixed grade school classes to get lower grades and achievement scores in high school. It is not clear whether these small negative relations really reflect a negative effect of attending racially mixed classes and, if so, why this effect should occur. It may be that black students in more racially mixed classes received less attention to their special academic needs than was true in predominantly black grade school classes.

It may be also, as Crain and Mahard (1977) suggest, that racial integration has a positive academic impact on black students only when it takes place by grade 2. Since our measure of class racial composition includes all the grade school years combined, it might not "pick up" such an effect, especially if this effect was quite small.

Another possibility is that, in most cases where blacks and whites had contact in grade school, these students were of similar (perhaps low) socioeconomic level, and had similar orientations toward school. If so, this may have reduced any positive impact of interracial contact on black students' academic achievement.

Unfortunately, we do not have information about the characteristics of those white schoolmates with whom black students in our own sample were in contact in grade school. We do have such information about their white schoolmates in high school. We will, therefore, pursue this issue further when we examine the relation between interracial contact and academic performance in high school.

Interracial Contact in High School

We turn next to the relation between interracial contact in high school and academic outcomes for black students. Studies of the relationship between the racial composition of high schools and the achievement of black students—like studies at the grade school level—have produced rather inconsistent results. Crain and Mahard (1978) reported that the achievement of Northern, but not Southern, high school students rose as the proportion of whites in their schools increased. Narot (1973) found that black boys tended to do better in racially balanced (40 to 70% white) schools than in either predominately black or predominately white schools. Jencks and Brown (1975) found no effect of school racial composition on estimated achievement increases between grades 9 and 12.

At the level of the classroom, results are more consistent in showing that increasing proportions of whites in classes had small but positive effects on the achievement of blacks (Cohen, Pettigrew, and Riley, 1972; McPartland, 1968; Crain and Mahard, 1978). However, there has been little evidence available about whether black achievement rises consistently over the entire range of the percentage of whites in classes. Also, the evidence concerning class racial composition has come from students' rough estimates, rather than from school records.

In this study we have available an unusually good measure of the racial composition of students' classes, based on school records. We also have more detailed data on social relations between blacks and whites than has been available in previous studies. Therefore, we can examine the relation between interracial contact and academic achievement with greater precision and depth than usually has been possible. We will examine the relevant data both for the total school and for individual students.

Duration of Interracial Contact and Outcomes

Before presenting the results concerning high school contact, we need to consider an important preliminary question. Was there enough time for interracial contact to have an effect on academic outcomes? Let us consider this question separately for the three key outcome measures: achievement scores, grades, and effort.

Our results on achievement tests are based on students who were freshmen or sophomores during the spring 1971 semester. Sophomores took achievement tests during that same semester (in March). Freshmen took the achievement tests one year later (March 1972), when they were sophomores. For all students, the measures of class racial composition and of types of interracial contact were obtained during the spring 1971 semester. However, a large majority of students were in the same school and in a total class of the same racial composition during both their freshman and sophomore years. Thus, almost all lowerclassmen were in classes of approximately the same racial composition for almost two school years prior to taking the standardized achievement tests. If class racial composition in high school is important for achievement, one would expect a discernible effect in that time.

It is less certain that the types of interracial contact (i.e., friendly or unfriendly) reported by black lowerclassmen for the semester in which they took the questionnaire also characterized their interracial contacts during their first two years of high school. However, since they were with the same group of classmates in the same school, it seems probable that their relations with white schoolmates generally would have been similar during this period. Therefore, the types of relationships with whites generally would have had about two years in which to affect achievement scores.

Current semester grades are a measure of performance during the same semester in which our data concerning class racial composition and types of interracial contact were obtained. Good grades depend in part on general abilities developed over a period of years. However, our data indicate that black students' grades were correlated more highly with their current semester effort than with the general cognitive abilities (IQ) they had on entering high school (see Chapter 10). Also, grades are dependent heavily on knowledge of the specific material taught during the current semester. Thus, if the amount and nature of interracial contact affects black students' school performance, we should expect some effect on their current semester grades.

Finally, our measure of students' effort is the performance measure which appears most susceptible to large influence by interracial contact.

While data on interracial contact and effort are for the same time period (spring 1971), effort can be change relatively easily in response to the current school situation.

Overall, then, our results concerning the relation between interracial contact and performance in high school are limited by the fact that our data were gathered over a short time period. However, there seems reason to believe that, if interracial contact does affect academic outcomes, some effects should be evident.

We will look first at the results concerning racial composition and then at those concerning the friendliness of interracial contact.

Racial Composition

Did the racial composition of the school affect academic outcomes for black students?

Schools. We related the percentage of blacks at each of the twelve school sites to the average effort, grades, and achievement scores of black students at that location (see correlations in Table 11.2). With respect to effort, a scatter plot of the data shows no consistent relation between school percent black and the average effort of black students. However, there was an overall tendency for average black effort to decline as the proportion of blacks in their school increased. With the average education of black students' parents and their own average IQ controlled, this negative correlation becomes somewhat stronger but the relationship is still modest and not statistically significant.

With respect to grades, a scatter plot shows no consistent relation between the racial composition of a school and the average grades of blacks in that school. However, there was a tendency for the average grades of black students to rise as the proportion of blacks in the school increased. The size of this small correlation is changed very little when the average IQ and average parental education of blacks at each school are controlled.

The average achievement scores of blacks tended to decrease as the proportion of blacks in their school increased. The only notable exception was the "academic" school, Highland, where there was a large proportion of blacks and where blacks had higher achievement scores than did blacks at any other school. When the average IQ and the average parental education of blacks in each school are controlled, the size of the negative correlation between school percent black and achievement scores becomes somewhat larger, though it still is only moderate, and not statistically significant for this small number of schools.

Overall, then, the average academic performance of black students was not related consistently to the racial composition of schools; but, as the percentage of black students in a school increased, effort and achievement scores tended to decline while grades tended to rise.

Individuals. We also related academic outcomes (effort, grades, achievement scores) for individual black students to the average racial

Table 11.2. School Racial Composition and Types of Contact Which Blacks Reported with White Schoolmates, as Related to Average Academic Outcomes for Blacks
(Pearson Correlations)

	School Percent Black	Average Friendly Contact with Whites	Average Total Unfriendly Experience with Whites
Average effort, blacks			
r	−.31	.57	−.45
Partial r^1	−.49	.66*	.16
N schools	(12)	(11)	(11)
Average current grades, blacks			
r	.39	.09	−.44
Partial r^1	.42	.07	−.56
N schools	(12)	(11)	(11)
Average achievement scores, black freshmen and sophomores			
r	−.21	.48	−.60*
Partial r^1	−.51	†	.03
N schools	(11)	(10)	(10)

1. Controls for partial correlations are average IQ and average parental education of black students.

* Significant at .05 level.
† Partial correlation could not be computed because of high correlations of average black IQ and average black parental education with average black achievement scores.

composition of their classes. Students' scores on each academic outcome were adjusted for their IQs, ability groups, and curriculum programs (academic or not). Thus, the effects of class racial composition cannot be attributed to the fact that students in more heavily black classes tended to be in low-ability groups and in nonacademic programs. (Moreover, the effects of class racial composition on academic outcomes did not differ significantly in different schools.)[2]

Figure 11.1 shows the relation between black students' effort and the racial composition of their classes. Effort among blacks generally was lower when the proportion of blacks in their classes was about half or more than when their classes were predominately white. This drop in effort with increasing proportions of blacks may reflect lower expectations

Figure 11.1 Class Racial Composition, as Related to
Black Students' Average Academic Effort, Adjusted for Effects
of IQ, Ability Group, and Program[1]

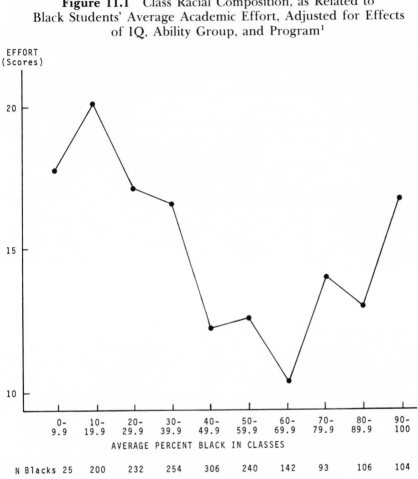

1. Difference in effort among those in different racial composition categories is significant at .05 level. The correlation ratio is .18. The correlation ratio after adjustment for other predictors is .13.

from teachers and/or a more lax student norm about academic behavior in heavily black classes.

While larger proportions of blacks in classes generally was associated with lower effort among black students, it generally was associated also with higher grades for black students (see Figure 11.2). This result may reflect a less stringent competition for grades in more heavily black classes. In addition, it may be that many teachers adopted more lenient standards of grading when they taught classes with large proportions of black students. Whatever the reasons, it appears that black students in heavily

Figure 11.2 Class Racial Composition, as Related to
Black Students' Average Current-Semester Grades, Adjusted for
Effects of IQ, Ability Group, and Program[1]

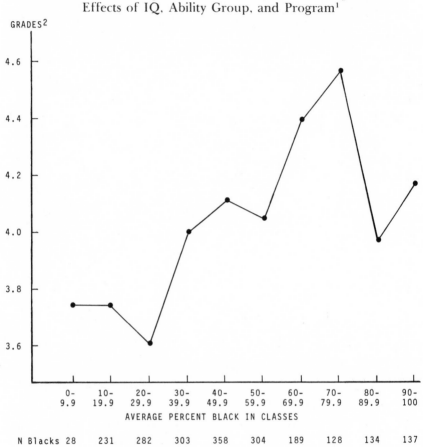

GRADES[2]

AVERAGE PERCENT BLACK IN CLASSES

	0- 9.9	10- 19.9	20- 29.9	30- 39.9	40- 49.9	50- 59.9	60- 69.9	70- 79.9	80- 89.9	90- 100
N Blacks	28	231	282	303	358	304	189	128	134	137

1. Differences in grades among those in different racial composition categories is
significant at .001 level. The correlation ratio is .17 and remains the same after adjustment for other predictors.
2. Grade code is as follows: F = 0, D = 2, C = 4, B = 6, A = 8.

black classes tended to get more positive feedback (in the form of grades)
than those in predominately white classes, despite their lower effort.

Next we consider the relation between the average racial composition of black students' classes and their achievement scores. Since
achievement scores for freshmen and sophomores were collected in different years and the results for the two groups differed somewhat, the
results for those in each year are shown separately (see Figure 11.3).

For both black freshmen and black sophomores, differences in
achievement scores among students with differing class racial composi-

Figure 11.3   Racial Composition of Classes of Black
Freshmen and Sophomores, as Related to Their Average Total
Scores on Metropolitan Achievement Tests[1], Adjusted for
Effects of IQ, Ability Group, and Program[2]

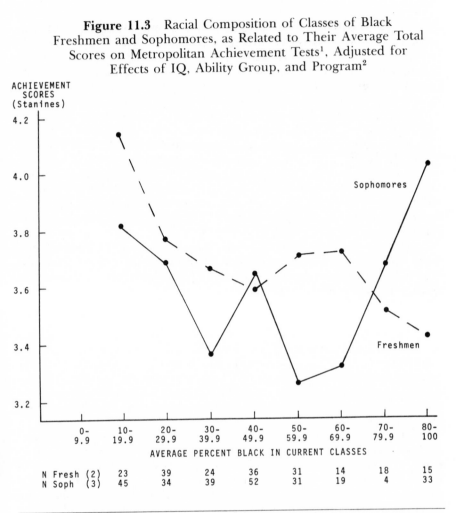

	0- 9.9	10- 19.9	20- 29.9	30- 39.9	40- 49.9	50- 59.9	60- 69.9	70- 79.9	80- 100
N Fresh (2)		23	39	24	36	31	14	18	15
N Soph (3)		45	34	39	52	31	19	4	33

AVERAGE PERCENT BLACK IN CURRENT CLASSES

1. All students took achievement tests in March of their sophomore year.
2. Differences in achievement scores among those in different racial composition categories are significant at the .09 level for freshmen and at the .08 level for sophomores. For freshmen, the correlation ratio is .39 but is reduced to .17 when other predictors are controlled. For sophomores, the correlation ratio is .56 and is reduced to .20 when other predictors are controlled.

tions were of marginal statistical significance (after adjustments for controls). However, for freshmen, there was a fairly steady decline in achievement scores as the proportion of blacks in classes increased. For sophomores, achievement scores also tended to decline as the proportion of blacks in classes increased, up to where classes averaged two-thirds black. But in the most heavily black classes, achievement scores for black sophomores rose again. Overall, these results indicate a tendency for black students' achievement scores to decline as the proportion of blacks in their classes increased; but this relation was not strong or consistent.[3]

The results just reported are based on students' total scores on the Metropolitan Achievement Test. Since racial integration sometimes has appeared to affect verbal and mathematical achievement differently (St. John, 1975), we also examined separately the relations between the racial composition of black students' classes and their scores on the Language Arts (English) and Mathematics portions of the MAT. There was no significant association between the racial composition of black students' classes and their achievement on Language Arts (i.e., reading, spelling, word usage, etc.). There was a small but statistically significant association between the racial composition of classes and the mathematics achievement of black students. However, this relation was curvilinear: blacks did best on math tests when the proportion of blacks in their classes was either smallest or largest.

Overall, the results relating class racial composition to academic outcomes indicate that as the proportion of blacks in their classes rose, the effort of black students generally declined (along with some indications of a drop in achievement scores), but their grades generally improved. These results are consistent with those for total schools, presented in the previous section.

However, inspection of Figures 11.1, 11.2, and 11.3 shows also that there was a deviation from this general pattern which deserves attention. The general trend for increasing proportions of blacks in classes to be accompanied by lower effort but by higher grades was reversed for students whose classes were almost all black. At that end of the continuum of racial composition, effort rose, achievement scores rose (for sophomores), and grades declined.

It may be that the trends in academic outcomes shown in Figures 11.1 through 11.3 were due to variations in the discipline and demands exerted in classes of differing racial proportions. As the proportions of blacks in classes rose, teachers generally may have reacted to the poorer preparation of students, difficulties in communication with students, and perhaps difficulties in controlling students, by relaxing their discipline and their standards. However, classes with very large black majorities often were in relatively stable settings where academic standards and/or discipline had been maintained at a fairly high level.[4] Thus, mostly academic Highland, which had many predominately black classes, had a well-deserved reputation for high standards. And Carver, the traditionally black school, had attempted over the years to maintain firm discipline and acceptable academic standards. (For evidence indicating the positive effects of high academic standards, see Brookover et al., 1979, and Rutter et al., 1979.)

We do not have quantitative evidence concerning the extent to which administrators and teachers attempted to maintain high academic standards in settings of varying racial composition. But we do have some evidence concerning disciplinary strictness

Figure 11.4 shows the disciplinary strictness perceived by students[5] who attended classes with different (average) racial compositions (with strictness adjusted for the effects of school program). As the proportion of blacks increased from under 20% to 70%, disciplinary strictness declined steadily, as perceived by both black students and white students. This decline parallels the decline in black students' effort over this range of class racial composition. As the proportion of blacks in classes rose above 70%, blacks perceived further declines in disciplinary strictness, but white students reported an upturn in strictness in these predominately black settings—especially in classes which were 80% or more black. Thus

Figure 11.4 Perceived Disciplinary Strictness (Mean Scores)[1] for Students in Classes of Different Racial Composition, Separately for Blacks and for Whites[2]

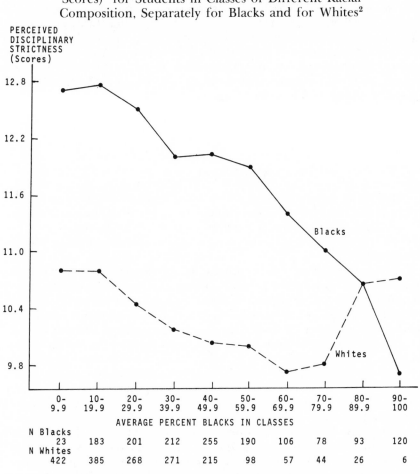

---

1. Scores on disciplinary strictness were adjusted for the effect of the program which students were following.
2. The effect of class racial composition on perception of strictness is significant for blacks (p < .001) and for whites (p < .001).

the perceptions of whites, though not of blacks. are consistent with the hypothesis that the upturn in black effort in predominately black classes might be related to stricter discipline in those settings. Another piece of evidence supporting this explanation is that disciplinary practices reported by the school principal at Carver (the almost all-black school) were among the strictest of all schools.

Overall, although the results are not completely consistent, they suggest that the relations found between class racial composition and black students' performance may be related to variations in disciplinary strictness.[6] In addition, expectations, demands, and support for achievement may differ in classes of different racial composition. Also, there is the possibility of differing influences by peers in classes of varying racial ·compositions. We will explore this last possibility later in this chapter.

Finally, while there are interesting, and in some cases statistically significant, associations between class racial composition and academic outcomes for individual black students, it is important to note that class racial composition explains very little of the total variation among black students on these outcomes. Specifically, after controls for the effects of IQ, ability group, and program, class racial composition accounts for less than four percent of the total variance on each of the academic outcomes.[7]

Nature of Interracial Contact

So far we have examined the relation between academic outcomes for black students and the racial composition of their schools and classes. Next we ask: Were the academic outcomes for blacks related to the types of contacts (friendly and unfriendly) they had with their white schoolmates?

Friendly Contact. On the questionnaire, we asked each black student how often during the present semester he had each of a variety of friendly contacts with white schoolmates (e.g., doing homework together, doing things together after school). On the basis of the student's responses, we computed an index showing the amount of friendly contact he had with white schoolmates (see Chapter 4 for more detail about this index).

Schools. The average level of friendly interracial contact was computed for the black students at each school site. These scores were then correlated with average academic outcomes for black students at each school site (see Table 11.2).

As the average level of friendly interracial contact reported by black students in a school increased, the average level of black effort also tended to increase. With the average IQ and the average parental education of black students controlled, this association becomes slightly stronger and statistically significant.

The average amount of friendly contact which blacks had with whites in a school had almost no association with the average grades for blacks. Friendly contact with whites did tend to be associated with higher achievement scores for black students. However, this moderate, nonsignificant association was due in part to the fact that, in schools where blacks had more friendly contact with whites, the blacks tended also to have a higher average IQ and a higher level of parental education (both of which were strongly related to average achievement scores).[8]

Overall, then, at the school level, a higher average level of friendly contact with whites tended to be associated with greater average effort by blacks but not with grades or achievement scores.

Individuals. Next we consider the results for individuals. Was the amount of friendly contact which individual black students had with white schoolmates associated with their academic outcomes?[9]

Table 11.3 shows the correlations between academic outcomes for black students and two measures of friendly interaction with whites. The first is the index of friendly contact with white schoolmates. The second is the measure of friendship with whites. (See Chapter 4 for details about these measures.) In each case, two types of partial correlations also are shown. The first shows the relations between friendly interaction and academic outcomes when differences in students' IQ scores are controlled. Since IQ was measured prior to interracial contact in high school, it could not have been affected by such contacts. The second set of partial correlations controls both for IQ and for other differences among students in high school which were related to academic outcomes (i.e., ability grouping, being in the academic program, and evaluation of teachers).[10,11]

The results show first that there was a tendency for blacks who had more friendly interaction with whites to exert greater academic effort. Though these relationships are very small, they remain statistically significant—especially for the friendship measure—when controls for IQ and for IQ plus relevant high school variables are applied.

Grades for black students were not associated significantly with the measure of friendly contact with white schoolmates, but did relate significantly to friendship with whites. This small relationship remains significant when IQ is controlled but not when IQ plus high school variables are controlled.

Achievement scores, like effort and grades, tended to be higher among black students who had more friendly interaction with whites. However, these associations generally were tiny and only the correlation between friendship and achievement scores for sophomores (without any controls) reaches statistical significance.

Overall, these results indicate that there was a tendency for more friendly interaction with whites—especially friendship—to be associated with more positive academic outcomes among black students. But these relationships are very small in size and tend to disappear almost entirely when other variables affecting academic outcomes are controlled.

Unfriendly Contact. What about unfriendly contact with whites in high school? Was this type of contact related to the academic effort and performance of black students?

Table 11.3 Friendly and Unfriendly Interaction with Whites in High School, as Related to Academic Outcomes for Black Students[1]

	Friendly Contact with Whites	Friendship with Whites	Total Unfriendly Experiences with Whites
Effort			
Correlation (r)	.10***	.11***	−.10***
Partial r, control on IQ	.08**	.10***	−.07*
Partial r, control on IQ plus high school variables[2]	.05	.06**	.00
(N)	(922)	(972)	(995)
Current Grades			
Correlation (r)	.04	.11***	−.15***
r, control on IQ	.01	.10***	−.12***
r, controls on IQ plus high school variables[2]	−.04	.05	−.05
(N)	(987)	(963)	(997)
Tenth Grade Total Achievement Scores, Freshmen			
Correlation (r)	.07	.10	−.09
Partial r, control on IQ	.08	.05	−.08
Partial r, control on IQ plus high school variables[2]	.03	.06	−.09
(N)	(154)	(228)	(205)
Tenth Grade Total Achievement Scores, Sophomores			
Correlation (r)	.08	.14*	−.17*
Partial r, control on IQ	.03	.11	−.10
Partial r, control on IQ plus high school variables[2]	.02	.04	−.06
(N)	(153)	(192)	(181)

1. Results are based on students for whom data on all variables used for partial rs were available. Zero-order correlations based on total sample are very close to those shown here.
2. Other variables controlled, as appropriate for each analysis, included evaluations of teachers, ability group, being in academic program, sex, and unfriendly contact with own race.

* Significant at .05 level; ** significant at .01 level; *** significant at .001 level.

Students were asked a series of questions concerning unfriendly contact with white schoolmates (e.g., being called bad names, being threatened, getting into fights). For each student, an index of total unfriendly experiences with white schoolmates was computed. (See Chapter 4 for more detail about this index.)

Schools. At each school, we computed the average amount of unfriendly interracial experiences which black students reported. These scores can be seen as reflecting the average level of overt hostility which black students experienced from whites at each school.

As the average amount of unfriendly contact experienced by black students rose, their average effort, grades, and achievement scores tended to decline (see Table 11.2). However, when the average IQ and average parental education of black students at each school are controlled, the associations of unfriendly contact with effort and with achievement scores are reduced to close to zero. With these controls, there remains a moderate, though nonsignificant, association between average unfriendly contact with whites and lower grades among black students. Overall, there appears to be only a weak relation between the general level of hostility from whites in a school and average academic outcomes for blacks.

Individuals. What about those individual black students who had the most unfriendly contact with white schoolmates? Did their academic outcomes differ from those of other blacks? For individual black students, correlations between scores on the index of unfriendly interracial experience and their academic effort, grades, and achievement test scores are shown in Table 11.3. The table also shows partial correlations when these associations are controlled for the effects of (1) students' IQs and (2) IQ plus sex and some differences in the high school situation (ability group, program, evaluation of teachers, and unfriendly contact with same-race schoolmates).[12]

There was a tendency for those black students who had more unfriendly contacts with whites to exert less academic effort. This association remains statistically significant, though tiny, when IQ is controlled, but declines to exactly zero when all control variables are applied.

A similar pattern is found for black grades. More unfriendly contact with whites was associated with lower grades. This association persists when IQ is controlled but declines to statistical nonsignificance when all control variables are applied.

There also was a tendency for black achievement scores to decline as unfriendly contact with white schoolmates increased. The zero-order correlation (without controls) was significant for sophomores but not for freshmen. When control variables (either IQ alone or IQ plus other controls) were applied, the correlation between unfriendly contact with whites and achievement scores was not significant for either freshmen or sophomores.

Thus, for all three academic outcomes (effort, grades, and achievement scores) the patterns of results are similar. There was a tendency for black students who had more unfriendly contact with white schoolmates to do less well in school. But these associations are weak and tend to disappear when other variables affecting academic outcomes are controlled.

More generally, the nature of the contact (either friendly or un-friendly) which black students had with their white schoolmates appeared to have only small effects on their academic outcomes. However, there was a tendency, both at the school and individual levels, for those blacks who had more friendly and fewer unfriendly interactions with whites to have better academic outcomes. This may reflect, in part, a small positive effect of friendly contact with white schoolmates. It may also reflect a tendency for those black students who are more academically able and motivated to form more friendly, and fewer unfriendly, relations with white schoolmates. We will consider further the possible mechanisms link-ing interracial contact to academic outcomes in the next section.

Interracial Contact under Varying Conditions

So far we have looked separately at the relation between academic outcomes and some specific aspects of interracial contact. Generally, we have found only small associations. But discussions of the relation of in-terracial contact to academic performance (see Chapter 1) have suggested that the effects of interracial contact on black students' achievement should vary with (1) the friendliness of their interracial contact, (2) their own characteristics (e.g., sex, social class, ability), and (3) the char-acteristics of the white students with whom they are in contact, as well as with other aspects of the school situation. In this section, we will consider whether the effects of interracial contact on academic outcomes for blacks did differ under such different circumstances.

The results summarized in this section are derived from a series of analyses which used the statistical technique of analysis of covariance. This method permits us to observe the separate and combined (interaction) effects on each academic outcome of (1) class racial composition, (2) friendship with whites, (3) each of a number of characteristics of black students, of their white peers,[13] and of the school setting (taken one or two at a time). For each of these analyses, the method also permits us to control for the effects of other variables which may affect academic outcomes.[14]

In each of these analyses, black students were divided into three categories, based on their average class racial compositions: (1) 0–34.9% black, (2) 35–54.9% black, and (3) 55–85.0% black. These categories were chosen on the basis of the results presented above which show that aca-demic outcomes tended to differ for black students in these categories.[15]

In those analyses where friendship with whites was included as a predictor of academic outcomes, students usually were divided into three "friendship" categories: (1) those who said that fewer than three white students are "friends" (and had no whites among their *closest* friends); (2) those who said three or more whites are "friends," but had no whites among their *closest* friends; and (3) those who said they belong to an inter-racial group with whom they "hang around a lot" and/or have one or more whites among their five best friends.

In summarizing the results of these analyses, we will focus on the extent to which the effects of interracial contact varied for black students with different characteristics and for those in different circumstances. (For more detailed results, see Patchen, Hofmann, and Brown, 1980; Patchen 1981.)

Class Composition and Friendship. It has been suggested by some writers (see Chapter 1) that black students will do well academically in predominately white schools only if they are socially accepted by their white peers. Such social acceptance, it is argued, will lead the blacks to use their white peers as role models. Moreover, when accepted, black students will not experience "social threat," which may result in anxiety and interfere with their school work. What do our results show on this subject?

First, the overall ("main") effects of class racial composition and of friendship with whites were independent of each other. With friendship with whites held constant, as the proportion of blacks in their classes rose, the grades of black students rose but their effort decreased. And with class racial composition held constant, more friendship with whites was associated with greater effort and higher grades among black students.

Were there any combined (interaction) effects between class racial composition and friendship with whites? Essentially, there were not. The effects of class racial composition did not vary for black students who had different amounts of friendship with whites. Conversely, the effects of friendship with whites did not vary for those in classes of differing racial composition.

There also was very little evidence that class racial composition and friendship with whites had combined effects for particular categories of black students. Thus, there was little indication of three-way interactions when the effects of class racial composition and of interracial friendship were analyzed together with the effects of (1) the student's sex, (2) the student's own parents' education and/or the average education of parents of his white peers, (3) the average academic values of white peers, or (4) the school program in which the student was enrolled.

Overall, we may conclude that—contrary to what some have predicted—the effects of class racial composition on academic outcomes for black students did *not* depend on the extent of their friendship with white peers.

Sex. Several studies have reported more positive (or less negative) effects of racial desegregation on the achievement of black girls than on that of black boys (Narot, 1973; Bryant, 1968; Lewis and St. John, 1974). Pursuing this matter further, we wished to see whether the effects of class racial composition, of friendship with whites, and of combinations of these two factors differed for black boys versus black girls.

While sex was itself related to academic outcomes, the effects of class racial composition on academic outcomes did not vary for black boys as compared to black girls. Nor did the effects of friendship with whites vary by sex. There were weak, statistically significant, three-way interactions among class racial composition, friendship with whites, and sex, as these factors related to grades and to achievement scores. However, inspection of the cell means showed no consistent pattern of results.

Overall, we may conclude that the effects of interracial contact were not different for the two sexes.

Contact in Grade School. It seems possible that the academic effects of contacts with whites in high school may depend on the amount of prior interracial contact which black students have in grade school. Perhaps those who attend grade school with whites are more psychologically open to the influences of white schoolmates in high school. Perhaps, also, interracial experiences must be long term and consistent in order to have their maximum effects. If this is the case, attending predominately white classes both in grade school and in high school might have a combined effect on black students' academic performance which is greater than the sum of the two separate (grade school and high school) influences.

Our results show, however, that this was not the case. There were no combined (interaction) effects of grade school and high school racial composition with respect to any of the academic outcomes. Regardless of the racial composition of black students' grade school classes, the racial composition of high school classes had similar associations with academic performance; that is, as the proportion of blacks in their classes increased, black students' grades rose but their effort and achievement scores declined. Thus we conclude that the effect of contact with whites in high school did *not* vary with the amount of such contact in grade school.

Education of Own Parents and Those of White Peers. It has been suggested by a number of writers that attending predominantly white classes will benefit black students academically, not because their schoolmates are white but because they are middle class (see Chapter 1). In such settings, it is argued, black students will be influenced by middle-class white schoolmates who hold positive academic values[16] and can serve as models of successful school behavior.

On the other hand, since middle-class peers tend to be higher than lower-class students in academic ability,[17] comparisons with these peers may lower the academic self-image of the minority student and his expectancy of being able to compete successfully with his schoolmates.

To provide further evidence on this subject, we investigated the separate and combined effects on academic outcomes of (1) class racial composition, (2) friendship with whites, (3) the education of black students' own parents, and (4) the average education of parents of white peers.

Our results show that the education of black students' own parents had no significant effect on any of the academic outcomes—though those whose parents were better educated tended to try harder. The average education of the parents of white peers also had no significant effects on any academic outcomes for blacks.

Of greatest interest for our purposes are the results concerning combined (interaction) effects among the predictors. These results may be summarized as follows:

1. The effects of contact with whites (either class racial composition or friendship) did *not* vary much with the education of black students' own parents.

2. The associations between black students' friendship with whites and academic outcomes did *not* vary much for blacks whose white peers came from families of different educational levels. The only significant combined effect of these factors was found for black students' grades. Friendship with whites was associated with slightly lower grades among blacks whose white peers came from medium-education families.

3. The effects of class racial composition on some academic outcomes for blacks did vary with the educational level of the families of their white peers. First, there was a combined effect of these factors on grades. The nature of this interaction is shown in Figure 11.5. Among black students whose white peers came from families of either high or medium education, grades declined as the proportion of whites in their classes rose to about half or more. But among black students whose white peers came from low-education families, grades were higher for those whose classes had half or more whites than for those in majority-black classes.

   The effect of class racial composition on black students' effort also varied with the educational level of their white peers' parents, in combination with the educational level of their own parents. The nature of this three-way interaction effect is shown in Table 11.4. Having larger proportions of whites in their classes was associated with greater effort among black students only when (a) the education of their own parents was low and (b) the education of the parents of their white peers was low or medium.

4. There were no significant four-way interaction effects among class racial composition, friendship with whites, own parents' education, and the education of the parents of white peers.

Overall, the results do not support the proposition that greater contact with white schoolmates will benefit students most when the whites are from high-status, well-educated families. Rather, being in classes with a substantial proportion of whites appeared to benefit only those blacks whose white peers (as well as they themselves) came from low-education families.[18]

Academic Values of Schoolmates. We noted in the previous section that the socioeconomic status (SES) of white peers may have at least two separate consequences. First, the SES background of white peers may affect the whites academic values. Secondly, it may affect the white peers' academic abilities. Since the values and abilities of white peers may have different effects on black students, it is desirable to consider each of these factors separately. Let us first consider the impact of peer values.

A basic assumption of many writers is that contact with white schoolmates will lead black students to adopt values and norms which emphasize the importance of hard work and doing well in school (e.g., Katz, 1968; Spady, 1976). If this assumption is correct, the effect should occur only when white schoolmates do, in fact, value success in school and work

Figure 11.5 Average Current-Semester Grades of Black
Students, as Related to Racial Composition of Their
Classes, Separately for Those Whose White Peers Come from
Families with Varying Education[1]

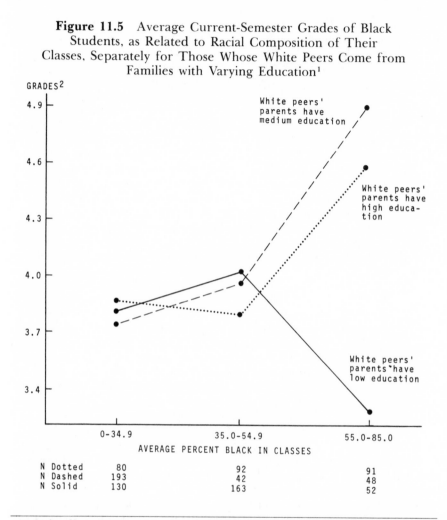

N Dotted	80	92	91
N Dashed	193	42	48
N Solid	130	163	52

1. Main effect of class racial composition is significant ($p < .001$), main effect of white parents' education is not significant and interaction of these two factors is significant ($p < .01$) in an analysis of covariance in which friendship with whites and own parents education are other factors, and IQ, sex, year in school, and education of parents of black peers are covariates.
2. Grade code is as follows: F = 0, D = 2, C = 4, B = 6, A = 8.

hard to achieve it. Such a normative effect of white students on their black
schoolmates would be expected to increase as the proportion of whites in
classes increases and as there is more friendly contact between blacks and
whites.

Academic values were assessed by asking students how important it
was to them to get good grades, to get a good education, and to go to
college (see Chapter 10). The average academic values of white peers

Table 11.4. Effort of Black Students, as Related to Class Racial Composition, Separately for Those with Different Combinations of Own Parents' Education and Education of Parents of White Peers

Own Parents' Education[1]	Average Education of Parents of White Peers[1]	Average Proportion of Blacks in Classes	N	Average Effort Score[2]
Low	Low	0–35	61	15.1
		35–55	87	12.8
		55–100	22	−8.3
Low	Medium	0–35	66	20.8
		35–55	11	8.0
		55–100	27	−0.5
Low	High	0–35	25	12.9
		35–55	42	12.8
		55–100	56	21.2
High	Low	0–35	48	19.4
		35–55	55	16.1
		55–100	19	15.9
High	Medium	0–35	83	18.1
		35–55	20	18.3
		55–100	14	14.5
High	High	0–35	53	18.5
		35–55	42	22.4
		55–100	75	19.4

1. Own parents' education was dichotomized into parents averaging less than completion of high school and those who completed high school or had more schooling. Average education of white peers was categorized at arbitrary cutting points to create equal numbers of peer groups in each category; those in the low category averaged less than high school completion; the medium group averaged close to high school completion; the high group averaged more than a high school education.
2. Interaction of own parents' education, education of parents of white peers, and class racial composition is significant at .01 level in analysis of covariance in which friendship with whites is fourth factor and IQ, sex, year in school, and average education of parents of black peers are covariates.

were related significantly to the grades and to the effort of black students. However, these relationships were not consistent. Grades were highest for the relatively small number of blacks whose white peers expressed the highest academic values. But those blacks whose white peers had medium academic values received somewhat lower grades than those whose white peers had the lowest values. With respect to effort, the greatest effort was displayed by those blacks whose white peers were medium in expressed academic values. Neither the academic values of blacks nor their achievement scores were related signficantly to the average academic values of their white peers.

Of particular interest are the results bearing on the question: Did the effects of class racial composition and/or of friendships with whites vary with the academic values of white peers? The results show that they did not. There were no combined (interaction) effects between the average values of white peers and either class racial composition or friendship with whites. Nor were there any combined effects among all three of those factors.

We also investigated whether the use of a behavioral, rather than a verbal, measure of the values of white peers would change the results. We therefore conducted another set of analyses in which we used the average effort of white peers as a measure of their academic values. The results were essentially the same as before. The findings are consistent, then, in indicating that the effects of interracial contact on the academic performance of black students did *not* depend on the values of white peers. Nor did the values of white peers exert a consistent effect of their own on academic outcomes for blacks.

However, while the academic values of *white* peers had little impact on black students, the academic values of their *black* peers appeared to be more important. Black students' effort and grades were related more strongly to the values of their black peers than to those of their white peers. Moreover, the relation of class racial composition to academic outcomes varied more consistently with the values of black peers than with those of white peers.[19] Most notably, attending classes with a larger proportion of blacks was associated with lower effort only among those black students whose black peers expressed low academic values (see Figure 11.6). Also, increasing proportions of blacks in classes was related to higher grades only among those blacks whose black schoolmates expressed high academic values. Thus, having larger proportions of blacks in their classes affected black students most adversely when their black peers attached low value to academic success.

These results suggest that one reason the values of white peers had little influence on blacks is that their black peer group was the more important reference group—i.e., the group against whose standards blacks judged their own behavior. In addition, the academic values of most black students were sufficiently high (see Chapter 10) that positive values among white peers often may not have differed much from the blacks' own values. Other factors—e.g., stimulation from teachers—may have been more important to arouse high motivation.

Own Ability and Ability of Peers. The effects of attending mostly white classes may depend in part on the (initial) ability of black students and on the ability of their white peers. Research on achievement motivation has shown that such motivation is highest when the expectancy of doing well, relative to others, is moderate (Atkinson and Feather, 1966).

Figure 11.6 Average Effort Scores of Black Students, as Related to Racial Composition of Their Classes, Separately for Those Whose Black Peers Differed in Academic Values[1]

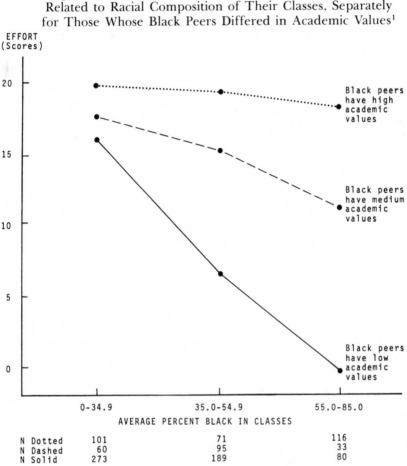

	0-34.9	35.0-54.9	55.0-85.0
N Dotted	101	71	116
N Dashed	60	95	33
N Solid	273	189	80

AVERAGE PERCENT BLACK IN CLASSES

1. Main effect of racial composition is significant at .05 level and main effect of black values is significant at .001 level; interaction is significant at .001 level. Results taken from analysis of covariance in which values of white peers was third factor and IQ, sex, parents' education, and year in school were covariates.

Black students' expectancies of doing well academically should be moderate when their initial academic skills are about equal to those of their classmates. Therefore, we might expect their achievement motivation to be highest in such situations. The impact of the black students' abilities relative to white peers should increase as the proportion of whites in their classes increases.

To explore this subject, we related academic outcomes to the separate and combined effects of (1) class racial composition, (2) the student's own academic ability on entering high school, as indicated by his IQ scores,[20] and (3) the average academic ability (IQ scores) of white peers.[21]

The results show first that the average IQ of white peers had a clear effect on black students' grades and smaller, but significant, effects on effort and achievement scores. As the average IQ of white peers increased, grades, effort, and achievement scores all rose among blacks. However, black students' expectations of being able to go to college were not related to the average IQ of their white peers. The general pattern of association between having high-IQ white peers and good academic outcomes may indicate that such schoolmates had a stimulating effect on black students. More important, probably, black students who had high-ability white peers were more likely to be in school settings (e.g., the the academic program) in which high standards of academic work were maintained.

Did the effects of class racial composition on academic outcomes for black students vary with their own IQ's? The results show that they did not. There were no significant combined (interaction) effects of class racial composition and black students' own IQ scores.

Nor did the effects of class racial composition depend on the average IQ of white peers. There was a very small, statistically significant interaction between these factors as they related to black achievement scores. However, inspection of the mean achievement scores of those with different combinations of class racial composition and white peer IQ reveals no clear pattern of results.

There is some indication that the effect of the average IQ of white peers varied with the student's own ability. However, the pattern of results does not support consistently the notion that black students will do better when their white peers are on about the same ability level (see Figure 11.7). Moreover, the effects of class racial composition did not vary with particular combinations of black students' own ability levels and those of their white peers.

Overall, these results do not support the expectation that the effects on blacks of attending predominately white classes will depend on the relative abilities of the two groups. One possible reason is that many black students may have defined academic success in absolute terms (e.g., getting a passing grade or a B) rather than in terms of their standing relative to classmates. Another possible explanation is that many black students may not have used white peers as a salient comparison group, even where classes were predominately white. They may have compared themselves to their black peers instead. In addition, any effects on students' motivation and achievement which stemmed from students' relative abilities may have been overshadowed by more powerful influences—such as pressures and rewards from teachers.

Program. Juniors and seniors in the Indianapolis high schools were enrolled in one of four curriculum programs: general, academic (college preparatory), fine and practical arts (FPA), or vocational (see Chapter 2). These programs differed with respect to the interests, aspirations, and abilities of students, in the types of courses offered, and in the expectations and demands of teachers.

Figure 11.7 Average Total Achievement Scores of Black Students (Freshmen and Sophomores), as Related to Average IQ Scores of Their White Peers, Separately for Those of Different Personal IQ Levels[1]

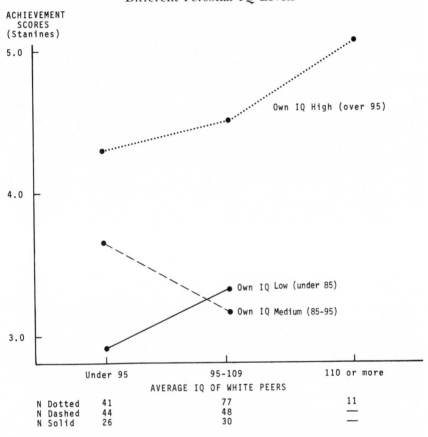

1. Effect of own IQ is significant (p < .001), effect of average IQ of white peers is significant (p < .05), and interaction of these factors is significant (p < .001). Results are from analysis of variance in which parents' education, sex, average IQ of black peers, and average values of peers of each race were covariates.

In view of these diverse differences among the programs, it was difficult to predict in which, if any, program(s) interracial contact would have the most beneficial effects on black students' performance. However, in view of the importance of programs, we wished to explore whether the academic effects of contact with whites might differ for black students in different programs. Only data for juniors and seniors were used since only these upperclassmen were formally enrolled in programs. Also, because of the small number of students in vocational programs, these students were omitted from these analyses.

We found first that students in different programs differed significantly with respect to all academic outcomes examined: values, effort, and grades. Those in the academic program were highest on all these criteria, those in the FPA program were next, and those in the general program were lowest in all three respects.

The effects of class racial composition on academic outcomes did not differ significantly for those in different programs. Nor did the effects of friendship with whites (or the combination of class racial composition and friendship) differ for blacks in different programs.

However, there was a strong tendency for an increasing proportion of blacks to lead to lower effort among black students more in the general program than in other programs (see Figure 11.8).[22] Thus, the general drop in effort which we found to accompany increasing proportions of blacks seems to have occurred mainly among those in the general program.

Relations with Teachers. A number of writers have suggested that the success of school racial integration will depend in considerable part on positive attitudes and positive actions by the school staff (see Chapter 1).

One aspect of staff behavior which might be important in affecting outcomes in racially mixed settings is the extent to which staff members show favoritism to students of one race (and are perceived by students as doing so). We do not have objective evidence concerning favoritism by school staff but we did obtain students' perceptions on this topic (see Chapter 8). Black students who saw the most staff favoritism toward whites had somewhat lower grades than other blacks, but they differed little in effort, achievement scores, or academic values.

Did the effects of interracial contact depend at all on black students' perceptions of staff discrimination? The results show a small interaction effect between class racial composition and perceived discrimination as these factors related to black students' grades. Inspection of the cell means shows that, among black students who saw little favoritism toward whites, being in classes with larger proportions of whites was associated with lower grades. Among blacks who saw greater favoritism toward whites, being in classes with more whites tended to be associated with higher grades. These results are contrary to the expectation that perceptions of equal treatment will make the effects of desegregation more positive for blacks.

The effects of class racial composition on other academic outcomes (effort, achievement scores, values) did not vary with black students' perceptions of discrimination. Nor did the effects of friendship with whites vary with perceived discrimination. Finally, there were no significant combined effects among class racial composition, friendship with white peers, and perceived staff discrimination on any of the academic outcomes. Overall, then, there is no evidence that interracial contact had the most positive effects on academic outcomes for black students when the students saw a relative absence of discrimination against their race by the school staff.

Another possibility is that, while the effects of biracial classrooms on black students may not depend specifically on perceptions of racial dis-

Figure 11.8 Average Effort Scores, as Related to Racial Composition of Their Classes, for Black Students (Juniors and Seniors) in Different Curriculum Programs[1]

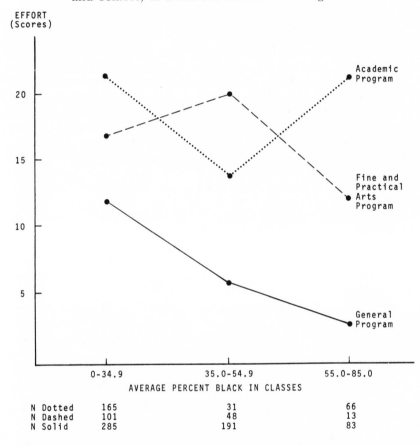

N Dotted	165	31	66
N Dashed	101	48	13
N Solid	285	191	83

1. Main effect of curriculum program is significant at .001 level; main effect of class racial composition is not significant; and interaction between these factors is marginally significant (p = .078) in analysis of covariance in which friendship with whites was third factor and IQ, sex, and parents' education were covariates.

crimination by teachers, they may depend on the black students' general relationships with their teachers. We do not have data on actual interactions between students and teachers but we do have a measure of students' evaluations of their teachers, based on their descriptions of teacher behaviors. Most of the items concern the extent to which the teacher is supportive of the student (e.g., "have shown an interest in me," "don't treat me with respect").

These results show that there was a small interaction effect between class racial composition and evaluation of teachers as these factors related to effort. Being in classes with greater proportions of whites was related to greater effort, regardless of students' evaluation of their teachers, but this effect was smallest when evaluation of teachers was medium, rather than either high or low.

Class racial composition and evaluation of teachers also had a small interaction effect on black students' academic values. Among blacks who evaluated their teachers highly, class racial composition had no relation to academic values. Among those who had low evaluations of their teachers, being in classes with greater proportions of whites was associated with slightly higher academic values.

The relation of class racial composition to grades and to achievement scores did not differ for blacks with different evaluations of their teachers. Nor did the relation of friendly contact with whites to any academic outcome differ significantly among blacks with different evaluations of their teachers. Finally, there were no three-way interaction effects among class racial composition, friendship with whites, and evaluation of teachers.

Overall, these results provide no indication that contact with white peers had the most beneficial effects on academic outcomes for black students when the blacks saw their teachers as supportive and had favorable attitudes toward them. A positive relation with teachers had beneficial effects in itself (see next section), but it did not appear to change the impact of interracial contact.

Conclusions about Conditions of Contact. The findings presented in this section indicate that black students who attended predominately white classes did not do better academically when they had white friends, or when their white peers came from high-SES families or had high academic values. Nor did the effect of class racial composition appear to be affected by the relative academic abilities of blacks and their white peers. These results indicate that the positive effects of attending predominately white classes which we observed previously were not the result of contact with, or influences from, white peers.

There was some evidence that attending predominately white classes was linked to better performance (especially effort) among those black students whose peers were *not* academically oriented (i.e., those whose black peers had low academic values and those in the general program). Also, attending predominately white classes appeared to lead to greater effort among those black students whose white peers' parents and whose own parents had little education.

Why should black students whose peers were not academically oriented and/or from low-SES backgrounds have tried less hard when their classes were heavily black than when their classes were predominately white? There is some evidence from prior studies that when teachers confront classes which are both (1) composed of students who are not academically oriented (usually also from poorly educated families) and (2) about half or more black, they tend to have lower expectations of, and place fewer demands on, the students than they do when both of these circumstances are not present together (see Weinberg, 1977). This may have occurred in the Indianapolis schools too.

Another possibility is that disciplinary problems may have been most severe in those classes which were both heavily black and had students who were not academically oriented and/or from low-SES backgrounds. These two possible causes may be related, since disciplinary problems (along with other factors, such as racial stereotypes) may contribute to teachers' having low expectations of students and making few demands on them.

Finally, the academic effects of contact with whites did not vary for black boys as compared to black girls, for those who attended grade schools of different racial compositions, and for those with different attitudes toward their teachers.

Interracial Contact in Context

The results presented so far show that the racial composition of classes and friendship with whites had some associations with academic outcomes for black students. The associations were stronger under certain conditions. But how sizable was the impact of interracial contact on academic outcomes?

One way of judging this impact is by including the interracial contact variables, together with other variables which might affect academic outcomes, in the same multiple regression analyses. Multiple regression permits us to see the impact of interracial contact variables relative to the impact of other variables. (See Chapter 9 for a brief description of multiple regression analysis.) These analyses also permit us to see whether the effects of interracial contact are significant when we control for a larger number of control variables than we have controlled for before.

Three outcomes were predicted: effort, grades, and achievement scores. We related each of these outcomes to the following set of possible predictors[23]:

A. *Interracial Contact*
   1. Racial composition of grade school classes
   2. Racial composition of high school classes[24]
   3. Friendly contact with whites in high school
   4. Unfriendly contact with whites in high school
B. *Home Background*
   1. Parents' education
   2. Family composition (both parents present, only mother present, etc.)
   3. Number of children in family
   4. Family concern about school work (as reported by student)
C. *High School Situation*
   1. Curriculum program
   2. Ability grouping of classes[25]

    3. Year in school
    4. Opportunity for contact with black faculty
    5. Participation in school activities
    6. Evaluation of teachers
  D. *Personal Information about Student*
    1. Sex
    2. IQ score (on entering high school)
    3. Time spent at a paying job
    4. Time spent helping family around the house
    5. Preference for different high school prior to attending present school
    6. Aggressiveness (unfriendly contact with same-race peers)

Table 11.5 shows which of these predictors made significant contributions to each academic outcome (with all the other predictors held constant) and the size of the independent contribution of each.

Effort. Being in the academic program (as compared to the general program) contributed most to greater effort. Those who chose this program of courses may have tended to be highly motivated when they entered. In addition, once in the academic program, students probably were encouraged to work hard by teachers and by other students in that program.

Evaluating teachers positively contributed second most to black students' effort. Students who saw their teachers as supportive were probably more likely to be encouraged and rewarded for greater effort by teachers. In addition, students who evaluated their teachers highly would have wanted to please their teachers.

Spending more time helping one's family around the house also helped predict greater effort. We had included this variable in the expectation that household chores might take time away from school work. But apparently the time spent on household tasks was taken from other activities than school work. Students who help more around the house may tend to be those who are more conventional, more oriented to adult values, and more generally responsible. In addition, their work at home may bring them more under the influence of adults in their family, who can be expected usually to encourage hard work in school.

Frequent unfriendly contacts with students of the same race contributed to lower effort in school. Frequent fighting in school probably is part of a general pattern of nonconformist behavior, which includes low effort and therefore low grades.

Finally, the weakest of the five significant predictors of effort is class racial composition. Being in classes with a substantial proportion of blacks (40 to 90%), as compared to being in predominately white classes, contributed to less effort among black students. (The drop was equal to .23 of a standard deviation on the effort scale.) This association between a large proportion of blacks and lower effort is familiar by now, and these results indicate that some association remains even when a large number of other variables are held constant simultaneously.

Table 11.5. Significant Predictors of Academic Outcomes
for Black Students (Partial Beta Coefficients)[1]

	Effort	Current Grades	Total Achievement Scores
Classes 40.0–89.9% black	−.11*	—	—
Positive evaluation of teachers	.15***	.23***	.08*
Taking academic program (or courses)	.17**	.19***	.20***
Time helping family around house	.13**	–	–
Unfriendly contact with same-race peers	−.12*	−.10*	–
Participation in school activities	–	.19***	–
IQ score	–	.11*	.51***
Sex female	–	–	−.14***
Higher ability grouping	–	–	.26***
Proportion of variance explained (R^2)	.17	.25	.64

1. Results taken from multiple regression analyses. Other variables included as predictors, which did not have significant effects on any outcome, are listed in text.

   Median N is about 1,600 for effort and grades and about 600 for achievement scores. N varies somewhat for each pair of variables, depending on number of cases with missing data.

   Achievement scores were analyzed only for freshmen and sophomores since juniors and seniors took these tests prior to the time the data on interracial contact were collected.

   Class racial composition was treated as a set of dummy variables in the analyses of effort and grades in order to reflect its nonlinear relations to these outcomes. For effort, 40–89.9 and 90–100% black each were compared to 0–39.9% black. For grades, 30.0–59.9, 60.0–79.9, and 80–100% black were compared to 0–29.9% black.

* Significant at .05 level; ** significant at .01 level; *** significant at .001 level; − indicates nonsignificant beta; — indicates variable to left not used to predict this outcome.

The nature of contact with white schoolmates (friendly and unfriendly) had no effect on black students' effort when all the other variables (including class racial composition) were controlled. Nor did any of the other predictor variables listed above affect the effort of black students. All together, the variables in this analysis were not very successful in explaining differences in effort among black students. Only 17% of the total variance was accounted for.

Grades. Evaluating teachers positively and being in the academic program—the two best predictors of effort—also were (in different order) the best predictors of grades. The greater effort of students in the academic program, and of those who evaluated teachers highly, probably contributed also to their getting higher grades—by leading to more learning and by evoking approval from teachers.

Participation in school activities also was associated relatively strongly with higher grades for black students. For some (though not most) activities, students had to have a minimum grade average in order to participate. Thus, higher grades would have enabled students to get into certain activities and some students may have been motivated to maintain a minimum grade average in order to enter, or remain in, activities that interested them. Students who participated more in activities also may have tended to have personal qualities (e.g., being outgoing and friendly) which contributed to their getting high grades.

Two other variables had smaller, but significant, effects on black students' grades. As would be expected, higher IQ contributed to higher grades. The small size of this contribution contrasts to the much larger effect of IQ on achievement scores. Apparently, while the general cognitive abilities measured by IQ do help to get good grades, other factors—such as completing assignments and doing work in the manner expected by teachers—may be more important.

Fighting frequently with students of one's own race also contributed to lower grades. We have already noted that students who fought often manifested lower effort. This low effort would have led to less learning. Moreover, both their low effort and their disruptive behavior would have led teachers to evaluate such students negatively.

None of the three aspects of interracial contact—class racial composition, friendly contact with white schoolmates, or unfriendly contact with white schoolmates—had a significant effect on black students' grades. These results are consistent with those reported earlier (Table 11.3) which showed that black students' grades were not correlated significantly with either friendly and unfriendly interracial contact when other relevant variables were controlled. However, the present results are *not* consistent with our earlier finding (Figure 11.2) of a significant association between black students' grades and the racial composition of their classes, even with IQ, ability group, and program controlled. The difference in results may be due to differences in the way class racial composition was categorized or to differences in the statistical tests used in the two analyses.[26] The different results also may be due to the fact that a much larger number of other variables are used as controls in the analysis shown in Table 11.5 than in that shown in Figure 11.2. While a large number of controls helps to prevent spurious associations from appearing, it also sometimes may mask real relationships.[27] In light of all the evidence—including the total amount of variance in grades explained (see below)—we are inclined to think that class racial composition does have some effect on black students' grades. However, the present results indicate that this association is not completely separate from that of other variables.

Table 11.5 indicates that some of the other variables listed above also did not affect grades. All together, the variables used in these analyses explained 25% of the total variance in current grades among black students.

Achievement Scores. For this analysis of achievement scores, freshmen and sophomores were combined. By far the best predictor of high achievement scores was high IQ. The strong effect of IQ indicates that the cognitive abilities developed at an earlier age have a great impact on later performance. This may occur in part because IQ tests and achievement tests tend to assess the same kinds of cognitive skills. The general cognitive skills acquired prior to high school probably also facilitate learning during high school. In addition, some students may have a facility for taking tests, which tends to raise scores in both types of tests.

Being in higher-level ability groups was the second largest contributor to high achievement scores. This association was not due to scores on achievement tests being used as a basis for placement into ability groups, since these scores were obtained later than the ability placement. It appears, therefore, that black students learned more in average (or, in a few cases, accelerated) ability groups than they did in slow classes. This may have been due to lower expectations and demands from teachers in slow classes, to teachers' covering less material in slow classes, to teachers' being less effective in slow classes, or to some combination of these factors.

Being in the academic program (as compared to the general program) was the third strongest contributor to higher achievement scores. This result is consistent with the greater effort and higher grades of those in the academic program, which we have already noted. It also is consistent with previous research showing that "tracking" has an independent effect on achievement (Rutter et al., 1979, p. 13).

Fourth in importance as a predictor of achievement scores was sex. Black boys did better than black girls on achievement tests. This is somewhat surprising since boys tended to try less hard and to get lower grades than girls. The reason for the better performance of boys on achievement tests is not apparent to us.

Finally, one other factor had a significant independent effect on achievement scores. The more positively black students evaluated their teachers, the higher their achievement scores tended to be. However, this effect was quite small.

None of the three aspects of interracial contact—class racial composition, friendly contact with white schoolmates, or unfriendly contact with white schoolmates—had a significant effect on black students' achievement scores when the effects of all other variables were controlled. These results are consistent with our earlier analyses which showed interracial contact to have only weak and inconsistent effects on black students' achievement scores.

A number of other factors among those listed above also did not have significant effects on achievement. The total set of predictor variables explained 64% of the variance in achievement scores among black students.

Overall, the total set of results for all academic outcomes indicates that the greatest influences on positive academic outcomes for black students were:

1. The cognitive skills the student had developed prior to high school (as indicated by IQ scores)

2. Curriculum and ability group placement in the school
3. The student's relations with his teachers
4. Personal characteristics of students which reflect conventional, responsible behavior (i.e., little fighting with same-race peers, helping one's family, participation in school activities).

Interracial contact generally had a very limited impact on academic outcomes for black students. Attending classes with greater proportions of whites did contribute somewhat to greater effort. But, with other relevant factors held constant, the racial composition of classes did not significantly affect black students' grades or achievement scores. Moreover, more friendly (or less unfriendly) contact with white schoolmates had no positive impact on academic outcomes for blacks.

Variance Explained. To provide an overall summary of the effects of the main interracial contact variables, we conducted a set of stepwise regression analyses. When the effects of grade school class racial composition, plus high school class racial composition, plus friendship with whites during high school were entered into the equations first, they explained together the following proportions of the total variance: effort, .011; grades, .100; achievement scores, .031; academic values, .012. When the three interracial contact variables were entered into the equations after other predictor variables,[28] they explained the following additional proportions of variance: effort, .004; grades, .080; achievement scores, .006; academic values, .010. Clearly, the impact of the interracial contact variables was quite small.[29]

Summary

Let us now sum up the results of our investigation into the effects of interracial contact on academic outcomes for black students.

First, our results have provided no support for the proposition that greater contact with whites in grade school will improve academic outcomes for blacks. Neither the amount nor the nature of interracial contact which blacks experienced in grade school had any impact on their general cognitive abilities at the end of grade school (as indicated by IQ scores). Nor did more interracial contact in grade school have a positive effect on black students' effort, grades, or achievement scores in high school.

The major portion of our investigation concerned the effects of interracial contact in high school. Academic outcomes for black students were not related consistently to the racial composition of their high schools. However, as the percentage of blacks in a school rose, effort and achievement scores of blacks tended to decline while their grades tended to rise. For individual students, results generally showed some of the same trends. As the racial composition of classes went from predominately white to those having larger proportions of blacks, effort among black students tended to decline, and achievement scores also tended to decline especially among freshmen. However, as the proportion of blacks in their classes rose, the grades of black students generally improved. Thus, black students generally appeared to be doing less but getting more positive feedback (in the form of grades) in mostly black, as compared to mostly white, classes.

The results for individual black students also indicate that effort and achievement scores did not decrease consistently, and grades did not increase consistently, as the proportion of blacks in classes rose. At the point where students' classes became almost all black, those overall trends were reversed: the effort of black students turned upward (and for sophomores, so did their achievement scores) while their grades declined. These results suggest that it is not the proportion of blacks *per se* that affected academic outcomes for black students but something else—perhaps lowered standards and laxer discipline—that tends to accompany increases in percentage black. Where high standards are maintained—as they appeared to have been in some all-black settings—high effort and achievement among black students can be maintained regardless of racial composition.

The nature of the contact which black students had with white schoolmates in high school generally had only small associations with academic outcomes. As blacks in a school had, on the average, more friendly contact with their white schoolmates, their average effort increased but their average grades and achievement scores did not seem to be affected. For individual black students, there was a tendency for those students who had more friendly interaction with whites—especially more friendship—to attain better academic outcomes. But these associations were quite small and tended to disappear when other variables affecting academic outcomes were held constant. Unfriendly contact with white schoolmates also generally had little association with academic outcomes among blacks, especially with other relevant variables held constant.

Did interracial contact have a greater impact on academic outcomes for certain types of black students or under certain conditions? In general, we found that the associations between academic outcomes for blacks and their contacts with white schoolmates varied little over a fairly wide range of conditions, including students' sex, their previous contact with whites in grade school, perceptions of supportiveness by teachers, and the relative ability of white peers.

Consistent with most other studies, we found that attending predominately white classes did *not* have more positive effects for blacks when they were friends with whites than when they lacked white friends. This was true even when white peers were from high-status families or had high academic values. These results suggest that the positive effects of attending predominately white classes which occurred for some blacks (specifically, higher effort) were *not* the result of contact with white peers.

Being in predominately white classes did appear to benefit those black students whose peers (of either race) were not academically oriented or came from low-education families. For these black students, it appears that there was something about being in predominately white classes that was beneficial, despite the low status and low academic orientation of their peers. It may be that academic standards remained relatively high in predominately white classes, even when students came from low-status families and/or were not academically oriented.

Finally, we compared the effect of interracial contact variables with those of other factors which may affect academic outcomes among black students. We found that the impact of interracial contact on academic outcomes was small relative to other factors. Also, the amount of variance in academic outcomes which was explained by interracial contact was quite small. Thus, the results indicate that the amount and nature of contact which black students had with whites had only a slight impact on their academic outcomes.

In this chapter, we have limited our attention to black students. In the next chapter, we turn to white students and consider the effects of interracial contact on academic outcomes for the whites.

12 | *Contact and Academic Outcomes: White Students*

Research concerning the effects of racial desegregation has focused on academic outcomes for minority—usually black—children (St. John, 1975, p. 34). This focus is understandable and justified, given the fact that poor school outcomes for minority children is a major societal problem. But there are reasons to be interested in the effects of interracial schooling on white students also. From a policy point of view, it is desirable to know if racially mixed schooling involves any costs with respect to white students' achievement and, if so, how great these costs are relative to any benefits for minority students. From a scientific point of view, we would like to know whether the processes which take place in interracial situations operate in the same way for whites as for blacks.

There has been some research concerning the effects of racial desegregation on academic outcomes for whites. The data of the national Equality of Educational Opportunity Survey indicated that verbal achievement test scores of white students declined as the proportion of blacks in schools increased, especially where schools had a black majority. However, this relationship was not substantial when the social background of individual students and of the total student body were taken into account (Coleman et al., 1966; U.S.C.C., 1967). A more recent study of Southern schools (Narot, 1973) found that, with students' social class controlled, the achievement scores of white tenth grade girls actually rose as the proportion of blacks in their schools increased. For white male tenth graders, and all fifth grade whites, there was little relation between school racial composition and achievement scores.

Eight longitudinal studies of desegregating school systems reviewed by St. John (1975, pp. 34–36) all showed that attending racially mixed schools had no negative effects on the achievement of whites. Moreover, six studies in which central city minority children were bused to outlying communities all showed no significant difference between the achievement of whites in classes that did or did not receive bused students. However, St. John notes that, in all these cases, white children remained in the majority in their schools and classrooms.

In the few studies of white students who attended majority-black schools, results have been more mixed. In a few cases, whites (usually self-selected) who attended majority-black schools did as well or better than those in mostly white schools (St. John, 1975). But at least two studies have shown an association between attendance at majority-black schools and lower achievement scores for whites (St. John and Lewis, 1971; Wrightstone et al., 1966).

Overall, the past evidence indicates that achievement of white students does not suffer when their classes have a minority of blacks. But past research is too sparse and too inconsistent to answer the question of whether attending majority-black classes has a detrimental effect on white achievement.

In this chapter we present additional data concerning the associations of school and class racial composition with academic outcomes for whites. We are able to examine these associations over a wide range of variation in class racial composition and for a number of academic outcomes. In addition, we will present evidence on several issues on which there has been an almost total lack of evidence to date. The first concerns the effect of close social relations with blacks. It has been argued that the achievement of black students will be influenced by white schoolmates more when they are friends with the whites (see Chapter 1). Similarly, one could argue that the achievement of white students will be influenced more by their association with black schoolmates when they are friends with the blacks. Is this true?

The effects of interracial contact also may vary with other circumstances. Again, this matter previously has been considered primarily from the perspective of black achievement (see Chapter 1). It has been suggested that the effects of contact with white peers may differ for blacks with different personal characteristics (e.g., sex, social class) and for blacks whose white peers have different characteristics (e.g., social class, IQ, values). Obviously, such variations in personal characteristics and in traits of the other-race group also may affect the outcomes of interracial contact among white students. We will present some evidence on these matters.

In general, the plan of this chapter and the results to be presented parallel those of Chapter 11, which examined the relationship of interracial contact and academic outcomes for blacks. In most cases we will not repeat for whites the details of measures and procedures described for blacks in Chapter 11.

We will begin by looking at the effects of interracial contact in grade school on academic outcomes for whites.

Interracial Contact in Grade School

We obtained from students information about the racial composition of their grade school classes and about the friendliness of the interracial contacts they had in grade school (see Chapter 5). To what extent was the amount and/or nature of interracial contact which white students had in grade school associated with their academic performance?

Relation to IQ

First, we may consider the associations between contact with blacks in grade school and white students' IQ scores. Since IQ scores measure general cognitive abilities, which may be substantially affected by school experiences, important differences in grade school environments would be expected to affect IQ scores at the end of grade school. (Almost all students in our sample took these tests in the eighth grade.)

However, Table 12.1 shows that there was almost no association between white students' IQ scores and the racial composition of their grade school classes. Nor was there any substantial association between white students' IQ scores and the friendliness of their contacts with blacks in grade school. The results shown in Table 12.1 control for the effects of parents' education and, in the case of friendly interracial contact, also for the effects of sex. But, even without these controls, the associations between whites' IQ scores and the measures of their contacts with blacks in grade school are tiny.

Could it be that the low correlation between grade school racial composition and white IQ scores is masking a relationship which is not a straight-line one? To check on this possibility, we divided the racial composition of grade school classes into four categories and obtained the average IQ scores for white students in each category, after adjusting for parents' education. The results show that average IQ scores were almost identical (averaging 105.6) for those white students who attended all-white classes, those who attended classes with "very few" blacks, and those who attended classes with "quite a few" blacks. However, among the relatively few (55) white students in our sample whose grade school classes generally did not have a white majority, the average IQ score (102.8) was slightly lower than the average for other whites.[1]

We also investigated the possibility that the effects of interracial contact in grade school would vary for white students from families of different educational levels. However, the results showed that this was not the case. Although white students' IQ scores were positively related to the education of their parents, there was no combined (interaction) effect between parents' education and the racial composition of grade school classes.

Table 12.1. Contact with Black Classmates in Grade School as Related to Academic Outcomes for White Students in Grade School and High School (Partial Correlations with Parents' Education and Sex Controlled)[1]

	Average Proportion Blacks in Grade School Classes		Friendly Contact with Blacks in Grade School	
	Partial r	*(N)*	*Partial r*	*(N)*
IQ scores	−.01	(1,543)	−.05*	(1,472)
Effort	−.01	(1,775)	.01	(1,698)
Current grades, high school	−.01	(1,823)	.00	(1,743)
Tenth Grade Achievement Scores, Freshmen and Sophomores				
MAT, total scores	−.11***	(787)	−.02	(766)
MAT, English Language	−.10***	(920)	.00	(894)
MAT, Mathematics	−.07*	(892)	.00	(867)
Tenth Grade Achievement Scores, Juniors and Seniors				
NEDT, total scores	−.11***	(798)	−.15***	(755)
NEDT, English Usage	−.12***	(798)	−.15***	(755)
NEDT, Math Usage	−.11***	(798)	−.12***	(755)

1. Parent education was controlled for all correlations. Parent education and sex were controlled for correlations of friendly contact with blacks with other variables.

* Significant at .05 level; *** significant at .001 level.

Relation to High School Outcomes

How about the associations between contact with blacks in grade school and academic outcomes for whites in high school? Is there evidence of any such long-term effects?

Table 12.1 shows the correlations between the interracial contact which whites had in grade school and their academic outcomes in high school. The correlations are controlled for the effects of the education of the students' parents.

The results show first that there were essentially no associations between white students' effort in high school and either the racial composition of their grade school or their friendly contact with blacks in grade school. Nor was there any association between current grades in high school and either of the measures of interracial contact in grade school.

However, the greater the proportion of black classmates in grade school, the lower the achievement scores of white students tended to be.

The size of these negative associations is small, explaining only about 1% of the variance in whites' achievement scores. But the associations are statistically significant, are found both for lowerclassmen and for upperclassmen (who took different batteries of achievement tests), and are found for total test scores, for the English-language portion, and for the math portion of the test battery.[2]

Among white juniors and seniors, friendly contact with blacks in grade school also was associated slightly with lower achievement scores in high school. However, among white freshmen and sophomores, no such associations were found.

The correlations presented in Table 12.1 are based on the assumption that any associations between interracial contact in grade school and academic outcomes in high school are linear (straight-line) relationships. But, as in the case of IQ, we may wonder whether there may be some nonlinear relationships between interracial contact in grade school and academic outcomes—for example, lower performance only among those who attended majority-black grade schools. A closer examination of the data indicates that this was not the case for either effort or grades.

However, the drop in white students' achievement scores occurred only when the proportion of blacks in their grade school classes exceeded a certain level. Figure 12.1 shows the achievement scores of whites on two batteries of achievement tests (the NEDT and the MAT), as these scores related to the racial composition of their grade school classes. (Scores are adjusted for the effects of parents' education and sex.) Total scores on the NEDT were low only for those white students who attended grade school classes which were half or more black. Inspection of more detailed results (not shown) indicates that this same pattern of results was generally present for various NEDT subtests, including English usage, math usage, social studies, and natural science.

For students who took the MAT achievement test, total scores dropped when the proportion of blacks in grade school classes exceeded just a few and declined further as the proportion of blacks rose to half or more. This same pattern tended to be true also for the various MAT subtests.

Overall, the results presented in this section indicate that the amount and friendliness of contact with black schoolmates in grade school had little effect on academic outcomes for white students—either in grade school or later in high school. There is some indication, however, that attending grade school classes which had a black majority was associated with slightly lower IQ scores and with slightly lower achievement scores in high school.

Why did this latter result occur? First, it may be that heavily black classes tended to be low-ability-group classes in which only white students with initially low ability were placed. Another possibility is that the achievement of white students in heavily black grade school classes was influenced in a negative way by their black classmates—e.g., as a result of whites' imitating black classmates who did not try hard. Still a third possibility is that teacher behavior may have been different in majority-

Figure 12.1 Racial Composition of Grade School Classes,
as Related to White Students' Total Achievement Scores in High
School (MAT or NEDT), Adjusted for Effects of Parents'
Education and Student Sex[1]

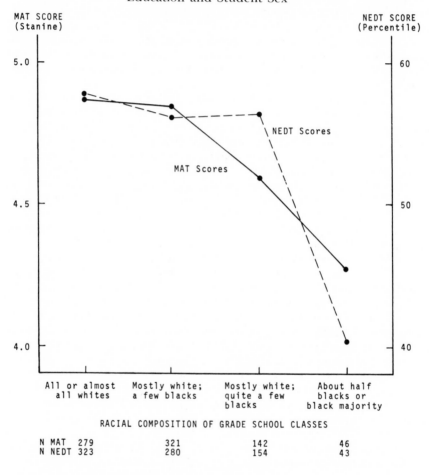

	All or almost all whites	Mostly white; a few blacks	Mostly white; quite a few blacks	About half blacks or black majority
N MAT	279	321	142	46
N NEDT	323	280	154	43

RACIAL COMPOSITION OF GRADE SCHOOL CLASSES

---

1. The relation between grade school composition and MAT scores is significant at .02 level; that with NEDT scores is significant at .001 level. Freshmen and sophomores (in 1970–71) took the MAT in their sophomore years. Juniors and seniors had taken NEDT in their sophomore years.

---

black classes than in other classes (e.g., lower teacher expectations and demands, fewer subjects covered).

It should be noted too that any effects of interracial contact in grade school on white students may vary under different circumstances. For example, it may be that any negative effects of attending classes with substantial proportions of blacks are greater when the blacks are of social class and initial ability levels far below those of the whites.

Unfortunately, we do not have several kinds of information—e.g., on pre-grade-school abilities of white students, on ability grouping of their grade school classes, and on the characteristics of their black classmates—which would help to interpret the association between achievement and contact with blacks in grade school. At the high school level, we do have information about these matters, as well as other relevant data, which will permit us to explore these issues in greater depth.

Interracial Contact in High School

Next we turn to the question of whether academic outcomes for white students were related to their interracial contacts in high school. We will consider first the impact of racial composition and then consider whether the nature of interracial contacts was important.

Racial Composition

Schools. Did the average academic performance of white students vary with the racial composition of the schools they attended?

To answer this question, we related the average effort scores, the average grades, and the average achievement scores of whites to the racial composition of their school (see Table 12.2).

The results show first that, as the percentage of blacks in a school increased, the average effort scores of whites in that school tended to decrease. When the average IQ scores of whites and the average education of their parents are controlled, this negative association becomes slightly stronger.

While these correlations are useful in giving us a rough estimate of the strength of the association, they are a little misleading because they assume a straight-line relationship between percent black and average effort. More detailed examination of the data shows that this relationship was not linear. Average effort among white students was uniformly high in all schools which were majority white, with one exception—John Price, the school with the poorest academic reputation. In contrast, at the three schools with a black majority, average white effort was lower than at the schools which were predominately white.

Despite the lower effort of whites in majority-black schools, average grades of whites tended to increase as the proportion of blacks in their school rose. However, this overall association was small and remained small when controlled for the average IQ and average parental education of whites. Moreoever, the pattern of results for individual schools was not consistent. In two of the three schools which had a black majority

Table 12.2. School Racial Composition and Types of Contact Which Whites Reported with Black Schoolmates, as Related to Average Academic Outcomes for Whites
(Pearson Correlations)[1]

	School Percent Black	Average Friendly Contact with Blacks	Average Total Unfriendly Experiences with Blacks
Average Effort, Whites			
r	−.68*	−.45	−.12
Partial *r*†	−.74*	−.65*	−.05
N schools	(11)	(10)	(10)
Average Current Grades, Whites			
r	.32	.40	.44
Partial *r*†	.31	.10	.80*
N schools	(11)	(10)	(10)
Average Achievement Scores, White Freshmen and Sophomores			
r	.09	.43	−.20
Partial *r*†	−.27	−.12	−.03
N schools	(11)	(10)	(10)

1. All-black school (Carver) not included in any correlations. Pershing High School omitted from correlations of friendly and unfriendly interaction with blacks because of small numbers of blacks there.

* Significant at .05 level.
† Controls for partial correlations are average IQ and average parental education of white students.

(Lakeview and Highland), average white grades were highest for whites in the various schools, but in the third majority-black school (Harrison), white grades were the lowest for whites at any school.

Average achievement scores for white students had little association with the racial composition of the high school they attended. When the average IQ and parental education of the whites were controlled, there was a tendency for whites to have lower achievement scores as the percentage of black students in their schools increased. But the correlation is very small. An examination of the results for individual schools shows *no* consistent tendency for a drop in average white achievement scores in majority-black schools.

Overall, then, our results which relate academic outcomes for white students to the racial composition of their high schools show that: (1) average effort of whites tended to be low in majority-black schools, and (2) there were no substantial associations between the average grades or the average achievement scores of whites and the racial composition of their schools.

Individuals. The racial composition of the entire school may have some importance because of its possible effects on the general academic climate of the school. However, individual students are likely to be affected more directly by the racial composition of their own classes. (We found also that the effects of class racial composition did not vary with the racial composition of the school.)[3]

What was the relation between academic outcomes for individual white students and the average racial composition of their classes?

Effort. Figure 12.2 shows the relationship between the racial composition of white students' classes and their effort in school. The effort scores are adjusted for the effects of students' IQ scores, their ability grouping, and whether or not they were taking an academic program of courses. The results show a curvilinear pattern. Effort among whites was highest for those who attended predominately white classes (i.e., 0–30% black). As the proportion of blacks increased beyond 30% effort among whites declined steadily, until the point where students' classes were 60 to 70% black. Then as the proportion of blacks in their classes rose above 70%, effort among whites rose again—though not to the level of those in predominately white classes.

The relationship between white students' effort and the racial composition of their classes was statistically significant ($p < .001$). However, racial composition explained only about 2.6% of the total variance in white students' effort scores.[4]

Grades. Figure 12.3 shows the relationship between the racial composition of white students' classes and their current grades. Like effort scores, grades are adjusted for the effects of students' IQ scores, ability group placement, and whether or not they were taking an academic program of courses.

The curve for grades is quite different from that for effort. As the proportion of blacks in their classes rose above 20%, white students' grades rose steadily, but only to the point where their classes were about half black. Then, as the proportion of blacks increased beyond the point of a black majority, white grades dropped again, reaching a low point when their classes were 60–70% black. With even larger proportions of blacks, whites' grades stayed at a generally low level.

The association between white students' grades and the racial composition of their classes is statistically significant, but explains only about 2.6% of the total variance in whites' grades.

Achievement Scores. Figure 12.4 shows the relationship between the racial composition of the classes of white lowerclassmen and their total scores on achievement tests.[5] Achievement scores were adjusted for the effects of students' IQs, ability grouping, whether or not they were taking an academic program of courses, and evaluation of teachers.

Achievement scores among whites generally tended to decline as the proportion of blacks in their classes increased. However, the curve was

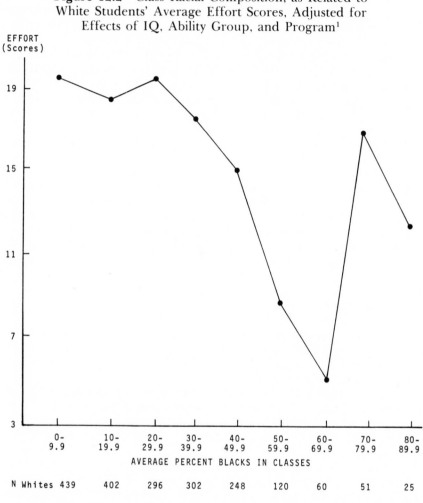

Figure 12.2 Class Racial Composition, as Related to White Students' Average Effort Scores, Adjusted for Effects of IQ, Ability Group, and Program[1]

| N Whites | 439 | 402 | 296 | 302 | 248 | 120 | 60 | 51 | 25 |

AVERAGE PERCENT BLACKS IN CLASSES

---

1. Difference in average effort scores among whites in classes with different racial compositions is significant at .001 level. The correlation ratio is .20 and the correlation ratio after adjustment for other predictors is .16.

neither regular nor consistent. For whites whose classes were 60–70% black, achievement scores dropped to the lowest point. But then, for the small number of whites in classes which were over 70% black, scores rose considerably above this low point.

The association between the total achievement scores of white students and the racial composition of their classes was statistically significant, but the racial composition of classes explained only about 1% of the total variance in white students' achievement scores.

Figure 12.3   Class Racial Composition, as Related to
White Students' Average Current-Semester Grades, Adjusted
for Effects of IQ, Ability Group, and Program[1]

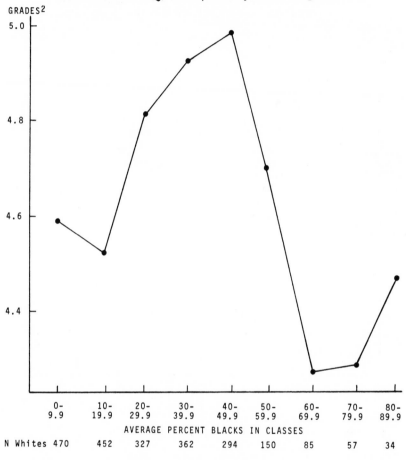

GRADES[2]

| N Whites | 470 | 452 | 327 | 362 | 294 | 150 | 85 | 57 | 34 |

AVERAGE PERCENT BLACKS IN CLASSES

1. Difference in average grades among whites in classes with different racial compositions is significant at .001 level. The correlation ratio is .20 and the correlation ratio after adjustment for other predictors is .16.
2. Grade code is as follows: F = 0, D = 2, C = 4, B = 6, A = 8.

We also looked at the separate associations between class racial composition and the English language and math subtests of the achievement test battery. In these analyses, scores on each subtest were adjusted for the effects of students' IQ, sex, and parents' education. Results (not presented in detail here) show that the relation between the racial composition of white students' classes and their language subscores was significant and followed the same general pattern as the relation between class racial composition and total achievement scores. The association between class

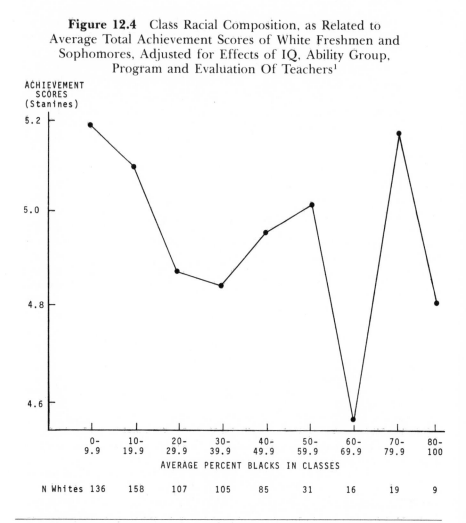

Figure 12.4 Class Racial Composition, as Related to
Average Total Achievement Scores of White Freshmen and
Sophomores, Adjusted for Effects of IQ, Ability Group,
Program and Evaluation Of Teachers[1]

1. Differences in average achievement scores among whites in classes with different racial
   compositions is significant at .01 level. Correlation ratio is .40 and correlation ratio after
   adjustment for other predictors is .10.

racial composition and math achievement scores, though statistically
significant, was weaker than that for language scores. There was a tendency for the math scores of whites to become lower as the proportion of
blacks in their classes increased, but the pattern was inconsistent.

In general, these results for whites are similar to those for blacks
presented in Chapter 11. For students of both races, lower effort and
achievement scores tended to accompany increasing proportions of blacks
in their classes. As we noted in Chapter 11, these results may reflect lesser
demands from teachers and laxer discipline in heavily black classes.

For both races also, as the proportion of blacks increased, there was a rise in grades, despite lower effort and achievement scores. This probably reflects in part a less stringent competition for grades in more heavily black classes (given the lower IQ scores and achievement scores of blacks reported in Chapter 10). What is somewhat more puzzling for white students is the general decline in their grades after blacks became a substantial majority. This result may indicate that the low level of effort of whites in majority-black classes led to their receiving relatively low grades despite the advantage in academic ability they tended to have over their black classmates.

Though the curves are not identical for the two races, the results for whites also parallel to some extent the reversal and upward movement of the effort and achievement curves for blacks when classes became almost all black (see Chapter 11). In the case of blacks, we suggested that educational standards probably were kept fairly high and discipline maintained fairly strictly in many predominately black settings. We would suggest the same kind of explanation for the upturn of effort and achievement scores for whites in predominately black settings. In any event, while there were general tendencies for effort and achievement to decline as the proportion of blacks in classes increased, higher percentages of blacks did not always lead to lower academic performance among students of either race.

Nature of Interracial Contact

Were academic outcomes for white students related to the nature of the contact they had with black schoolmates?

Schools. Again, we examine first the data for total schools. For all white students at each of ten school sites,[6] we computed average scores on the indices of friendly and unfriendly contact with blacks.

The correlations between average scores on these indices of interracial contact and average academic outcomes for whites in a school are shown in Table 12.2. Partial correlations with controls for average IQ and the average education of white students' parents also are shown.

There was an overall tendency for average effort among whites to become lower in schools where whites had more friendly contact with blacks. However, this relationship was due primarily to the effect of Highland High School. At that school, white students had an unusually high level of friendly contact with black schoolmates and also had a fairly low average level of effort.

The relatively low effort of white students at Highland probably was not caused by their friendly contact with blacks, since blacks at that academic school had a high average level of effort themselves. The relatively low level of effort of whites at Highland may have been due, at least in part, to their high level of ability. (They had the highest average IQ of any white student group.) Because of their unusually high ability, white students at Highland may not have had to try very hard. Also, there was a "hippie" segment among whites at Highland, who were more interested in personal development and radical political action than in getting good grades.

The average level of friendly contact which whites had with black schoolmates had only fairly small associations with average white grades and achievement scores. When the average IQ and the average parental education of whites are controlled, friendly contact with blacks had very little relationship to either average grades or average achievement scores.

What about unfriendly contact? The average amount of unfriendly contact which white students in a school had with black schoolmates had little association with either their average effort or their average achievement scores. There was a substantial correlation between whites' having more unfriendly contact with blacks and whites' getting higher grades, after the average IQ and parental education of whites were controlled. However, a detailed examination of the data shows that this was not a general association. Rather, it was due to the effect of one school, Lakeview. At this school, to which most white students were being bused against their wishes (see Chapter 2), whites had by far the most unfriendly contacts with blacks. Whites at this school also got unusually high grades, in view of their fairly low average IQ and low parental education. High grades for white students at Lakeview probably were due to special circumstances there, stemming in part from a hurried and somewhat disorganized creation of a new campus. The association of high grades with much unfriendly contact with blacks at Lakeview probably was coincidental.

Overall, the results indicate very little association between average academic outcomes for whites in a school and the nature of their social relations with blacks. The correlations generally are quite small and, in the two cases where they are more sizable, reflect the influence of a single unusual school, rather than a general association.

Individuals. Were academic outcomes for individual students related to their social relationships with black schoolmates?

Preliminary analyses showed that these relationships were essentially straight-line ones.[7] Therefore, correlation analyses are appropriate. Table 12.3 shows the correlations between academic outcomes for white students and their friendly contact, unfriendly contact, and friendship with blacks. Partial correlations also are presented, showing these relationships after the effects of other relevant variables are controlled. The control variables, applied as appropriate to each relationship, include IQ score, parents' education, evaluation of teachers, sex, ability grouping, following an academic program of courses, and amount of unfriendly contact within one's own racial group.

The results show first that the kinds of interpersonal relations which white students had with black schoolmates had very little relationship to their level of effort in school. There was a tendency for whites who were friends with blacks to exert greater effort in school, even after control variables are applied. But this association is so tiny that it is trivial.

The grades which white students attained also were not associated with either friendly contacts or unfriendly contacts with blacks, especially after other relevant variables were controlled.

Table 12.3. Friendly and Unfriendly Interaction with Blacks in High School, as Related to Academic Outcomes for White Students[1]

	Friendly Contact with Blacks	Friendship with Blacks	Total Unfriendly Experiences with Blacks
Effort			
Correlation (*r*)	.03	.07**	−.10***
r, control on other variables[2]	.00	.07**	.05
(*N*)	(1,338)	(1,358)	(1,469)
Current Grades			
Correlation (*r*)	.03	.05*	−.13***
r, control on IQ	−.03	.03	†
r, control on IQ plus other variables[2]	−.05	.03	.02
(*N*)	(1,000)	(1,335)	(1,455)
Achievement Scores, Freshmen			
Correlation (*r*)	.13*	.11*	−.13*
r, control on IQ	.08	.07	.00
r, controls on IQ plus other variables[2]	.02	.05	.07
(*N*)	(219)	(255)	(262)
Achievement Scores, Sophomores			
Correlation (*r*)	.22***	.07	−.11*
r, control on IQ	−.02	−.03	−.12*
r, controls on IQ plus other variables	−.03	.00	−.07
(*N*)	(259)	(278)	(232)

1. Results are based on students for whom data on all variables used for partial *r*s were available. Zero-order correlations based on total sample are very close to those shown here.
2. Other variables controlled, as appropriate for each analysis, included evaluation of teachers, ability group, being in academic program, sex, parents' education, unfriendly contact with own race, and participation in school activities.

* Significant at .05 level; ** significant at .01 level; *** significant at .001 level.
† IQ not used as control for this correlation because IQ and unfriendly contact are essentially uncorrelated (*r* = −.06).

Total achievement scores for white students (freshmen and sophomores) tended to be higher among those who had friendly contacts with
blacks and lower among those who had unfriendly contacts with blacks.
However, these correlations—quite small to begin with—decline to negligible size and statistical nonsignificance when other variables related to
achievement are controlled.

In other analyses, we examined the relationship between friendship
with blacks and scores on the English language and math portions of the
achievement test battery. These relationships were controlled for the effects of students' IQ scores, parents' education, and sex. The results
showed *no* significant association between white students' friendships with
blacks and their scores on either the language or the math achievement
tests.

Overall, the results of our analyses for individual white students
show little relationship between any of their academic outcomes and any
measure of their social contact with black schoolmates. These results are
consistent with those for total schools (presented above), which also
showed a general lack of association between academic outcomes for
whites and their social relations with blacks.

Interracial Contact under Varying Conditions

As we have pointed out in previous chapters (see Chapters 1 and
11), the effects of varying racial composition may differ for students who
are friends with classmates of the other race as compared to those who
stay aloof from the other race. Moreover, the effects of class racial composition and of interracial friendship on white students may depend on
(1) the characteristics of particular whites, (2) the characteristics of their
black peers, and (3) various aspects of the school situation.

Did interracial contact in fact have different effects on the academic
outcomes of white students under different conditions? To obtain information on this general question, we conducted a series of analyses of
covariance for white students parallel to those conducted for black students (see Chapter 11). These analyses explored the separate and combined effects on each academic outcome of (1) class racial composition, (2)
friendship with blacks, and (3) each of a number of characteristics of
white students, their black peers, and the school setting (taken one or two
at a time).

The racial composition of white students' classes was categorized as
follows: 0–19.9% black, 20–39.9% black, and more than 40% black.[8] Interracial friendship was categorized in a way parallel to that used for black
students. As in the analyses for black students, we controlled the effects of
those factors being studied at any one time for the effects of other variables which might affect academic outcomes.[9]

In summarizing the results of this extensive set of analyses, we will
focus on the extent to which the effects of contact with blacks varied
under different circumstances. (For more detailed results, see Patchen,
1981.)

Class Composition and Friendship. If a large proportion of blacks in classes has any negative effect on academic outcomes for white students, it can be argued that such a negative effect would occur primarily among those who establish most friendship with their black peers. To the extent that black students tend to behave in ways that are not helpful for academic success (e.g., coming late to class), those whites who are most friendly with blacks might be most influenced in a negative way. However, it might be argued on other grounds that friendship with black peers would tend to eliminate any negative effects of being in heavily black classes. To the extent that such negative impact is due to anxiety about acceptance by classmates or even anxiety about personal safety, white students who are most friendly with blacks would suffer fewer detrimental effects.

What do our results show on this question? First, holding constant friendship with blacks does not change the effects of class racial composition reported previously. As the proportion of blacks in their classes increased, the effort and achievement scores of white students still decreased.

Friendships with blacks also had an effect which was independent of class racial composition. Specifically, more friendship with blacks was related to *greater* effort among white students. However, friendship with blacks was not related to any other academic outcomes for white students—i.e., not to grades, achievement scores, or academic values.

Was there a combined (or interaction) effect between class racial composition and friendship with blacks? Basically, there was not. The effects of class racial composition on academic outcomes for whites did not vary much with the amount of friendship with blacks. There were no significant combined effects on grades, achievement scores, or academic values. Moreover, while there was a weak interaction effect on effort, detailed inspection of these results shows that increases in the proportion of whites in classes, and increases in friendship with blacks, were related consistently to higher effort—regardless of the level of the other factor.

There also was little evidence that class racial composition and friendship with blacks had combined effects for particular types of students. Thus, there was little evidence of three-way interactions when the effects of class racial composition and of friendship with blacks were analyzed together with the effects of (1) the student's sex, (2) the student's own parents' education and/or the average education of parents of his black peers, (3) the average academic values of black peers, or (4) the school programs in which the student was enrolled.

Overall, we may conclude that the effects of class racial composition on academic outcomes for whites did *not* depend on the extent of friendship with blacks. Conversely, the effect of friendship with black peers did not vary with class racial composition.

Sex. Compared to white girls, white boys tended to experience more friction in their relationships with black schoolmates (see Chapter 6). This result might lead us to suspect that interracial contact would have different academic effects on white boys and girls. Also, as noted above, Narot (1973) found that increases in the proportion of blacks in schools had more positive effects on the achievement of white high school girls than of white high school boys. What do our own results show?

First, sex affected all the academic outcomes. Girls put forth more effort, got higher grades, and valued academic success more than boys did, although boys got higher achievement test scores. However, the effects of class racial composition on academic outcomes for white students did not differ for white boys as compared to white girls. Nor did the effect of friendship with blacks vary much for the two sexes. Finally, the effects of different combinations of class racial composition and friendship with blacks did not differ much for white boys and white girls.

Overall, then, we may conclude that while sex itself had some fairly sizable effects on academic outcomes for whites, the effect of contact with black schoolmates did not differ for the two sexes.

Contact in Grade School. It is possible that the effect of attending racially mixed classes in high school varies for white students who attended grade schools with differing racial compositions. Perhaps any negative effects occur only for those who attended heavily black classes throughout their school careers. Or perhaps those who attended racially mixed classes in grade school are accustomed to being with black schoolmates and therefore experience fewer negative effects (or more positive effects) than do other whites.

Our results do not support either of these speculations. There is little evidence of interaction effects between the racial composition of classes at the grade school and high school levels. The only significant (though small) interaction was with respect to effort. Inspection of the detailed data shows that being in heavily black high school classes (i.e., over 40% black) was associated with lower effort among whites regardless of the racial composition of their grade school classes. However, the negative effect of heavily black classes on white effort was slightly greater for those who also attended grade schools with substantial proportions of blacks.

Overall, these results indicate that the effect of class racial composition in high school did not vary much for whites who attended grade schools with different racial compositions.

Education of Own Parents and Those of Black Peers. If the academic performance of white students is affected negatively by attending classes with large proportions of blacks, one might expect that any such impact would vary with the relative social class of black schoolmates. Blacks from families of low socioeconomic status (especially low education) may tend to assign low importance to academic goals,[10] may present little competitive academic challenge to most whites,[11] and may lead teachers to cover less material and demand less from students than they usually do.

The effect of attending classes with blacks might depend also on the educational level of white students' own families. The role of this factor is hard to predict, however. On the one hand, whites from the best-educated families potentially can be "pulled down" the most, in terms of academic values, level of class material, etc., by attending classes with lower-class blacks. On the other hand, whites from the best-educated families may have developed strong values and abilities which are less easily affected by interracial contact than those of whites from less-well-educated families.

What do our data show on this subject? First, the general tendency for whites to show lower effort and achievement scores as the proportion of black students rose was *not* affected by the education of the parents of black peers. Nor were these associations affected by any combination of own-family education and the education of black peers' families. Similarly, the relation between friendship with blacks and academic outcomes for whites did not change as the education of white students' own parents or the education of the parents of their black peers varied.

There was one indication that relative social class counts. The effort of white students who came from the best-educated families was low (compared to other white students) only when their black peers came from the lowest-education families. However, this was true only among those whites who reported *little* friendship with blacks (see Table 12.4). Since the absence, rather than the presence, of friendship with blacks contributed to low effort, apparently it was not direct influence from lower-class blacks that led to low effort among the higher-class whites. It may be that white students who were very different in background from their black schoolmates, and who were not friendly with the blacks, felt alienated from their school environment. However, white students having this particular combination of characteristics did not differ from other whites with respect to academic values, grades, or achievement scores. These latter results are consistent with our more general finding that the academic effects of contact with black schoolmates were *not* affected much by the social class background of their black peers, by the social class of their own families, or by the combination of these two factors.[12]

Values of Black Peers. As we have noted previously, one reason the social class background of school peers may be important is that peers from lower-class families may value academic success less than those of higher social class. Since the social class background (specifically parents' education) of black peers was only modestly related to their academic values, it is desirable to look more directly at the possible impact of the values of black peers. (See Chapter 10 for description of the measure of academic values.)

Did the effect of interracial contact on whites depend on the values of their black peers? Our results show the effect of class racial composition on white students' grades did differ as the academic values of their black peers differed (see Figure 12.5). Among those whites whose black peers had high academic values, grades rose when the proportion of blacks in classes went above 20% and then stayed high. Among those white students whose black peers expressed low or medium academic values, grades dropped when the proportion of blacks went above 40%.

In general, whites would be expected to get higher grades as the proportion of blacks in their classes increased, since there was less stiff academic competition from blacks (see Chapter 10). The fact that this

Table 12.4. Effort of White Students, as Related to Combinations of Own Parents' Education, Education of Parents of Black Peers, and Friendship with Blacks[1]

Own Parents' Education[2]	Average Parents' Education, Black Peers[3]	Friendship with Blacks[4]	Average Effort Scores	(N)
Low	Low	Low	12.5	(169)
Low	Low	High	13.7	(78)
High	Low	Low	4.0	(36)
High	Low	High	19.9	(15)
Low	Medium	Low	13.2	(217)
Low	Medium	High	17.1	(69)
High	Medium	Low	19.1	(104)
High	Medium	High	14.2	(48)
Low	High	Low	18.6	(101)
Low	High	High	18.9	(35)
High	High	Low	17.7	(102)
High	High	High	20.9	(54)

1. Main effect of education of parents of black peers (A) is significant at .05 level. Main effects of own parents' education (B) and of friendship with blacks (C) are not significant. Interaction of A x B and of A x B x C are significant at .05 level. Results are taken from analysis of covariance in which class racial composition was fourth factor and IQ, sex, year in school, and average education of parents of white peers were covariates.
2. Parents who (on the average) had some schooling beyond high school were categorized as high in education.
3. Groups of black peers were divided into three approximately equal groups according to their average parental education. Parents of the lowest group averaged less than high school or only a little high school; parents of the medium group averaged some high school; parents of the high group ranged from about completion of high school to schooling beyond high school.
4. Those who had one or more blacks among their closest friends and/or belonged to an interracial group of friends were categorized as high in friendship.

expected rise in grades did not occur in heavily black settings when black schoolmates had low academic values (and that, in fact, white grades dropped) may indicate that the performance of whites was depressed by the low academic values of their black peers and/or by the lesser expectations of teachers in such settings. Another possibility is that teachers tended to give low grades routinely in classes which they defined as academically poor.

Although the effect of class racial composition on white students' grades varied with the values of their black peers, this was not true for other outcomes—i.e., for effort, academic values, or achievement scores. Most notably, the major effects of class racial composition on whites which we have observed—i.e., the tendency for effort and achievement scores to decline as the proportion of blacks increased—did not depend on the

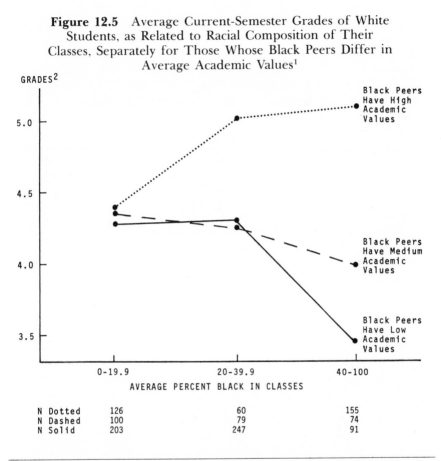

Figure 12.5   Average Current-Semester Grades of White Students, as Related to Racial Composition of Their Classes, Separately for Those Whose Black Peers Differ in Average Academic Values[1]

1. Main effect of academic values of black peers is significant at .01 level but main effect of class racial composition is not significant. Interaction of these factors is significant at .05 level. Results taken from analysis of covariance in which friendship with blacks was third factor; IQ, parents' education, average academic values of white peers, average IQ of white peers, and average IQ of black peers were covariates.
2. Grade code is as follows: F = 0, D = 2, C = 4, B = 6, A = 8.

academic values of black peers. Nor did the general tendency for academic outcomes to be higher among whites who had black friends depend on black peers having high academic values. Nor were there any three-way interaction effects among class racial composition, friendship with blacks, and the academic values of peers. In general, then, the effects of interracial contact on white students do not appear to be the result of their adopting the academic values of their black peers.

Own Ability and Ability of Black Peers. According to the theory of achievement motivation, the aroused need for achievement will be highest when chances of success are moderate, and low when success is almost certain (Atkinson and Feather, 1966). The former situation provides a challenge while the latter does not. On this basis, we would expect white students in racially mixed classes to try hardest when their black peers have about the same academic abilities as themselves and therefore provide effective competition for grades, academic honors, etc. When black peers are lower in academic abilities, they would not provide a competitive challenge.

It is possible that there may be other negative effects of attending classes with those of lower ability. In particular, if teachers go at a slower pace to meet the needs of some students, those of high ability may be exposed to less course material. If attending classes with black students of lower ability does reduce the motivation and/or the learning of white students, this effect should become more pronounced as the proportion of blacks in classes increases.

Whatever the plausibility of these speculations, our results show that the effects of class racial composition on academic outcomes for white students did *not* vary appreciably for those whose black peers were at different IQ levels.[13] Also, interaction effects between white students' own IQ levels and those of their black peers were absent or inconsistent.[14] In addition, there were no significant three-way interaction effects of class racial composition, own IQ, and the average IQ of black peers, as these factors related to any of the academic outcomes for whites.

Overall, these results indicate that the impact of class racial composition, on white students, was affected very little by their own ability, by the average ability of their black peers, or by the combination of these factors.

Why should white students have been affected so little by the absolute or relative academic ability of their black peers? Several possible reasons may be mentioned. One is that white students may have used other whites, rather than blacks, as their primary comparison group, regardless of the proportion of blacks in their classes. If so, they may have perceived a competitive challenge (from other whites) even when black peers were below them in basic academic skills. A second possibility is that most whites may have defined academic success in absolute, rather than comparative, terms. Thus, getting an A or a B in a course may have been the goal of most students, rather than getting a better grade than their classmates. If the standard of success is an absolute one, success would be far from certain, regardless of the performance of black peers, and therefore the incentive for achievement would remain high.

With respect to the effect of low-ability peers on course content, it may be that teachers covered about the same amount of material regardless of the ability of their students (perhaps because of standard requirements) and/or that high-ability students tended to make up for any classroom deficiencies by efforts made and input received (from extra reading, parents' help, etc.) outside of class.

Program. Students following different curriculum programs not only took different courses, but also were exposed to different academic expectations and standards from teachers and from peers. It seemed possible therefore that contact with black schoolmates would have different effects on academic outcomes for white students in different programs. Our results show that the program in which students were enrolled had sizable associations with their academic outcomes. Academic values, effort, and grades were highest among white students in the academic program, lowest for those in the general and vocational programs, and intermediate for those in the fine and practical arts (FPA) program.[15]

Did the effects of interracial contact vary for whites in different programs? First, being in classes with a large proportion of blacks tended to be associated with low grades more for whites in the general program than for those in other programs (see Figure 12.6). This result seems consistent with our finding that whites who attended heavily black classes got low grades when the academic values of their black peers were low. But class racial composition did not have different effects on the effort or on the academic values of white students in different programs.[16] Nor did the associations between friendship with blacks and academic outcomes vary for those in different programs. Finally, there were no three-way interaction effects among class racial composition, friendship with blacks, and program, as these factors related to academic outcomes for whites. In sum, a large proportion of blacks, but not friendship with blacks, had the most negative effect on whites in the general program; this effect was limited to grades.

Attitudes toward Teachers. Finally, we will consider briefly whether the academic effects of interracial contact varied with white students' attitudes toward their teachers.

Some white students thought that the school staff tended to discriminate in favor of blacks—especially by letting black students "get away with" things that would not be permitted for whites (see Chapter 8). Did the effect of class racial composition on academic outcomes for white students depend at all on whether whites perceived such "reverse discrimination" to be taking place?

Our results show that neither the effects of class racial composition nor of friendship with blacks varied with differences in white students' perceptions of discrimination against their race. There was a significant (though weak) three-way interaction between class racial composition, friendship with blacks, and perceived favoritism toward blacks, as these factors related to achievement scores. This result is hard to interpret because of the large number of categories and the small number of students in some categories. However, there is some indication that the usual decline in achievement scores for whites whose classes were over 40% black did not occur for those whites who were friends with blacks and who also perceived little discrimination against whites. The tendency for achievement scores to remain high for this category of whites may reflect a general sense of belonging in the heavily black school situation.

We also examined the possibility that the effect of contact with black schoolmates on academic outcomes might differ for white students who had a generally favorable attitude toward their teachers as compared to those with a generally negative attitude.

Figure 12.6 Average Current-Semester Grades of White
Juniors and Seniors, as Related to Racial Composition of
Their Classes, Separately for Students in Different
Curriculum Programs[1]

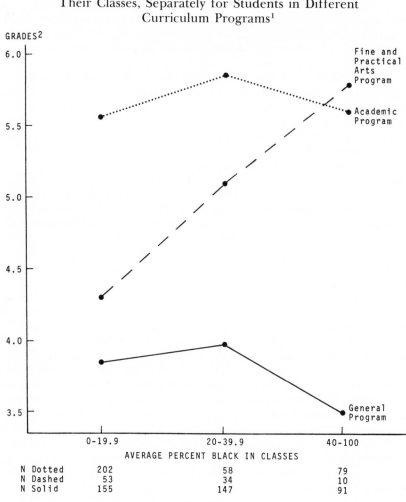

	0-19.9	20-39.9	40-100
N Dotted	202	58	79
N Dashed	53	34	10
N Solid	155	147	91

1. Main effects of both program and racial composition are significant (p < .001) and
interaction is significant (p = .01) with interracial friendship, IQ, sex, and parents'
education controlled.

We have seen that white students' general evaluations of their
teachers were related positively to all of their academic outcomes (see
Chapter 10). However, the effects of class racial composition on academic
outcomes for whites did not vary with how highly the whites evaluated
their teachers. Nor did the effects of friendship with blacks depend on
whites' evaluation of their teachers. Nor were there any three-way in-

teractions among class racial composition, friendship with whites, and evaluation of teachers.

Overall, we may conclude that the effects of contact with black schoolmates on academic outcomes did not vary appreciably for white students who had different attitudes toward the school staff—either with respect to racial discrimination or in terms of their more general attitudes toward teachers.

Conclusions concerning Conditions of Contact. Let us now summarize the results presented in this section. They indicate first that the effects of class racial composition on academic outcomes for whites did not depend on the extent of their friendship with blacks, or vice versa. They show also that the effects of interracial contact in high school did not differ much for white boys as compared to white girls; for those who attended grade schools of varying racial composition; or for those who had different attitudes concerning their teachers.

Generally, the academic effects of interracial contact on whites also were affected relatively little by the social class background, the academic values, or the academic ability of their black peers. Most notably, the small declines in white students' effort and achievement scores which were associated with increasing proportions of blacks occurred regardless of variations in these characteristics of black peers. However, white students got especially low grades when they attended classes with large proportions of blacks and their schoolmates were not academically oriented— i.e., had low academic values or were in the general program.

This latter result is consistent with those for black students in showing that the poorest academic outcomes occurred for those who were in heavily black classes and who also had peers who were not academically oriented. As was the case for blacks, too, the sum of the evidence for whites suggests that this result was *not* due to direct influences from peers. (If negative influences from black peers were operating, whites who were friends with low-SES or nonacademically oriented blacks should have done most poorly.) As we suggested when discussing the results for blacks (see Chapter 11), the tendency for poorer performance by students in heavily black classes—especially classes whose members are not academically oriented—may be due to lower academic standards and laxer discipline in such settings.

Interracial Contact in Context

We have seen that as the proportion of blacks in their classes increased, the effort and achievement scores of whites tended to decline. But how important was interracial contact relative to other factors which were associated with academic outcomes for white students? And how sizable were the effects of interracial contact?

To explore the relative importance of interracial contact and other variables as predictors of academic outcomes for whites, we conducted a set of regression analyses. The following variables were included as possible predictors of academic outcomes for white students.

A. *Interracial Contact*
  1. Racial composition of grade school classes
  2. Racial composition of high school classes
  3. Friendly contact with blacks in high school
  4. Unfriendly contact with blacks in high school
B. *Home Background*
  1. Parents' education
  2. Family composition
  3. Number of children in family
  4. Family concern about school work (as reported by students)
C. *High School Situation*
  1. Curriculum program
  2. Ability level of student's classes
  3. Year in school
  4. Opportunity for contact with black faculty
  5. Participation in school activities
  6. Student's evaluation of teachers
D. *Personal Information about Student*
  1. Sex
  2. IQ score
  3. Time spent at a paying job
  4. Time spent helping family around the house
  5. Preference for different high school prior to attending present school
  6. Aggressiveness (unfriendly contact with same-race peers)

The variables in the above list which had significant associations with each academic outcome (with the effects of all the other variables controlled) are shown in Table 12.5. The partial beta coefficients in each column indicate the relative importance of the variables as predictors of the particular outcome. Let us review these results.

Effort. The best predictors of greater effort among white students were (1) positive evaluation of teachers, (2) being female, and (3) following an academic program (as compared to the general program). The racial composition of white students' classes also affected their effort. Being in classes which averaged from 50 to 70% black contributed to less effort among whites, as compared to being in classes of less than 40% black. (Those in classes of 40 to 50% black and those in classes over 70% black did not differ significantly in effort from those in predominately white classes, though effort of whites in these kinds of classes also tended to be lower than in predominately white classes.) These results are consistent with our previous findings that effort among whites tended to drop as the proportion of blacks in classes increased, and indicate that this effect remains even when a large number of other factors which may affect effort are held constant. The effect of class racial composition on effort was not large, but was not trivial either. Specifically, those in classes of 50–70% black were .41 of a standard deviation lower on the effort measure than those in predominately white classes.

The only other two variables which had a significant independent effect on white students' effort were parents' concern about the student's school work (more parental concern, more student effort) and the amount of time the student spent around the house helping the family (more time, more effort in school). These latter results suggest that close relations with parents, especially where parents encourage school success, contribute to greater student effort.

While class racial composition had an effect on white students' effort, the nature of their interracial contacts did not. Neither the amount of their friendly contact with black schoolmates nor the amount of their unfriendly contact with black schoolmates had a significant effect on effort. Nor did any of the other variables listed above.

The total set of variables explains statistically about 25% of the total variance in white students' effort.

Grades. Two of the variables which were most closely related to white students' effort—taking an academic program and evaluating teachers positively—also were the best predictors of high grades. Next in importance as predictors of higher grades for white students were (3) higher IQ scores, (4) participating more in school activities, and (5) being female.

Being in classes which averaged 30 to 40% black (as compared to classes of less than 20% black) made a small but significant contribution to higher grades for whites. Whites in classes which were 30 to 40% black had an average grade of 4.95 (where C = 4 and B = 6), as compared to an average grade of 4.45 for whites in classes having fewer than 20% blacks. (The increment is .26 of one standard deviation in grades among all whites.) Being in classes with other substantial proportions of blacks (20–30 or 40–50%) also tended to increase whites' grades (as compared to being in almost-all-white classes), but not significantly so. Being in classes with a black majority hardly affected white grades at all—again in comparison to those in almost-all-white classes.

Other variables which contributed slightly to higher grades among whites were: being in the fine and practical arts program or in the vocational program (rather than the general program); being in higher-ability group classes; more parental education; and spending less time on a job away from home.

Neither the amount of friendly contact with black schoolmates nor the amount of unfriendly contact with blacks had an independent effect on white students' grades. Nor did any of the other variables listed above which have not been mentioned.

The total set of variables used in this analysis accounted for 43% of the variance in grades among white students.

Achievement Scores. By far the strongest predictor of achievement scores among white lowerclassmen was their IQ scores. This strong association is even more impressive because it appears when the effect of IQ is controlled for the impacts of program and ability group, both of which have substantial positive correlations with IQ.

The strong association between IQ test scores and achievement scores probably reflects the fact that performance on each type of test

Table 12.5. Significant Predictors of Academic Outcomes for White Students (Partial Beta Coefficients)[1]

	Effort	Current Grades	Total Achievement Scores
Classes 50–69.9% black	−.13**	—	—
Classes 30–39.9% black	—	.10*	—
Classes 20–39.9% black	—	—	−.11***
Classes 40–59.9% black	—	—	−.07*
Classes 60–69.9% black	—	—	.05*
Unfriendly contact with black schoolmates	–	–	−.08***
IQ	–	.19***	.61***
Taking academic program (or course)	.19***	.24***	.18***
Taking fine and practical arts program (or course)	–	.09*	.05*
Taking vocational program (or course)	–	.09*	–
Higher ability grouping	–	.09*	.13***
Sex female	.19***	.12***	−.16***
Participation in school activities	–	.15***	–
Positive evaluation of teachers	.20***	.24***	.08***
Parents' educational level	–	.08*	–
Living with mother only	–	–	−.04*
Living with parent substitutes	–	–	.05*
Time helping family around house	.10**	–	–
Parents' concern about school work and career	.11**	–	−.06**
Time spent on job	–	−.07*	–
Higher year in school	–	–	−.04*
Proportion of variance explained (R^2)	.25	.43	.80

1. Results taken from multiple regression analyses. Other variables included as predictors which did not have significant effects on any outcomes are listed in text.

 Median N is about 1,800 for effort and grades and about 700 for achievement scores. N varies somewhat for each pair of variables, depending on number of cases with missing data. Achievement test scores were analyzed only for freshmen and sophomores, since juniors and seniors took these tests prior to the time the data on interracial contact were collected.

 Class racial compositin was treated as a set of dummy variables in order to reflect its requires the same types of cognitive abilities. Thus, from one perspective, this result indicates that performance on one type of achievement test (IQ), taken at one point in time (usually eighth grade), predicts performance on another set of achievement tests taken later, in the tenth grade. This may be in part because the earlier abilities are reflected again at the later time and partly because greater early development of cognitive abilities helps the student to learn better during the first two years of high school.

Next in importance as predictors of high achievement scores (though far less important than IQ) are (1) taking an academic program of courses, (2) being male (despite the advantage that females had in effort and grades), and (3) being in classes of higher ability grouping.

Class racial composition had some effects on white students' achievement scores, but these effects were not completely consistent. Being in classes which averaged 20 to 39.9% black (as compared to classes with fewer blacks) contributed to somewhat lower achievement scores for whites. Similarly, being in classes averaging 40 to 59.9% black (compared to less than 20% black) contributed, though more slightly, to lower achievement scores for whites. However, attending classes which averaged 60 to 69.9% black (again compared to those with less than 20% black) had a slight *positive* impact on white students' achievement scores.

When compared with white students in almost-all-white classes, being in classes averaging 20–39.9% black brought a decrease of .38 of one stanine (or .24 of one standard deviation) in achievement scores; being in classes averaging 40–59.9% black brought a decrease of .25 of a stanine (.16 of a standard deviation); and being in classes with 60–69.9% black brought an increase of .40 of a stanine (.24 of a standard deviation) in achievement scores. Attending classes with more than 70% blacks had no significant effect on whites' achievement scores.

Overall, these results indicate that increases above 20% in the proportion of black students in their classes tended to lower the achievement scores of white students but that this negative effect was not found (or even slightly reversed) where blacks were a large majority.

With respect to the nature of whites' contact with black schoolmates, more unfriendly contact with blacks was related slightly to lower achievement scores. However, the amount of friendly contact with blacks had no significant effect on achievement.

---

nonlinear relation to each outcome. For effort, 40–49.9, 50–69.9, and 70% or more were compared to 0–39.9% black. For grades, 20–29.9, 30–39.9, 40–49.9, 50–59.9, and 60% or more were compared to less than 20% black. For achievement scores, 20–39.9, 40–59.9, 60–69.9, 70–79.9, and more than 80% were compared to less than 20% black.

Students in each program were compared to those taking a general program of courses.

* Significant at .05 level; ** significant at .01 level; *** significant at .001 level; – indicates nonsignificant beta; — indicates variable to left not used to predict this outcome.

A number of other variables made very small, but statistically significant, contributions to whites' achievement scores. Achievement scores tended to be higher (everything else equal) when students: (1) evaluated their teachers more highly; (2) were taking fine and practical arts courses (rather than general courses); (3) lived with parent substitutes (rather than two parents); (4) did not live with a mother only (rather than with two parents); (5) were freshmen rather than sophomores in 1970–71; and (6) had parents who talked to them less about their school work and careers. The last result may indicate that parents of students who did well academically felt less need to discuss matters related to school with their children.

The total set of variables used in the analysis explained 80 % of the variance in achievement scores among white students.

Overall, the results of the three analyses concerning effort, grades, and achievement scores indicates that the greatest impact on academic outcomes for white students in high school came from (1) the development of cognitive abilities prior to high school — as indicated by IQ scores; (2) following a college preparatory (academic) program, with the extra encouragement to learning which is likely to come from teachers and peers in such a program; and (3) having positive relationships with teachers.

Interracial contact did have some effect on academic outcomes for whites. However, the effects of interracial contact were small compared to the effects of other factors.

Variance Explained by Interracial Contact. To provide a summary of the size of the effects of interracial contact on white students, we conducted an additional set of regression analyses. First, we saw how well each academic outcome could be predicted by the following set of variables relevant to interracial contact: grade school class racial composition, high school class racial composition, and friendship with whites during high school (with no controls for other variables). The three interracial contact variables together explained the following proportions of the total variance in academic outcomes for white students: academic values, .027; effort, .049; grades, .037; achievement scores, .162.

Next, we wished to see how much variance the interracial contact variables explained in addition to that which could be explained by other variables. (Other variables used here were IQ, parents' education, sex, curriculum program, and year in school.) The interracial contact variables explained the following additional proportions of variance: academic values, .022; effort, .024; grades, .020; achievement scores, .007. These results indicate that interracial contact explains very little of the variance in academic outcomes among white students which is not explained by characteristics of the students and their school programs.[17]

Summary

Our results indicate that—even with other variables controlled—academic outcomes generally were poorer for white students who attended classes with a substantial proportion of blacks than they were in predominately white settings. Whites who attended majority-black grade school classes obtained slightly lower IQ scores at the end of grade school and slightly lower achievement scores in high school than did those who attended predominately white grade school classes. In majority-black high schools, the average effort of white students was lower than that of whites in majority-white schools. As the proportion of blacks in white students' high school classes rose above about one-third, the effort of the whites declined. And achievement scores generally were lower among white students in classes with more than 20% blacks than among whites in classes with fewer black students.

These results are contrary to the frequently made assertion that racial desegregation has no negative academic effects on white students; they support the findings of a few previous studies which indicated a possible academic cost to white students in majority-black settings. On the other hand, there are some intriguing findings which suggest that academic outcomes do not necessarily become poorer for whites as they attend classes with increasing proportions of blacks. Among whites whose classes had a large majority of blacks, effort and achievement scores were higher than among whites in classes with about an equal number of blacks and whites or a small black majority. These results generally parallel those for black students (see Chapter 11) and we suggested the same explanation that we did for black students. The performance of students probably depends primarily on the academic standards of administrators and teachers—i.e., what they require of the students and how well they arrange to have their requirements met. A drop in academic standards (including discipline) appears generally to occur with increasing proportions of blacks in classes. But where academic standards are maintained—as they were in many predominately black settings—academic outcomes for students of both races may be relatively good.

Were academic outcomes for white students related to the friendliness or unfriendliness of the contacts they had with black schoolmates? In general, there was little relationship. However, there was some tendency for friendship with blacks to be associated with greater effort and for unfriendly contact with blacks to be associated with lower achievement scores among whites. The effects of class racial composition on academic outcomes for whites did not vary with the amount of friendship which the whites had with blacks. These results suggest that it was *not* close social relations with blacks that led to declines in white effort and achievement in substantially black classes. To the contrary, the effects of friendly contact with blacks—though very slight—tended to work in a positive direction.

Did the effects of interracial contact on academic outcomes for white students vary under different circumstances? Our results suggest that the effects of class racial composition and of friendship with blacks (or the combination of these factors) differed little for white boys as compared to white girls, for those who attended grade schools of different racial compositions, and for those who had differing evaluations of their teachers (both in general and with respect to possible favoritism toward blacks).

In general, the effects of interracial contact on whites also did not vary greatly with the characteristics of their black peers—i.e., with the blacks' ability level, their academic values, or the education of their families. However, there were some indications—similar to results for black students—that being in heavily black classes had the most negative effects when schoolmates were not academically oriented. We suggested—as in the case of blacks—that the tendency for poorer performance by white students in heavily black classes whose members are not academically oriented may reflect lower academic standards and laxer discipline in such settings.

Finally, we found that interracial contact (especially class racial composition) continued to show significant effects when many other factors affecting academic outcomes were held constant. But the effects of interracial contact were much smaller than those of other factors. Also, the interracial contact variables explained very little of the variation in academic outcomes beyond which can be explained by other variables.

With this chapter, we have concluded our discussion of the effects of interracial contact on social and academic outcomes for students of both races. In the next, final chapter, we will summarize the findings presented in the total book and will suggest some policy implications which it seems reasonable to draw from the findings.

Overview

13 | *Summary and Policy Implications*

In the preceding chapters we presented an extensive and detailed set of findings concerning the patterns, determinants, and effects of interracial contact in one city's public high schools. In this final chapter, we will not attempt to summarize all of the findings and conclusions presented earlier. Instead, we will state in a somewhat more general way what we have learned which may help to answer the questions with which we started this investigation. We also will suggest some policy implications of our findings.

The general questions with which we began were the following:

1. When does contact between black students and white students result in good social relations between students of the two races and when does it result, instead, in mutual avoidance or friction?
2. Under what conditions does attending classes with white schoolmates result in improved academic outcomes for black students? And what about the academic effects on white students of attending racially mixed classes? Do these effects vary under different circumstances?
3. Are the conditions which lead to good social relations between black students and white students the same ones, or different ones, than those which lead to good academic outcomes?
4. In general, what are the advantages—social and/or academic—to black students and to white students of attending racially mixed classes? Are there any disadvantages for students of each race?

We will discuss each of these subjects in turn.

Determinants of Social Relations between the Races

What factors determine the extent to which black students and white students in a school will get along well together? In trying to answer this broad question, we looked separately at attitudes of blacks and whites toward schoolmates of the other race, at their changes in racial opinions during high school, and at several aspects of interracial behavior (avoidance, friendly contact, friendship, and unfriendly contact).

These varied aspects of interracial attitudes and behavior appear to have some common determinants. Most notably, all appear to be affected by the student's early interracial contacts (in his grade school and neighborhood) and by the racial attitudes of the student's family and peers. On the other hand, each of the specific aspects of social relations between the races has some unique determinants. For example, among black students, high educational aspirations contributed significantly to friendship with whites but not to a more general measure of friendly contact with whites and not to any other aspects of social relations with whites.

Despite the presence of some common determinants and some unique determinants of specific attitudes and behaviors, it is useful to distinguish among three broad types of social outcomes: (1) students' reactions to the other-race group as a whole—including attitudes toward other-race schoolmates, avoidance of schoolmates of that race, and changes in opinion of other-race people; (2) friendly interaction with particular schoolmates of the other race (including both general friendly contact and friendships); and (3) unfriendly interaction with schoolmates of the other race. These three types of social outcomes tend to be related to different aspects of the school situation and to different student characteristics. Let us consider, in turn, each of the three.

General Reaction to Other-Race Schoolmates

The general reactions which students of one race have toward their schoolmates of another race stem from their perceptions of the good and bad traits of most of the members of that group and from the closely related feelings (liking, disliking, anger, and fear) which accompany such perceptions. But the traits of other-race schoolmates which were seen as important, and which often caused resentment, differed somewhat for blacks and for whites.

When black students expressed negative attitudes toward white schoolmates, these negative attitudes generally centered on the perception that whites didn't want to be friendly and/or were "stuck up" and acted as if they were superior. Thus, the key issue for blacks was whether white schoolmates generally were willing to accept them as equals.

White students who expressed negative attitudes toward black schoolmates had some of the same complaints which many blacks had against whites—i.e., what they saw as a lack of friendliness and even an attitude of superiority by many blacks. However, the main focus of negative white attitudes was the perception of many black schoolmates as dangerous and disruptive.

The circumstances under which students of each race reacted most positively or negatively to schoolmates of the other race appeared to be related to these basic concerns. One of the circumstances which contributed to more negative black reactions toward whites (especially more avoidance) was being in classes in which blacks were a clear numerical minority. This was particularly true among those black students who had little friendly contact with whites prior to high school. It is likely that black students in such circumstances—being in a numerical minority and lacking positive past experiences—would be particularly uncertain about acceptance by white peers.

On the other hand, reactions toward white schoolmates were unusually positive in settings where (1) blacks were not a clear numerical minority and also (2) the racial attitudes of white peers were positive. In such settings, black students had little need to be doubtful about social acceptance by whites.

Black students also had more positive attitudes toward their white schoolmates when they perceived fair treatment by school administrators and teachers—especially an absence of discrimination against blacks.

In general, then, the types of circumstances in which blacks expressed the most positive attitudes toward white schoolmates, and were most willing to associate with them, appeared to be those in which blacks were most likely to feel accepted and treated on an equal basis by both white students and the school staff.

What were the circumstances in which white students reacted most positively, or most negatively, to their black schoolmates as a group? One "circumstance" which made a difference for the white student was his or her sex. White boys had more negative attitudes toward black schoolmates and avoided them more often than did white girls. Our results suggest strongly that this sex difference is due to the fact that white boys were more likely than white girls (and more likely than blacks of either sex) to be the target of physical attack and more likely than other students to be fearful of violence by other-race schoolmates.

Among all white students, seeing blacks as having more power than whites in their school (which usually meant seeing physical dominance by blacks) also contributed to negative attitudes toward, and the avoidance of, blacks. In addition, whites who were in classes with a large black minority—which usually occurred in the context of a growing black proportion in the school—tended to avoid black schoolmates more than did other whites. Whites in such settings often were concerned not only with perceived physical threats from blacks, but with the prospect of blacks' "taking over" their school.

In general, then, the circumstances in which white students reacted most positively to black schoolmates as a group appeared to be those in which they felt least threatened by blacks, either physically and/or in terms of a growing black presence in the school. Conversely, whites had the most negative attitudes toward black schoolmates, and tended to avoid contact with blacks most, in circumstances where they felt most threatened.

For students of both races, general reactions toward schoolmates of the other race also were related to the racial attitudes of both families and peers. Family and peers often help to shape students' perceptions of what other-race schoolmates are like and what to expect from association with them. For example, black families and peers who are hostile to whites may lead the black student to expect hostility, rebuff, and "putdown" from whites. White families and peers who are hostile to blacks may influence the white student to believe that contact with blacks is likely to be danger-ous and unpleasant. In addition, parents and peers may reward the kind of behavior toward the other group (e.g., avoidance) which they believe correct and punish behavior which they believe to be wrong.

Early experiences with members of the other race also affected gen-eral reactions toward other-race schoolmates. Among both black students and white students, those who had friendly contacts with people of the other race in their grade schools and/or neighborhoods were most likely to have positive attitudes toward their other-race schoolmates in high school. On the other hand, those who had unfriendly (or no) interracial contact at an early age were most likely to avoid members of the other group. Friendly interracial contact at an early age would lead the student to have more positive perceptions of the other group—e.g., that they are friendly—and to expect further interracial association in high school to be pleasant. Unfriendly early contacts would lead the student to expect further contact to be unpleasant.

It is important to note also several aspects of the interracial contact situation which had *little* effect on students' general reactions to school-mates of the other race.

First, attitudes toward, and willingness to associate with, students of the other race had little relation to the amount of opportunity which stu-dents had for contact with the other race, as indicated by class racial com-position. Having more exposure to schoolmates of the other race did not, in itself, lead to more favorable attitudes or to less avoidance. The cir-cumstances under which interracial contact occurred, and the background of the student, had much more impact.

The extent of similarity in status between students and their schoolmates of the other race had only a slight effect on their general reactions. Among black students, neither their socioeconomic status nor their grades, relative to white schoolmates, affected their attitudes toward or general avoidance of the whites. Among whites, higher socioeconomic status, relative to blacks, contributed only slightly to more negative atti-tudes toward blacks (though not to avoidance).

Similarity of status may have important implications for interaction in some settings (e.g., where one person has authority over another). But, for students in these schools, the pleasantness or unpleasantness of in-teraction probably was affected much more by the behavior of other-race schoolmates (e.g., their offering help in homework, pushing others, being disruptive in class) than by their relative position on formal status criteria. Important behaviors sometimes are linked to relative position on status dimensions (like SES), but in other settings—including the schools we studied—this connection appears to be weak. Thus, similarity of status may have only a small impact on general reactions toward members of another group.

In sum, for students of both races, general reactions to schoolmates of the other race appear to be shaped in part by the attitudes of important others (family and peers) and by the nature of early experiences with people of the other race. In addition, these general reactions are influenced by features of the present school situation which make other-race schoolmates as a group seem more or less attractive. For blacks, the aspects of the school situation which appear to be most important are those which affect the extent to which they feel accepted and treated on an equal basis by whites. For whites, the most important aspects of the school situation appear to be those which affect whites' feelings of threat from blacks.

Friendly Contact

The amount of friendly contact which students had with school-mates of the other race did not necessarily depend on their general reactions toward members of this group as a whole (though there were small to moderate associations among these outcomes). Moreover, unlike general attitudes and avoidance, friendly contact depended a good deal on the amount of opportunity for interracial contact (as indicated by racial composition and by proximity to other-race schoolmates in class). The larger the proportion of other-race schoolmates in their classes, the more frequently students had friendly contacts with, and formed friendships with, individuals from the other-race group. Being in the same classes apparently led, or in some cases even forced, black students and white students to interact with one another—checking on assignments, comparing answers to questions, etc. Many students found at least some of these interactions to be rewarding and thus repeated them and even extended them outside of class. However, being in more racially mixed classes had a stronger effect on friendly contact among white students than among blacks. For blacks—who may have been more cautious in taking friendly initiatives—being physically near to whites in classes, and not merely in the same classes, appeared important in facilitating friendly interaction.

Opportunity for interracial contact in classes did not lead equally to more friendly interracial contact under all circumstances. Among white students, being in classes with substantial proportions of blacks led to friendly contacts with blacks most clearly among those whose white peers had positive racial attitudes. Peers with such attitudes are likely to facilitate friendly interracial contact (e.g., by drawing the student into an interracial conversation) and to support such contact. Peers with negative racial attitudes may frown on friendly interaction between the races and so students may not use the opportunity for friendly contact for fear of peer disapproval or even ostracism.

In addition to opportunity for contact, friendly contact between the races also appears to depend on the extent to which students are involved in cooperative activities. One important area for such cooperative activity is extracurricular groups—sports teams, clubs, musical groups, theater groups, etc. Among both black students and white students, participating in such groups contributed substantially to more friendly contact with students of the other race. Working together with students of another race in task subgroups within classes also contributed to friendly interracial contact—especially for black students.

Besides providing additional opportunity for interracial contact, working together on common activities probably contributes to friendly contact between the races because it makes the contact which occurs more rewarding. This is likely to be true especially when the activities reflect common interests and values, when students share in the rewards of group success, and when students must help one another in order to reach their common goals.

However, among white students, those who participated in interracial task subgroups in classes were likely to form interracial friendships only when the racial attitudes of their peers were relatively positive. These results indicate that a combination of both working toward common goals and social support for friendly interaction may be necessary for positive ties between the races to occur.

Factors other than the immediate school situation also affected the amount of friendly interracial contact which students had in school. Among both black students and white students, those who had more friendly contacts with people of the other race in their grade schools and neighborhoods also had more friendly contacts with schoolmates of the other race in high school. As we have already noted, friendly early contact leads to more positive racial attitudes and, therefore, to the expectation that contact with schoolmates of the other race will be rewarding. In addition, patterns of friendly behavior toward people of the other race—and toward particular individuals whom students may meet again—are likely to carry over from earlier situations into the high school setting.

Family racial attitudes also played a role in determining friendly interracial contact, just as they did with respect to other social outcomes. The more positive the racial attitudes of the student's family, the more friendly contact and friendship he or she reported with schoolmates of the other race. This association reflects two separate effects of parents on students' interracial behavior. The first is an indirect one, through parents' influence on students' own racial attitudes prior to high school. The second is a more direct effect at the present time—resting in part, no doubt, on the sanctions (approval, disapproval, punishments, etc.) which parents can bring to bear on the student. It should be noted, however, that opportunity for interracial contact in students' grade schools and neighborhoods generally led to more friendly contact even among those students whose families had the most negative racial attitudes (though not as much as for students whose parents had positive attitudes).

What about the relative status of black students and white students? Does this affect the amount of friendly contact they have with each other? Our results indicate that equality of socioeconomic status is not necessary for friendly contact to occur. In fact, the most friendly contact between the races tended to occur in that school where black students and white students differed most with respect to parents' education. Moreover, the position of individual students, relative to schoolmates of the other race, with respect to socioeconomic status, grades, and IQ, was not related to the amount of friendly interracial contact they reported. Apparently, differences in SES or in academic status or ability do not necessarily affect the extent to which contact between blacks and whites is pleasant for students involved.

There was an indication that students' own personal characteristics did have some effect on friendly contact with the other race. Among black students, those who exerted greatest effort in school and those who had high educational aspirations were most likely to report friendships with whites. These academically involved black students probably were most likely to find contact with white peers to be rewarding (since whites generally did well academically), and white students, in turn, probably found contact with this type of black student most rewarding. Again, as in the case of other social outcomes, friendly interracial contact appears to depend little on students' similarity with respect to formal status characteristics and more on the extent to which their values and behaviors in the particular situation are compatible.

To sum up, students appear to be most likely to have friendly contact with schoolmates of the other race when (1) they have sufficient opportunity for such contact; (2) previous experiences have led them to expect such interaction to be pleasant and have taught them patterns of friendly behavior toward the other race; (3) the school situation in which contact takes place—especially insofar as it requires students of both races to cooperate on tasks of common interests toward common goals—tends to make interracial contact rewarding; (4) values and behavior of students—as manifested in the present situation—are compatible; and (5) the racial attitudes and norms of important others—especially peers and family—support, rather than oppose, friendly contact between the races.

Unfriendly Contact

The amount of unfriendly contact (i.e., fighting and arguing)[1] which students had with schoolmates of the other race was essentially independent of the amount of friendly contact they had with members of that group. Many students had a good deal of both friendly and unfriendly interracial contact (usually with different individuals) and many students had little of either type of contact. (Unfriendly contact did have moderate associations with interracial attitudes and with interracial avoidance.)

There was a tendency for students of both races to fight most with each other in classroom settings which were about 30–50% black. This finding may reflect the tensions, and perhaps struggle for control, which occur when there is a large (and usually growing) black minority. But the racial composition of students' classes did not have a significant effect on unfriendly contact when other factors were held constant. In addition, most other differences in the school situation had little or no impact. For both blacks and whites, unfriendly contact was not related to the average ethnocentrism of schoolmates of the other race, or to perceived favoritism by the school staff. Moreover, unfriendly contact had only very slight associations with students' status relative to other-race schoolmates, or to their perceptions of power imbalance in the school. Thus, unfriendly interracial contact did not appear to be caused to any great extent by a school situation which was unusually unpleasant, frustrating, or provocative.

The amount of unfriendly contact in which students actively participated appeared to depend primarily on their personal characteristics. For both blacks and whites, by far the best predictor of how often a student had fights and arguments with schoolmates of the *other* race was how often he had fights and arguments with schoolmates of his *own* race. Thus, interracial fighting appears to reflect some students' general patterns of behavior toward peers. Unfriendly interracial contact also was considerably more frequent among boys than among girls of both races. Again, this sex difference seems to reflect more general patterns of behavior, since boys in our culture generally use more physical violence than do girls in their interpersonal relations.

These findings do not indicate that interracial fighting has no racial motivation or significance. Rather, they suggest that in situations where some racial prejudice and some racial frictions exist—as they did to some extent in all the school situations we studied—those students who react in an overtly aggressive way toward schoolmates of the other race are likely to be those who also react aggressively in interpersonal situations that are not biracial.

The importance of personal aggressiveness varied with the racial composition of students' classes. Among the most aggressive black students, unfriendly contact with white schoolmates fell off markedly when the blacks attended classes with a clear black majority. While this may have been due partly to the presence of fewer whites, the pattern of results suggests that it also reflected lesser hostility to whites among blacks in majority-black settings.

Hostility toward the other race may also stem from past experiences. Among white students, those who had unfriendly contacts with blacks in their neighborhood prior to high school had more unfriendly contact with blacks in high school as well (even with personal aggressiveness and other variables controlled). Their negative past experiences probably caused these whites to be hostile toward the blacks whom they met in high school.

As with other interracial behaviors, unfriendly contact also appeared to be influenced by the racial attitudes of others. Among black students and white students, more negative racial attitudes by students' families contributed to more unfriendly contacts. Among white students, more ethnocentric racial attitudes by students' peers, and the perception of less positive racial attitudes among teachers, also contributed to more unfriendly contact with blacks. It seems likely that negative racial attitudes by students' families and peers, and the perception of weak support for good racial relations among teachers, provide an atmosphere in which students feel relatively free to give overt expression to whatever hostile feelings they may have. In some cases, showing one's own "toughness" in fights with schoolmates of the other race may even be a way of gaining social prestige.

In summary, unfriendly interaction with schoolmates of another race appeared to occur primarily among those students who (because of their personalities and their sex) were often aggressive in their interpersonal relations. This was especially true of those students who—because they were part of a not-fully-accepted minority or because of previous negative experiences—probably felt hostile to students of the other race. Negative racial attitudes by others also contributed to unfriendly behavior, probably mainly by making such behavior more socially acceptable.

Policy Implications

What do our findings indicate needs to be done in order to improve social relations between black students and white students in racially mixed schools? It is not our aim to lay out a comprehensive or detailed program for improving race relations in the schools. But, based on our findings, we would like to suggest some general directions for policymakers in the schools and in the broader community to consider. We will discuss especially the composition of student bodies in schools, ways in which racial tensions in schools can be reduced, and ways in which friendly contacts between the races can be promoted.

Racial Proportions. Some writers have suggested that it is best to create racially mixed schools in which whites are a majority but blacks are a substantial minority, rather than merely a small token group. For example, Pettigrew (1979, p. 127) states that a proportion of 20 to 35% black "seems optimal at this time in schools," explaining that this proportion "seems to avoid blacks' fears of tokenism and whites' fears of being in an unaccustomed minority status."

Our own results indicate that, when students attended classes which had a large black minority, friendly contact between blacks and whites was fairly frequent. However, the greatest tensions between the races (as indicated by general racial attitudes, avoidance, and unfriendly contact) also occurred when racial compositions were in this range (about 20–50%).

Many blacks appear to be sensitive to possible rejection as members of an unwelcome minority while many whites appear to feel threatened by the large black minority.

There often may be good reasons for having classes with a large black minority—including those which Pettigrew notes. However, school administrators and staff should be aware that it is in this range of racial proportions that the greatest tensions between the races seem likely to occur. If other considerations dictate such a racial composition, school personnel need to be especially ready to take steps to reduce such tensions. (See below for some suggested steps.)

Our results indicate that settings in which there is a very small proportion of black students (especially under 10%) have the disadvantage that white students are exposed to little contact with blacks and change their opinions of black people less positively than do whites in other settings. However, black students had more positive and fewer negative interactions with white schoolmates under these circumstances than they did when blacks were a larger minority. Thus, while having a small black minority does not provide all the potential advantages of more extensive racial mixing, it seems to bring less interracial tension than occurs when there is a larger black minority.

We found that the best social relations between blacks and whites (in all respects) occurred where there was a black majority—provided that the white student group was not ethnocentric and accepted the principle of racial integration. These results indicate that majority-black classes are not necessarily bad. Such a racial composition has some possible disadvantages, including a possible academic disadvantage to black students (see below) and the possibility of "white flight" from a majority-black setting. However, there are some situations in which there is a small, relatively stable black majority in a school (or class or program) and where a black majority is not likely to be academically damaging because students are highly motivated to do well. In such circumstances, it may be a mistake to assume automatically that majority-black classes should be eliminated because they do not match the racial composition of the school or the community. The best social relations between the races may be occurring in such settings.

Reducing General Tensions. How can tensions between blacks and whites in school be reduced? Our results suggest that black students will have more positive attitudes toward their white schoolmates and be more willing to associate with them when they feel that the whites (and white administrators as well) accept them fully as equals of the white students. Thus, an important aim of school administrators and teachers—especially where blacks are a minority and/or are new to the school—is to provide a school structure and atmosphere which will make blacks feel accepted as equals.

There are a variety of specific ways in which this may be accomplished. Examples include: role-playing, to make white students more aware of the problems of acceptance faced by minorities; visits with incoming students by biracial teams of older students; making extracurricular activities more accessible to blacks (e.g., by changing meeting times and grade requirements); election and selection procedures which facilitate black representation in school government and prestigeful school activities (e.g., cheerleaders); having a substantial number of black teachers and administrators; inclusion of material about minorities in courses taken by all students; and disciplinary procedures which are sufficiently standardized to avoid perceptions of racial favoritism. The best strategies and techniques can vary with specific circumstances, so long as the goal is kept in mind—creating a situation where black students are in fact, and thus perceive themselves to be, accepted as equals of their white schoolmates.

At the same time that the special concerns of black students are being addressed, attention has to be given to the needs of white students. Many white students—especially in schools where there is a substantial and growing black minority—feel that their interests and well-being, physical and otherwise, are being threatened.

As a first requirement, school administrators need to make sure that all students are physically safe in and around the school. Only when they feel safe from physical attack can students have the security to reach out in friendship toward strangers of the other race.

School administrators also need to take steps to assure white students that the quality of their education and of their school activities is not being threatened by the biracial character of their school. Thus, if a small number of black students are disruptive in classes (as many white students claim), such disruption should not be tolerated. If black students violate school rules, they should be penalized in the same way as whites. And the attempt to involve black students in school activities and entertainments should be done in addition to, not at the expense of, activities and entertainments which may be more popular with white students.

Thus, we are suggesting a two-pronged strategy for reducing general interracial frictions in the school by (1) making blacks feel more accepted as equals and (2) reassuring whites that their own well-being is not threatened by racial integration. These two strategies should be complementary and mutually reinforcing. The more that black students feel accepted, the less aggressive they will be toward white schoolmates. And the less threatened white students feel by black schoolmates, the more they will accept the blacks fully.

Promoting Friendly Relations. It is not sufficient for schools to reduce the irritants which may lead to hostility between the races. They also need to take steps to facilitate positive biracial experiences.

Our results indicate that getting black students and white students to work together on tasks of common interest, toward common goals, is an especially important tool for building ties of friendship. Extracurricular activities seem to be a particularly important area in which friendly contact between black students and white students is developed.

Usually, school activities have contributed to more friendly interracial contact by accident rather than design. But schools can and should do many things to make school activities a more effective tool for this purpose. For example: Requirements that students have a minimum grade average in order to join some activities (which tend to work more against blacks) might be eliminated where not essential; the times that activities meet might be changed (e.g., to the middle of the school day, as was done in one Indianapolis school) to permit more students—especially blacks— to participate; new activities which meet the interests of students of both races might be started; where some activities have tended to be limited to those of one race, efforts might be made to bring more students of the other race into these groups.

Attention needs to be paid, also, to the types of experiences which students have when participating in an activity. The goal should be to make interaction between students as pleasant and rewarding as possible. Among the ways to accomplish this are minimizing competition among members of the activity; emphasizing cooperative rather than individualistic tasks; permitting influence from all students on the way activities are conducted; and trying to see that all students gain some rewards (e.g., publicity and recognition) from success in their joint activities.

As our results indicate, cooperation in activities within classes also may contribute to friendship between students of different races. But in most schools and classes, existing arrangements emphasize individualistic effort or competition between students. Much more can be done to encourage cooperative activity in the classroom. For example, students may be assigned to racially mixed subgroups which are asked to work together on some course project. Efforts should be made to make such projects interesting for students and to structure them in such a way that students of both races can make meaningful contributions. At least part of students' grades should be based on the joint product of such groups.

At the same time that cooperative effort between blacks and whites is facilitated, competition in the classroom can be reduced. One important way to accomplish this is to reduce the extent to which grades are assigned on a competitive basis (i.e., on a "curve"). Assigning grades on the basis of each student's own performance (e.g., based on his accomplishment of course objectives) should help to reduce the competitive atmosphere which often leads to bad feelings between black students and white students.

Strengthening Social Support for Good Race Relations. Our results indicate that students' interracial attitudes and behaviors are influenced substantially by the racial attitudes of their close associates—especially their families and peers. These findings suggest that we need to address our change attempts not only at students as individuals but also at the social groups in which they are located.

Family attitudes are not easily changed. But schools can take steps to enlist more parents—especially those with unformed or moderate views—in support of efforts to improve black–white relations in the schools. Such steps might include more communication with parents about problems and opportunities in the school; involving more parents in discussion, advisory, or decision-making groups; and efforts to mobilize greater support for interracial cooperation in the total community.

To take proper account of the influence of peers, schools need to try to influence students not only as individuals (e.g., by providing information to them about other racial groups) but also as members of peer groups which may have norms about proper racial attitudes and behaviors. Such efforts might include special attention to enlisting the support of prestigeful and influential students (team captains, student government leaders, etc.) and group discussions aimed at producing group consensus on constructive interracial actions.

The racial attitudes of school administrators and teachers also should not be ignored. Our own limited evidence on this topic indicates that teacher racial attitudes (as perceived by students) were not as influential as those of families or peers, but that support for racial integration by teachers did contribute to less negative behavior by white students toward black schoolmates. Some teachers to whom we spoke said that they did not want to preach to or coerce students concerning their interracial behavior. While it is probably unwise to be too heavy-handed in this matter, our results indicate that the staff should make clear its support of friendly and equalitarian contact between the races.[2] Such support can help create a school norm concerning what kind of behavior is appropriate and put the sanctions (especially approval and disapproval) of teachers and administrators on the side of positive interracial behavior.

Promoting Positive Interracial Contact at an Early Age. Among both black students and white students, having friendly contact with people of the other race prior to high school—i.e., in grade schools and neighborhoods—contributed to more positive interracial attitudes and behavior in high school.

These results suggest that efforts to promote friendly interracial contact need to begin when children are young—in grade schools, neighborhoods, and community activities. However, it is not enough simply to provide the opportunity for interracial contact at an early age. Our results show that attending racially mixed grade schools and living in racially mixed neighborhoods had little effect on later attitudes and behavior. Only when early exposure involved friendly interaction with other-race people was there a positive impact on later attitudes and behavior. Thus, while early experiences are important, the problem of how to promote friendly interracial contacts must be faced in the grade school and other early-contact settings, just as it must be confronted in the high school. Involving students of both races in cooperative activities of common interest—in grade schools, Ys, Boy Scouts, recreation centers, summer camps, etc.—seems to offer particular promise of leading to friendly interactions in children's early years.

Similarity of Black Students and White Students. The degree to which blacks and whites were similar with respect to socioeconomic status, academic ability (IQ), or school performance (grades) had little effect on their attitudes and behavior toward one another. These results indicate that schools can bring together blacks and whites from different socioeconomic backgrounds and different academic achievement levels without this necessarily making it difficult for students of the two races to get along with each other. This conclusion is important because, in most situations where racial integration of schools is contemplated, the black student group, on the average, is below the white student group with respect to socioeconomic status and/or school performance.

While the similarity of blacks and whites on formal status criteria (SES, school performance) was not important, there were indications that similarity of blacks and whites with respect to important values and behavior in school (e.g., school effort, fighting, college aspirations) did have an impact on their relationships. Our own limited data on this topic, plus other research results (e.g., Rokeach and Mezei, 1966; Byrne, 1971), suggest that schools should try to bring together black students and white students who have common interests and common values. For example, it may be desirable to group students in high school on the basis of their main school interests. This probably would involve placing increased emphasis on varied school programs and further development of specific programs which would engage the interests of students of both races.

Effects of Interracial Contact on Academic Outcomes

We turn now to our findings bearing on academic outcomes for students. The average grades of black students and their average scores on standardized achievement tests were far below the averages for white students. These large differences between the races were paralleled by large differences in average IQ scores between the races but *not* by any large racial differences in educational or occupational goals, in expectancies of being able to reach these goals, in school effort, or in attitudes toward teachers. Thus, the sizable racial difference in academic performance in high school appeared to reflect primarily a difference in the early development of cognitive abilities (as measured by IQ), rather than differences in school attitudes and motivation.

There also was wide variation in grades and in achievement scores *within* each racial group. These variations were related to differences in IQ scores but also to differences within each racial group, which reflected varying motivation and effort.

Black Students

To what extent were differences in academic outcomes among black students (especially in effort, in grades, and in achievement scores) related to their contacts with white schoolmates?

Black students who attended predominately white classes in grade school did not have higher IQ scores (prior to high school) and did not do better academically in high school than those who attended mostly black grade school classes. (In fact, their achievement scores were slightly lower.) Also, friendly contact with white schoolmates in grade school was not associated with better academic outcomes in high school.

The racial composition of the classes which black students attended in high school did have a significant, though small, impact on their academic outcomes. As the proportion of black students in their classes increased (especially when it rose above about 40%), the effort of black students generally decreased. Black students' achievement scores also tended to decrease as the proportion of blacks in their classes increased. At the same time as their effort (and to some extent their achievement scores) were decreasing, the grades of black students generally rose. Thus, blacks who were in classes with large proportions of blacks tried less hard in school, tended to get lower achievement scores, but got higher grades than blacks in predominately white classes. The impression given by these results is that there generally was a laxer academic atmosphere in mostly black settings, so that black students did less but got rewarded (by grades) more in such settings than did black students in predominately white settings.

However, this general tendency was reversed in those settings which were most heavily (75–100%) black. At this end of the continuum of class racial composition, the effort and achievement scores of black students rose while their grades declined, relative to blacks whose classes averaged about 45 to 75% black. We suggested that these results probably reflect the fact that academic standards were kept fairly high in most predominately black settings. Academic standards—though they may be related to racial composition—are likely to be more crucial for academic outcomes than are racial proportions *per se.*

Conditions of Contact. A key question for our investigation was whether the impact of contact with whites was greater for some types of black students, and in certain types of school situations, than under other circumstances.

It has been argued by some that black students will benefit most from racial integration where they attend classes with middle-class, rather than lower-class, whites. The assumption is that blacks will use high-achieving middle-class whites as role models and/or will be influenced by the presumably pro-academic norms of white students from a middle-class background. Our results do *not* support these expectations. Attending predominately white classes did not lead to better academic outcomes when white schoolmates were of high, rather than low, social class background or when white schoolmates held the most positive academic values. Nor did friendship with whites have more positive effects under these conditions.

The seeming unimportance of the academic values of white peers may stem from several circumstances. One is that, contrary to what many people have assumed, the academic values of blacks—e.g., the importance they assigned to good grades and going to college—generally were as strong as those of whites. Thus, where whites had strong academic values, their black classmates often had similarly high values from the start. Secondly, some of our results indicate that, even in predominately white classes, blacks were influenced more by the academic values of their black peers than by those of white peers.

Our results also are *not* consistent with predictions derived from the theory of achievement motivation. That theory predicts that black students will try hardest when their own academic ability is about equal to that of their peers (and thus their chances of success in competition are moderate) and will try less hard when their ability is low relative to their peers (and thus their chances of success are low).

However, the effects of class racial composition on academic outcomes for black students did *not* depend on the average ability of their white peers (as indicated by average IQ). Nor did the effects of class racial composition depend in any consistent way on black students' own IQs or on the combination of their own IQ and the average IQ of white peers. That the effects of class racial composition depended so little on the relative ability of white peers may indicate that, even in predominately white classes, black students tended to compare their performance (especially grades) to other blacks, rather than to whites. Another possibility is that students judged their performance primarily by an absolute standard (e.g., getting a passing grade) rather than by a comparative standard.

The link between interracial contact and academic outcomes for blacks also did not depend on several other conditions. Neither class racial composition nor friendship with whites (nor combinations of these factors) had different effects on black girls as compared to black boys, on blacks who attended grade schools of varying racial composition, and on blacks with differing attitudes toward their teachers.

However, there were some circumstances under which attending predominately white classes did have especially positive effects on academic outcomes (especially effort) among black students. Among those blacks whose parents had little education and whose white peers also came from poorly educated families, school effort was highest when they attended mostly white classes. Also, among black students whose peers were not academically oriented (i.e., had low academic values or were in the general program), performance (especially effort) was highest when they attended predominately white classes. Since the positive academic outcomes for blacks cannot be attributed to the influence of white peers, there must have been something else in predominately white settings which promoted high effort. Probably this "something" was the maintenance of fairly high academic standards, even when students came from low-SES backgrounds and were not academically oriented.

Academic effort and performance among blacks were lowest when two conditions were both present: (1) students were low in SES and/or not academically oriented and (2) classes were mostly black. Evidence from other studies suggests that these are precisely the conditions under which the expectations and demands of administrators and teachers are likely to be lowest (see Weinberg, 1977, Chapter 9). Low expectations and demands may stem in part from stereotypes associated with a low-achieving, mostly black class. They probably stem even more from the special problems which often arise in such settings—including discplinary problems, a low level of basic skills among many students, and difficulties for teachers in relating to students of a different subcultural background. But the especially poor performance of black students in such settings was not due to the mostly black composition of their classes. When the academic orientation of students was high—and high academic standards presumably were maintained—black students did as well in majority-black classes as in predominately white classes.

White Students

How about white students? What effects, if any, did contact with black schoolmates have on academic outcomes for whites?

Consistent with previous research, we found that, when classes were predominately white, small increases in the proportion of blacks had little effect on the effort, grades, or achievement scores of white students. However, when the proportion of blacks in classes became substantial, declines in academic outcomes for whites did occur. Those whites who attended grade school classes which were about half or more black tended to get slightly lower scores on IQ tests (in grade school) and on achievement tests (in high school) than those who attended mostly white grade school classes. White students who attended high school classes which were over 40% black exerted lower effort than whites in predominately white classes. And achievement scores generally were lower for whites in classes with over 20% blacks than for whites in classes with fewer blacks. On the other hand, for the relatively small number of whites who attended classes with large (over 70%) black majorities, effort and achievement scores generally were higher than for those in classes with small black majorities.

This pattern of results for whites is very similar to the pattern for black students. For students of both races, academic performance generally was lower for students in classes with a large proportion of blacks than in predominately white classes, but there was an upturn in effort and achievement scores for students in classes with the largest proportions of blacks. For whites, as for blacks, these results probably reflect a tendency for administrators and teachers to have had relatively low academic standards when there were large proportions of black students, but for these standards to have been moderately high in some almost-all-black settings.

While attending classes with large proportions of blacks generally had a slight negative effect on academic outcomes for whites, the amount of friendly contact which they had with black schoolmates had little effect on the whites' academic outcomes. The small associations which did occur were positive—i.e., whites who were more friendly with black schoolmates tended to do better academically. (This was true regardless of the racial composition of classes.) These results suggest that whatever negative academic effects occurred for whites in classes with large proportions of blacks were *not* due to close association with, and direct influence from, blacks.

It might be expected that any negative academic effects for whites will occur most strongly when they have close contact with blacks who come from lower-class backgrounds. Black students from such backgrounds, it can be argued, are most likely to provide bad models of school behavior (e.g., by being noisy, having poor study habits) and also may influence white peers to value academic activities and goals less. If these processes operate, they should be most evident for whites who have large proportions of blacks in their classes and who are most friendly with the blacks.

There were a few indications consistent with the propositions that negative academic effects will occur most when whites have contact with blacks of low family status or low academic values. Whites who were in classes with large (over 40%) proportions of blacks and whose black peers had low academic values tended to get low grades. And effort tended to be low among whites who came from high-education families and had black peers from low-education families. But, in the latter case (i.e., of whites who came from much higher social class backgrounds than black peers), effort was lowest among those who had *least* friendship with blacks. In addition, the decline in effort and in achievement scores associated with large proportions of blacks in classes did not vary for whites whose black peers came from families of different educational levels, or for those whose black peers differed in academic values. Nor did the effects of friendship with blacks vary with the family education or with the academic values of black peers. Thus, the sum of the evidence indicates that the small negative effects on whites of attending heavily black classes did *not* stem from their close contacts with blacks of lower social status and/or lower academic values.

Another possibility is that white students will suffer negative academic effects from close contact with blacks when the blacks are much lower than the whites in their academic abilities. In these circumstances, it may be argued, white students will not try hard because things are too easy for them; they will not feel challenged by competition from classmates.

Our findings do *not* support these predictions. The effects of class racial composition did not depend on the average ability level (IQ) of black schoolmates or on the combination of the average black ability level and the whites' own ability level. It may be that white students were not using black students as a basis for comparison and/or that they tended to judge their academic success against an absolute standard (e.g., a grade of A or B) rather than a comparative one.

The effect of interracial contact on academic outcomes for whites also did not differ for boys as compared to girls; for those who attended grade schools of different racial compositions; or for those who had different attitudes toward their teachers. Students' curriculum programs did make some difference. Being in classes which had large proportions of blacks was associated with lower grades among whites in the general program more than among those in other school programs.

How can we explain the fact that whites generally exerted less effort and got lower achievement scores when they attended classes which had a substantial proportion of blacks? Since the evidence indicates that these effects were not due to close contact with black peers, it appears that they were due to other differences in the school situation. As in the case of blacks, academic outcomes for whites tended to be low when there was a combination of (1) a high percentage of blacks in classes and (2) low academic orientation among students (in the case of whites, low academic values among black peers and being in the general program). In the case of blacks, we argued that teachers and administrators in such situations tend to lower their expectations of, and demands upon, students. This explanation seems equally applicable to white students. It appears that they accomplish less in heavily black classes not because of their contact with blacks but because there tend to be low academic standards in these school settings.

Policy Implications

Our results have indicated that, although interracial contact has only small effects on academic outcomes, both black students and white students tend to try hardest and (especially among whites) achieve best in predominately white settings. These results might suggest that, for the best academic results, communities and schools should attempt to provide a racial mixture in schools and classes which is predominately white.

However, this conclusion is too general and too superficial to be maximally useful. First, classes with large proportions of blacks appear to have negative academic effects on students (of both races) only when students in such classes are not academically oriented. In settings where students are well-motivated academically, the racial composition of classes does not appear to matter. Thus, on academic grounds at least, schools and communities need not be concerned about having classes with large numbers of blacks if—by virtue of the way students are selected or the quality of the school program—students are involved in their school work.

But what should be done in settings in which there is a large proportion of blacks, and students are not academically oriented? Our results indicate that poor academic outcomes for students in such settings are not due directly to their contacts with blacks. Rather, they probably are due to low academic standards, and perhaps lax discipline, in these settings—i.e., to low demands from administrators and teachers.

One possible way to change academic standards of teachers and administrators is to change the racial composition of their schools and classes. Their own preconceptions, and those of others in the school and community, may lead them to expect and require more of students in predominately white classes. Moreover, there often may be fewer practical difficulties (of discipline, poor preparation, and communication) in maintaining high academic standards in predominately white settings.

But being in a predominately white school does not mean that students are exposed automatically to high academic standards. Standards are low in many mostly white schools. Nor is there any reason why majority-black schools cannot have high standards. One case in point is the school included in our study (Highland) which was both of high quality academically and mostly black at the time of our study. Although this school was selective in its admissions, there are other cases in which primarily black schools which draw a much broader range of black students are able to maintain high academic standards and produce well-educated graduates (Sowell, 1974).

The problems of maintaining high academic standards generally are tougher in schools with large proportions of blacks than in mostly white schools for reasons we have mentioned. But, even if predominately white schools are deemed preferable, they are not feasible in many cities which have a majority of black pupils. Thus, the challenge in many localities is to raise academic standards in majority-black schools, even in those whose students are not initially able or motivated academically. We can give no exact prescriptions about how to do this, but an effective policy probably should include these elements: (1) placing demands on students which are high but realistic (in light of progress to date); (2) making school effort as rewarding as possible to the student, in terms of its intrinsic content and the approval of teachers, peers, and parents; (3) providing feedback to students on their progress and raising future goals when students meet current ones; (4) maintaining reasonable standards of discipline with fairness but firmness.[3] While greater racial integration often is desirable for a variety of reasons, there is no inherent reason why black schools need to be bad schools.

Social Outcomes versus Academic Outcomes

We have assumed that the factors which affect students' relations with schoolmates of another race and those which affect their academic outcomes are not necessarily the same. Therefore, we have examined a different set of determinants of social, as compared to academic, outcomes. However, there is some overlap between these two sets of determinants. Of particular interest, we have examined the relation of both social and academic outcomes to (1) class racial composition and (2) the characteristics of, and similarity between, black students and white students. To what extent do these factors have consistent effects on the social and academic outcomes of interracial contact, and to what extent do their effects differ for the two types of outcomes?

Racial Proportions

First let us consider the effects of different racial mixtures on social versus academic outcomes. Where there was a small black minority (especially under 10%), social frictions between the races were relatively low (though whites had little chance for contact with blacks) and academic outcomes for both races were relatively good. Where there was a larger black minority (up to about 40%), frictions between the races generally increased considerably, but academic outcomes (especially effort) remained relatively high for both races. Where the number of blacks and whites was about equal, both social relations and academic outcomes tended to be poor. And finally, when there was a clear black majority (over 60%), social relations between the races generally were at their best while academic outcomes generally were. low.

These results indicate that the effects of class racial composition on social relations and on academic outcomes were not always the same. Thus, community and school officials planning for different racial mixtures in school and classes should consider separately their probable social and academic effects. In general, situations where there is a small black minority seem to be satisfactory on both social and academic criteria. Situations in which the numbers of blacks and whites are about equal appear generally to be poor on both criteria. However, these are general tendencies and should not be expected to hold true in all cases. As our results make clear, the effects of class racial composition on both social and academic outcomes depend also on other circumstances. (See Chapters 7, 11, and 12.)

Characteristics of Blacks and Whites

The extent to which students of either race were similar to schoolmates of the other race with respect to socioeconomic status had little effect on either their social relations with schoolmates of the other race or on their academic outcomes. Also, similarity in cognitive skills (IQ) to schoolmates of the other race had little effect on students' social or academic outcomes. These results suggest that, when making pupil assignment plans, school administrators need not be greatly concerned about bringing together black students and white students who differ considerably in socioeconomic status and/or in their initial level of academic ability.

However, there are some indications that the orientation of students toward school may make a difference for both social and academic outcomes. Moreover, the effects of this student characteristic may be different for the two types of outcomes.

Black students who were *most* academically oriented—e.g., those who tried hardest in school and had the highest educational aspirations—were most likely to get along well with their white schoolmates.

However, the most academically oriented black students (e.g., those in the academic program) did *not* benefit academically from attending predominately white classes.

Those students who were *least* academically oriented tended to get along least well socially with their white schoolmates. But this type of student (e.g., those in the general program) benefited most academically from attending predominately white classes.

These results suggest that those black students who will get along best with white schoolmates will derive the least academic benefit from interracial contact. On the other hand, those blacks who might benefit most academically from attending mostly white classes (because of the high academic standards there) will probably have the hardest time forming good social relations with white schoolmates.

In the case of groups of academically oriented black students, sending them to mostly white classes may be justified in terms of the positive interracial experiences it is likely to provide for students of both races—but not on academic grounds.

For black students who are not academically oriented, there may be a tradeoff between some academic benefit and some social difficulties as a result of their attending predominately white classes. Where this is the case, two basic strategies are possible. The first is pressing ahead with racial desegregation involving groups of black students who are not academically oriented and attempting to counter social problems which may arise between the races. The second strategy is to attempt to improve academic outcomes for nonacademically oriented blacks by means other than sending them to predominately white schools—i.e., by raising academic standards in majority-black settings. The choice between these strategies will depend on a complex set of other factors, including political pressures in the community and the personal preferences of the decision makers.

Benefits and Costs of Racial Integration

What do our findings suggest about the benefits of increased interracial contact in the schools? And are there costs as well?

As we have seen, differences in class racial composition had rather complex effects on academic outcomes and these effects varied for students who differed in the strength of their academic orientation. But, in general, black students were stimulated to the greatest effort and tended to get the highest achievement scores when they attended predominately white high school classes. On the other hand, probably because of stiffer competition, black students generally got poorer grades in predominately white than in mostly black settings.

Among white students, effort and achievement generally were higher for those in predominately white classes than for those in classes with a large proportion of blacks.

Overall, then, the results indicate that there generally was an academic advantage to students of both races of attending predominately white classes. However, the size of these effects was quite small. Similarly, the effects of friendly interracial contact (and friendship) on academic outcomes were quite small. Moreover, even when the effects of class racial composition and of interracial friendship were considered (singly and together) under a wide range of varying circumstances, these effects remained small. We found also that factors other than interracial contact—e.g., early cognitive development (IQ), curriculum program, relations with teachers—had a much greater impact on academic outcomes than did interracial contact.

These results suggest that, although changes in racial composition can bring some academic benefits in some circumstances, racial mixing should not be relied upon as a major tool to bring large improvements in the academic achievement of minorities. To rely on this approach may not only bring disappointment but may cause neglect of approaches that promise to have a greater impact. While our research has not investigated methods of improving academic performance, the results suggest that improving students' cognitive abilities at an early age, providing stimulating school curricula, and improving relations between teachers and students are among the most promising directions to pursue.

While the potential academic benefits of different racial mixtures appear to be small, the potential social advantages are larger. There is a great deal of difference between not knowing any people of another race (and probably being suspicious of them) and having a close friend of another race. And our results show that as opportunity for interracial contact increased, the amount of friendly contact (and friendship) between the races increased considerably too.

This is not to say, of course, that attending schools and classes with schoolmates of another race always leads to good social relations with members of that group. Most students had varied interracial experiences—both friendly and unfriendly—with schoolmates of the other race. And school settings in which there was considerable racial mixture (especially a large black minority) often were scenes of considerable racial friction—hostile attitudes, avoidance, and fighting.

Whether the positive social effects of interracial contact in schools will outweigh the negative effects will vary with particular locations. In the Indianapolis high schools, the great majority of students reported that their interracial experiences, on the whole, were fairly friendly. Also, a large majority of blacks, and a smaller majority of whites, said that they had changed their opinions of other-race people for the better since coming to high school. But there were several schools in which a majority of white students said they had changed their opinions of blacks for the worse since coming to high school. Moreover, results from other studies also indicate that the overall social effect of interracial contact in schools is not always positive.

The balance of social outcomes in any situation will depend on a variety of circumstances which we have discussed—racial proportions;

family, peer, and teacher racial attitudes; early racial experiences of students; the extent to which black students and white students participate in common activities; etc. The challenge for community leaders and for school personnel is to try to create the conditions under which the negative social effects of interracial contact are minimized and the positive effects are maximized. To the extent that such efforts are successful, the result will be that students of different races will come to relate to one another just as all people do—with some frictions but with bonds of friendship forming often as well. The potential contribution of such school experiences to our society is great.

Appendices

Appendix A. Sample of Students at Various Schools[1]

School	*N* Blacks	*N* Whites
Pershing	21	245
Jefferson	147	329
Eastern	199	231
Southwest	226	245
Emerson	240	240
Hillcrest	245	254
Roosevelt	245	260
John Price	243	285
Harrison	324	303
Lakeview	154	120
Highland	235	234
Carver	215	0
Total	2,494	2,746

1. Data shown represent most of the sample originally chosen. (Another 239 cases were included in the total original sample but are not included in table because we did not obtain all identifying data on these additional cases.)

For information about the proportion of cases in the total original sample for whom questionaires were obtained, see Table 2.6.

Appendix B. School Means (and Standard Deviations) for Blacks and for Whites on Interracial Attitude Measures

School	Index of Attitude toward Other-Race Schoolmates[1]		Change in Opinion of Other-Race People[2]	
	B	**W**	**B**	**W**
Pershing	.43	—	2.7	2.6
	(1.60)	—	(1.2)	(0.9)
Jefferson	−.25	.09	2.7	3.0
	(1.50)	(1.60)	(1.1)	(1.1)
Eastern	.39	.33	2.4	2.6
	(1.20)	(1.50)	(1.1)	(1.1)
Southwest	−.40	.14	2.9	2.8
	(1.50)	(1.50)	(1.1)	(1.1)
Emerson	−.41	−.83	2.7	3.4
	(1.40)	(1.50)	(1.1)	(1.3)
Hillcrest	.27	−.71	2.5	3.4
	(1.30)	(1.60)	(1.1)	(1.3)
Roosevelt	−.27	−.19	2.6	2.8
	(1.40)	(1.40)	(1.0)	(1.1)
John Price	−.43	−.01	2.6	2.9
	(1.20)	(1.30)	(1.0)	(1.1)
Harrison	.41	.03	2.4	2.6
	(1.20)	(1.50)	(1.0)	(1.2)
Lakeview	.07	−.45	2.4	2.8
	(1.10)	(1.70)	(0.9)	(1.3)
Highland	.98	.91	2.6	2.5
	(1.20)	(1.30)	(0.9)	(1.1)
Carver	—	—	2.8	—
	—	—	(1.1)	—

Notes: For each entry, mean is above and standard deviation is below, in parentheses. Differences among mean scores for black students in various schools on both measures are significant at beyond .001 level; the same is true for differences among means of whites in various schools.

1. Computation of attitude index is described in Chapter 3, note 4. Positive scores reflect more favorable scores on attitude components relative to mean of all students of same race; negative scores reflect less favorable relative scores.
2. Scores on opinion change were as follows: gotten much better—1; gotten a little better—2; stayed about the same—3; gotten a little worse—4; gotten a lot worse—5.

Appendix C. School Means (and Standard Deviations) for Blacks and for Whites on Indices of Interracial Avoidance and of Friendly Interracial Interaction

	Avoidance		Friendly Contact		Friendship	
School	B	W	B	W	B	W
Pershing	19.1	—	96.8	—	2.8	1.8
	(21.6)	—	(84.7)	—	(1.2)	(1.0)
Jefferson	25.4	16.3	35.4	25.9	2.2	1.9
	(24.4)	(16.7)	(35.4)	(26.7)	(1.1)	(1.0)
Eastern	19.5	16.6	43.0	25.5	2.6	1.9
	(22.4)	(17.0)	(37.6)	(22.0)	(1.1)	(1.0)
Southwest	31.0	17.5	42.1	28.5	2.2	2.1
	(28.0)	(18.3)	(44.3)	(31.1)	(1.1)	(1.0)
Emerson	23.4	22.1	36.3	23.9	2.2	1.9
	(23.0)	(20.2)	(39.8)	(26.4)	(1.1)	(0.9)
Hillcrest	20.0	19.9	50.2	34.7	2.5	2.3
	(20.8)	(15.8)	(50.4)	(35.2)	(1.1)	(1.0)
Roosevelt	22.2	21.1	37.5	34.3	2.1	2.2
	(23.1)	(20.4)	(35.4)	(32.3)	(1.0)	(1.0)
John Price	29.9	20.4	33.5	34.0	2.1	2.3
	(28.1)	(19.7)	(32.0)	(42.5)	(1.1)	(1.1)
Harrison	17.6	18.4	43.7	36.6	2.3	2.5
	(17.9)	(18.0)	(46.6)	(33.7)	(1.1)	(1.1)
Lakeview	16.2	30.5	33.1	30.3	2.3	2.2
	(15.2)	(26.4)	(31.1)	(28.0)	(1.1)	(1.0)
Highland	14.3	13.1	42.0	72.8	2.3	3.0
	(13.2)	(10.4)	(45.0)	(54.2)	(1.0)	(1.1)
Carver	—	—	—	—	—	—

Notes: For each entry, mean is above and standard deviation is below, in parentheses. Range of scores on each index is as follows: avoidance, 7–112; friendly contact, 9–232; friendship, 1–4. Differences among mean scores for black students in various schools on all indices are significant at beyond .001 level; the same is true for differences among means of whites in various schools.

Appendix D. School Means (and Standard Deviations) for Blacks and for Whites on Indices of Unfriendly Interracial Interaction

School	Participation In Unfriendly Contact		Total Unfriendly Experiences	
	B	W	B	W
Pershing	10.5	—	10.6	—
	(7.5)	—	(6.7)	—
Jefferson	12.9	8.2	13.0	18.1
	(12.3)	(9.1)	(11.5)	(19.8)
Eastern	7.8	6.1	9.8	12.1
	(7.1)	(5.8)	(7.5)	(11.9)
Southwest	10.1	6.7	11.7	16.4
	(10.1)	(7.3)	(9.1)	(17.8)
Emerson	9.2	6.9	11.8	18.9
	(8.4)	(7.5)	(12.7)	(18.4)
Hillcrest	9.2	6.5	10.3	23.5
	(9.7)	(6.4)	(9.3)	(21.9)
Roosevelt	9.7	8.2	12.1	18.8
	(9.5)	(8.3)	(11.8)	(19.3)
John Price	13.1	7.2	13.4	18.9
	(12.5)	(7.3)	(10.5)	(20.0)
Harrison	8.9	7.2	9.7	19.2
	(9.9)	(6.8)	(8.7)	(19.0)
Lakeview	8.3	9.9	8.9	30.5
	(6.8)	(8.7)	(6.9)	(27.8)
Highland	6.0	6.5	7.0	14.7
	(6.0)	(5.3)	(3.9)	(13.8)
Carver	—	—	—	—

Notes: For each entry, mean is above and standard deviation is below, in parentheses. Range of scores on each index is as follows: participation in unfriendly contact, 3–48; total unfriendly experiences, 5–109. Differences among mean scores for black students in various schools on both indices are significant at beyond .001 level; the same is true for differences among means of whites in various schools.

Appendix E. School Means (and Standard Deviations) for Blacks and for Whites on Academic Effort and Performance

School	Academic Effort Index		Current Semester Grades		Achievement Test Scores (MAT)	
	B	**W**	**B**	**W**	**B**	**W**
Pershing	.20	.17	3.9	4.6	4.0	5.0
	(.19)	(.18)	(1.2)	(1.6)	(1.1)	(1.3)
Jefferson	.06	.17	3.3	4.5	3.7	5.1
	(.31)	(.19)	(1.5)	(1.6)	(1.4)	(1.6)
Eastern	.16	.17	3.4	4.3	3.8	5.1
	(.22)	(.19)	(1.5)	(1.8)	(1.3)	(1.5)
Southwest	.17	.18	3.5	4.0	3.5	4.7
	(.19)	(.20)	(1.6)	(1.8)	(1.2)	(1.5)
Emerson	.14	.17	3.2	4.5	3.4	5.5
	(.21)	(.21)	(1.4)	(1.6)	(1.3)	(1.6)
Hillcrest	.16	.18	3.5	4.9	3.7	5.5
	(.24)	(.24)	(1.6)	(1.9)	(1.1)	(1.5)
Roosevelt	.13	.18	3.7	4.4	3.2	4.2
	(.22)	(.21)	(1.7)	(2.0)	(0.9)	(1.3)
John Price	.03	.12	3.8	4.5	2.4	3.3
	(.24)	(.26)	(1.8)	(1.8)	(0.9)	(1.5)
Harrison	.07	.11	3.0	3.8	3.1	4.3
	(.22)	(.27)	(1.8)	(2.2)	(1.3)	(1.4)
Lakeview	.09	.14	4.5	5.0	3.2	4.6
	(.22)	(.20)	(1.7)	(1.7)	(1.1)	(1.4)
Highland	.18	.13	4.2	5.0	4.4	6.3
	(.24)	(.20)	(1.8)	(2.0)	(1.4)	(1.6)
Carver	.08	—	3.9	—	2.8	—
	(.25)	—	(2.0)	—	(1.1)	—

Notes: 1. For each entry, mean is above and standard deviation is below, in parentheses.
2. For content of items in effort index, see Chapter 10; for computation of index, see Patchen (1975, Appendix). Sign of scores has been reversed here.
3. Code for grades is F = 0, D = 2, C = 4, B = 6, A = 8.
4. Achievement test scores are mean stanine scores for freshmen and sophomores, since only these groups took Metropolitan Achievement tests. For data on upperclassmen, see Patchen (1975).
5. For each race, differences among the mean scores of students at the different schools on effort, grades, and achievement scores are all significant ($p < .001$).

Appendix F. Pearson Correlations for Total Schools[1]

	Avoidance by		Friendly Contact Reported by		Participation in Un-friendly Contact by		Positive Opinion Change by	
	B	W	B	W	B	W	B	W
Ethnocentrism								
Blacks	.68	.05	−.07	−.29	.24	−.04	−.72	−.14
Whites	.44	.74	−.38	−.82	.42	.45	.13	−.13
Parents' Education								
Blacks	−.17	−.35	.12	.39	−.29	−.27	−.40	−.32
Whites	−.46	−.37	.11	.50	−.53	−.37	−.03	−.22
Black–White difference	−.44	−.49	.00	.66	−.60	−.56	.08	−.14
Participation in Activities								
Blacks	−.25	−.61	.35	.83	−.49	−.61	−.16	.32
Whites	−.10	−.57	.11	.66	−.33	−.63	−.27	−.19
Percent in Academic Program								
Blacks	−.59	−.35	.26	.86	−.63	−.15	.11	.48
Whites	−.48	−.43	.16	.66	−.63	−.41	−.07	−.02
Black–White difference	.07	−.19	−.08	−.19	−.12	−.45	−.27	−.76
Grades, current semester								
Blacks	−.34	.40	.09	.47	−.26	.48	.33	.29
Whites	−.43	.28	.05	.40	−.25	.27	.10	−.07
Black–White difference	−.04	−.23	−.07	−.16	.07	−.35	−.35	−.50

Percent ever on Honor Roll								
Blacks	-.02	-.01	-.32	.66	-.27	.04	-.40	.25
Whites	-.44	.21	-.25	.68	-.42	.14	-.09	-.06
Black–White difference	-.02	.15	.23	-.44	.02	-.07	.15	-.41
IQ Scores								
Blacks	-.63	-.48	.17	.72	-.78	-.36	-.03	.07
Whites	-.49	-.40	.17	.45	-.59	-.42	-.27	-.36
Black–White difference	.02	-.03	.24	-.22	.05	-.27	-.24	-.78
Educational Aspirations								
Blacks	-.27	-.51	-.27	.70	-.59	-.49	-.10	-.20
Whites	-.52	-.28	.24	.46	-.52	-.33	-.25	-.40
Black–White difference	.59	.08	.28	-.24	.41	-.32	-.33	-.09
Occupational Aspirations								
Blacks	-.10	-.20	.17	.40	-.41	-.49	-.46	-.15
Whites	-.40	-.36	.25	.42	-.45	-.48	-.29	-.47
Black–White difference	-.03	-.30	.02	.30	.06	-.36	-.26	-.78
Academic Effort								
Blacks	-.30	-.29	.56	.28	-.58	-.49	-.27	.06
Whites	.26	-.05	.26	-.44	.11	-.17	-.25	-.36
Black–White difference	.25	-.02	-.34	.03	.63	.39	.26	-.30
Accept conventional norms								
Blacks	.80	-.09	-.17	-.24	.67	-.07	-.02	-.74
Whites	-.29	-.41	-.16	.63	-.53	-.43	-.02	-.13
Black–White difference	.48	-.33	-.10	.16	.38	-.07	-.31	-.24

Continued

Appendix F. *Continued*

	Avoidance by		Friendly Contact Reported by		Participation in Un-friendly Contact by		Positive Opinion Change by	
	B	W	B	W	B	W	B	W
Unfriendly Intraracial Contacts								
Blacks	.50	.04	-.80	-.22	.45	.36	-.05	-.19
Whites	-.20	.48	-.45	.07	-.33	.35	.28	-.03
Black–White difference	.43	-.30	.22	-.24	.74	.06	-.11	.15
Proportion Living in Segregated Neighborhoods								
Blacks	-.15	.49	-.83	-.16	-.30	.48	.60	.03
Whites	.44	.25	.10	-.93	.55	.14	-.06	.23
Overall School	.25	.21	.13	-.80	.39	.24	.04	.01
Proportion of Other-Race Students in Grade School Classes								
Blacks	.18	-.35	.83	-.01	.43	-.29	-.52	-.01
Whites	-.14	-.23	-.16	.80	-.22	-.12	.02	.22
Overall School	.18	-.26	-.19	.56	.07	-.29	-.17	-.12
Friendly Interracial Contact in Grade School								
Blacks	.05	-.56	.88	.20	.31	-.39	-.35	-.21
Whites	-.28	-.04	-.23	.80	-.28	.19	-.15	.21
Overall School	-.06	-.15	-.23	.69	-.09	.00	-.28	.00

Positive Family Attitudes							
Blacks	-.72	.00	.78	.27	-.49	-.22	.37	.27
Whites	-.55	-.51	.19	.88	-.44	-.15	.35	.47
Overall School	-.81	-.15	.12	.83	-.65	.01	.36	.26
Positive Opinion of Other Race Prior to High School							
Blacks	-.33	.03	.89	.68	-.06	-.16	-.05	.29
Whites	-.27	-.67	.45	.83	-.07	-.36	-.19	.23
School Average	-.08	-.65	.75	.51	.27	-.29	-.36	.12
Percent Black Students in High School	-.52	.14	-.45	.78	-.55	.17	.51	.14
Strictness of Disciplinary Rules	.18	-.04	-.21	-.29	.28	.05	.19	-.14
Student Council Ratio of Representatives to Total Students							
Blacks	-.22	.37	.68	.17	.08	.68	-.16	.47
Whites	-.32	-.63	-.05	.79	-.48	-.63	-.23	-.27
Black–White difference	-.50	-.08	.44	.40	-.41	-.34	-.33	-.40

1. Correlations are based on N of all 12 schools, where dependent variables are opinion change by either race. N is 11 schools for blacks and 10 schools for whites, where the dependent variable is avoidance, friendly contact, or unfriendly contact by that race. (Schools where whites or blacks had little interracial contact were omitted for that race.) Where the predictor variable is a difference between the mean scores for blacks and for whites, an absolute difference was used.

Notes

Chapter 1

1. A recent volume, edited by Rist (1979), contains some reports of biracial interaction in schools. However, these studies are impressionistic descriptions and contain almost no systematic data about such interactions.

2. Crain and Mahard (1978) found that, in the North, black students' achievement was highest in predominately white schools. However, in the South, black achievement was not related to school racial composition.

3. NORC data, as analyzed by Narot (1973), show that black boys, but not black girls, dropped in achievement in predominately white schools. Among whites, girls, but not boys, achieved better in primarily black schools, when student background variables were controlled.

Chapter 2

1. The names used for specific high schools are pseudonyms.

2. Population data are from the U.S. 1970 census.

3. See Patchen and Davidson, 1973, p. 52, for further data on modes of transportation.

4. The proportion of students in the academic program at Highland was much lower among freshmen than among those in other classes, since the selective admission policy at that school had been ended just prior to the admission of the freshman class.

5. At Lakeview, which technically was part of Carver, a white assistant principal was the on-the-spot administrative head.

6. The larger number of teachers, in proportion to students, at John Price probably stemmed from the relatively large proportion of students with low academic ability who needed special help at that school and the relatively large emphasis on vocational programs there. The large proportion of teachers at

Lakeview apparently was a response to the special problems of serving only freshmen under trying conditions (e.g., high initial racial tension) in a new facility.

7. In 1970–71, 51 fights at Harrision, 43 of them interracial, were reported to the central school administration. The next highest were John Price with 16 and Emerson with 12. (See Patchen and Davidson, 1973, p. 57, for detailed data on recorded fights.)

8. The construction of indices from items on the questionnaires is described in an appendix to this report and in an appendix to a second report (Patchen, 1975).

9. Mean scores and standard deviations on a wide variety of measures, for the total sample of individual students (by race), are available elsewhere (Patchen, 1981).

10. A subsample of teachers within each school was given a questionnaire which was lengthier than the standard one.

Chapter 3

1. Findings on the dimensions of interracial perceptions are based on the results of factor analyses (see Patchen, Hofmann, and Davidson, 1976). Additional descriptive results concerning specific interracial perceptions, as well as results concerning the accuracy of interracial perceptions, also are presented in that paper.

2. For information about several other minor dimensions, see Patchen, Hofmann, and Davidson, 1976.

3. These results also are based on factor analyses (Patchen, Hofmann, and Davidson, 1976).

4. For black students and for white students separately, standardized scores, based on our total sample, were computed for an index of perception (14 items), for liking, for anger, and for fear. These standard scores were summed, with the perception index given a weight of 3, so that perceptions and emotions had equal weight in the overall attitude index.

5. A scatter plot shows that, with Highland omitted, there is a close-to-zero correlation between the average racial attitude scores of blacks and the average racial attitude scores of whites in the same schools.

6. Correlations between change in opinion of other-race people and attitudes toward other-race schoolmates were .36 for black students and .52 for white students.

7. Mean scores and standard deviations on opinion change for blacks and for whites in different schools are shown in Appendix B. Proportions of each race in each school who reported positive, negative, or no opinion change are presented in Patchen and Davidson (1973, pp. 111–112).

8. A scatter plot shows that there was little overall association between average opinion-change scores of black students and of white students in the various schools.

Chapter 4

1. A rare exception is the work of Chadwick (1972).

2. Additional information on interracial behavior in these schools may be found in Patchen and Davidson (1973).

3. The construction of this index, and of other indices of interracial behavior, is described in Patchen and Davidson (1973).

4. The items were weighted according to the intimacy of the friendly contact. See Patchen and Davidson (1973).

5. Sixty-two percent of blacks and 68% of whites said they belonged to an informal group of friends.

6. For a description of the interracial friendship scale, see Patchen, Hofmann, and Brown (1980). The scale was developed and used by Hofmann (1973).

7. Items not shown in Figure 4.4 are (1) "made fun of you . . ." and (2) "stole something from you . . ." These items, along with those in Figure 4.4, were included in the index of total unfriendly contact. Items were weighted by the severity of the behavior (see Patchen and Davidson, 1973).

8. The correlation between the average amount of participation in unfriendly interracial contact reported by blacks and by whites in the same schools was .20 (not statistically significant).

9. Correlations among measures of interracial behavior also were computed separately for students in each school. The medians of these correlations, presented elsewhere (Patchen and Davidson, 1973, p. 120), are very similar to those presented in Table 1.

10. There also were substantial correlations between average interracial avoidance in a school and average participation in unfriendly interracial contacts, both for blacks ($r = .76$) and for whites ($r = .75$).

11. At the school level also, the correlations between average friendly interracial contact and average unfriendly interracial contact were very small, both for blacks and for whites.

12. At the school level, the correlation for blacks between average interracial avoidance and average friendly interracial contact also was small ($-.23$); for whites, the correlation was somewhat larger ($-.43$) but nonsignificant.

Chapter 5

1. Other revelant information and analysis of these data concerning early experiences are presented in the doctoral dissertation by William R. Brown (1974).

2. We also asked each student: "How old were you when you first got to know any [other-race] kids pretty well?" For results concerning these data, see Brown (1974).

3. Other research (e.g., Campbell, 1971; Schuman and Hatchett, 1974) indicates that racial attitudes are more related to education than to occupation or income. However, we also obtained information about parents' occupations and computed a measure of parents' SES, based on education and income level (estimated) of occupation.

4. It may be also that there are joint effects of early background factors on behavior or attitudes in high school. These possibilities were not investigated be-

cause of the very large number of possible interactions which would have had to be checked and because joint effects on more immediate outcomes were judged to be more important.

5. Although IQ scores usually were obtained just prior to high school, we also examined possible joint effects of early interracial experiences and IQ, on the assumption that IQ scores probably were fairly consistent during grade school years for students of both races. The relation between (a) grade school racial composition and friendly interracial contacts in grade school, (b) grade school racial composition and early racial attitudes, (c) neighborhood segregation and friendly interracial contact in the neighborhood, and (d) neighborhood segregation and early racial opinions did not differ significantly for blacks or for white students of different IQ levels.

6. In a two-way analysis of variance, the effect of grade school racial composition on friendly grade school contact was significant ($p < .001$), the effect of sex was not significant, and the interaction was significant ($p < .05$).

7. The correlation ratio (eta) between the racial composition of neighborhood and total friendly interracial contact prior to high school was .29 for blacks and .31 for whites; eta between neighborhood racial composition and opinion of the other race prior to high school was .13 for blacks and .13 for whites.

8. Constructing joint variables would sacrifice some detail in the component measures and would introduce greater complexity into the analyses.

9. These are treated as sets of "dummy variables," in the language of regression analysis.

10. For whites, the relation between neighborhood racial composition and the friendliness of neighborhood contacts with blacks was treated as linear, since it deviated for only a small number of students at the extreme of the curve.

11. Friendly contacts in grade school and in the neighborhood were kept separate in preliminary analyses, which used a two-stage, bloc-recursive technique to take account of reciprocal causation between these variables. However, extreme multicollinearity made the result uninterpretable.

12. See Patchen (1981). Direct, indirect, and joint effects can be calculated from the basic correlations presented in that document.

13. Although sex was included as a factor in the path analyses (primarily to control for its effects), we will not discuss the effects of sex here, since these are discussed in the next chapter.

14. To compute the indirect effect, the path coefficient of each link in the causal chain must be multiplied by that for the next link in the chain.

15. However, those who reported no early contact with whites in the neighborhood had slightly less friendly contact with whites in high school than did the small number of those who had unfriendly early contact with whites.

16. The path coefficient from prior opinion to change in opinion is $-.25$.

17. Two-way analyses of variance were performed. One predictor used was a summary measure of friendly contact prior to high school. For black students, the second predictor was the average ethnocentrism of same-race peers; for white students the second measure combined the ethnocentrism of both same-race and other-race peers.

18. Among white students, a combination of high parent education and a high proportion of blacks in classes was associated with particularly positive racial attitudes. However, this result appears to reflect the liberal racial attitudes of white students at Highland, where black students were academically outstanding and white parents were unusually liberal.

19. Data were included for each race only for those schools where there were more than just a few schoolmates of the other race.

20. Tests of statistical significance are not strictly applicable to the set of schools studied since they are not a random sample of schools from a specified universe. However, significance levels do provide one rough guide to the meaningfulness of the correlations.

Chapter 6

1. For blacks, two-way analyses of variance show large main effects of both sex and (within-race) aggressiveness on unfriendly interracial contact but no significant interaction between sex and aggressiveness.

2. Among white girls, the tallest were significantly less fearful of blacks than were smaller girls; however, there was no association between sex and avoidance or other behavior.

3. The measure of general satisfaction had only a very small correlation with the measure of aggressiveness ($-.05$ for blacks, $-.11$ for whites).

4. The great majority of students (93.4%) took the California Test of Mental Maturity in the eighth grade. The remainder of students took this or another IQ test during the sixth grade (1.9%) or during the ninth grade (4.7%).

5. A three-way analysis of variance also showed the effects of black students' IQs on their attitudes toward white schoolmates to be independent of the blacks' educational aspirations and effort in school.

6. Analyses of variance showed no significant interactions, for blacks, between IQ and class racial composition as these affected any interracial behaviors or opinion change. There was a small interaction of IQ and class racial composition with respect to racial attitudes, such that high-IQ blacks in heavily black classes (primarily at Highland) had especially positive attitudes toward whites.

7. A two-way analysis of variance of friendly contact with blacks showed significant effects for class racial proportions ($p < .001$), IQ ($p < .001$), and for the interaction between racial proportions and IQ ($p < .002$). With peer racial norms as a third predictor in a three-way analysis of variance, the interaction between racial proportions and IQ remained significant.

8. Among whites, higher IQ tended only slightly to be associated with more positive opinions of black people prior to high school ($r = .10$).

9. Appendix F also shows a sizable positive correlation between the average IQ of blacks in a school and the average amount of friendly interracial contact reported by whites. However, this correlation is due almost entirely to Highland, where black IQ and friendly contact among whites were both unusually high.

10. Among black students, IQ was correlated .26 with educational aspirations and .19 with effort. Among white students, IQ was correlated .47 with educational aspirations and .14 with effort.

11. Among black students, educational aspirations correlated .32 with participation in school activities.

12. Academic aspirations and effort may have explained, jointly with other variables, some of the variance in interracial behavior and attitudes. They may also have served to some degree as intervening variables between some other variables and interracial behavior and attitudes.

13. Appendix F also shows a sizable positive correlation between the average educational aspirations of blacks in a school and the average amount of friendly interracial contact reported by whites. However, this association was due entirely

to Highland, where black educational aspirations and friendly contact among whites were both unusually high.

Chapter 7

1. Our data on racial composition of classes are of unusually good quality. Unlike many studies which rely on student reports, they are derived from school records.

2. While there was no overall association between the racial composition of a school and the average amount of interracial avoidance by blacks, avoidance by blacks was lowest in the three schools which had the largest percentage of blacks.

3. Correlations also were computed between change in the proportion of blacks in each of ten schools from 1965–1970 (and from 1969–1970) and average interracial behaviors and opinion change. The only sizable correlations were that, for whites, the larger the change in percentage black from 1965 to 1970, the more avoidance of blacks ($r = .70$) and the less positive the change in racial opinion ($r = .72$). Scatter plots show the relation with avoidance, but not that for opinion change, to hold generally for the entire set of schools.

4. In a series of two-way analyses of variance, performed separately for black students and for white students, there were no significant interactions between the school the student attended and the racial composition of his classes, with respect to any of the interracial behavior or attitude measures.

5. The association of class racial composition and interracial friendship also was investigated. For black students, there was no consistent association. For white students, interracial friendship increased steadily as the average percentage of blacks in classes increased. This relationship was significant ($p < .001$).

6. To see the effects of class racial composition with other variables relevant to race relations controlled, see Tables 9.1 and 9.2.

7. Correlations between interracial proximity in classes and interracial avoidance are $-.04$ for blacks and $-.09$ for whites.

8. The interaction effect of class racial composition and parents' education on white students' racial attitudes was found even when the students' racial attitudes prior to high school, their IQs, and the racial ethnocentrism of peers were, in turn, held constant. However, other special conditions—such as the high academic motivation of black schoolmates at Highland—may have accounted for the positive attitudes of whites from well-educated families in majority-black situations.

9. Among whites, the interaction of class racial composition and IQ was significant at the .01 level for both friendly contact and racial attitudes.

10. A combined measure of the racial ethnocentrism of both same-race and other-race peers was used as a control where friendly interracial contact was the dependent variable. A measure of the ethnocentrism of same-race peers was used when racial attitude was the dependent variable.

11. For black students, the racial attitudes of same-race peers were used. For white students, a combination of the racial attitudes of same-race and other-race students was used.

12. The interaction effect of class racial composition and white peers' ethnocentrism on black students' racial attitudes was found even when variations in the aggressiveness of black students were controlled.

13. With the aggressiveness of black students controlled, the interaction between class racial composition and white peers' ethnocentrism falls short of statistical significance. However, the interaction effect described tends to occur regardless of black students' aggressiveness.

14. For whites there was a significant three-way interaction between class racial composition, peers' racial attitudes, and family racial attitudes, as these variables affected friendly contact. However, the Ns in many cells are very tiny and the results are not interpretable.

15. These data were available for 250 black students and 320 white students—i.e., those who participated in one or more activities and for whose activities data from teacher advisors were available.

16. A very small but statistically significant association between opportunity for contact with black faculty and white change in racial opinion is reduced to nonsignificance when other factors affecting opinion change are controlled.

Chapter 8

1. An exception is the study by Hough et al. (1969), who obtained information about racial attitudes both from students and from their parents.

2. Chadwick (1972) has studied the relations between the racial attitudes of family and peers, as perceived by students, and their "integrative behavior" toward, and avoidance of, other-race schoolmates.

3. School-level correlations between the average racial ethnocentrism of students of each race and their average interracial behaviors and opinion change are shown in Appendix F. It is not possible to know the extent to which these correlations reflect group influences on individuals versus the extent to which they reflect merely the average relation between individuals' own ethnocentrism and their behavior and opinion change.

4. The small effect of the ethnocentrism of same-race peers for blacks as compared to whites probably is due, in part at least, to the fact that the dispersion (standard deviation) of scores for blacks on this variable was less than half that of scores for whites.

5. There was, however, a tendency for whites to have less friendly contact with blacks when the average ethnocentrism of black schoolmates was high rather than low or medium.

6. In the multiple regression analysis, greater ethnocentrism by black peers was associated slightly with more positive racial attitudes among whites. Since no causal connection seems plausible, this result probably is coincidental and due to variables not controlled in this analysis.

7. For both races, there were statistically significant interactions between same-race ethnocentrism and other-race ethnocentrism with respect to some behavioral or attitudinal outcomes. However, inspection of the cell means revealed no consistent and meaningful patterns.

8. Forehand et al. (1976, p. 190) found white students' perceptions of their teachers' racial attitudes "highly congruent" with the racial attitudes expressed by teachers. Black high school students also tended to perceive the racial attitudes of the teachers correctly.

9. Perceptions of family and teacher racial attitudes were included in the multiple regression analyses (Tables 9.1 and 9.2) but only objective measures of peer racial attitudes were included in these analyses. With other variables con-

trolled, perceived family racial attitudes had significant effects on interracial relations for both races. Perceived racial attitudes of same-race teachers had significant effects on avoidance, unfriendly contact, and attitudes for white students.

10. Forehand et al. asked students whether they would like more friends of another race. It is not clear whether this indicates positive racial attitudes (as assumed) or whether those students with positive racial attitudes feel they already have enough other-race friends.

11. Only those freshmen and sophomores in all regular-ability classes were included in these analyses. For those who attended classes of varying ability levels, the background of peers was likely to be more variable.

12. Since one school site was almost all black and another school was almost all white, two of the twelve school sites are not included for this purpose.

13. For an analysis of the relation between overall "racial climate" in a school and the relative social and academic statuses of the black and white student bodies, see Davidson, Hofmann, and Brown (1978).

14. In our samples, relative SES correlated with amount of in-group fighting: .01 for blacks and .00 for whites, with educational aspirations .03 for blacks and .25 for whites. Relative grades correlated with in-group fighting, −.10 for blacks and −.16 for whites, with educational aspirations .23 for blacks and .44 for whites.

15. These data need to be interpreted cautiously. Since in some cases students may have chosen their coworkers, rather than being assigned without regard to their preference, the association may be inflated spuriously. On the other hand, the association may be reduced because the measure does not assess the total amount of participation in interracial class subgroups which the student had throughout high school.

16. Perceptions of goal-helpfulness were not included in the multiple regression analyses reported in Tables 9.1 and 9.2, since this measure overlaps objective measures of being in cooperative situations. However, in other analyses (Patchen and Davidson, 1973, pp. 254–271), perception of goal-helpfulness was found to have significant effects on interracial behavior even after a variety of other relevant factors was controlled.

17. The interaction between perceptions of goal facilitation by other-race students and perceptions of relative social status of the races was investigated only for white students, since perceived relative status was more important for whites.

18. Teacher items were weighted according to the proportions of white teachers and black teachers at each school. The administrator item was weighted one-fourth and the security-guard item was weighted one-eighth, the sum of teacher weights.

19. Blacks scored somewhat higher than whites on the index of perceived discrimination against their race. Also, the standard deviation of scores was slightly higher for blacks.

Chapter 9

1. For a fuller description of multiple regression analysis, see Blalock (1972).

2. The units for the different variables have been made comparable by "standardizing" all scores—i.e., by dividing each raw score on a measure by the standard deviation of that measure.

3. For a description of "dummy variables," see Blalock (1972), pp. 498–502.

4. In some cases negative behavior by the students themselves (including avoidance) may have led other-race schoolmates to act in an unfriendly way toward them. Often, the process probably was a circular one. Because the direction of causation is not completely clear, unfriendly experience was not included as a predictor in the multiple regression analyses.

5. Friendly interracial contact was correlated with positive change in opinion of other-race people, .13 for blacks and .26 for whites. Total unfriendly experience was correlated with positive change in opinion, −.12 for blacks and −.30 for whites.

6. Measures of the nature of interracial contact were not included as predictors of opinion change because we cannot be sure whether the contact or the change in opinion came first.

Chapter 10

1. More detailed information about academic performance measures, by race and school, and their relationship to subjective (and other) factors is presented in a previous report (Patchen, 1975).

2. The correlations between cumulative grades and composite scores on the Metropolitan Achievement Tests (MAT) were .41 for blacks and .62 for whites. Correlations between current grades and composite MAT scores were .39 for blacks and .54 for whites. Correlations between grades and National Educational Development Tests scores were very similar to those between grades and MAT scores.

3. A stanine is a value on a simple nine-point scale of normalized standard scores. Conversion to stanine scores, when averaging MAT tests results, is recommended by the test authors (Durost et al., 1964). The conversion of percentile ranks to stanines is as follows: 96 and above = 9, 89–95 = 8, 77–88 = 7, 60–76 = 6, 40–59 = 5, 23–29 = 4, 11–22 = 3, 4–10 = 2, below 4 = 1.

4. At Pershing, too, grades of blacks were substantially lower than those of whites, though the difference was not statistically significant.

5. IQ scores for 93.4% of students are based on the California Test of Mental Maturity, taken in the eighth grade. The remainder took this or another IQ test during the sixth grade (1.9%) or during the ninth grade (4.7%).

6. MAT scores are emphasized in our analyses because they were obtained at the same time or later than our measures of interracial contact. Current grades are emphasized because they are closer in time than cumulative grades to other information obtained.

7. The index of academic values was correlated with educational aspirations, .36 among blacks and .47 among whites. Academic values correlated with occupational aspirations, .13 among blacks and .28 among whites.

8. Our measures of academic values and of effort were correlated .25 for blacks and .38 for whites.

9. There are, however, only very small correlations between our measure of effort and expectations of educational success ($r = .09$ for blacks and .14 for whites) and between effort and expectations of occupational success ($r = .08$ for blacks and .06 for whites).

10. For details on construction of the effort index, see Patchen, 1975, Appendix B.

11. Liking for white teachers and liking for black teachers are not included in this set of correlations because students differed in the number of white and black teachers they had.

Chapter 11

1. More detailed inspection of these data showed that, though the relations were not completely linear, black students' high school grades and total MAT achievement scores (for lowerclassmen) became lower as the proportion of whites in their grade school classes increased. The relation between total NEDT scores (for upperclassmen) and proportion of whites in grade school classes was less consistent, although NEDT scores were lowest for those who attended grade school classes with the most whites.

2. In a series of two-way analyses of variance, the average racial composition of students' classes and the schools they attended were related, in turn, to each of the academic outcomes. There were no significant interaction effects between class racial composition and school attended.

3. The different results for freshmen and sophomores may be related to the fact that no freshmen attended Carver, the almost-all-black school.

4. Among students in our sample whose classes averaged 70% or more black, about 46% were at Highland (with freshmen overrepresented) and 29% were at Carver.

5. See Chapter 8 for description of the strictness measure.

6. It may be that less disciplinary strictness by staff leads to less effort. On the other hand, it may be that where students do not try hard, and also are unruly, discipline is relaxed because it is more difficult to maintain. A circular process may ensue.

7. The estimate or percent of variance explained was obtained by squaring the beta, which is the correlation ratio after adjusting for other predictors. While useful for such an estimate, beta^2 should not be viewed as showing the exact amount of variance explained by a single variance (Andrews et al., 1973).

8. No partial correlation could be computed because of high correlations among the variables.

9. The associations between friendly interracial contact and academic outcomes were essentially linear and therefore correlation analyses are appropriate.

10. Sex also was controlled in one partial correlation analysis.

11. The student's high school situation may exert independent effects on academic outcomes but it may, in turn, be influenced by such outcomes. The partial correlations in which high school factors are used as controls represent conservative estimates of the relation between interracial contact and academic outcomes.

12. Parents' education and school program were not used as controls because they were not related substantially to both unfriendly interracial contact and academic outcome variables.

13. We defined peers in terms of those with whom the student would be in most frequent contact. For juniors and seniors, peers were defined as those in the same program in the same school. For freshmen and sophomores in all average-ability classes, peers were defined as those in the same school and year who also were in all average-ability classes. Those lowerclassmen in any slow (or accelerated) classes were not given scores concerning peers since the characteristics of their peers were likely to differ in their "special," as compared to their average-ability, classes.

14. Sex was controlled in all analyses. IQ was controlled in every analysis except those involving grade school racial composition (since IQ scores were obtained at the end of grade school). Own parents' education was always controlled, except for analyses involving average values of white peers (due to its small effect on academic outcomes and computer limitations). Where a characteristic of white peers was being studied, the average score of black peers on the same characteristic was controlled. When either the average academic values or the average IQ of white peers was studied, the other variable was controlled. In addition, year in school was an added control in some analyses where computer program limitations permitted.

15. Those whose classes averaged over 85% black were omitted from most analyses because results presented previously indicated that their academic outcomes differed from those of blacks in majority-black classes. They could not be treated as a separate category since their small numbers and the fact that they had few contacts with whites would have resulted in few or no cases in some cells of the analyses. For the four-factor analyses involving parents' education, all blacks in classes with more than 55% black were included in one category, but very few blacks in classes of over 85% black actually were represented even in this analysis, since most were not asked questions about white friends and/or did not have scores concerning white peers.

16. Our own data show, however, a lack of association ($r = -.04$) between the average education of whites' parents and the average expressed values of whites. See Patchen, Hofmann, and Brown (1980) for correlations between all variables used in these analyses.

17. In this study, average education of white peers' parents correlated .58 with the average IQ of white peers.

18. There were two other interactions which reached a low level of statistical significance in these analyses (see Patchen, Hofmann, and Brown, 1980), but inspection of the cell means showed inconsistent patterns of results.

19. These results are based upon a set of analyses of covariance in which the factors were class racial composition, average academic values of white peers, and average academic values of black peers.

20. Black students' own IQs were categorized as low for blacks (below 85), about average (85–95), and high for black (above 95). The average IQ of white peer groups was trichotomized to produce about equal numbers of groups in each category: below 100, 100–108, above 108.

21. The average IQ of white peers was correlated .35 with their average academic values and .58 with the average education of their parents.

22. This interaction ($p = .078$) is just short of the usual criterion of statistical significance, but reaches this criterion ($p = .05$) when friendship with whites is not used as a third factor.

23. The average values, intelligence, and parental education of peers were not included as predictors in these analyses because these variables were correlated substantially with students' own IQ, ability grouping, and program, as well as with each other.

24. To take account of the nonlinear relation between class racial composition and effort, and between class racial composition and grades, racial composition was treated as a set of dummy variables for the regressions predicting effort and grades. Since students in the all-black school were not included in these analyses (because of their lack of scores on the measures of friendly and unfriendly contact), the relation between class racial composition and achievement scores was approximately linear and so racial composition was treated as an ordinary variable for the achievement regression.

25. Students, usually lowerclassmen, were divided into general, slow, or accelerated classes in some courses (especially English and Math). Scores were assigned students, ranging from 7 for those with two or more accelerated classes to 3 for those with two or more slow classes.

26. In the analyses shown in Figure 11.2, analysis of variance was used to test the overall significance of differences in mean grade scores among ten class composition categories. In the analysis shown in Table 11.5, multiple regression analysis was used to test the separate effect on grades of each of three dummy variables (classes 30–59.9% black, 60–79.9% black, 80% and over black), in comparison to the effect of being in classes averaging under 30% black.

27. For example, if A and B jointly explain some portion of the variance in C, neither A nor B will receive "credit" for this effect when the effect of A is controlled by B, and vice versa.

28. Other predictor variables in these analyses were IQ, parents' education, year in school, sex, and curriculum program.

29. In each of the series of analyses of covariance summarized earlier, the proportion of total variation explained by class racial composition, plus friendship with whites, plus the characteristics of white peers, plus the interactions among these factors, was computed (see Patchen, Hofmann, and Brown, 1980). Usually much less than 10% of the variation was explained by these factors, except in two cases where a number of nonsignificant and/or inconsistent interaction effects brought the "explained" variation slightly above 10%.

Chapter 12

1. A *t* test of the significance of the difference in average IQ between whites who attended grade school classes with a white majority and those who did not showed the difference to be significant at the .05 level (one-tailed test). With IQ scores adjusted by parents' education and sex, the difference between those in white-majority classes and others remained almost exactly the same, though it did not reach statistical significance in an analysis of covariance.

2. Total achievement scores were based on scores on other subtests (e.g., social science and science), in addition to scores on English Lanugage and Math subtests (see Chapter 10).

3. In a series of two-way analyses of variance, the racial composition of students' classes and the school which they attended were related to their effort, grades, achievement scores, and academic values. No significant interaction effects were found.

4. The estimate of percent of variance explained was obtained by squaring the beta, which is the correlation ratio after adjustment for other predictors. Though beta^2 is useful for such an estimate, it should not be viewed as showing the exact amount of variance explained by a single variable (Andrews et al., 1973).

5. Juniors and seniors were not included in these analyses because their achievement scores were obtained prior to the year that the racial composition data were obtained.

6. Two schools were omitted from these analyses—Pershing, because the small proportion of blacks restricted whites' opportunities for interracial contact there, and Carver, because there were only a few whites there.

7. The shape of the associations of outcomes with friendly and interracial contact and with unfriendly interracial contact, but not with friendship, was examined.

8. Class racial composition was categorized in this way because results presented earlier indicate that academic outcomes tended to differ for white students in these categories.

9. IQ, sex, and parents' education were used as controls (covariates) in most analyses. IQ, measured at the end of grade school, was omitted as a control when the effect of grade school racial composition was studied. Where the effect of a characteristic of black peers was studied, the average score of white peers on the same characteristic was included as a control. Where the effect of the average academic values of black peers or the average IQ of black peers was studied, the other was included as a control. Year-in-school was an additional control where computer limitations permitted.

10. The average parental education of black peers correlates .22 with the average expressed academic values of black peers.

11. The average parental education of black peers correlates .41 with the average IQ scores of black peers.

12. In the four-way analyses of covariance in which class racial composition, friendship with blacks, average education of black peers' parents, and own parents' education were related to whites' academic outcomes, there were several other statistically significant but weak interaction effects. However, in each case, inspection of the cell means showed no consistent patterns of results.

13. There was a small significant interaction between class racial composition and the average IQ of black peers, as these factors related to expectancies of attending college; but the detailed results showed no consistent pattern.

14. There was a significant interaction effect of these factors on grades. Higher personal IQ scores contributed to higher grades regardless of average IQ scores of black peers, but the effect of white students' own IQ was strongest among those whose black peers had a high average IQ level; the effect of one's own IQ was least strong among those whose black peers had a medium IQ level. There was also a small significant interaction effect of one's own IQ and the average IQ of black peers, as these variables related to achievement scores, but no consistent pattern was evident.

15. Because of the small number of students in the vocational program, they were combined with those in the fine and practical arts program for these descriptive comparisons and were omitted from the analyses of covariance.

16. Achievement test scores were not included in these analyses since they were limited to juniors and seniors, who took achievement tests prior to the year in which our data on class racial composition and friendship were collected.

17. In each set of analyses reported above, in the section "Interracial Contact under Varying Conditions," we computed the proportion of variance in a particular outcome which was explained by class racial composition, plus friendship with blacks, plus the characteristics of black peers, plus the interactions of these factors with each other and with any other factor included in the analyses. Though the results vary somewhat with each particular analysis, they show consistently that only small proportions of variance in academic outcomes for white students can be accounted for by their contact with black schoolmates (see Patchen, 1981).

Chapter 13

1. The discussion in this section is based on results from our measure of the student's own active participation in unfriendly contact. A second measure, labeled "total unfriendly contact," was affected much more by unfriendly actions which other-race schoolmates initiated toward the student, without there necessarily being any unfriendly action by himself.

2. See Forehand and Ragosta (1976) for a discussion of the role of staff in making school desegregation effective.

3. See Brookover et al. (1979), Rutter et al. (1979), and Clark (1972) for discussions of ways in which schools can be more effective in raising student achievement.

References

Allport, G. W. 1958. *The Nature of Prejudice.* Garden City, N.Y.: Addison-Wesley, Anchor Books Edition.

Amir, Y. 1969. Contact Hypothesis in Ethnic Relations. *Psychological Bulletin* 71:319–342.

———. 1976. The Role of Intergroup Contact in Change of Prejudice and Ethnic Relations. In *Toward the Elimination of Racism,* ed. P. A. Katz, New York: Pergamon Press.

Andrews, F. M., J. N. Morgan, J. A. Sonquist, and L. Klein. 1973. *Multiple Classification Analysis.* 2d ed. Ann Arbor: Institute for Social Research.

Armor, D. J. 1972a. School and Family Effects on Black and White Achievement: A Re-examination of the USOE Data. In *On Equality of Educational Opportunity,* eds. F. Mosteller and D. P. Moynihan. New York: Vintage Books, pp. 168–229.

———. 1972b. The Evidence on Busing. *The Public Interest* 28:90–126.

Aronson, E., N. Blaney, J. Sikes, C. Stephan, and N. Snapp. 1975. Busing and Racial Tension. *Psychology Today* 8:43–120.

Atkinson, J. W., and N. T. Feather, eds. 1966. *A Theory of Achievement Motivation.* New York: Wiley.

Bain, R., and J. G. Anderson. 1974. School Context and Peer Influence on Educational Plans of Adolescents. *Review of Educational Research* 44:429–445.

Bandura, A. 1973. *Aggression: A Social Learning Analysis.* Englewood Cliffs, N.J.: Prentice-Hall.

Blalock, H. M., Jr. 1967. *Toward a Theory of Minority-Group Relations.* New York: John Wiley.

———. 1972. *Social Statistics.* 2nd ed. New York: McGraw-Hill.

Bouma, D. H. and J. Hoffman. 1968. *The Dynamics of School Integration.* Grand Rapids, Michigan: Eerdmans.

Brookover, W., C. Beady, P. Flood, J. Schweitzer, and J. Wisenbaker, 1979. *School Social Systems and Student Achievement: Schools Can Make a Difference.* New York: Praeger.

Brown, W. R. 1974. Experiences Prior to and Outside High School As These Affect the Inter-Racial Perceptions and Behaviors of High School Students. Ph.D. Dissertation, Purdue University.

Bryant, J. C. 1968. Some Effects of Racial Integration of High School Students on Standardized Achievement Test Scores, Teacher Grades, and Dropout Rates in Angleton, Texas. Ph.D. Dissertation, University of Houston.

Bullock, C. S., III. 1976. *School Desegregation, Interracial Contact and Prejudice*. Houston: University of Houston.

Byrne, D. 1971. *The Attraction Paradigm*. New York: Academic Press.

————. 1961. The Influences of Propinquity and Opportunities for Interaction on Classroom Relationships. *Human Relations*. 14: 63–69.

———— and J. A. Buehler. 1955. A Note on the Influence of Propinquity upon Acquaintanceships. *Journal of Abnormal and Social Psychology* 51:147–148.

Campbell, A. 1971. *White Attitudes toward Black People*. Ann Arbor: Institute for Social Research, University of Michigan.

Carithers, M. W. 1970. School Desegregation and Racial Cleavage, 1954–1970: A Review of the Literature. *Journal of Social Issues* 26:25–48.

Carrigan, P. M. 1969. School Desegregation via Compulsory Pupil Transfer: Early Effects on Elementary School Children. Final report for project no. 6–1320, U.S. Office of Education.

Chadwick, B. A. 1972. Factors Relevant to Interracial Avoidance or Acceptance Behavior in an Integrated High School. Paper presented at 67th Annual Meeting of American Sociological Association.

————, H. M. Bahr, and R. C. Day. 1971. Correlates of Attitudes Favorable to Racial Discrimination among High School Students. *Social Science Quarterly* 51:873–888.

Clark, K. B. 1972. *A Possible Reality: A Design for the Attainment of High Academic Achievement for Inner-City Students*. New York: Emerson Hall.

Cohen, A. R. 1964. *Attitude Change and Social Influence*. New York: Basic Books.

Cohen, D. K., T. F. Pettigrew, and R. T. Riley. 1972. Race and the Outcomes of Schooling. In *On Equality of Educational Opportunity*, eds. F. Mosteller and D. P. Moynihan. New York: Random House.

Coleman, J. S., E. Campbell, C. Hobson, J. McPartland, A. Mood, F. Weinfeld, and R. York. 1966. *Equality of Educational Opportunity*. Washington, D.C.: U.S. Government Printing Office.

Cook, S. W. 1970. Motives in a Conceptual Analysis of Attitude-related Behavior. In *Nebraska Symposium on Motivation*, eds. W. J. Arnold and D. Levine. Lincoln: University of Nebraska Press.

Coulson, J. E. 1977. Overview of the National Evaluation of the Emergency School Aid Act. Santa Monica, Cal.: System Development Corp.

Crain, R. L., and R. E. Mahard. 1978. School Racial Composition and Black College Attendance and Achievement Test Performance. *Sociology of Education* 51:81–100.

————. 1977. *Desegregation and Black Achievement*. Santa Monica, Cal: The Rand Corp.

Davidson, J. D., G. Hofmann, and W. R. Brown. 1978. Measuring and Explaining High School Interracial Climates. *Social Problems* 26:50–70.

Deutsch, M. 1949. Experimental Study of the Effects of Cooperation and Competition upon Group Processes. *Human Relations* 2:199–232.

———— and M. E. Collins. 1951. *Interracial Housing*. Minneapolis: University of Minnesota Press.

DeVries D., and K. Edwards. 1972. Student Teams and Instructional Games: Their Effects on Cross-Race and Cross-Sex Interaction. ERIC Document No. ED 070–808.

Drake, S. C., and H. R. Cayton. 1962. *Black Metropolis* (rev. ed.). New York: Harper and Row.

Durost, W., W. Evans, J. Leake, H. Bowman, C. Cosgrove, and J. Read. 1964. *Guide for Interpreting Metropolitan Achievement Tests: High School Battery.* New York: Harcourt, Brace and World.

Dwyer, R. J. 1958. A Report on Patterns of Interaction in Desegregated Schools. *Journal of Educational Sociology* 31:253–256.

Feagin, J. R. 1978. *Racial and Ethnic Relations.* Englewood Cliffs, N.J.: Prentice-Hall.

Feshbach, S. 1970. Aggression. In *Carmichael's Manual of Child Psychology,* vol. 2, ed. P. H. Mussen. New York: Wiley.

Ford, W. 1972. *Interracial Public Housing in Border City.* Lexington, Mass.: Lexington Books.

Forehand, G., and M. Ragosta. 1976. *A Handbook for Integrated Schooling.* Washington, D.C.: U.S. Office of Education.

———, ———, and D. A. Rock. 1976. Conditions and Processes of Effective School Desegregation, 2 vols. Washington, D.C.: Educational Resources Information Center (ED131155).

Fox, D. J. 1966. Free Choice Open Enrollment-Elementary Schools. Mimeo. New York: Center for Urban Education.

Freud, S. 1938. *The Basic Writings of Sigmund Freud.* New York: Random House.

Gerard, H. B., T. D. Jackson, and E. S. Conolley. 1975. Social Contact in the Desegregated Classroom. In H. B. Gerard and N. Miller, *School Desegregation.* New York: Plenum Press.

Harding, J., H. Proshansky, B. Kutner, and I. Chein. 1969. Prejudice and Ethnic Relations. In *Handbook of Social Psychology,* eds. G. Lindsey and E. Aronson. 2d ed. Vol. 5. Reading, Mass.: Addison-Wesley.

Herman, B. E. 1967. The Effect of Neighborhood upon the Attitudes of Negro and White Sixth Grade Children toward Different Racial Groups. Ph.D. dissertation, University of Connecticut.

Hildebrandt, C. A. 1962. The Relationship of Some Personal and Social Variables of School Children to Preferences for Mixed Schools. Ph.D. dissertation, Ohio State University. Columbus, Ohio.

Hodge, R. W., P. M. Siegel, and P. H. Rossi. 1964. Occupational Prestige in the United States, 1925–1963. *American Journal of Sociology* 70:286–302.

Hofmann, G. 1973. Interracial Fraternization: Social Determinants of Friendship Relations between Black and White Adolescents. Ph.D. dissertation, Purdue University.

Honzik, M. P. 1973. The Development of Intelligence. In *Handbook of General Psychology,* ed. B. B. Wolman. Englewood Cliffs, N.J.: Prentice-Hall.

Hough, R., G. Summers, and J. O'Meara. 1969. Parental Influence, Youth Contraculture, and Rural Adolescent Attitudes toward Minority Groups. *Rural Sociology* 34:383–386.

Huffman, D. M. 1969. Interpersonal Attraction as a Function of Behavioral Similarity. Ph.D. dissertation, University of Texas.

Hunt, C., and L. Walker. 1974. *Ethnic Dynamics.* Homewood, Ill.: Dorsey.

Jencks, C., and M. Brown. 1975. The Effects of Desegregation on Student Achievement: Some New Evidence from the Equality of Educational Opportunity Survey. *Sociology of Education* 48:126–140.

Justman, J. 1968. Children's Reactions to Open Enrollment. *The Urban Review* 3:32–34.

Kaplan, H. K., and A. J. Matkom. 1967. Peer Status and Intellectual Functioning of Negro School Children. *Psychology in the Schools* 4:181–184.

Katz, I. 1968. Factors Influencing Negro Performance in the Desegregated School. In *Social Class, Race, and Psychological Development,* eds. M. Deutsch, I. Katz, and A. Jensen. New York: Holt, Rinehart and Winston.

Kiesler, C. A., and S. B. Kiesler. 1969. *Conformity.* Reading, Mass.: Addison-Wesley.

Kriesberg, L. 1973. *The Sociology of Social Conflicts.* Englewood Cliffs, N.J.: Prentice-Hall.

Kupferer, H. J. 1954. An Evaluation of the Integration Potential of a Physical Education Program. *Journal of Educational Sociology* 28:89–96.

Lachet, M. 1972. A Description and Comparison of the Attitudes of White High School Seniors toward Black Americans in Three Suburban High Schools. Ph.D. dissertation, Teachers College, Columbia University.

Laue, J. 1971. A Model for Civil Rights Change through Conflict. In *Racial Conflict,* ed. G. Marx. Boston: Little, Brown, pp. 256–262.

Lewis, R. 1971. The Relationship of Classroom Racial Composition to Student Academic Achievement and the Conditioning Effects of Interracial Social Acceptance. Ph.D. dissertation, Harvard Graduate School of Education.

——— and N. St. John. 1974. The Contribution of Cross-Racial Friendship to Minority Group Achievement in Desegregated Classrooms. *Sociometry* 37:79–91.

Lieberson, S. 1961. A Societal Theory of Race and Ethnic Relations. *American Sociological Review* 26:902–910.

Loehlin, J. C., G. Lindzey, and J. N. Spuhler. 1975. *Race Differences in Intelligence.* San Francisco: W. H. Freeman.

Lombardi, D. N., 1963. Factors Affecting Changes in Attitudes toward Negroes among High School Students. *Journal of Negro Education,* 32:129–136.

London, O. H. 1967. Interpersonal Attraction and Abilities: Social Desirability or Similarity to Self? M.A. thesis, University of Texas.

McClelland, D. C. 1951. *Personality.* New York: Wm. Sloan Assoc.

McPartland, J. 1968. The Segregated Student in Desegregated Schools: Sources of Influence on Negro Secondary Students. Center for the Study of Social Organization of Schools, Baltimore, Md. The Johns Hopkins University, Report No. 21.

——— and R. York. 1967. Further Analyses of Equality of Educational Opportunity Survey. In U.S. Commission on Civil Rights, *Racial Isolation in the Public Schools.* Vol. 2. Washington, D.C.: U.S. Government Printing Office.

Maccoby, E. E., and C. N. Jacklin. 1974. *The Psychology of Sex Differences.* Stanford, Cal.: Stanford University Press.

Mahan, T. W. 1968. *Project Concern: 1966–1968.* Hartford Public Schools.

Maisonneuve, J., G. Palmade, and G. Fourment. 1952. Selective Choices and Propinquity. *Sociometry* 15:135–140.

Meer, B., and E. Freedman. 1966. The Impact of Negro Neighbors on White Home Owners. *Social Forces* 45:11–19.

Minard, R. D. 1952. Race Relationships in the Pocohantos Coal Field. *Journal of Social Issues* 8:29–44.

Moreno, J. 1934. Who Shall Survive? A New Approach to the Problem of Human Inter-relations. Washington, D.C.: Mental Disease Publishing.

Morrison, E. B., and J. A. Stivers. 1971. *A Summary of the Assessments of the District's Integration Programs, 1964–1971.* Research Report No. 9 of series 1971–1972. Sacramento City Unified School District, Sacramento, Cal.

Mussen, P. J. 1950. Some Personality and Social Factors Related to Changes in Childrens' Attitudes toward Negroes. *Journal Abnormal and Social Psychology* 45:423–441.

Namboodiri, N. K., L. F. Carter, and H. M. Blalock, Jr. 1975. *Applied Multivariate Analysis and Experimental Designs.* New York: McGraw-Hill.

Narot, R. E. 1973. The Effects of Integration on Achievement. In National Opinion Research Center, *Southern Schools.* Vol. 1. University of Chicago.

National Opinion Research Center. 1973. *Southern Schools: An Evaluation of the Effects of the Emergency School Assistance Program and of School Desegregation*, 2 vols. University of Chicago.

Nelson, J. 1972. High School Context and College Plans: The Impact of Social Structure on Aspirations. *American Sociological Review* 37:143–149.

Newcomb, T. 1963. Stabilities Underlying Changes in Interpersonal Attraction. *Journal of Abnormal and Social Psychology* 66:376–386.

Newcomb, T. M., R. H. Turner, and P. E. Converse. 1965. *Social Psychology*. New York: Holt, Rinehart and Winston.

O'Connor, P., J. W. Atkinson, and M. S. Horner. 1966. Motivational Implications of Ability Grouping in Schools. In *A Theory of Achievement Motivation*, eds. J. W. Atkinson and N. T. Feather. New York: Wiley.

O'Reilly, R. P. 1970. *Racial and Social Class Isolation in the Schools*. New York: Praeger.

Patchen, M. 1965. *Some Questionnaire Measures of Employee Motivation and Morale*. Ann Arbor: Survey Research Center.

———. 1981. Supplementary Tables for Study of Black–White Contact in Schools. Department of Sociology and Anthropology, Purdue University.

———, in collaboration with J. D. Davidson, G. Hofmann, and W. R. Brown. 1975. The Relation of Interracial Contact and Other Factors to Outcomes in the Public High Schools of Indianapolis. W. Lafayette, Ind.: Purdue University (ERIC Doc. No. ED 118–716).

——— and J. Davidson, in collaboration with G. Hofmann, with assistance of W. Brown. 1973. Patterns and Determinants of Interracial Interaction in the Indianapolis Public High Schools. W. Lafayette, Ind.: Purdue University (ERIC Doc. No. ED 095–252).

———, G. Hofmann, and W. R. Brown. 1980. Academic Performance of Black High School Students under Different Conditions of Contact with White Peers. *Sociology of Education* 53:33–51.

———, ———, and J. D. Davidson. 1976. Interracial Perceptions among High School Students. *Sociometry* 39:341–354.

Patterson, G. R., R. A. Littman, and W. Bricker. 1967. Assertive Behavior in Children: A Step toward a Theory of Aggression. *Monographs of the Society for Research in Child Development* 32, No. 5.

Petroni, F. 1970. Uncle Toms: White Stereotypes in the Black Movement. *Human Organization* 29:260–266.

———, E. Hirsch, and C. L. Petroni. 1970. *2, 4, 6, 8. When You Gonna Integrate?* New York: Behavioral Publications.

Pettigrew, T. 1969a. The Negro and Education: Problems and Proposals. In *Race and the Social Sciences*, eds. I. Katz and P. Gurin. New York: Basic Books, pp. 49–112.

———. 1969b. Racially Separate or Together? *Journal of Social Issues* 25:43–70.

———. 1979. Racial Change and Social Policy. *Annals of American Academy of Political and Social Science* 441:114–131.

———, E. L. Useem, C. Normand, and M. S. Smith. 1973. Busing: A Review of "The Evidence." *The Public Interest*, no. 30, pp. 88–118.

Proshansky, H. M. 1966. The Development of Intergroup Attitudes. In *Review of Child Development*, vol 2. Eds. L. W. and M. L. Hoffman. New York: Russell Sage Foundation.

Reagor, P. A., and G. L. Clore. 1970. Attraction, Text Anxiety and Similarity-Dissimilarity of Test Performance. *Psychonomic Science* 18:219–220.

Riordan, C. 1975. The Conditions and Effects of Equal-Status Contact: A Critical

Review. Paper presented at annual meeting of American Sociological Association.

Rist, R., ed. 1979. *Desegregated Schools. Appraisals of an American Experiment.* New York: Academic Press.

Robinson, J. W., and J. D. Preston. 1976. Equal-Status Contact and Modification of Racial Prejudice. *Social Forces* 54:911–924.

Rock, W. C., J. E. Long, H. R. Goldberg, and L. W. Heinrich. 1968. A Report on a Cooperative Program between a City School District and a Suburban School District. Rochester School District, Rochester, N.Y.

Rokeach, M., and L. Mezei. 1966. Race and Shared Belief as Factors in Social Choice. *Science* 151:167–172.

Rotter, J. B., J. E. Chance, and E. J. Phares. 1972. *Applications of a Social Learning Theory of Personality.* New York: Holt, Rinehart and Winston.

Rudwick, E. 1964. *Race Riot at East St. Louis, 1917.* Carbondale, Ill.: Southern Illinois University Press.

Rutter, M., B. Maughan, P. Mortimore, and J. Ouston, 1979. *Fifteen Thousand Hours: Secondary Schools and Their Effects on Children.* Cambridge, Mass.: Harvard University Press.

Sartain, J. A. 1966. Attitudes of Parents and Children toward Desegregation. Ph.D. dissertation, Vanderbilt University.

Schermerhorn, R. A. 1970. *Comparative Ethnic Relations.* New York: Random House.

Schmuck, R. A., and M. B. Luzski. 1969. Black and White Students in Several Small Communities. *Applied Behavioral Science* 5:203–220.

Schofield, J. W. 1978. School Desegregation and Intergroup Relations. In *Social Psychology of Education: Theory and Research,* eds. D. and L. Saxe. New York: Wiley.

————. 1975. To Be or Not to Be (Black). Paper presented at annual meeting of American Psychological Association. Chicago.

———— and H. A. Sager. 1977. Interracial Behavior in a "Magnet" School. Paper presented at meetings of American Psychological Association. San Francisco.

Schuman, H., and S. Hatchett. 1974. *Black Racial Attitudes.* Ann Arbor: Institute for Social Research, University of Michigan.

———— and M. P. Johnson. 1976. Attitudes and Behavior. In *Annual Review of Sociology,* eds. A. Inkeles et al. Palo Alto, Cal.: Annual Reviews.

Science Research Associates. 1969. *National Educational Development Tests: Interpretive Manual, Grades 9–10.* Chicago, Ill.

Sewell, W. H. 1967. Review Symposium. *American Sociological Review* 32:475–479.

Shaw, M. E. 1973. Changes in Sociometric Choices Following Forced Integration of an Elementary School. *Journal of Social Issues* 29:143–157.

Sherif, M., and C. W. Sherif. 1953. *Groups in Harmony and Tension.* New York: Harper.

Shuey, A. M. 1966. *The Testing of Negro Intelligence.* New York: Social Science Press.

Silverman, I., and M. Shaw. 1973. Effects of Sudden Mass Desegregation on Interracial Interaction and Attitudes in One Southern City. *Journal of Social Issues* 29:133–142.

Singer, D. 1967. The Influence of Intelligence and an Interracial Classroom on Social Attitudes. In *The Urban R's,* eds. R. A. Dentler, B. Mackler, and M. E. Marshaver. New York: Praeger.

Sowell, T. 1974. Black Excellence: The Case of Dunbar High School. *The Public Interest,* pp. 3–21.

Spady, W. 1976. The Impact of School Resources on Students. In *Schooling and Achievement in American Society,* eds. W. Sewell, R. Hauser, and D. Featherman. New York: Academic Press.

St. John, N. H. 1963. Defacto Segregation and Interracial Association in High School. *Journal of Education* 37:326–344.

———. 1975. *School Desegregation: Outcomes for Children.* New York: Wiley Interscience.

——— and R. G. Lewis. 1971. The Influence of School Racial Context on Academic Achievement. *Social Problems* 19:68–78.

Thorpe, J. G. 1955. A Study of Some Factors in Friendship Formation. *Sociometry* 18:207–214.

U. S. Commission on Civil Rights. 1967. *Racial Isolation in the Public Schools,* 2 vols. Washington, D.C.: Government Printing Office.

———. 1976. *Fulfilling the Letter and Spirit of the Law: Desegregation of the Nation's Public Schools.* Washington, D.C.: Government Printing Office.

———. 1973. *School Desegregation in Ten Communities.* Washington, D.C.

Webster, S., 1961. The Influence of Interracial Contact on Social Acceptance in a Newly Integrated School. *Journal of Educational Psychology,* 52:292–296.

Weigel, R., P. Wiser, and S. Cook. 1975. The Impact of Cooperative Learning on Ethnic Relations and Attitudes. *Journal of Social Issues* 31:219–243.

Weinberg, M. 1977. *Minority Students: A Research Appraisal.* Washington, D.C.: National Institute of Education.

Weissback, T. A. 1976. Laboratory Controlled Studies of Change of Racial Attitudes. In *Toward the Elimination of Racism,* ed. P. Katz. New York: Pergamon.

White Plains High Schools. 1967. *White Plains Racial Balance Plan Evaluation.* White Plains, N.Y.

Whitmore, P. G., Jr. 1957. A Study of School Desegregation: Attitude Change and Scale Validation. Ph.D. dissertation, University of Tennessee.

Wicker, A. W. 1969. Attitudes versus Actions: The Relationship of Verbal and Overt Behavioral Responses to Attitude Objects. *Journal of Social Issues* 25:41–78.

Willie, C. V., with J. Beker. 1973. *Race Mixing in the Public Schools.* New York: Praeger.

Wilson, W., and N. Miller. 1961. Shifts in Evaluations of Participants Following Intergroup Competition. *Journal of Abnormal and Social Psychology* 63:428–431.

Winter, J. A., 1977. *Continuities in the Study of Religion.* New York: Harper and Row.

Witte, P. H. 1972. The Effects of Group Reward Structure on Interracial Acceptance, Peer Tutoring and Academic Performance. Ph.D. dissertation, Washington University.

Wrightstone, J. W., S. D. McClelland, and G. Forleno. 1966. Evaluation of the Community Zoning Programs. New York: Bureau of Educational Research, Board of Education.

Yarrow, M. R. (issue ed.). 1958. Interpersonal Dynamics in a Desegregation Process. *Journal of Social Issues* 14:3–63.

Zdep, S. M., and D. Joyce. The Newark-Verona Plan for Sharing Educational Opportunity. PR 69–13. Princeton, N.J.: Educational Testing Service.

Subject Index

Ability, relative to other race: effect on academic outcomes, 10–11; 280–282, 315–316; effect on social relations, 180–181

Ability grouping: and outcomes for blacks, 287–292; and outcomes for whites, 319–324

Ability, own. *See* IQ

Absences: data, 31; frequency by race, 247–249

Academic orientation: effect on social relations, 130–135; perceptions of other race, 44, 48–49. *See also* Peers, other race; Peers, own race

Achievement tests: description of, 31, 236–237; predictors of blacks' scores, 290–292; predictors of whites' scores, 321–323; scores of blacks vs. whites, 237–239

Activities, school: and academic outcomes; 287–292; 319–324; and social relations, 160–161

Administration of school: disciplinary strictness of, 195–196; questionnaires for, 30–31; role in problem-solving, 203–204. *See also* Principals

Aggressiveness: effect on academic outcomes, 287–289, 319–322; effect on social relations, 123–125, 154–155

Anger at other race: by blacks, 45–46; by whites, 50–52

Aspirations of students: blacks vs. whites, 242–244; and academic outcomes, 244; and social relations, 130–135

Attitude change. *See* Opinion change

Attitudes toward other race: data, 38–39; description of, 40–51; determinants of, 223–226, 330–333; differences among schools, 51, 53; summary measure, 51–53. *See also* Liking for other race; Perceptions of other race

Avoidance of other race: determinants of, 211–212, 214–216, 330–333; frequency of, 58–60

Behavior toward other race, 56–80; correlation among types of, 73–74; relation to attitudes, 74–76; relation to attitude change, 76. *See also* Avoidance; Friendly contact; Unfriendly contact

Contact, interracial: benefits and costs, 350–352; duration of, 262–263; rationale for, 3–4; research on academic effects, 9–14; research on social effects, 5–9; theory of, 5–7. *See also* Racial Composition

Cooperative situations: in activities and social relations, 190–192; in classes and social relations, 158–160, 187–189, perceptions of and social relations, 192–195

Curriculum program: by race and school, 22–23; as related to academic outcomes, 282–284; 289, 316–317, 322

Desegregation: pressures for, 16. *See also* Racial Composition

Discipline: effects on social relations, 195–196; relation to racial composition, 268–270

385

Early experiences, 83–114; combined effects of factors, 90–91; differences among schools, 111–112; and high school situation, 110–111. *See also* Grade school interracial contact; Neighborhood interracial contact

Effort: of blacks vs. whites, 247–249; predictors of, 288–289, 320–321; and social relations, 130–135

Ethnocentrism. *See* Peers, own race; Peers, other race

Expectancy of success: blacks vs. whites, 245–246; relation to performance 246–247, 280–282, 315–316

Facilities: adequacy, by school, 24–25

Faculty: contact with black faculty and academic relations, 287–289, 319–322; contact with black faculty and social relations, 161–162; percent black, 23–24; ratio to students, 24–25. *See also* Teachers

Family characteristics: impact on academic outcomes, 287–292, 319–324. *See also* Socioeconomic status

Family racial attitudes: effects on social relations, 102–103, 107–108; measures of, 89; reasons for impact of, 102–103; trying to influence, 340–341

Favoritism by staff: and social relations, 201–202, 213, 216

Fear of other race: and academic outcomes, 250–251, and avoidance, 120, extent of, 45–46, 50–52

Feelings, interracial: of black students, 44–46; of white students, 50–52

Fighting: incidents in schools, 17. *See also* Unfriendly contact

Friendliness by other race: student perceptions of, 42–43, 49

Friendly contact between races: and academic outcomes: 270–271, 287–292, 308–310, 319–324, determinants of, 217, 220–221, 333–335; frequency of, 60–64; ways of promoting, 339–340

Friendship, interracial: and academic outcomes, 275–311; determinants of, 221; frequency of, 65–67

Grades: of blacks vs. whites, 239–240; data concerning, 31; predictors for blacks, 253, 289–290; predictors for whites, 253, 321; relative to other race and social relations, 179–180

Grade school interracial contact: and academic outcomes in high school, 260–261, 287–292, 298–301, 319–324; differences in effects by sex and family, 92–95; and social relations in high school, 85, 99–101, 104–106; measures of, 86; relation to IQ, 258–260, 297

Height: effect on social relations, 119–120

Indianapolis: population, 18; school problems, 16–17

Interviews, 25–26

IQ scores: of blacks vs. whites, 240–241; data used, 31; effect on academic outcomes, 241, 287–292, 319–324; effect on social relations, 125–130, 154–156; interpretation of, 240; relative to other race and social relations, 180–181

Job: time spent on and academic outcomes: 287–289, 319–324

Liking for other race: by blacks, 45–46; by whites, 50–52. *See also* Attitudes toward other race

Neighborhood interracial contact: differences in effects by sex and family, 95–97; effects on social relations, 101–102, 106–107; measures of, 87–88; possible effects of, 87. *See also* Early Experiences

Norm violations: perceptions by blacks, 43; perceptions by whites, 48–49

Opinion change: description of, 53–54; determinants of, 226–228

Parents' education: effects on academic outcomes, 276–277, 287, 289, 312–313, 319–320, 322; effects on social relations, 103, 108, 151–152; measure of, 89–90; possible effects of, 89; by school and race, 20–21. *See also* Socioeconomic status

Peers, other race: ability of and academic outcomes, 10–11, 280–282, 315–316; academic values of and academic outcomes, 10, 277–280, 313–315; feelings toward and academic outcomes, 250–251; racial attitudes of and social relations, 167–169, 171–175; social class of and academic outcomes, 11–12, 276–277, 312–313

Peers, own race: academic values of and academic outcomes, 280; influencing racial attitudes of, 340–341; racial attitudes of and relations with other race, 156–158, 166–167, 169–175

Perceptions of other race: by blacks, 40–44; by whites, 45, 47–50

Power: perceptions of, 189–201; in student councils, 197–198

Principals: race of, 24. *See also* Administration of school

Prior friendly contact: effect on social relations, 103–104, 108–109, 152–153; importance of promoting, 341. *See also* Early experiences; Grade school interracial contact; Neighborhood interracial contact

Prior opinion of other race: effects on social relations, 104, 109; measure of, 90

Problem-solving in schools: and social relations, 203–204

Proximity to other race: effects on social relations, 148–151

Questionnaires: for students, 26–29; for teachers, 29–30; for administration, 30–31

Racial composition, general: policy implication of findings, 337–338; social vs. academic effects, 348–350. *See also* Contact, interracial

Racial composition of classes: data on, 31; effects on academic outcomes, 263–270, 275–292, 303–324; effects on social relations, 141–148. *See also* Contact, interracial

Racial composition of schools: description of, 18–19; as related to academic outcomes, 263, 301–303; as related to social relations, 140–141. *See also* Contact, interracial

Religious involvement: effect on social relations, 135–136

Sample, of students, 27–28, 353

Satisfaction of students: as related to social relations, 122–123

School preference: by race and school, 19–20; as related to academic outcomes, 287–289, 319–322

Security guards, 24–25, 202

Sex: effect on academic outcomes, 275–276, 287–292, 311–312, 319–324; effect on social relations, 115–119, 153–154; inclusion in analyses of effects of early experiences, 90

Similarity to other race: effects on social relations, 158, 177–186; policy implications of findings, 341–342, 349–350

Social acceptance: relation to achievement, 10. *See also* Friendly contact between races

Socioeconomic status: by race and school, 20–22; relative to other race and social relations, 177–179. *See also* Parents' education.

Statistical methods: for predicting academic outcomes, 274, 287–288, 292, 310, 319–320, 324; for predicting social outcomes, 97–99, 209–211

Teachers: attitudes of students toward, 251–252; behavior of and student achievement, 12; importance of support for integration, 341; student attitudes toward and academic outcomes, 251–254, 287–292, 319–324; perceived racial attitudes of and students' social relations, 171–173, 213, 215. *See also* Faculty; Favoritism by staff

Tensions: ways of reducing, 338–339

Toughness: perceptions of, 44, 50

Transportation to school, 18–20

Unfriendliness by other race: perceptions by blacks, 43–44; perceptions by whites, 48–49

Unfriendly contact: and academic outcomes, 273–274, 287–292, 307–310, 319–324; determinants of, 221–223, 335–357; frequency of, 67–73. *See also* Fighting

Values, academic: blacks vs. whites, 242–244; as related to academic outcomes, 244

Variance explained: in academic outcomes, 292, 324; in social relations, 288–230

Year in school: and academic outcomes, 288–289, 320–324